KEEPING CURRENT WITH
TEXAS
REAL ESTATE MCE

CHARLES J. JACOBUS
DREI, CREI

JOHN P. WIEDEMER
HOUSTON COMMUNITY COLLEGE

JOSEPH E. GOETERS
HOUSTON COMMUNITY COLLEGE

CENGAGE
Learning

Australia • Brazil • Japan • Korea • Mexico • Singapore • Spain • United Kingdom • United States

CENGAGE
Learning™

Keeping Current with Texas Real Estate MCE, 9e

Charles J. Jacobus, John P. Wiedemer, Joseph E. Goeters

Vice President/Editor-in-Chief:

Dave Shaut

Executive Editor: Scott Person

Acquisitions Editor: Sara Glassmeyer

Senior Marketing Manager: Mark Linton

Developmental Editor: Michelle Melfi

Content Project Manager:

Corey Geissler

Frontlist Buyer, Manufacturing:

Charlene Taylor

Art Director: Pamela Galbreath

Production Service:

Internal Designer: Chris Miller,

Cmiller Design

Cover Designer: Chris Miller,

Cmiller Design

Cover Image: iStockphoto.com/ Brandon Seidel

Library of Congress Control Number: 2008943682
ISBN-13: 978-0-324-78751-1
ISBN-10: 0-324-78751-0

Cengage Learning
5191 Natorp Boulevard
Mason, OH 45040
USA

Cengage Learning products are represented in Canada by Nelson Education, Ltd.

For your course and learning solutions, visit **academic.cengage.com**
Purchase any of our products at your local college store or at our preferred online store **www.ichapters.com**

Printed in Canada
1 2 3 4 5 6 7 12 11 10 09 08

Contents

Foreword

Chapters 1 and 2 of this book contain the mandatory TREC material. They consist of three hours of legal update and another three hours of ethics. All licensees are required to receive this same, up-to-date information. Instructors are required to be certified to teach the courses.

The second half of Chapter 2 begins the discussion and teachings of the authors. Chapter 3 is an extended discussion on legal topics by the authors. Chapter 4 focuses on finance and Chapter 5 on commercial real estate and environmental issues (all approved to complete the full 15 hour required MCE).

Updates to this material can be found on the web site for this text, **www.cengage.com/realestate/jacobus**.

We cannot emphasize this enough... education for professionals is ongoing; there is always more to learn; things keep changing. That's what makes this business so exciting. Thank you for participating!

Chuck Jacobus
Jack Wiedemer
Joe Goeters

Legal Update

Pre-Assessment Evaluation

Please answer the following questions.

1. The current education requirement for salesperson licensure is 90 hours and the core hours required for broker licensure is 180 hours.

   True   False

2. Title companies can legitimately sponsor events for Licensee's business promotion if licensees consistently bring business to the title company.

   True   False

3. If the title company chooses to accept it, an existing survey may be used instead of requiring a new one.

   True   False

4. A professional inspector license applicant under the alternate education track will be required to complete 128 hours in core education courses and 320 additional education hours.

   True   False

5. A person conducting business as a builder in Texas must hold a certificate of registration from the Residential Construction Commission.

   True   False

Texas Real Estate Commission Legal Update MCE

Edition 3.1

Prepared By

**Compiled and Edited
by Denise Whisenant**

December 2008

Acknowledgments

MCE Advisory Committee

Jan Agee, Arlington, TX
Loretta Dehay, Austin, TX
Louise Hull, Victoria, TX
Chuck Jacobus, Bellaire, TX
Larry Jokl, Brownsville, TX
Kathleen McKenzie-Owen, Pipe Creek, TX
Tom Morgan, Austin, TX
Minor Peeples, Corpus Christi, TX
Ron Walker, Austin, TX
Avis Wukasch, Georgetown, TX

Real Estate Center Staff

Gary W. Maler, Director
Denise Whisenant, Education Coordinator
David S. Jones, Communications Director
Nancy McQuistion, Associate Editor
Kammy Baumann, Assistant Editor
Robert P. Beals II, Art Director
JP Beato III, Graphics Designer
Brian Pope, Associate Editor

Foreword

In cooperation with the Texas Real Estate Commission, the Real Estate Center at Texas A&M University developed this real estate legal update curriculum with the assistance of an advisory committee of active licensees, attorneys and education providers. Real estate licensees are encouraged to acquire additional information and to take courses in specific, applicable topics.

This curriculum has been developed using information from publications, presentations and general research. The information is believed to be reliable, but it cannot be guaranteed insofar as it is applied to any particular individual or situation. The laws discussed in this curriculum have been excerpted, summarized or abbreviated. For a complete understanding and discussion, consult a full version of any pertinent law. This curriculum contains information that can change periodically. This curriculum is presented with the understanding that the authors and instructors are not engaged in rendering legal, accounting or other professional advice. The services of a competent professional with suitable expertise should be sought.

The authors, presenters, advisory committee, Real Estate Center and Texas Real Estate Commission disclaim any liability, loss or risk personal or otherwise, incurred as a consequence directly or indirectly from the use and application of any of the information contained in these materials or the teaching lectures and media presentations given in connection with these materials.

When using this course for three hours of Legal Update MCE credit as required by the Texas Real Estate Commission, the student course manual must be reproduced and used in its entirety, without omission or alteration.

Contents

1

Legislative and Regulatory Changes

Changes in the Real Estate License Act (TRELA) in 2007

Fingerprints

An applicant for a license or renewal of an unexpired license must submit a complete and legible set of fingerprints, on a form prescribed by the commission, to the commission or to the Department of Public Safety for the purpose of obtaining criminal history record information from DPS and the Federal Bureau of Investigation. If the applicant refuses to do so, the commission must refuse to issue the license. [TRELA 1101.3521]

Commissioner Training

A person who is appointed to serve as a Commissioner may not vote, deliberate, or be counted as member in attendance at a meeting of the Commission until that person completes a training program that complies with state law. [TRELA 1101.059]

Complaint Provision

The commission is required to maintain a system to act promptly and efficiently on complaints filed with the commission and must maintain a file on each complaint. The commission must also ensure that it gives priority to the investigation of complaints filed by a consumer and an enforcement case resulting from the consumer complaint. The commission is required to assign priorities and investigate complaints using a risk-based approach based on the degree of potential harm to the consumer, potential for immediate harm to a consumer, overall severity of the allegations and the complaint, number of license holders potentially involved in the complaint, previous complaint history of the license holder, and number of potential violations in the complaint. [TRELA 1101.203]

Notes

1

Refund to Consumer

In addition to suspension and revocation, the commission may order a licensee to pay a refund to a consumer as provided in an agreement resulting from an informal settlement conference or an enforcement order, in addition to imposing an administrative penalty or other sanctions. [TRELA 1101.659]

Informal Proceedings

The commission is also required to adopt procedures governing informal disposition of the contested case. An informal disposition must provide the complainant and the license holder the opportunity to be heard. The proceeding requires the presence of a public member of the commission for a case involving a consumer complaint and at least two staff members of the commission with experience in the regulatory area that is the subject of the proceeding.

Temporary Suspension

The presiding officer of the commission for a case involving a consumer is also required to appoint a disciplinary panel, consisting of three commission members, to determine whether a person's license to practice should be temporarily suspended. If the disciplinary panel determines that the licensee constitutes a threat to the public by continuing to practice, or the licensee constitutes a continuing threat to the public welfare, the panel shall temporarily suspend the license of that person. [TRELA 1101.660]

Required Course for Broker License

Of the eighteen semester hours of core real estate courses, two semester hours must include "real estate brokerage" as defined under the Texas Real Estate License Act. [TRELA 1101.356(a)]

Financial Responsibility of Inspectors

Real Estate inspectors must now maintain liability insurance with a minimum limit of $100,000 per occurrence. [TRELA 1102.114]

License Renewal

A person whose license has been expired for ninety days or less may renew the license by paying a fee equal to 1 ½ times the renewal fee. If the license has been expired for more than ninety days but less than one year, the person may renew the license by paying a fee equal to two times the renewal fee.

Notes

2

If a person's license has been expired for one year or longer, the person may not renew the license. The person may obtain a new license by complying with the requirements and procedures for obtaining an original license. Under existing law, however, the commission by rule may waive all or part of the licensing requirements for an applicant who was licensed with the commission within six years preceding the date the application is filed. By rule the commission has waived the examination requirement for an applicant who was licensed no more than two years prior to the filing of the application.

Online Courses

An online course may not be completed in fewer than 24 hours [TRELA 1101.455(k)].

Other Legislative Changes

JP Jurisdiction

The justice of the peace court jurisdiction was raised from $5,000 to $10,000, exclusive of interest. The courts still maintain exclusive jurisdiction for forcible entry and detainer proceeding, foreclosures of mortgages, and enforcement of liens on personal property within the court's new limits. (Section 27.031(a), Texas Government Code)

Seller Disclosure Notice

A Seller disclosure notice must contain

- ☑ whether or not the seller knows the home was previously used for the manufacture of methamphetamines;

- ☑ whether or not the seller knows if the property has smoke detectors and smoke detectors for the hearing impaired, carbon monoxide detectors, and emergency escape ladders;

- ☑ an acknowledgement by the buyer that the property complies with smoke detector requirements of Chapter 766, Health and Safety Code or if it doesn't comply, the buyer waives his rights to have the smoke detectors installed;

- ☑ a notice that if the property is located seaward of the Gulf Intracoastal Waterway or within one thousand feet of the mean high tide bordering the Gulf of Mexico, the property may be subject to the Open Beaches Act or the Dune Protection Act.

Notes

3

Chapter 766 of the Health and Safety Code provides that the property must contain smoke detectors that comply with the local building code.

Homesteads; Judgment Liens

When a person cannot pay a judgment, an abstract of judgment constitutes a lien on and attaches to all real property owned by the defendant in the county in which the abstract is filed. An exception is for real property exempt under Texas Homestead laws. This new law provides that a judgment debtor may, at any time, file an affidavit in the Real Property Records in the county in which the judgment debtor's homestead is located, and it serves as its release of record of a judgment lien. A bona fide purchaser or mortgagee, successor, or assigns may rely conclusively on this affidavit if it includes evidence that:

☑ the judgment debtor is sent a letter and a copy of the affidavit notifying the judgment creditor of the affidavit and judgment debtor's intent to file the affidavit; and

☑ the letter and the affidavit were sent by registered or certified mail, return receipt requested, 30 or more days before the affidavit was filed to

   (i) the judgment creditor's last known address,

   (ii) the address appearing on the judgment creditor's pleadings,

   (iii) the judgment creditor's last known attorney, and

   (iv) the address of the judgment creditor's last known attorney as shown in the records of the State Bar of Texas, if that address is different from those pleadings.

The affidavit does not serve as a release of record if the judgment creditor files a contradicting affidavit in the real property records of the county asserting that:

☑ the debtor's affidavit is untrue; or

☑ states another reason exists as to why the judgment lien attaches to the judgment debtor's property (Section 52.0012, Texas Property Code).

Title Insurance

A new provision under the insurance code allows title insurance companies to insure personal property, departing from Texas' long-standing tradition of insuring only real property. The statute defines personal property as "what is defined as personal property under Section 1.04 of the Texas Tax Code." Section 1.04 defines personal property as "property that is not real property." This change will have most application on commercial transactions in which personal property plays a significant part (motels, apartments, etc.). It may have applications on other transactions as well.

Notes

4

This allows boats, airplanes and a number of other items of personal property to be insured (Section 2751.002, Texas Insurance Code).

Landlord and Tenant Issues

A number of changes were made to the landlord and tenant statutes in the 2007 Legislature. Some of the changes that are more significant to real estate brokers are outlined below.

Lock-Out Procedures

A landlord may not intentionally prevent a tenant from entering the leased premises except by judicial process unless the tenant is delinquent in paying at least part of the rent. The amended statute states that the landlord cannot lock out a tenant unless the right to change the locks is specified in the tenant's lease and the provision is underlined or in bold print. The tenant has a right to receive a key to the new lock at any hour, regardless of whether the tenant pays the delinquent rent. This applies only to residential premises (Section 92.0081, Texas Property Code).

The landlord cannot prevent a tenant from entering a common area of residential real property.

In addition, the landlord may not change the locks on the door of a tenant's dwelling when the tenant or any other legal occupant is in the unit. Locks cannot be changed more than once during a rental period. This is an incentive to start eviction proceedings immediately rather than changing locks multiple times (Section 92.0081(k), Texas Property Code).

Note: One who uses lock-outs needs to be familiar with the statutory procedures and exercise care to comply.

Late Payment Fee

Landlords may not charge tenants late fees for failing to pay rent, unless the

- ☑ notice of the fee is included in the written lease;
- ☑ the fee is a reasonable estimate of the landlord's uncertain damages that cannot be calculated precisely and result from late payment of rent; and
- ☑ the rent remains unpaid two days after the rent was originally due (the third day).

The late fee may include an initial fee and a daily fee for each day the rent continues to remain unpaid. If a landlord violates this section, the landlord is liable to the tenant for $100 and three times the amount of the late fee charged. Any provision in the lease that purports to waive this right of the tenant is void (Section 92.019, Texas Property Code).

Notes

5

Emergency Phone Number

If a landlord has an onsite management or superintendent's office for residential property, the landlord must provide a 24-hour emergency telephone number for reporting conditions that materially affect the physical health or safety of the tenant. The landlord is required to post the phone number prominently outside the manager's or superintendent's office (Section 92.020, Texas Property Code). If there is no onsite manager or superintendent, the landlord must provide the tenant a telephone number for the purposes of reporting emergencies.

Changes to Leases

A lease must contain language in underlined or bold print that informs the tenant of the remedies available under Sections 92.056 and 92.0561 (tenant repair and deduct remedies) of the Texas Property Code.

Rental Applications

When a rental application with a non-refundable application fee is submitted, the landlord must provide the applicant a printed notice of the landlord's tenant selection criteria and the grounds for which the application may be denied. This may include the applicant's

- ☑ criminal history;
- ☑ previous rental history;
- ☑ current income;
- ☑ credit history; or
- ☑ failure to provide accurate or complete information on the application form.

The applicant must sign the acknowledgement indicating that the notice was available. If this acknowledgement is not signed, there is a rebuttable presumption that the notice was not made available to the applicant. The acknowledgement must contain a statement substantially similar to:

"Signing this acknowledgement indicates that you have had the opportunity to review the landlord's tenant selection criteria. The tenant selection criteria may include factors such as criminal history, credit history, current income and rental history. If you do not meet the selection criteria, or if you provide inaccurate or incomplete information, your application may be rejected and your application fee will not be refunded."

Notes

6

This acknowledgement may be part of the rental application. If it is, it must be underlined or in bold print.

Mortgage Fraud

A bill passed to help combat mortgage fraud, discussed in Chapter Five.

Conveyance of Encumbered Real Estate

Due to high default rates, most lenders put in "due on transfer" clauses in their deeds of trust to allow them to foreclose on the property if the original obligor ever conveyed it without notifying the lender (assumptions, etc.). In an effort to curb violations of the due-on-sale clauses, the 2007 Legislature created a new Property Code provision. The statute provides the person may not:

☑ convey an interest, or

☑ enter into a contract to convey an interest in residential property that will be encumbered by a recorded lien at the time the interest is conveyed <u>UNLESS</u>, on or before the earlier of the

(i) effective date of the conveyance (execution of deed), or

(ii) execution of the executory binding contract for sale to purchase the property the seller provides the purchaser and each lien holder a separate written disclosure statement in at least 12-point type that contains specific information required by Section 5.016 of the Property Code. It must contain a notice that if the property is transferred without the lender's consent, the lender could demand payment and foreclosure.

To purchase the property, the seller must provide the purchaser and each lien holder a separate written disclosure statement in at least 12-point type that contains specific information as required under Section 5.016 of the Property Code, including a notice that if the property is transferred without the lender's consent, the lender could demand payment and foreclosure. The new statute is likely to have little impact on brokers who use the TREC forms (or other standard Association forms) because the statute does not apply to a transaction in which the buyer will receive a title insurance policy. If a licensee notes that a buyer will not receive a title insurance policy, the licensee should refer to requirements under this new provision in the Property Code.

Stopping Another Scam?

There has been a practice promoted by some that encourages property owners to file a Declaration of Covenants, Conditions, and Restrictions which purports to put a lien on all future conveyances of the property by deed restricting the seller's property and requiring a transfer fee (a percentage of the sales price) every time the property is subsequently transferred. The Texas Legislature responded by passing a new Section 5.017 of the Texas Property Code to provide that a deed restriction or other covenant running with the land that requires a

Notes

7

transferee of residential real property or the transferee's heirs, successors, or assigns to pay a Declarant or other person opposing the deed restriction on the property, is prohibited and is void and unenforceable. It applies only to residential real property and specifically does not apply to deed restrictions imposed by property owner's associations, an entity organized under section 501(c)(3) of the Internal Revenue Code, or a governmental entity.

Regulatory Update

Corporations and Limited Liability Companies

The Real Estate License Act (the Act) and the Rules of the Commission require a corporation or limited liability company (LLC) to be licensed as a real estate broker if it provides real estate brokerage services or represents to others that it is engaged in the business of real estate brokerage. Corporations and LLCs licensed as brokers have the same authority as individuals licensed as brokers. A corporation or LLC may sponsor persons and is responsible for the acts and conduct of any persons it sponsors. The general rule is that only a corporation or LLC created under the laws of Texas may obtain a Texas resident broker license. However, a corporation or LLC formed under the laws of another state may be licensed if the corporation or LLC has its principal place of business in Texas; all of its assets are located in Texas; and all of its officers, directors, managers and members are Texas residents. Also, a non-resident corporation or LLC lawfully conducting real estate brokerage in another state may qualify for a broker's license as a nonresident.

Section 1101.453 of the Act requires a corporation or LLC to designate one of its officers or managers to act for the corporation or LLC. Each designated officer or manager must be licensed as an active real estate broker. The designated officer or manager is the person through which the corporation or LLC applies and qualifies for its broker license. A licensed broker may serve as the designated officer or manager for an unlimited number of corporations or LLCs. A salesperson or unlicensed person may own all or part of a corporation or LLC that holds a real estate broker license. While the designated person must be an officer of the corporation or manager of the LLC, he or she is not required to own an interest in the corporation or LLC. However, the designated person remains responsible for all real estate activity conducted by or through the corporation or LLC, much as an individual broker is liable for the acts of the persons sponsored by the broker. A complaint filed against a corporation or LLC or any of its sponsored persons is deemed a complaint against the designated person of the corporation or LLC. If the license status of the designated person changes to inactive, expired, revoked, or suspended; or if he or she dies or leaves, the corporation or LLC must cease conducting its real estate business until a qualified replacement is named. This is done by submitting a *Change of Designated Officer or Manager* form and the correct fee to TREC. The corporation or LLC can then resume its real estate activities.

Notes

8

2

News Briefs

RESPA & Procedural Rule P-53

One of the primary reasons the Real Estate Settlement Procedures Act (RESPA) was enacted several decades ago was to stop settlement service providers from giving rebates and kick-backs to each other in real estate transactions involving federally-related mortgages (Section 8, RESPA). A settlement service provider is anyone who provides service in connection with a real estate settlement (title companies, attorneys, surveyors, lenders, appraisers, inspectors, brokers, residential service companies, etc.).

In May 2003, the U.S. Department of Housing and Urban Development (HUD) investigated several title companies in Texas for allegedly violating Section 8 by providing free virtual tour services to brokers. Subsequently, the Texas Department of Insurance (TDI) implemented Procedural Rule 53 (P-53), which prohibits title companies and agents from directly or indirectly paying referral fees or subsidizing the business expenses of any producer. A producer is, essentially, a settlement service provider. Section 8 of RESPA and Procedural Rule P-53 are similar. RESPA is broader in its application as it governs the relationships between all settlement service providers. Rule P-53 governs only the relationships between title companies and producers.

In recent years the primary violations of RESPA and Rule P-53 have occurred when a settlement service provider pays a business expense of another settlement service provider as an inducement to direct business to them. For example, a mortgage company delivered free listing brochures and signs to an agent to induce the agent to refer business to the mortgage company. In another example, a title company paid or provided free MCE classes to a brokerage firm.

After clarifying Rule P-53, TDI has adopted a rule that mirrors provisions in RESPA. Under both RESPA and Rule P-53, a title company or any settlement service provider may not pay or subsidize the business expenses of another settlement service provider or producer. A "business expense" reflects its common definition. Anything that is deducted on income tax as a business expense is presumed to be a business expense.

Notes

9

A broker should not accept, nor should a title company (or any settlement service provider) offer to give a broker, anything that is an item of value or that constitutes the payment of a business expense.

Settlement service providers may engage in legal promotional activities only. Settlement service providers can purchase bona fide advertising from each other at market rates, however, the regulators will highly scrutinize these arrangements.

Do-Not-Call, Do-Not-Fax, Do-Not-Spam

The following is a quick reminder that solicitations or advertisements communicated by phone, fax, or e-mail are now governed by several federal and state statutes. Brokers, especially those brokers who make cold calls or send out advertisements by fax or e-mail, need to be aware of these statutes and may need to seek additional education.

Do-Not-Call

Real estate licensees who make cold calls must comply with the requirements of the National Do-Not-Call registry and Do-Not-Call rules. Specifically, before making a cold call, a licensee must verify whether the number is on the national do-not-call registry. Licensees may not make cold calls to numbers in the registry. The licensee needs to update any download of the registry at least every 31 days.

A licensee may call a person whose number is on the do-not-call registry if the licensee has an established business relationship (EBR) with the person called (unless the number is on the firm's internal do-not-call list). An EBR exists with someone who was party to a transaction with the broker's company in the last 18 months or with someone who made an inquiry with the broker's company within the last three months. Additionally, licensees may call if a consumer grants prior written permission.

The rules require that a brokerage that permits agents to make cold calls must maintain an internal do-not-call list. Requests to be placed in the internal list must be honored for five years. The internal list applies to all agents in the firm. The firm should maintain a central list into which each agent may input names and check before making calls. If a name is on the internal list, the agent may not call that number even if the number is not on the national do-not-call registry.

Notes

10

Do-Not-Fax

The federal rule governing faxes prohibits sending unsolicited faxes that contain any type of advertising. One may send faxes containing advertisements only to individuals who have given their expressed consent to receive the fax.

The federal rule also provides that the sender of the fax containing advertisement must give the receiver the right to opt out, even if an EBR exists. The opt-out mechanism must be included in faxes, must be clear and conspicuous, must be on the first page (cover sheet), and must contain specific language that the FCC rule mandates.

All fax messages, including those faxes that do not contain advertisements, must contain the date and time that the message is sent as well as the identification of the business entity or individual sending the message and the telephone number of the machine sending the message or of the business entity or individual sending the message.

To be safe, one should: (1) not send a fax containing an advertisement unless the sender can document that he has permission to do so; (2) eliminate cover sheets that contain inadvertent advertisements; and (3) eliminate inadvertent advertisements in agent newsletters that are sent by fax.

Anti-Spam

When sending out e-mails with advertisements, real estate licensees in Texas must comply with both the federal statute (Federal CAN-SPAM Statute) and the state statute (Chapter 46, Business and Commerce Code) governing e-mail solicitations. Both statutes apply to any e-mail that contains advertising. Both statutes prohibit: (1) the falsification of routing or sending information in any e-mail; and (2) any false, misleading or deceptive statements in the subject line.

The Texas statute requires the sender of an e-mail with an advertisement to precede the subject message with "ADV:" unless there is an existing business relationship (EBR). The federal statute provides that the sender's message must contain clear and conspicuous notice that the message is an advertisement or solicitation. The federal statute also requires the sender's message to include a valid physical postal address.

Both statutes require that e-mails containing advertisements must contain unsubscribe features. The Texas statute requires that the unsubscribed request be honored in three days. The federal statute requires that it be honored in ten days. The federal statute also requires that the unsubscribe feature remain active for 30 days after the message is sent.

Notes

11

Builders — Texas Residential Construction Commission

The Texas Residential Construction Commission (TRCC) governs the registration of builders and has adopted limited warranties that builders must provide to home owners along with building performance standards. It also operates a dispute resolution procedure under which home owners who have disputes with their builders need to follow. Builders who fail to follow the statute and rules that TRCC administers may face disciplinary action by TRCC.

A "builder" is one who is compensated for constructing, supervising or managing the construction of: (1) a new home; (2) a material improvement to a home, except a roof; or (3) an improvement to the interior of an existing home, if the cost is greater than $10,000. A broker or manager who arranges or supervises construction for an owner is not required to register.

A homeowner who has a dispute with a builder over a construction defect must first submit a written notice of the alleged defect to the builder. The homeowner must give the builder an opportunity to inspect the alleged defect. Thirty days after sending the written notice, the homeowner (or builder) may submit a request to TRCC for dispute resolution. TRCC will appoint a third-party inspector to inspect the alleged defect. Either the homeowner or the builder can appeal to the commission for review of the inspector's findings. Costs for the inspection may apply. After the process is complete, the homeowner and builder will receive a final determination as to whether a construction defect exists. If one exists, the builder and the homeowner should be able to settle the claim at that point. If a satisfactory settlement is not reached, the parties may pursue their legal remedies before a court of law.

It is critical that a homeowner follow TRCC procedures because the final determination creates a rebuttal presumption as to whether or not a construction defect exists. The determination of this rebuttal presumption will likely have a significant impact on prevailing in any lawsuit. Additionally, obtaining the determination from TRCC is a prerequisite for filing a lawsuit against a builder for an alleged construction defect.

Notes

12

Concerns Over Mineral Rights in Some Residential Transactions

In the past, buyers and sellers of residential property generally have not been concerned about rights to minerals or royalties under a lease of the mineral estate. This has been especially true for the typical residential property within the city limits of a mid-size or large city. In most cases, the mineral estate was severed a long time ago, or the value of the mineral estate is insignificant. There is usually little risk that the owner of the mineral estate will access the property to drill for minerals, because such activity is heavily regulated within a city's limits.

Reflecting this state of affairs, the TREC residential contract forms do not specifically address rights to the mineral estate as does the TREC Farm and Ranch Contract form. The residential contract form simply provides that the seller will convey to the buyer all rights, including the mineral estate (subject only to those items listed in Paragraph 6A or as otherwise stated in the contract).

In recent years, a couple of developments have caused concern in certain transactions involving residential property near or just outside a city's boundaries. With the increase in oil and gas prices and the growth of many cities, drillers are now drilling in areas that are closer to a city's limits. Some of these areas have been developed into residential subdivisions featuring acreage lots — for example, a single-family subdivision with one- to five-acre lots.

In one dispute, a seller was angered when learning, after the sale, that the owner of the mineral estate started paying royalties of several hundred dollars a month, and that the new owner was receiving the royalties.

In another situation, a seller signed a contract without a reservation of rights to royalties. The seller then refused to sign the deed at closing, claiming that he wanted the right to receive any future royalties.

In a third case, the owner of the mineral estate constructed a rig about 500 feet from the buyer's property. The buyer was angered by the noise, trucks, and lights.

Trying to write a proper reservation clause or a clause that limits executory rights of the holder of the mineral estate in Special Provisions might constitute the unauthorized practice of law. Additionally, the residential contract forms are adequate for the vast majority of residential transactions as the minerals are not typically at issue. In residential transactions

Notes

13

where the minerals might be an issue, the licensees should advise their clients that: (1) the residential contract form provides for the seller to convey all rights to the property, including the mineral estate; (2) the owner of the executory rights is, most likely, entitled to use the property to reasonably access the mineral estate or may use a nearby property to do so; and (3) if a party wishes to address the matter differently, that person should seek the assistance of an attorney to properly address the issue in the contract.

Executory Contracts, Contracts for Deed, & Lease-Purchase Agreements

The 2005 legislature made additional efforts to protect consumers in transactions involving executory contracts. In the statute, an executory contract is a contract involving the sale of a residence in which closing occurs later than 180 days after execution. Contracts for deed and lease-purchase transactions meet this definition. These contracts were already subject to strong consumer-protection provisions in the Property Code and were sufficiently complex as to require the assistance of changes to further strengthen consumer protections. Perhaps the most dramatic change is that the Property Code now considers lease-purchases to be executory contracts and treats them in much the same way as contracts-for-deed. An option-to buy that includes, or is combined or executed concurrently with, a residential lease is now an executory contract under the law. The portion of the new law that treats lease-purchases and lease-options like executory contracts will only apply to lease-purchases executed on or after January 1, 2006.

Under an executory contract, there are significant penalties for a seller who does not strictly comply with Subchapter D of Chapter 5 of the Property Code. The best course of action for a real estate licensee is to advise clients not to enter into a contract-for-deed, lease-purchase or lease-option transaction without seeking the assistance of an attorney. Do not attempt to use the TREC forms or other such standard forms to create lease-purchase or lease-option contracts. Do not attempt to write a lease-option clause into a standard residential lease agreement without having the parties seek the assistance of an attorney.

Neither TREC nor any real estate trade association in Texas drafts standard forms to be used as executory contracts. Real estate licensees should advise clients and customers to seek the assistance of an attorney when entering into or desiring to enter into an executory contract, contract for deed, lease purchase contract, or a lease-option contract.

Notes

14

Mold Assessment and Remediation

Remediation Process

Mold assessment involves inspection of a building to evaluate whether mold growth is present, and to what extent. The mold assessment consultant will develop a mold remediation plan that will specify the estimated quantities and location of materials to be remediated, appoint methods to use and develop clearance criteria that must be met. Mold remediators must follow the mold remediation protocol described above and their own mold remediation work plan that provides specific instructions and/or standard operating procedures for how the remediation will be achieved. The mold assessment consultant must conduct a post assessment. This is an inspection to ensure that the work area is free from all visible mold and wood rot, that the work was completed in compliance with the remediation protocol and the work plan, and that the remediation meets all clearance criteria specified in the protocol. The assessor must give the property owner a passed clearance report documenting the results of the inspection.

Certificate of Mold Remediation

No later than ten days after a mold remediation has passed a clearance inspection, the remediation contractor will give the property owner a Certificate of Mold Remediation. The licensed mold assessment consultant who conducted the post remediation assessment must also sign the certificate. The consultant is required to state on the certificate whether the underlying cause of the mold problem has, with reasonable certainty, been corrected. All certificates of mold remediation issued within the previous five years must be furnished to the buyer when the property owner sells the property.

Insurance

Section 3 under Article 21.21-11, Insurance Code, prohibits an insurer from making an underwriting decision based on previous mold damage or a previous mold claim if

- ☑ the applicant has property eligible for residential property insurance;

- ☑ the property has had mold damage;

- ☑ mold remediation has been performed; and

- ☑ a Certificate of Mold Remediation was issued stating the underlying cause of the mold has been corrected or the property was inspected by an independent assessor or adjustor who determined that the property does not contain evidence of mold damage.

Notes

15

CLUE Reports

Most insurance companies participate in the Comprehensive Loss Underwriting Exchange (CLUE) and obtain a CLUE report to evaluate the claims history of the property and the applicant and to help the insurance company in its underwriting decisions. A CLUE report contains information about the claims history of the applicant and the property. Insurance companies use the CLUE report in different ways.

While CLUE reports are generally accurate, there may be errors in the reports. Most commonly, property owners who have made inquiries about coverage have found that insurance companies have classified such inquiries as claims and reported this information to CLUE. Federal law permits a person to challenge inaccurate information. One may contact the administrator of the CLUE report to correct information in a CLUE report. Section 551.113 of the Insurance Code prohibits an insurance company from considering an "inquiry" as a basis to decline to insure. An inquiry means a call or communication made to the insurance company that does not result in an investigation or claim and that is in regard to general terms or conditions of coverage under the insurance policy. The term includes a question concerning the process for filing a claim and whether a policy will cover a loss, unless the question concerns specific damage that has occurred and that has results in an investigation or claim.

If the buyer has the option to terminate the contract, the buyer should make sure that the buyer and the insurance agent have completed these steps before the option expires:

1. contact one or more insurance agents;

2. submit an application for insurance with the insurance agent of the buyer's choice;

3. ask for written confirmation from the insurance agent that the insurance company will issue a policy; and

4. verify that the insurance coverage the buyer chooses is acceptable to the buyer's lender.

Notes

16

3

Signatures, Records & Completing Forms

Electronic Transactions Signatures

The Uniform Electronic Transactions Act (UETA) was published by the National Conference of Commissioners on Uniform State Laws (NCCUSL) in 1999. It was adopted in Texas in 2001 (effective 1/1/2002) and is codified as Chapter 43, Business and Commerce Code. UETA removes barriers to electronic commerce by establishing electronic records and signatures as being the legal equivalent to paper writings and manual signatures.

UETA is a procedural law that permits electronic records and signatures without changing existing substantive laws; however, UETA does not require the use of electronic signatures. UETA defines an electronic signature as "an electronic sound, symbol, or process attached to or logically associated with a record and executed or adopted by a person with the intent to sign the record."

Both parties to a transaction must agree to conduct the transaction electronically. UETA also allows a party who has agreed to an electronic transaction to withhold consent in connection with other transactions. This would apply specifically to a provision in an agreement that required a party to consent to using electronic signatures in future transactions.

E-Sign Signatures

There is a federal statute, the Electronic Signatures in Global and National Commerce Act (E-Sign), which the U.S. Congress enacted in 2000. E-Sign overlaps with UETA, but it is not identical to UETA. E-Sign specifies the legal effect and enforceability of electronic contracts and electronic signatures, but it does not address how to establish the authenticity or validity of those signatures. Under E-Sign, if a state has adopted UETA, the state's law will preempt E-Sign and will govern electronic transactions.

Notes

17

Consumer's Consent for Electronic Signature

Both UETA and E-Sign require the consumer's consent to conduct the transaction electronically, and E-Sign requires that consent itself be communicated electronically. Initial consent may be given on paper or electronically. Since the definition of an electronic signature is broad, it appears that consent could be established by any reasonable means. A court might hold that "reasonable means" could include the click of a mouse, or it might require a more sophisticated means of establishing consent. Most experts are suggesting that secure platforms involving verifiable signatures be employed, for example, VeriSign or Entrust. Under UETA, the consumer may decline to use electronic means to transact. E-Sign specifically allows a consumer to withdraw consent to the use of electronic records at any point in the transaction. If a consumer who initially gives consent to the use of electronic records withdraws that consent, the parties will need to complete the rest of the transaction in paper and ink format. Brokers will need to obtain the consent of both the buyer and the seller to conduct the transaction electronically. If only one party consents, the broker may continue to have an electronic relationship with him or her; however the relationship with the other party would need to be handled in paper format.

Privacy is a critical issue. Before relying on electronic signatures in a transaction, it seems prudent to:

☑ obtain the necessary consents to the electronic transaction at the outset (both consent to the receipt of electronic records and consent to the use of electronic signatures);

☑ disclose to consumers that they have the right to withdraw their consent at any point in the transaction; and

☑ provide adequate means to withdraw the consent (providing notice of any ramifications, such as additional costs or a delay in the transaction because of switching to a paper system).

Technology

The law is technology neutral. The parties must agree on the method for digitally authenticating the documents of the transaction, and consumers must consent electronically, thereby proving they can access the information that is the subject of the consent.

Records Retention

Records can be retained electronically. The storage method used must ensure that the record can be accurately reproduced for later reference by all parties who are entitled to retain the record.

Notes

18

Signatures for Divorced Parties

What happens when the parties to a divorce wish to sell a property? If a divorce decree has been entered, the decree or a property settlement agreement will establish the respective ownership rights of each of the former spouses. It is not prudent to rely on the oral statements of a divorced spouse concerning rights to sell the property. A better practice is to see a copy of the divorce decree or settlement agreement. If that is not clear as to who is entitled to sell or own the property, consult an attorney.

At times, a divorce decree will give one party the right of possession but will not give full ownership to the one in possession. The former spouses could be co-owners. In that case, both spouses should sign the listing agreement and the earnest money contract. The title company will require both spouses to sign the deed, unless there are separate managing rights given in the decree or property settlement agreement.

Sometimes, the court will appoint a receiver to sell the property for the parties. A real estate broker may be appointed as receiver. The broker acting as receiver must obtain the court's authorization to accept an offer, as well as an order of the court authorizing the consummation of the sale. A receiver must file an oath and a bond with the court and obtain instructions from the court.

Occasionally, one spouse wants to purchase property while a divorce is pending. In this situation, the spouse should not enter into a contract to buy a property without clear guidance from an attorney.

Signatures in Foreclosures

If a bank or any corporate entity owns the property, the broker must exercise care to deal with a person or officer who is authorized to sign for the owner. The broker may ask for a copy of certified resolutions of the bank or other entity. These resolutions authorize the person to bind the property owner. The title company will require evidence of such an authorization at closing. Do not rely on oral statements from an unauthorized bank employee who tells the broker to market the property. If such an employee signs a listing agreement without authority, it may be unenforceable.

Pending Foreclosures

What happens when the property owner is delinquent in his or her mortgage payments and the property has been posted or is likely to be posted for foreclosure? The owner can sell the property until the time he ceases to be the property owner. A property owner who is behind

Notes

19

in his mortgage payment may be "under water" (meaning that the balance of the indebtedness secured by the property is greater than the value of the property), or the owner will be unable to net enough money to sell the property and pay all costs of the transaction. The broker will want to discuss various scenarios with owners in such cases and carefully review available proceeds to cover costs.

Many times lenders are willing to engage in "short sales" in which the lender will allow the borrower to sell the property for less than the amount owed and either forgive the borrower the deficiency or work out some other arrangement with the borrower. The borrower will need to have discussions with the lender about such possibilities. Offers to purchase such properties will need to be made subject to lender approval. Brokers should be careful when drafting such clauses in the standard forms and suggest that the parties consult an attorney when drafting such contingencies in the standard forms.

Relocation Companies

Many times the relocation company does not take title to the property from the employee who was transferred. If the relocation company operates under power of attorney from the property owner, the broker should have a copy of that power of attorney at the time the listing is taken. The title company will require the power of attorney to be filed of record at the time the property is sold. The power of attorney should be specific and clearly identify the property by legal description. If a power of attorney is involved in the transaction, send a copy to the title company to see if the form is acceptable.

Bankruptcy

If a broker is taking a listing from owners who have filed bankruptcy, different rules apply depending upon whether the bankruptcy is a Chapter 7, Chapter 11 or Chapter 13 proceeding. In a Chapter 7 proceeding, the broker will want to see a copy of the schedules filed by the debtor to determine whether or not the property is exempt. If the debtor claims it as exempt, listing the property is usually unaffected (barring any unforeseen circumstances). A creditor could still object to such a claim. In this type of situation, the debtor may be in default under a mortgage which could mean that foreclosure is likely. Ask if the loan is current or delinquent. If the proceeding is under Chapter 11 or Chapter 13, the debtor should have an order from the court authorizing the debtor to sign the listing agreement. Any offer which is submitted to the debtor should contain a provision making the contract subject to approval by the bankruptcy court. The transaction may not close until the debtor has obtained an order of the court authorizing the sale. Be prepared for delays as other creditors may object to the sale and request hearings in the bankruptcy court.

Notes

20

Common Mistakes When Completing Contract Forms

Effective Date

The broker forgets to insert the effective date in the contract. The effective date is critical because it is the date by which most other time periods in the contract are measured. Insert the date of final acceptance as the effective date. At the time final acceptance is communicated to the other party or the other party's agent, tell the other broker in the transaction that you have inserted the effective date.

Contract Modifications

The broker fails to have the parties enter into written amendments when the contract is modified. Modifying a contract that has changed since its original preparation is something many parties and brokers say they will do, and then they forget. If the parties agree to modify (for example, extend the closing date), the broker should suggest that the parties execute an amendment. Oral agreements to modify or extend time periods have been the subject of litigation.

Notes

21

4

Recent Cases

Lewis v. Foxworth

170 S.W. 3d 900; 2005 Tex. App.

The parties executed a contract for the sale of approximately 450 acres for almost $1.7 million in cash. The buyer deposited $50,000 in earnest money. Closing was to take place on January 15. Under special provisions, the contract stated:

> Both Seller and Purchaser agree that there are items of Personal Property which will be removed from the Property and that all fixtures which are attached to the Property will remain with the Property, said fixtures including, but not limited to fences, working pens, gates, chutes, water well fixtures, and tanks.

The seller removed several — but not all — personal items from the property before closing. The buyer did not close on the scheduled closing date. Two days after the scheduled closing, the seller sent the buyer a letter stating they were willing to extend the time for closing to January 21. The buyer did not close on January 21. The seller informed the buyer the next day by letter that they were terminating the contract. The title company refused to release the earnest money to the seller without a signed release from the buyer. The seller sent two requests to the buyer asking him to sign the release but received no reply. The seller then sued for the earnest money.

The buyer argued that his obligation to close was excused because the seller failed to remove personal items before closing. In the charge, the jury was asked to determine if the buyer's failure to perform was excused because the seller failed to comply with a material obligation under the contract or if the seller had repudiated the contract. Repudiation occurs when one party indicates to the other that, by actions or words, he is not going to fulfill the obligations of the contract, thereby renouncing the agreement. The jury found that the buyer failed to comply with the contract and that the failure was not excused. The jury awarded the seller the earnest money.

Notes

23

On appeal, the buyer argued that the contract required that the seller remove all personal property, and some personal property was left. The appellate court found that the contract did not require the removal of all personal property, but instead allowed removal of personal items from the property. The court stated that the evidence showed unequivocally that this was done.

The appellate court held that any failure to remove all personal items was not material enough to excuse the buyer from performing. The court found that by offering to extend the closing, the seller clearly demonstrated a desire to go forward with the sale and, therefore, did not demonstrate any intention to repudiate the contract. The appellate court upheld the jury award.

Aguiar v. Segal

167 S.W.3d 443; 2005 Tex. App.

This case involves a dispute between a buyer and seller over whether a closing date was or was not extended by oral agreement. In a few cases, courts have enforced oral extensions of deadlines in contracts. Enforcement has been difficult, however, because in most cases, the proof needed to establish an oral extension is inadequate. Hence, the preferred practice is to document all extensions, even the seemingly small ones.

In this case, the parties signed five separate contracts for the purchase of four apartment complexes and one duplex. Time was of the essence. Each contract contained an integration clause; one that provides that there are no other agreements between the parties regarding the sale.

The original closing date in each contract was July 15th. An automatic 15-day extension applied under a financing addendum if the buyer's lender had not completed the lender's closing requirements, such as an appraisal, by the closing date. The appraisals of the five properties were not completed on time, and the closing date was automatically extended until July 30th. On July 30th, the appraisals remained incomplete. The closing date was extended by an oral agreement, but the parties disagree as to the duration of the agreed upon extension.

The agent, who had acted as an intermediary, testified that she asked the seller on July 30th to hold out for one more week, and he agreed to do so. The agent stated that the seller called her to terminate the contracts on August 6th. She tried to talk him out of it and told him the bank was almost ready to close. The seller refused and said he had been willing to extend the closing only by one week after July 30th.

The seller testified he agreed to a one-week extension of the closing, but it was his understanding that all five properties would close within a week. The seller assisted with the

---

Notes

24

scheduling of the appraisals within the one-week extension, and he notified his tenants that a sale was imminent. The lender was not able to close on August 6th and was not prepared to fund the loans until August 25th. When the seller learned that the closing would not take place on August 6th, he notified the agent that he was terminating the contracts. He executed earnest money releases on August 6th. The buyers did not sign the releases.

The buyer's testimony confirmed that the lender was not ready to close on July 30th. The buyer testified that no consideration was given to the seller to extend the closing date, and there was no written agreement concerning any extension. However, according to the buyer, he was ready to pay cash on July 30th and August 5th. When asked whether he thought he had an oral agreement with the seller to extend the time for closing past July 30th, the buyer answered, "yes." However, the buyer did not testify as to any specifics concerning the alleged oral agreement. Instead, the buyer believed that the contract had been extended by a "reasonable period of time," which would allow the appraisals to be completed. The buyer argued that the seller did not object after the July 30th date had passed, that there was not a specific grant of a one-week extension, and that the seller had acted in a way after July 30th that indicated he agreed the contract was still in effect.

The trial court ruled in favor of the buyers, awarding them specific performance and attorney's fees. The trial court ruled that the sellers never objected to any delays in obtaining the loan commitment, never requested that the contract be terminated on this basis, and elected by their silence, conduct and words to treat the contracts as continuing.

The seller appealed. The appellate court noted the uncontroverted evidence that the contracts were orally extended for one week until August 6th. Specifically, the court ruled that the evidence did not support the trial court's findings and, in fact, the agent's and the seller's testimony concerning the oral agreement to extend the closing of the contracts until August 6 directly contradicts the trial court's findings. The appellate court remanded the case for entry of a new judgment that would award the seller the earnest money, post-judgment interest and attorney's fees.

Bentley v. Peace & Quiet Realty 2 LLC

367 F. Supp. 2d 341; 2005 U.S. Dist.

A federal court in New York let a suit proceed to trial in order to decide whether a disabled tenant's request to move to a more accessible apartment in the same building for the same rent is reasonable.

The tenant was a 66-year old cancer patient who lived on the fourth floor of a building. She had to climb stairs to reach her apartment. Her rent was fixed by law at $820.64 per month.

Notes

25

Surgeries made it difficult for her to climb stairs. She asked the landlord for a first floor apartment. The landlord agreed but increased the rent to $1000.30 (the maximum permitted under law).

The tenant sued under the Fair Housing Act, claiming that the landlord failed to make a reasonable accommodation based on her disability. Under the Fair Housing Act, a landlord must make a reasonable accommodation to a disabled tenant when the accommodation is necessary to afford an equal opportunity to use and enjoy the building. Whether a request is "reasonable" is determined on a case-by-case basis weighing the costs to the landlord and the benefit to the disabled individual.

The landlord attempted to have the case dismissed without the necessity of trial. The landlord argued that there was no discrimination against the tenant. Instead, he argued that his decision as to the amount of the rent was neutral and was not based on one's disability. The landlord argued that the tenant request was not based on her disability, but was based on her inability to pay market rent for the specific apartment she desired.

The court rejected the landlord's arguments as a basis to dismiss the lawsuit and allowed the matter to proceed to trial. The court said that:

1. a disability-neutral policy or decision could be "trumped" by the need to reasonably accommodate a particular disabled person; and

2. moving to a lower floor, in this case, could qualify as an accommodation in this case.

The question left for the trial was whether the accommodation was reasonable under the circumstances; specifically, the court would need to weigh the costs to the landlord against the benefit to the disabled person.

The point of this case is that even those policies that appear neutral on their face may be subject to the requirement to make a reasonable accommodation.

Huntley v. Enon Limited Partnership

197 S.W.3d 844; 2006 Tex. App.

Huntley entered into a Commercial Contract of Sale with Enon to purchase a shopping center. The contract provided that if the contract were properly terminated by Huntley, he was entitled to the return of the earnest money. The contract provided for assumption of the existing loan and that, if the assumption was not approved by the lender, Huntley had the right to terminate. An amendment to the assumption provision extended the time for obtaining approval. A second amendment provided that the lender's approval had to be free of any obligation on Huntley's part for environmental matters and further extended the time for lender approval.

Notes

26

On September 28th, just before the date for lender approval to be obtained, the lender sent a letter stating that approval had been given. The letter did not indicate the terms of the assumption. When the commitment letter arrived on October 3rd (after the expiration of the assumption approval period), it included a requirement that Huntley execute an environmental indemnity. Enon signed the commitment letter, but Huntley did not. A month later, Huntley sent a letter terminating the contract and requesting the return of the earnest money. Two days after the termination letter was received, the lender sent a new commitment letter deleting the environmental indemnity requirement. Again, Enon accepted and signed the document; Huntley did not.

Huntley argued that he had a right to terminate the contract when the lender required an environmental guaranty. Enon argued that Huntley did not have a right to terminate the contract and that Huntley's subsequent termination constituted a breach of the contract because the lender approved Huntley's assumption of the loan. The court held that Enon's argument, however, was unpersuasive because it ignored the second amendment's requirement that Huntley assume the loan without any liability for environmental issues.

Although the September 28th approval notice indicates that the lender had approved the loan assumption, it does not indicate any of the terms or conditions upon which the loan assumption had been approved. Conversely, the letter faxed by the lender on October 3rd set forth the conditions upon which the loan assumption had been approved, including that Huntley assume liability for environmental issues. The September 28th letter did not serve as the lender's approval of the loan assumption absent a requirement that Huntley assume liability for environmental issues as required by the second amendment but was directly contrary to the express requirement of the second amendment that the loan assumption be free of any such assumption of environmental liability. The lender withdrew its requirement that Huntley assume environmental liability in the November 8th letter, but this was more than a month after the September 30th deadline set by the second amendment, two days after Huntley had provided written notice terminating the contract.

Norris v. Thomas

215 S.W.3d 851; 2007 Tex. App.

The Texas Supreme Court responded to an inquiry from the 5th Circuit Court of Appeals to determine whether a boat qualifies as a homestead under the Texas Constitution. The Texas Supreme Court held that the Constitution has been interpreted to mean that improvements to real property must include improvements to real property as spelled out in Article 16, Section 51 of the Constitution, and that there can be no homestead rights in personal property until it is annexed to the real estate, and even at that, it must be a permanent improvement.

Notes

27

The court analogized the situation to a house trailer, mounted on wheels and moved into a backyard of a residence. The court noted that the house trailer was a homestead only because it was permanently attached to the real estate and set alongside the house, essentially becoming an extra room, and that house trailers without the characteristics of permanent fixtures are not protected homesteads.

In this case, despite dock-based connections to utilities and plumbing that are sufficient for a mobile home or house trailer, the boat retains its independent, mobile character. Even when attached to the dock-based amenities, the boat has self-contained utility and plumbing systems and has its own propulsion. The court further noted that the legislature is certainly free to put a proposed amendment before the Texas voters to include boats.

Pulley v. Milberger

198 S.W.3d 418; 2006 Tex. App.

This is a landlord-tenant case involving a dispute related to the return of a security deposit. The landlord was neither a professional landlord nor a property manager.

The landlord leased the property to a tenant under a one-year lease. The tenant gave the landlord a $3,700 security deposit. The landlord had installed new carpet in the home about four months before the tenant occupied the property and the evidence indicated that the home was in good condition at the time of the lease.

The landlord programmed the sprinkler system to water the yard regularly and instructed the tenant that the sprinkler system should remain on. The landlord paid for the maintenance of the yard.

The tenant stayed in the property a total of six years. Near the end of the tenancy, the tenant sent a notice notifying the landlord that he would vacate the property. The tenant also told the landlord that the sprinkler system was not working properly.

When the landlord's agent went to view the property to list it for lease, the agent noted the grass in the front yard was dead. The landlord had the yard resodded and told the tenant that it had to be watered or the grass would die. The landlord learned that the sprinkler system had been turned off. He turned it back on and wrapped a tie around it. Later that evening the landlord learned that the tie wrap was removed, and the system was turned off.

The agent had problems showing the property. It was difficult to schedule showings and, once inside, the prospects soon left because of a urine smell in the master bedroom. The landlord took the property off the market.

When the tenant finally vacated the home, the tenant left a handwritten note in the house advising the landlord of his forwarding address. The landlord inspected the property two

---

Notes

28

days after the tenant vacated the property. A few days later, he inspected the property again with his agent. In addition to the lawn, they observed that the foundation was cracked, the built-in china cabinet had several severe scratches, the garage had a deep oil stain, the carpet was stained in several places, there was a urine smell throughout, and there were other damages to the property. The landlord took photographs and obtained estimates to make repairs.

The landlord sent the tenant a letter describing the damages and stated, "As a result of the damages to the property that exceed what is considered reasonable wear and tear the resultant cost of repairs has exceed[ed] the [security] deposit."

The tenant did not respond to the letter. The landlord tried several times to call the tenant, but the tenant did not take the landlord's calls. After 30 days had passed from the date the tenant vacated, the tenant sent a letter to the landlord demanding that the landlord return the security deposit. The landlord invited the tenant to meet with him. The tenant did not respond. The landlord had the damage repaired, which took approximately three months.

About one year after the tenant had notified the landlord that he would vacate the property, the tenant sued the landlord to recover his security deposit. The tenant alleged that the landlord

☑ failed to return their security deposit within 30 days;

☑ failed to account for the security deposit because he did not furnish them with a written description and itemized list of the deductions; and

☑ improperly accounted for the security deposit because he did not itemize the deductions and that the sums were deducted for normal wear and tear.

The tenant claimed the landlord acted in bad faith. The landlord denied the allegations and filed a counterclaim for $2,000 in damages above the security deposit.

The trial court found for the landlord and awarded the landlord the amount under his counterclaim plus attorney fees.

Section 92.109 of the Texas Property Code provides a tenant with a cause of action against his landlord when the landlord fails to return a security deposit or to provide a written description of the damages and an itemized list of the deductions by the 30th day after the tenant surrenders the premises. After a tenant proves the landlord did not comply with Section 92.109, the landlord must then show that he did not act in bad faith; otherwise the landlord will have to pay, in addition to the security deposit, a penalty of $100 plus three times the amount wrongfully withheld. Bad faith is presumed when the landlord fails to return the security deposit or provide a written description of the damages within 30 days after the tenant surrenders the property. However, the 30-day period does not begin until after the

---

Notes

tenant has vacated the property and has given the landlord a written statement of the tenant's forwarding address for the purpose of returning the security deposit.

A landlord may deduct damages to the property from the security deposit as authorized by the lease but may not deduct for normal wear and tear to the property. The tenant claimed that the landlord did not provide him with a written itemization of the damages and that the failure to provide the itemization proves that the landlord acted in bad faith.

To determine if the landlord acted in good faith, the court must determine if the landlord had a reasonable basis to believe that he had the right to retain the security deposit. The appellate court noted that:

- ☑ the landlord was an amateur landlord;

- ☑ the landlord believed he was entitled to retain the security deposit to cover the damages;

- ☑ there was evidence showing damage to the property beyond normal wear and tear; and

- ☑ the landlord did send a letter to the tenant stating that there was damage and invited the tenant to discuss the damages with him, which the tenant refused to do.

Therefore, the appellate court upheld the trial court's determination that the landlord did not act in bad faith. The appellate courted noted that the landlord presented evidence at trial of the damages to the property. The tenant did not provide any contrary evidence. The appellate court reviewed the evidence presented by the landlord and determined that it was sufficient to uphold the trial court's finding that the deductions were reasonable. The appellate court concluded that the charges were reasonable and that the landlord had a reasonable excuse for failing to give an itemized list of the deductions.

It is important to note that this case may distinguish between a professional and amateur landlord in reaching its findings as to whether a landlord acted in good faith or in bad faith.

Belew v. Rector

202 S.W.3d 849; 2006 Tex. App.

A real estate agent had an oral agreement with his broker that he would receive a percentage of the commission from his sales. The agent had worked for the broker about three years. The broker assisted a developer in developing a subdivision. The developer paid the broker a development fee. The agent received one-half of the development fee because the agent had done much of the legwork. The agent believed the broker also agreed to pay him one-half of any commission for any lot sold in the subdivision.

Notes

The agent produced evidence that ten lots had sold in the subdivision during the time he was associated with the broker, which would have entitled him to a commission of $4,618.50. The broker claimed the agent was not entitled to a commission on the sale of the ten lots as that transaction was unfunded. The lots had sold to one entity that intended to build homes on the lots. The broker testified that the sale of the ten lots was subject to a side agreement under which the purchaser was not required to pay for a lot until it was occupied by a house and the house sold. The broker testified that her company received no commission on the sale of the ten lots. The broker owned a portion of the entity that bought the ten lots. The trial court found for the agent and awarded him his claimed commissions plus attorney fees.

The broker appealed. The broker argued that the alleged agreement to pay the agent on the sale of lots that had not been funded lacked any type of consideration. She argued that the agent had not done anything to earn the commission on the sale of the ten lots as he was not involved in that sale. The agent did not argue that he earned the commission on the ten lots by performing any services on the sale. Instead, he argued that his agreement with the broker was that, while he was associated with the broker, he was entitled to one-half of the commission of any lot sale in the subdivision regardless of whether he sold it or not.

The decision in this case depended on whether the parties had one or two agreements covering lot sales in the subdivision. The agent claims they had one agreement, under which he had already performed his obligations and was simply awaiting payment. The broker claimed that there was one agreement covering the initial development fee and a second agreement covering the subsequent lot sales. The appellate court noted that there was conflicting testimony as to this issue. Because the trial court is the judge of the credibility of the witnesses and the weight to be given to the testimony, the appellate court had to defer to the trial court's determination on this issue. The trial court ruled that the evidence was sufficient to establish that there was only one oral agreement for the commissions.

The broker also argued that since there was no evidence that she received any commission on the sale of the ten lots during the time the agent was associated with her, the agent was not entitled to be paid. The appellate court noted that the broker was a sole proprietor and also owned an interest in the entity that bought the lots and that she could easily facilitate a deferred commission payment. The court also recalled that a clear distinction must be made between earning and receiving a commission. Specifically, the commission was earned on the date the lots sold. Apparently, the oral agreement between the broker and the agent did not draw this distinction. Therefore, the appellate court deferred to the trial court's determination that the commission had been earned and was payable.

Notes

31

Probus Properties v. Kirby

200 S.W.3d 258; 2006 Tex. App

In 2001, a commercial tenant leased space under a three-year term. The lease gave the tenant a one-year option to buy the property for $200,000. The tenant also had the right to extend the option to buy for two more years "by paying, on or before January 1st of each respective year, an additional annual Option Fee . . ." If the tenant failed to make any annual payment of option fees, the tenant would forfeit any option fees previously made.

The tenant made the original option fee and the first annual option fee payments by personal checks delivered to the landlord. The tenant paid the next annual option fee with a personal check. The landlord deposited the check on January 2nd. On January 6th, the tenant's bank returned the check unpaid with the notation "Drawn Against Uncollected Funds." The landlord then sent the tenant notice that the option had expired due to nonpayment of the option extension fee.

The tenant explained that he had two checking accounts, and he had mistakenly made deposits at the wrong bank. He realized he had made the mistake on January 2nd and drove to the bank on which the check was drawn to make a deposit to cover the check but had car trouble along the way. On January 3rd, the tenant deposited a check to cover the option fee check. Because of inactivity in the account and the size of the deposit, the bank placed a two-day hold on the deposit. The tenant was unaware that the bank would put a hold on the deposit. He did not contact his bank officer about the deposit.

The tenant sued the landlord claiming that he performed the conditions necessary to extend the option, or, as an alternative, that under the circumstances, equity would relieve him of the obligation to satisfy the strict conditions.

The jury found for the tenant, holding that he had met the conditions to extend the option and that equity gave him relief to strictly comply. The court awarded specific performance to the tenant.

The landlord appealed. The appellate court noted that, in general, options must be exercised in strict compliance with the terms of the option agreement. In this case, the lease required the tenant to pay an additional option fee on or before January 1st to extend the option. Although the lease did not contain an express statement that "time is of the essence," the nature of the option and the language requiring timely payment of the option fees makes time essential to the extension and exercise of the option.

The check was delivered to the landlord on January 1st. The efficacy of the check as payment is critical in this case. The court noted that, unless otherwise agreed, an uncertified check is merely a conditional payment for an obligation and payment is made absolute when the

---

Notes

32

check is presented and honored. If the check is dishonored, the original obligation remains. The tenant's dishonored check established that payment was never made. The tenant could not cure the "dishonorment" because the time by which payment had to be made to extend the option had expired. The tenant had waited until the last day to make payment. The appellate court concluded that there was no evidence to support the jury's finding that the tenant performed the required obligations to extend the option.

The court then looked to whether equity excused the tenant from strict compliance. "Equity" is a remedy that a court may grant where "the failure was the result of an honest and justifiable mistake, any delay was slight, any loss to the optionor was slight, and cancelling the option would result in unconscionable hardship to the optionee." The appellate court looked at prior cases granting such relief and established that the facts in each case were clearly different. In those prior cases, there were some unusual events, relating to the landlord, that did not exist in this case.

The appellate court reversed the trial court's judgment and remanded the case to the trial court to enter judgment that the tenant take nothing and that the landlord recover attorney's fees, costs and interest (allowing for proper credits).

Coldwell Banker Whiteside Associates v. Ryan Equity Partners, Ltd.

181 S. W. 3d 879; 2006 Tex. App.

The Parkmont apartment project was built in 1964 when zoning allowed multifamily uses. The sellers bought the property in 1972. In 1978, the property was rezoned to single family but allowed multifamily to continue as legal nonconforming. In 1988, the area was rezoned again, making multifamily housing nonconforming. This zoning change went unrecognized until 1994, when residents petitioned the city to close various multifamily housing uses.

The Dallas City Council then passed an ordinance creating a Planned Development District (PDD) that included the property. Under the PDD, multifamily housing uses larger than six units were prohibited unless owners obtained a special-use permit. Failure to obtain a special-use permit required the nonconforming use to be abated by the city's board of adjustment on the application of any citizen.

Abatement of the nonconforming use meant that the nonconforming property would have to become a single-family residence or cease to operate. In 1995, the sellers applied for a special-use permit from the city, but their application was denied. However, they continued to operate the property as a 31-unit apartment complex, and no one applied to abate the nonconforming use.

Notes

33

In 1998, Ryan Equity started looking for properties in East Dallas to buy and renovate. It contacted Coldwell Banker as a broker, which recommended the Parkmont as a suitable investment. One of the partners in Ryan Equity asked Coldwell Banker about the zoning, and Coldwell Banker said Parkmont was a grandfathered legal nonconforming use. Ryan Equity made no independent investigation of the zoning nor did it seek confirmation of Coldwell Banker's representation of the extent to which the property was grandfathered. Ryan Equity did not ask sellers about the zoning, nor did it tell them the intended use of the property. After looking at the property and deciding it could be rehabilitated according to the plan, Ryan Equity offered to purchase the property. The contract for the sale of the property stated that the sellers were "not aware of…any material defects to the Property." The sale closed on November 24, 1998.

Ryan Equity planned to renovate the property after renovating another, but it planned to use the rental income from the property to maintain it until the renovations could begin. Ryan Equity, however, was soon cited for the property's multiple building code violations. Ryan Equity's attorney discovered the PDD ordinance and determined that unless Ryan Equity obtained a special-use permit, the property would be forced to cease operation as multifamily housing on the application of any citizen to the board of adjustment.

An application for abatement of the nonconforming multifamily use of the property was filed with the board of adjustment. Since the property did not have a legal right to exist as multifamily housing, Ryan Equity was unable to obtain the building permits and financing necessary to repair the major problems with the property. Ryan Equity incurred fines of over $167,000 for building code violations.

The City of Dallas brought two suits, one seeking demolition of the buildings for building code violations and the other seeking abatement of the nonconforming use of the property. In June 2001, Ryan Equity settled the suits with the city by agreeing to tear down the apartments in exchange for the city waiving the fines. Ryan Equity demolished the buildings in August 2001.

Ryan Equity sued the sellers and Coldwell Banker for breach of the duty of good faith and fair dealing, common-law and statutory fraud, and breach of contract. Ryan Equity also sued Coldwell Banker for breach of fiduciary duty. The trial court found the sellers were not liable and found Coldwell Banker liable only for breach of contract.

Ryan Equity contended that the nondisclosure of the status of the zoning and the denial of the special-use permit were nondisclosures of material defects with the property. The trial court concluded, "The status of the property's zoning does not constitute a 'material defect' under the terms of the contract."

Notes

34

Whether nonconformance to zoning ordinances constitutes a "material defect" requiring disclosure under a real estate contract is an issue of first impression in Texas. The term "material defect" is not defined in the purchase contract, nor is it defined in the statutes governing the sale of real property. According to the dictionary, a "defect" is "an irregularity in a surface or a structure that spoils the appearance or causes weakness or failure." Thus, a "defect to the property" would be some irregularity in "a surface or a structure" of the property that mars its appearance or causes some aspect of the property to weaken or fail. The definition addresses tangible aspects of the property, whether its physical appearance or its physical structure. This definition is in line with the plain understanding and usage of the term: when something is labeled defective, we mean it is blemished, broken, deficient, or imperfect in some physical sense.

Given this plain understanding of the language at issue, the court concluded that the zoning status of the property was not a material defect to the property within the meaning of the purchase contract. Zoning laws neither cause nor result from physical imperfections or deficiencies in real property itself. The zoning law at issue does not relate to the exact physical condition of the property. Instead, the zoning law regulates the use of the property, giving it a discernible legal status. The denial of sellers' application for a special-use permit was a determination of the property's legal status pursuant to the zoning ordinance, not a material defect to the property.

Finally, having concluded that the zoning information related to legal status and not to any defective condition of the property, the court addressed whether that legal status nonetheless had to be disclosed by the sellers. Ryan Equity contended the sellers had the duty to inform it of the zoning laws and to interpret the effect of those laws for it. Ryan Equity cited no authority for the proposition that a seller of commercial real estate has a duty to identify the applicable zoning laws or explain their effect to a sophisticated, experienced real estate investor who makes no inquiry to the seller of the zoning status and receives no express representation from the seller of the zoning status. Courts presume the parties to a contract know and take into consideration the laws affecting matters about which they contracted, unless the contrary clearly appears in the terms of the contract.

In its second issue, Ryan Equity contended the trial court erred in concluding the sellers did not commit fraud against it. For common-law fraud, the plaintiff must prove

☑ a material misrepresentation was made and was false when made;

☑ the misrepresentation was known by the speaker to be false when it was made or that it was made recklessly as a positive assertion without knowledge of its truth;

☑ that the speaker made the misrepresentation with intent that it should be acted upon;

Notes

35

☑ the party justifiably relied on the representation; and

☑ the party was injured as a result.

To prove statutory fraud in a real estate transaction, a plaintiff must show:

☑ a false representation of a past or existing material fact, when the false representation is made to a person for the purpose of inducing the person to enter into a contract and relied on by that person in entering into that contract; or

☑ a false promise to do an act, when the false promise is

- material,

- made with the intention of not fulfilling it,

- made to a person for the purpose of inducing that person to enter into a contract, and

- relied on by that person in entering into that contract (Section 27.01(a), Texas Business & Commerce Code).

A misrepresentation may consist of the concealment or nondisclosure of a material fact when there is a duty to disclose. The duty to disclose arises when one party knows that the other party is ignorant of the true facts and does not have an equal opportunity to discover the truth.

It is undisputed that the sellers did not discuss the zoning or special-use permits with Ryan Equity's principals and made no affirmative representations regarding the zoning. Thus, their liability for fraud depends on their having a duty to disclose those facts. A seller of real estate is under a duty to disclose any material fact that would be not be discoverable by the purchaser's exercise of ordinary care and diligence or which a reasonable investigation would not uncover.

Ryan Equity does not explain why the zoning status and denial of the application for the special-use permit were not discoverable through the exercise of ordinary care, reasonable diligence or a reasonable investigation. Ryan Equity's lawyer testified that he discovered the zoning status and the denial of the application for the special-use permit through examining the publicly available zoning records at city hall. No witness testified that these records were not discoverable through a reasonable investigation. The lawyer's testimony did not indicate that the investigation yielding the facts was unreasonable or went beyond the exercise of ordinary care and reasonable diligence. Because the sellers had no duty to disclose the facts, their failure to do so was not fraud.

Notes

36

5

Mortgage Fraud

To help curb mortgage fraud, several changes have been made to the Texas Finance Code. A new section provides that the lender, mortgage banker or licensed mortgage broker must provide each home loan applicant a written notice at closing. The notice must be provided on a separate document, be at least fourteen-point type and have the following or substantially similar language:

"WARNING": Intentionally or knowingly making a materially false or misleading written statement to obtain property or credit, including a mortgage loan, is a violation of Section 32.32, Texas Penal Code, and, depending on the amount of the loan or value of the property, is punishable by imprisonment for a term of 2 years to 99 years and a fine not to exceed $10,000.00.

"I/We, the undersigned home loan applicant(s), represent that I/we have received, read, and understand this notice of penalties for making a materially false or misleading written statement to obtain a home loan.

"I/We represent that all statements and representations contained in my/our written home loan application, including statements or representations regarding my/our identity, employment, annual income, and intent to occupy the residential real property secured by the home loan, are true and correct as of the date of loan closing."

_____

Name:_____

SUBSCRIBED AND SWORN TO before me on this _____ day of _____, _____, by _____.

_____

Notary Public, State of Texas

Notes

37

On receipt of the notice, the loan applicant must verify the information and execute the notice (Section 343.105, Texas Finance Code).

Another change to the Government Code provides that if anyone who determines or reasonably suspects that fraudulent activity has been committed or is about to be committed, that person must report this information to an authorized governmental agency, such as the attorney general, local or state law enforcement agency, prosecuting attorney, or Texas Department of Banking. The agency receiving such a report may not disclose to any person involved in the fraudulent activity that the fraudulent activity has been reported (Section 402.031, Government Code).

The state has also established a residential mortgage taskforce consisting of various state office holders. This task force focuses its efforts on sharing information and resources and enforces administrative and criminal actions against perpetrators of mortgage fraud. A concurrent change with the Code of Criminal Procedures extends the statute of limitations for prosecution for mortgage fraud to seven years (Article 12.01, Texas Code of Criminal Procedure).

Difference between Mortgage Fraud, Sub-Prime Lending, and Predatory Lending

In some discussions about mortgage fraud, the distinctions between the terms *mortgage fraud*, *sub-prime lending*, and *predatory lending* can become blurred. It is important to note the differences.

Mortgage fraud is typically any activity involving a mortgage that constitutes a violation of a criminal or penal statute and involves an attempt to defraud someone. Fraud usually involves a material representation that was false, which the perpetrator knows is false (or made recklessly), and which the perpetrator intends for the victim to act on.

Subprime lending is a type of lending that is considered to be "risky" as it typically serves borrowers who cannot obtain credit in the prime market. It is sometimes called "B-paper." It is typically defined by the status of the borrower. Subprime loans are risky for both borrowers and lenders. Typically, these loans contain higher interest rates and higher fees. Some argue that subprime lending has a legitimate place in the market as it may provide credit to those who would otherwise not have access to the credit. Critics of subprime lending point out that many lenders take advantage of unsophisticated borrowers, increase foreclosure rates by introducing too many unqualified borrowers into the market, and cause long-term instability in the market.

Predatory lending involves unfair or deceptive practices by lenders who seek to make legitimate loans to consumers but who seek to take advantage of the consumer. The predatory

Notes

38

lender is usually targeting subprime borrowers. Predatory lending typically involves at least one of the following:

- ☑ making loans based predominantly on the liquidation value of a borrower's collateral rather than on the borrower's ability to repay the mortgage (which may end up stripping the borrower of any equity he may have had);

- ☑ inducing a borrower to repeatedly refinance a loan in order to charge high points and fees each time the loan is refinanced (loan flipping);

- ☑ charging excessive fees, which may be packed into the loan amount without the borrower understanding the effect (loan packing); or

- ☑ engaging in fraud or deception to conceal the true nature of the loan obligation or ancillary products from an unsuspecting borrower.

Home Loan Corporation v. Texas American Title Company

191 S.W.3d 728 (Tex. App. – Houston [14th Dist.] pet. Den.)

Texas American Title Company (TATCO) acted as a settlement agent for the closing of a residential mortgage loan funded by Home Loan. Home Loan sold the loan in a secondary market; no payments were made on it, and Home Loan was obligated to repurchase it. Home Loan filed suit against TATCO alleging that they breached fiduciary duties owed Home Loan by failing to: (1) inform Home Loan that the seller had requested over half of the seller's proceeds be paid to the mortgage loan broker; (2) inform Home Loan that the seller had requested that those proceeds be paid to the principal of the mortgage loan broker; and (3) accurately disclose in the HUD-1 settlement statement how the seller's proceeds would be or had been disbursed.

The court noted that even though no formal escrow agreement had been entered into, a title company normally accepts funds for disbursement in a closing transaction for a fee and owes the party remitting those funds a duty of loyalty, a duty to make full disclosure, and a duty to exercise a high degree of care to conserve the money and pay it only to those who are entitled to receive it. The difference is what that fiduciary duty and full disclosure requires.

The court noted that ordinarily a fiduciary duty of full disclosure requires disclosure of all material facts known to the fiduciary that might affect the rights of the person to whom the duty is owed. The court went on to note that there is a variation on how the disclosure duty is handled in the various states. TATCO argued that an escrow agent is required to remain neutral under Texas law, and while they owe a fiduciary duty to buyer and seller, these duties

Notes

39

are strictly limited to its role as an escrow agent as defined by the escrow agreement. [Equisource Realty Corp. vs. Crown Life Ins. Co., 854 S.W.2d 691, 697 (Tex. App. —Dallas 1993, no writ)].

This court, however, held that despite the language of the Equisource case, they could find no Texas decision that has directly addressed any limitation on the scope of an escrow or other settlement agent's fiduciary duties to disclose.

The court did note, however, that Home Loan suffered no loss from the disbursement because it had already funded the loan to TATCO. Their disbursement to TATCO was irrevocable, and Home Loan would have had no recourse to prevent the disbursement. The real damage, the court noted, was that the underlying loan transaction was a sham, and Home Loan would have suffered the resulting loss even if TATCO had disbursed the funds directly to the seller as set out in the HUD-1 statement.

Notes

40

6

TREC Forms

The following forms have been updated since December 2006.

9-7 Unimproved Property Contract (amended June 2008)

The changes are the same as those listed for 20–8 except

- Paragraph 2 – reformatted but not amended

- Paragraph 7B – changes referenced in 20-8 7D are made to 7B

- Paragraph 22 – check box not added regarding addendum containing required notices under §5.01, §420.001, and §420.002, Texas Property Code

PROMULGATED BY THE TEXAS REAL ESTATE COMMISSION (TREC)   06-30-08

EQUAL HOUSING OPPORTUNITY

UNIMPROVED PROPERTY CONTRACT
NOTICE: Not For Use For Condominium Transactions

1. PARTIES: The parties to this contract are _____ (Seller)
and _____ (Buyer). Seller agrees
to sell and convey to Buyer and Buyer agrees to buy from Seller the Property defined below.

2. PROPERTY: Lot _____, Block _____
_____ Addition, City of
_____, County of _____
Texas, known as_____
(address/zip code), or as described on attached exhibit together with all rights, privileges and
appurtenances pertaining thereto, including but not limited to: water rights, claims, permits,
strips and gores, easements, and cooperative or association memberships (the Property).

3. SALES PRICE:
   A. Cash portion of Sales Price payable by Buyer at closing.................. $_____
   B. Sum of all financing described below (excluding any loan funding
        fee or mortgage insurance premium) .... $_____
   C. Sales Price (Sum of A and B) .... $_____

4. FINANCING: The portion of Sales Price not payable in cash will be paid as follows: (Check
   applicable boxes below)
   ☐ A. THIRD PARTY FINANCING: One or more third party mortgage loans in the total amount of
        $_____ (excluding any loan funding fee or mortgage insurance premium).
        (1) Property Approval: If the Property does not satisfy the lenders' underwriting
             requirements for the loan(s), this contract will terminate and the earnest money will be
             refunded to Buyer.
        (2) Financing Approval: (Check one box only)
             ☐ (a) This contract is subject to Buyer being approved for the financing described in the
                   attached Third Party Financing Condition Addendum.
             ☐ (b) This contract is not subject to Buyer being approved for financing and does not
                   involve FHA or VA financing.
   ☐ B. ASSUMPTION: The assumption of the unpaid principal balance of one or more promissory
        notes described in the attached TREC Loan Assumption Addendum.
   ☐ C. SELLER   FINANCING: A promissory note from Buyer to Seller of $_____,
        secured by vendor's and deed of trust liens, and containing the terms and conditions
        described in the attached TREC Seller Financing Addendum. If an owner policy of title
        insurance is furnished, Buyer shall furnish Seller with a mortgagee policy of title insurance.

5. EARNEST MONEY: Upon execution of this contract by all parties, Buyer shall deposit
   $_____ as earnest money with _____
   as escrow agent, at _____
   (address). Buyer shall deposit additional earnest money of $_____ with escrow
   agent within _____ days after the effective date of this contract. If Buyer fails to deposit the
   earnest money as required by this contract, Buyer will be in default.

6. TITLE POLICY AND SURVEY:
   A. TITLE POLICY: Seller shall furnish to Buyer at ☐Seller's ☐Buyer's expense an owner policy of
      title insurance (Title Policy) issued by _____
      (Title Company) in the amount of the Sales Price, dated at or after closing, insuring Buyer
      against loss under the provisions of the Title Policy, subject to the promulgated exclusions
      (including existing building and zoning ordinances) and the following exceptions:
      (1) Restrictive covenants common to the platted subdivision in which the Property is located.
      (2) The standard printed exception for standby fees, taxes and assessments.
      (3) Liens created as part of the financing described in Paragraph 4.
      (4) Utility easements created by the dedication deed or plat of the subdivision in which the
           Property is located.
      (5) Reservations or exceptions otherwise permitted by this contract or as may be approved by
           Buyer in writing.
      (6) The standard printed exception as to marital rights.
      (7) The standard printed exception as to waters, tidelands, beaches, streams, and related
           matters.
      (8) The standard printed exception as to discrepancies, conflicts, shortages in area or boundary
           lines, encroachments or protrusions, or overlapping improvements. Buyer, at Buyer's expense,
           may have the exception amended to read, "shortages in area".
   B. COMMITMENT: Within 20 days after the Title Company receives a copy of this contract, Seller
      shall furnish to Buyer a commitment for title insurance (Commitment) and, at Buyer's
      expense, legible copies of restrictive covenants and documents evidencing exceptions in the

Initialed for identification by Buyer_____ _____ and Seller _____ _____   TREC NO. 9-7

41

10-5 Addendum for Sale of Other Property by Buyer (amended April 2007)

The revisions to Paragraphs A & B of TREC No. 10-5, Addendum for Sale of Property by Buyer, remove references to a specific time of day in the definition of Contingency and in the deadline date to waive the Contingency. Paragraph D is rewritten for clarity and deletes extraneous language regarding Buyer's failure to obtain loan or assumption approval.

04-23-07

PROMULGATED BY THE TEXAS REAL ESTATE COMMISSION (TREC)

ADDENDUM FOR
SALE OF OTHER PROPERTY BY BUYER

TO CONTRACT CONCERNING THE PROPERTY AT

_____
(Address of Property)

A. The contract is contingent upon Buyer's **receipt of the proceeds** from the sale of Buyer's property at_____ (Address) on or before _____, 20_____ (the Contingency). If the Contingency is not satisfied or waived by Buyer by the above date, the contract will terminate automatically and the earnest money will be refunded to Buyer.

NOTICE: The date inserted in this Paragraph should be no later than the Closing Date specified in Paragraph 9 of the contract.

B. If Seller accepts a written offer to sell the Property, Seller shall notify Buyer (1) of such acceptance **AND** (2) that Seller requires Buyer to waive the Contingency. Buyer must waive the Contingency on or before the _____ day after Seller's notice to Buyer; otherwise the contract will terminate automatically and the earnest money will be refunded to Buyer.

C. Buyer may waive the Contingency only by notifying Seller of the waiver and depositing $_____ with escrow agent as additional earnest money. All notices and waivers must be in writing and are effective when delivered in accordance with the contract.

D. If Buyer waives the Contingency and fails to close and fund solely due to Buyer's non-receipt of proceeds from Buyer's sale of the Property described in Paragraph A, Buyer will be in default. If such default occurs, Seller may exercise the remedies specified in Paragraph 15 of the contract.

E. For purposes of this Addendum time is of the essence; strict compliance with the times for performance stated herein is required.

_____   _____
Buyer   Seller

_____   _____
Buyer   Seller

TREC No. 10-5

42

11-6 Addendum for "Back-up" Contract (amended April 2007)

The blank line for the Buyer's name is removed from Paragraph A of TREC No. 11-6, Addendum for "Back-Up" Contract. Paragraphs B & C are rewritten and combined for clarity. In Paragraph B, the reference to a specific time of day is deleted consistent with the revisions to TREC No. 10-5; the reference to a Contingency Date is deleted in the last sentence of Paragraph B, which defines the Amended Effective Date for purposes of performance of the Back-Up Contract. Therefore, the Amended Effective Date hinges solely on the date the Buyer receives notice of termination of the First Contract.

PROMULGATED BY THE TEXAS REAL ESTATE COMMISSION (TREC) 04-23-07

ADDENDUM FOR "BACK-UP" CONTRACT

TO CONTRACT CONCERNING THE PROPERTY AT

_____
(Address of Property)

A. The contract to which this Addendum is attached (the Back-Up Contract) is binding upon execution by the parties, and the earnest money and any Option Fee must be paid as provided in the Back-Up Contract. The Back-Up Contract is contingent upon the termination of a previous contract (the First Contract) dated _____, 20_____, for the sale of Property. Except as provided by this Addendum, neither party is required to perform under the Back-Up Contract while it is contingent upon the termination of the First Contract.

B. If the First Contract does not terminate on or before _____, 20_____, the Back-Up Contract terminates and the earnest money will be refunded to Buyer. Seller must notify Buyer immediately of the termination of the First Contract. For purposes of performance, the effective date of the Back-Up Contract changes to the date Buyer receives notice of termination of the First Contract (Amended Effective Date).

C. An amendment or modification of the First Contract will not terminate the First Contract.

D. If Buyer has the unrestricted right to terminate the Back-Up Contract, the time for giving notice of termination begins on the effective date of the Back-Up Contract, continues after the Amended Effective Date and ends upon the expiration of Buyer's unrestricted right to terminate the Back-Up Contract.

E. For purposes of this Addendum, time is of the essence. Strict compliance with the times for performance stated herein is required.

_____   _____
Buyer   Seller

_____   _____
Buyer   Seller

This form has been approved by the Texas Real Estate Commission for use with similarly approved or promulgated contract forms. Such approval relates to this form only. TREC forms are intended for use only by trained real estate licensees. No representation is made as to the legal validity or adequacy of any provision in any specific transactions. It is not suitable for complex transactions. Texas Real Estate Commission, P.O. Box 12188, Austin, TX 78711-2188, 1-800-250-8732 or (512) 459-6544 (http://www.trec.state.tx.us) TREC No. 11-6. This form replaces TREC No. 11-5.

TREC No. 11-6

43

12-2 Addendum for Release of Liability on Assumed Loan and/or Restoration of Seller's VA Entitlement (amended April 2007)

The amendments to TREC No. 12-2, Addendum for Release of Liability on Assumed Loan and/or Restoration of Seller's VA Entitlement, change the title to more accurately reflect the purpose and use of the addendum. Redundant phrases in Paragraphs A.2, B.2, and the Notice are removed. The paragraph that addresses payment of costs for obtaining the release and restoration, which includes a sentence regarding negotiation of payment of such costs that exceed a specified amount, is amended to delete the sentence so that seller pays all such costs under the addendum.

PROMULGATED BY THE TEXAS REAL ESTATE COMMISSION (TREC)   04-23-07

ADDENDUM FOR
RELEASE OF LIABILITY ON ASSUMED LOAN
AND/OR RESTORATION OF SELLER'S VA ENTITLEMENT

TO CONTRACT CONCERNING THE PROPERTY AT

_____
(Address of Property)

❑ **A. RELEASE OF SELLER'S LIABILITY ON LOAN TO BE ASSUMED:**

Within _____ days after the effective date of this contract Seller and Buyer shall apply for release of Seller's liability from (a) any conventional lender, (b) VA and any lender whose loan has been guaranteed by VA, or (c) FHA and any lender whose loan has been insured by FHA. Seller and Buyer shall furnish all required information and documents. If any release of liability has not been approved by the Closing Date: (check one box only)

❑ (1) This contract will terminate and the earnest money will be refunded to Buyer.

❑ (2) Failure to obtain release approval will not delay closing.

❑ **B. RESTORATION OF SELLER'S ENTITLEMENT FOR VA LOAN:**

Within _____ days after the effective date of this contract Seller and Buyer shall apply for restoration of Seller's VA entitlement and shall furnish all information and documents required by VA. If restoration has not been approved by the Closing Date: (check one box only)

❑ (1) This contract will terminate and the earnest money will be refunded to Buyer.

❑ (2) Failure to obtain restoration approval will not delay closing.

NOTICE: VA will not restore Seller's VA entitlement unless Buyer: (a) is a veteran, (b) has sufficient unused VA entitlement and (c) is otherwise qualified. If Seller desires restoration of VA entitlement, paragraphs A and B should be used.

Seller shall pay the cost of securing the release and restoration.

Seller's deed will contain any loan assumption clause required by FHA, VA or any lender.

_____   _____
Buyer   Seller

_____   _____
Buyer   Seller

TREC No. 12-2

44

15-4 Seller's Temporary Residential Lease (amended December 2006)

Paragraph 12 of TREC No. 15-4, Seller's Temporary Lease, is revised to require the tenant to provide the landlord with door keys and access codes to allow access to the property during the term of the lease. Paragraph 24 is revised to include a blank for e-mail addresses. The blank line for the execution date is removed as the execution date is provided for in the contract to which the lease is attached.

PROMULGATED BY THE TEXAS REAL ESTATE COMMISSION (TREC)   12-04-06
(NOTICE: For use only when SELLER occupies the property for no more than 90 days AFTER the closing)

SELLER'S TEMPORARY RESIDENTIAL LEASE

1. **PARTIES:** The parties to this Lease are_____
   (Landlord) and _____(Tenant).

2. **LEASE:** Landlord leases to Tenant the Property described in the Contract between Landlord as Buyer and Tenant as Seller known as _____
   _____(address).

3. **TERM:** The term of this Lease commences on the date the sale covered by the Contract is closed and funded and terminates _____, unless terminated earlier by reason of other provisions.

4. **RENTAL:** Tenant shall pay to Landlord as rental $_____ per day (excluding the day of closing and funding) with the full amount of rental for the term of the Lease to be paid at the time of funding of the sale. Tenant will not be entitled to a refund of rental if this Lease terminates early due to Tenant's default or voluntary surrender of the Property.

5. **DEPOSIT:** Tenant shall pay to Landlord at the time of funding of the sale $_____ as a deposit to secure performance of this Lease by Tenant. Landlord may use the deposit to satisfy Tenant's obligations under this Lease. Landlord shall refund any unused portion of the deposit to Tenant with an itemized list of all deductions from the deposit within 30 days after Tenant (a) surrenders possession of the Property and (b) provides Landlord written notice of Tenant's forwarding address.

6. **UTILITIES:** Tenant shall pay all utility charges except _____
   which Landlord shall pay.

7. **USE OF PROPERTY:** Tenant may use the Property only for residential purposes. Tenant may not assign this Lease or sublet any part of the Property.

8. **PETS:** Tenant may not keep pets on the Property except _____.

9. **CONDITION OF PROPERTY:** Tenant accepts the Property in its present condition and state of repair at the commencement of the Lease. Upon termination, Tenant shall surrender the Property to Landlord in the condition required under the Contract, except normal wear and tear and any casualty loss.

10. **ALTERATIONS:** Tenant may not alter the Property or install improvements or fixtures without the prior written consent of the Landlord. Any improvements or fixtures placed on the Property during the Lease become the Property of Landlord.

11. **SPECIAL PROVISIONS:**

12. **INSPECTIONS:** Landlord may enter at reasonable times to inspect the Property. Tenant shall provide Landlord door keys and access codes to allow access to the Property during the term of Lease.

13. **LAWS:** Tenant shall comply with all applicable laws, restrictions, ordinances, rules and regulations with respect to the Property.

14. **REPAIRS AND MAINTENANCE:** Except as otherwise provided in this Lease, Tenant shall bear all expense of repairing and maintaining the Property, including but not limited to the yard, trees and shrubs, unless otherwise required by the Texas Property Code. Tenant shall promptly repair at Tenant's expense any damage to the Property caused directly or indirectly by any act or omission of the Tenant or any person other than the Landlord, Landlord's agents or invitees.

Initialed for identification by Landlord _____ and Tenant_____   TREC NO. 15-4

45

16-4 Buyer's Temporary Residential Lease (amended December 2006)

Paragraph 12 of TREC No. 16-4, Buyer's Temporary Lease, is revised to require the tenant to provide the landlord with door keys and access codes to allow access to the property during the term of the lease. Paragraph 14 is revised to add equipment and appliances to the list of specific expenses of repairing, replacing and maintaining the property that the buyer/tenant will bear. Paragraph 24 is revised to include a blank for e-mail addresses. The blank line for the execution date is removed as the execution date is provided for in the contract to which the lease is attached.

PROMULGATED BY THE TEXAS REAL ESTATE COMMISSION (TREC)   12-04-06
(NOTICE: For use only when BUYER occupies the property for no more than 90 days PRIOR the closing)

BUYER'S TEMPORARY RESIDENTIAL LEASE

1. PARTIES: The parties to this Lease are_____
(Landlord) and _____(Tenant).

2. LEASE: Landlord leases to Tenant the Property described in the Contract between Landlord as Seller and Tenant as Buyer known as _____
_____(address).

3. TERM: The term of this Lease commences _____ and terminates as specified in Paragraph 18.

4. RENTAL: Rental will be $_____ per day. Upon commencement of this Lease, Tenant shall pay to Landlord the full amount of rental of $ _____ for the anticipated term of the Lease (commencement date to the Closing Date specified in Paragraph 9 of the Contract). If the actual term of this Lease differs from the anticipated term, any additional rent or reimbursement will be paid at closing. No portion of the rental will be applied to payment of any items covered by the Contract.

5. DEPOSIT: Tenant has paid to Landlord $_____ as a deposit to secure performance of this Lease by Tenant. If this Lease is terminated before the Closing Date, Landlord may use the deposit to satisfy Tenant's obligations under this Lease. Landlord shall refund to Tenant any unused portion of the deposit together with an itemized list of all deductions from the deposit within 30 days after Tenant (a) surrenders possession of the Property and (b) provides Landlord written notice of Tenant's forwarding address. If this Lease is terminated by the closing and funding of the sale of the Property, the deposit will be refunded to Tenant at closing and funding.
NOTICE: The deposit must be in addition to the earnest money under the Contract.

6. UTILITIES: Tenant shall pay all utility connections, deposits and charges except _____
_____, which Landlord shall pay.

7. USE OF PROPERTY: Tenant may use the Property only for residential purposes. Tenant may not assign this Lease or sublet any part of the Property.

8. PETS: Tenant may not keep pets on the Property except _____.

9. CONDITION OF PROPERTY: Tenant accepts the Property in its present condition and state of repair, but Landlord shall make all repairs and improvements required by the Contract. If this Lease is terminated prior to closing, Tenant shall surrender possession of the Property to Landlord in its present condition, as improved by Landlord, except normal wear and tear and any casualty loss.

10. ALTERATIONS: Tenant may not: (a) make any holes or drive nails into the woodwork, floors, walls or ceilings (b) alter, paint or decorate the Property or (c) install improvements or fixtures without the prior written consent of Landlord. Any improvements or fixtures placed on the Property during the Lease become a part of the Property.

11. SPECIAL PROVISIONS:

12. INSPECTIONS: Landlord may enter at reasonable times to inspect, replace, repair or complete the improvements. Tenant shall provide Landlord door keys and access codes to allow access to the Property during the term of the Lease.

13. LAWS: Tenant shall comply with all applicable laws, restrictions, ordinances, rules and regulations with respect to the Property.

14. REPAIRS AND MAINTENANCE: Except as otherwise provided in this Lease, Tenant shall bear all expense of repairing, replacing and maintaining the Property, including but not limited to the yard, trees, shrubs, and all equipment and appliances, unless otherwise required by the Texas Property Code. Tenant shall promptly repair at Tenant's expense any damage to the Property caused directly or indirectly by any act or omission of the Tenant or any person other than the Landlord, Landlord's agents or invitees.

Initialed for identification by Landlord _____ and Tenant_____   TREC NO. 16-4

46

20-8 One to Four Family Residential Contract (Resale) (amended June 2008)

- Paragraph 1
  - o Reformatted to extend the blank lines before Buyer and Seller
  - o Rewritten to define the parties to the contract
- Paragraph 2
  - o 2A is reformatted
  - o 2D has added text to clarify that improvements and accessories retained by seller must be removed prior to delivery of possession
- Paragraph 5 – "both" is replaced by "all"
- Paragraph 6C
  - o "any lender" and "Buyer's lender" are changed to "Buyer's lender(s)"
  - o Last sentence is bolded
- Paragraph 6D – sentence that addresses the time for buyer to object is rewritten for clarity
- Paragraph 6E(2)
  - o "Mandatory owners' association" is changed to "mandatory membership" in a property owners' association"
  - o Amended to indicate that the residential community in which the property is located is identified in Paragraph 2
  - o Last sentence is bolded
- Paragraph 7D – amended to provide check boxes to choose whether buyer accepts property in its present condition or in its present condition with specific repairs
- Paragraph 9
  - o Subparagraphs C and D are moved to Paragraph 19
  - o New clause, (4), is added to subparagraph B regarding seller's representations
  - o Text for the new clause is moved from Paragraph 19
- Paragraph 12A(1)(b) – reference to the Veterans Housing Assistance Program is changed to a reference to the Texas Veterans Land Board
- Paragraph 17 – amended to substitute "Buyer, Seller, Listing Broker, Other Broker or escrow agent who prevails" for "The Prevailing Party"
- Paragraph 18D – amended to clarify that damages for wrongfully failing or refusing to sign a release of earnest money include the sum of the earnest money, three times the earnest money, reasonable attorney's fees and all costs of suit
- Paragraph 19 – revised to add text that was deleted from subparagraphs 9© and (D)

47

- Paragraph 22

  o Revised to add a check box for the Addendum Containing Required Notices Under §5.01, §420.001, and §420.002, Texas Property Code

  o Revise the title of "Addendum for Property Subject to Mandatory Membership in a Property Owners' Association."

  o The Seller's Temporary Lease is added to the list of addenda

- Paragraph 23 – amended to clarify that if the buyer fails to pay the Option Fee to seller within the time prescribed, the option paragraph will not be a part of the contract

---

06-30-08

PROMULGATED BY THE TEXAS REAL ESTATE COMMISSION (TREC)

ONE TO FOUR FAMILY RESIDENTIAL CONTRACT (RESALE)

NOTICE: Not For Use For Condominium Transactions

1. PARTIES: The parties to this contract are _____ (Seller) and _____ (Buyer). Seller agrees to sell and convey to Buyer and Buyer agrees to buy from Seller the Property defined below.

2. PROPERTY:
   A. LAND: Lot _____ Block _____, _____, County of _____ Addition, City of _____ Texas, known as _____ (address/zip code), or as described on attached exhibit.
   B. IMPROVEMENTS: The house, garage and all other fixtures and improvements attached to the above-described real property, including without limitation, the following permanently installed and built-in items, if any: all equipment and appliances, valances, screens, shutters, awnings, wall-to-wall carpeting, mirrors, ceiling fans, attic fans, mail boxes, television antennas and satellite dish system and equipment, heating and air-conditioning units, security and fire detection equipment, wiring, plumbing and lighting fixtures, chandeliers, water softener system, kitchen equipment, garage door openers, cleaning equipment, shrubbery, landscaping, outdoor cooking equipment, and all other property owned by Seller and attached to the above described real property.
   C. ACCESSORIES: The following described related accessories, if any: window air conditioning units, stove, fireplace screens, curtains and rods, blinds, window shades, draperies and rods, controls for satellite dish system, controls for garage door openers, entry gate controls, door keys, mailbox keys, above ground pool, swimming pool equipment and maintenance accessories, and artificial fireplace logs.
   D. EXCLUSIONS: The following improvements and accessories will be retained by Seller and must be removed prior to delivery of possession: _____

   The land, improvements and accessories are collectively referred to as the "Property".

3. SALES PRICE:
   A. Cash portion of Sales Price payable by Buyer at closing .... $ _____
   B. Sum of all financing described below (excluding any loan funding fee or mortgage insurance premium) .... $ _____
   C. Sales Price (Sum of A and B) .... $ _____

4. FINANCING: The portion of Sales Price not payable in cash will be paid as follows: (Check applicable boxes below)
   ☐ A. THIRD PARTY FINANCING: One or more third party mortgage loans in the total amount of $ _____ (excluding any loan funding fee or mortgage insurance premium).
      (1) Property Approval: If the Property does not satisfy the lenders' underwriting requirements for the loan(s), this contract will terminate and the earnest money will be refunded to Buyer.
      (2) Financing Approval: (Check one box only)
        ☐ (a) This contract is subject to Buyer being approved for the financing described in the attached Third Party Financing Condition Addendum.
        ☐ (b) This contract is not subject to Buyer being approved for financing and does not involve FHA or VA financing.
   ☐ B. ASSUMPTION: The assumption of the unpaid principal balance of one or more promissory notes described in the attached TREC Loan Assumption Addendum.
   ☐ C. SELLER FINANCING: A promissory note from Buyer to Seller of $ _____, secured by vendor's and deed of trust liens, and containing the terms and conditions described in the attached TREC Seller Financing Addendum. If an owner policy of title insurance is furnished, Buyer shall furnish Seller with a mortgagee policy of title insurance.

5. EARNEST MONEY: Upon execution of this contract by all parties, Buyer shall deposit $ _____ as earnest money with _____ as escrow agent, at _____ (address). Buyer shall deposit additional earnest money of $ _____ with escrow agent within _____ days after the effective date of this contract. If Buyer fails to deposit the earnest money as required by this contract, Buyer will be in default.

6. TITLE POLICY AND SURVEY:
   A. TITLE POLICY: Seller shall furnish to Buyer at ☐ Seller's ☐ Buyer's expense an owner policy of title insurance (Title Policy) issued by _____ (Title Company) in the amount of the Sales Price, dated at or after closing, insuring Buyer against loss under the provisions of the Title Policy, subject to the promulgated exclusions

Initialed for identification by Buyer _____ _____ and Seller _____ _____   TREC NO. 20-8

48

23-8 New Home Contract (Incomplete Construction) (amended June 2008) and

24-8 New Home Contract (Completed Construction) (amended June 2008)

The changes are the same as those listed for TREC No. 20-8 except:

In December 2007, the disclosure on Page 8 of the contract required by §27.007(a), Texas Property Code was revised because the disclosure was amended by House Bill 3147, 80th Legislature, R.S. (2007).

In June 2008, additional changes were made and are the same as those listed for TREC No. 20–8 except:

- Paragraph 2 is reformatted but not amended

- Paragraph 7D is not amended

- The check box added to Paragraph 22 regarding the Addendum Containing Required Notices Under §5.01, §420.001, and §420.002, Texas Property Code is pre-checked and a parenthetical is included to explain that the addendum must be attached and Paragraphs B and C must be completed

PROMULGATED BY THE TEXAS REAL ESTATE COMMISSION (TREC)   06-30-08

NEW HOME CONTRACT
(Completed Construction)

NOTICE: Not For Use For Condominium Transactions or Closings Prior to Completion of Construction

1. **PARTIES:** The parties to this contract are _____ (Seller) and _____ (Buyer). Seller agrees to sell and convey to Buyer and Buyer agrees to buy from Seller the Property defined below.

2. **PROPERTY:** Lot _____, Block _____
_____ Addition, City
of _____, County of _____,
Texas, known as _____
(address/zip code), or as described on attached exhibit, together with: (i) improvements, fixtures and all other property located thereon; and (ii) all rights, privileges and appurtenances thereto, including but not limited to: permits, easements, and cooperative and association memberships. All property sold by this contract is called the "Property".

3. **SALES PRICE:**
   A. Cash portion of Sales Price payable by Buyer at closing .... $_____
   B. Sum of all financing described below (excluding any loan funding fee or mortgage insurance premium) .... $_____
   C. Sales Price (Sum of A and B) .... $_____

4. **FINANCING:** The portion of Sales Price not payable in cash will be paid as follows: (Check applicable boxes below)
   ☐ A. THIRD PARTY FINANCING: One or more third party mortgage loans in the total amount of $_____ (excluding any loan funding fee or mortgage insurance premium).
      (1) Property Approval: If the Property does not satisfy the lenders' underwriting requirements for the loan(s), this contract will terminate and the earnest money will be refunded to Buyer.
      (2) Financing Approval: (Check one box only)
         ☐ (a) This contract is subject to Buyer being approved for the financing described in the attached Third Party Financing Condition Addendum.
         ☐ (b) This contract is not subject to Buyer being approved for financing and does not involve FHA or VA financing.
   ☐ B. ASSUMPTION: The assumption of the unpaid principal balance of one or more promissory notes described in the attached TREC Loan Assumption Addendum.
   ☐ C. SELLER FINANCING: A promissory note from Buyer to Seller of $_____, secured by vendor's and deed of trust liens, and containing the terms and conditions described in the attached TREC Seller Financing Addendum. If an owner policy of title insurance is furnished, Buyer shall furnish Seller with a mortgagee policy of title insurance.

5. **EARNEST MONEY:** Upon execution of this contract by all parties, Buyer shall deposit $_____ as earnest money with _____, as escrow agent, at _____ (address). Buyer shall deposit additional earnest money of $_____ with escrow agent within _____ days after the effective date of this contract. If Buyer fails to deposit the earnest money as required by this contract, Buyer will be in default.

6. **TITLE POLICY AND SURVEY:**
   A. TITLE POLICY: Seller shall furnish to Buyer at ☐ Seller's ☐ Buyer's expense an owner policy of title insurance (Title Policy) issued by _____ (Title Company) in the amount of the Sales Price, dated at or after closing, insuring Buyer against loss under the provisions of the Title Policy, subject to the promulgated exclusions (including existing building and zoning ordinances) and the following exceptions:
      (1) Restrictive covenants common to the platted subdivision in which the Property is located.
      (2) The standard printed exception for standby fees, taxes and assessments.
      (3) Liens created as part of the financing described in Paragraph 4.
      (4) Utility easements created by the dedication deed or plat of the subdivision in which the Property is located.
      (5) Reservations or exceptions otherwise permitted by this contract or as may be approved by Buyer in writing.
      (6) The standard printed exception as to marital rights.
      (7) The standard printed exception as to waters, tidelands, beaches, streams, and related matters.
      (8) The standard printed exception as to discrepancies, conflicts, shortages in area or boundary lines, encroachments or protrusions, or overlapping improvements. Buyer, at Buyer's expense, may have the exception amended to read, "shortages in area".
   B. COMMITMENT: Within 20 days after the Title Company receives a copy of this contract, Seller shall furnish to Buyer a commitment for title insurance (Commitment) and, at Buyer's expense, legible copies of restrictive covenants and documents evidencing exceptions in the

Initialed for identification by Buyer _____ _____ and Seller _____ _____   TREC NO. 24-8

50

25-6 Farm and Ranch Contract (amended June 2008)

Changes are the same as those listed for 20-8 except

- Paragraph 2E - amended rather than Paragraph 2D
- Paragraph 6D - not amended
- Paragraph 6E – not amended

PROMULGATED BY THE TEXAS REAL ESTATE COMMISSION (TREC) · 06-30-08

FARM AND RANCH CONTRACT

1. PARTIES: The parties to this contract are _____ (Seller) and _____ (Buyer). Seller agrees to sell and convey to Buyer and Buyer agrees to buy from Seller the Property defined below.

2. PROPERTY: The land, improvements, accessories and crops are collectively referred to as the "Property".
   A. LAND: The land situated in the County of _____, Texas, described as follows:_____
   _____
   or as described on attached exhibit, also known as _____ (address/zip code), together with all rights, privileges, and appurtenances pertaining thereto, including but not limited to: water rights, claims, permits, strips and gores, easements, and cooperative or association memberships.
   B. IMPROVEMENTS:
      (1) FARM and RANCH IMPROVEMENTS: The following permanently installed and built-in items, if any: windmills, tanks, barns, pens, fences, gates, sheds, outbuildings, and corrals.
      (2) RESIDENTIAL IMPROVEMENTS: The house, garage, and all other fixtures and improvements attached to the above-described real property, including without limitation, the following permanently installed and built-in items, if any: all equipment and appliances, valances, screens, shutters, awnings, wall-to-wall carpeting, mirrors, ceiling fans, attic fans, mail boxes, television antennas and satellite dish system and equipment, heating and air-conditioning units, security and fire detection equipment, wiring, plumbing and lighting fixtures, chandeliers, water softener system, kitchen equipment, garage door openers, cleaning equipment, shrubbery, landscaping, outdoor cooking equipment, and all other property owned by Seller and attached to the above described real property.
   C. ACCESSORIES:
      (1) FARM AND RANCH ACCESSORIES: The following described related accessories: (check boxes of conveyed accessories) ❑ portable buildings ❑ hunting blinds ❑ game feeders ❑ livestock feeders and troughs ❑ irrigation equipment ❑ fuel tanks ❑ submersible pumps ❑ pressure tanks ❑ corrals ❑ gates ❑ chutes ❑ other:_____
      _____
      (2) RESIDENTIAL ACCESSORIES: The following described related accessories, if any: window air conditioning units, stove, fireplace screens, curtains and rods, blinds, window shades, draperies and rods, controls for satellite dish system, controls for garage door openers, entry gate controls, door keys, mailbox keys, above ground pool, swimming pool equipment and maintenance accessories, and artificial fireplace logs.
   D. CROPS: Unless otherwise agreed in writing, Seller has the right to harvest all growing crops until delivery of possession of the Property.
   E. EXCLUSIONS: The following improvements, accessories, and crops will be retained by Seller and must be removed prior to delivery of possession: _____
   _____
   F. RESERVATIONS: Seller reserves the following mineral, water, royalty, timber, or other interests:_____
   _____

3. SALES PRICE:
   A. Cash portion of Sales Price payable by Buyer at closing .... $_____
   B. Sum of all financing described below (excluding any loan funding fee or mortgage insurance premium) .... $_____
   C. Sales Price (Sum of A and B) .... $_____
   D. The Sales Price ❑ will ❑ will not be adjusted based on the survey required by Paragraph 6C. If the Sales Price is adjusted, the Sales Price will be calculated on the basis of $_____ per acre. If the Sales Price is adjusted by more than 10%, either party may terminate this contract by providing written notice to the other party within _____ days after the terminating party receives the survey. If neither party terminates this contract or if the variance is 10% or less, the adjustment will be made to the amount in ❑ 3A ❑ 3B ❑ proportionately to 3A and 3B.

Initialed for identification by Buyer_____ _____ and Seller _____ _____   TREC NO. 25-6

51

26-5 Seller Financing Addendum (amended December 2006)

A blank line is added to Paragraph C of TREC No. 26-5, Seller Financing Condition Addendum, for the interest rate of the note; a provision addressing the interest rate of matured unpaid amount is added; subparagraphs (2) and (3) provide for a choice of monthly installments rather than an option to fill in the blanks on the type of installment; a note is added to subparagraph D(1) which states that the buyer's liability to pay the note will continue unless the buyer obtains a release of liability from the Seller; subparagraph D(2)(a) is revised by adding "ad valorem" before "taxes."

PROMULGATED BY THE TEXAS REAL ESTATE COMMISSION (TREC)   12-04-06

SELLER FINANCING ADDENDUM
TO CONTRACT CONCERNING THE PROPERTY AT

_____

(Address of Property)

A. CREDIT DOCUMENTATION. To establish Buyer's creditworthiness, Buyer shall deliver to Seller within_____days after the effective date of this contract, ☐ credit report ☐ verification of employment, including salary ☐ verification of funds on deposit in financial institutions ☐ current financial statement and ☐ _____.

Buyer hereby authorizes any credit reporting agency to furnish copies of Buyer's credit reports to Seller at Buyer's sole expense.

B. CREDIT APPROVAL. If the credit documentation described in Paragraph A is not delivered within the specified time, Seller may terminate this contract by notice to Buyer within 7 days after expiration of the time for delivery, and the earnest money will be paid to Seller. If the credit documentation is timely delivered, and Seller determines in Seller's sole discretion that Buyer's credit is unacceptable, Seller may terminate this contract by notice to Buyer within 7 days after expiration of the time for delivery and the earnest money will be refunded to Buyer. If Seller does not terminate this contract, Seller will be deemed to have approved Buyer's creditworthiness.

C. PROMISSORY NOTE. The promissory note (Note) described in Paragraph 4 of this contract payable by Buyer to the order of Seller will bear interest at the rate of _____% per annum and be payable at the place designated by Seller. Buyer may prepay the Note in whole or in part at any time without penalty. Any prepayments are to be applied to the payment of the installments of principal last maturing and interest will immediately cease on the prepaid principal. The Note will contain a provision for payment of a late fee of 5% of any installment not paid within 10 days of the due date. Matured unpaid amounts will bear interest at the rate of 1½% per month or at the highest lawful rate, whichever is less. The Note will be payable as follows:

☐ (1) In one payment due _____ after the date of the Note with interest payable ☐ at maturity ☐ monthly ☐ quarterly. (check one box only)

☐ (2) In monthly installments of $ _____ ☐ including interest ☐plus interest (check one box only) beginning _____ after the date of the Note and continuing monthly thereafter for_____ months when the balance of the Note will be due and payable.

☐ (3) Interest only in monthly installments for the first _____ month(s) and thereafter in installments of $_____ ☐ including interest ☐ plus interest (check one box only) beginning _____ after the date of the Note and continuing monthly thereafter for _____ months when the balance of the Note will be due and payable.

D. DEED OF TRUST. The deed of trust securing the Note will provide for the following:

(1) PROPERTY TRANSFERS: (check one box only)

☐ (a) Consent Not Required: The Property may be sold, conveyed or leased without the consent of Seller, provided any subsequent buyer assumes the Note.

☐ (b) Consent Required: If all or any part of the Property is sold, conveyed, leased for a period longer than 3 years, leased with an option to purchase, or otherwise sold (including any contract for deed), without Seller's prior written consent, which consent may be withheld in Seller's sole discretion, Seller may declare the balance of the Note

Initialed for identification by Buyer_____ and Seller_____   TREC NO. 26-5

52

28-1 Environmental Assessment, Threatened or Endangered Species, and Wetlands Addendum (amended April 2007)

The amendments to Standard Contract Form TREC No. 28-1, Environmental Assessment, Threatened or Endangered Species, and Wetlands Addendum, remove redundant text and make non-substantive conforming changes consistent with current forms.

PROMULGATED BY THE TEXAS REAL ESTATE COMMISSION (TREC)   04-23-07

ENVIRONMENTAL ASSESSMENT, THREATENED OR ENDANGERED SPECIES, AND WETLANDS ADDENDUM

TO CONTRACT CONCERNING THE PROPERTY AT

_____

(Address of Property)

❏ A. ENVIRONMENTAL ASSESSMENT: Buyer, at Buyer's expense, may obtain an environmental assessment report prepared by an environmental specialist.

❏ B. THREATENED OR ENDANGERED SPECIES: Buyer, at Buyer's expense, may obtain a report from a natural resources professional to determine if there are any threatened or endangered species or their habitats as defined by the Texas Parks and Wildlife Department or the U.S. Fish and Wildlife Service.

❏ C. WETLANDS: Buyer, at Buyer's expense, may obtain a report from an environmental specialist to determine if there are wetlands, as defined by federal or state law or regulation.

Within _____days after the effective date of the contract, Buyer may terminate the contract by furnishing Seller a copy of any report noted above that adversely affects the use of the Property and a notice of termination of the contract. Upon termination, the earnest money will be refunded to Buyer.

_____   _____
Buyer   Seller

_____   _____
Buyer   Seller

TREC No. 28-1

53

30-7 Residential Condominium Contract (Resale)
(amended June 2008)

Changes are the same as those listed for 20-8 except

- Paragraph 2A

  o Not reformatted

  o Text added to 2A(4) instead of 2D regarding improvements and accessories

- Paragraph 6C is amended rather than 6D regarding the time for buyer to object

- Paragraph 6E2 – not amended

- Paragraph 22

  o Revised to add check box for the Addendum Containing Required Notices Under §5.01, §420.001, and §420.002, Texas Property Code

  o The Seller's Temporary Lease is added to the list of addenda

PROMULGATED BY THE TEXAS REAL ESTATE COMMISSION (TREC)   06-30-08
NOTICE: Not For Use Where Seller Owns Fee Simple Title To Land Beneath Unit

RESIDENTIAL CONDOMINIUM CONTRACT (RESALE)

1. **PARTIES:** The parties to this contract are _____
(Seller) and _____ (Buyer).
Seller agrees to sell and convey to Buyer and Buyer agrees to buy from Seller the Property defined below.

2. **PROPERTY AND CONDOMINIUM DOCUMENTS:**
   A. The Condominium Unit, improvements and accessories described below are collectively referred to as the "Property".
   (1) CONDOMINIUM UNIT: Unit _____, in Building _____
   of _____, a condominium project, located at
   _____ (address/zip code).
   City of _____ County of _____
   Texas, described in the Condominium Declaration and Plat and any amendments thereto of record in said County; together with such Unit's undivided interest in the Common Elements designated by the Declaration, including those areas reserved as Limited Common Elements appurtenant to the Unit and such other rights to use the Common Elements which have been specifically assigned to the Unit in any other manner. Parking areas assigned to the Unit are:_____
   (2) IMPROVEMENTS: All fixtures and improvements attached to the above described real property including without limitation, the following permanently installed and built-in items, if any: all equipment and appliances, valances, screens, shutters, awnings, wall-to-wall carpeting, mirrors, ceiling fans, attic fans, mail boxes, television antennas and satellite dish system and equipment, heating and air conditioning units, security and fire detection equipment, wiring, plumbing and lighting fixtures, chandeliers, shrubbery, landscaping, outdoor cooking equipment, and all other property owned by Seller and attached to the above described Condominium Unit.
   (3) ACCESSORIES: The following described related accessories, if any: window air conditioning units, stove, fireplace screens, curtains and rods, blinds, window shades, draperies and rods, controls for satellite dish system, controls for garage door openers, entry gate controls, door keys, mailbox keys, and artificial fireplace logs.
   (4) EXCLUSIONS: The following improvements and accessories will be retained by Seller and must be removed prior to delivery of possession: _____

   B. The Declaration, Bylaws and any Rules of the Association are called "Documents". (Check one box only):
   ☐ (1) Buyer has received a copy of the Documents. Buyer is advised to read the Documents before signing the contract.
   ☐ (2) Buyer has not received a copy of the Documents. Seller shall deliver the Documents to Buyer within _____ days after the effective date of the contract. Buyer may cancel the contract before the sixth day after Buyer receives the Documents by hand-delivering or mailing written notice of cancellation to Seller by certified United States mail, return receipt requested.

   C. The Resale Certificate from the condominium owners association (the Association) is called the "Certificate". The Certificate must be in a form promulgated by TREC or required by the parties. The Certificate must have been prepared no more than 3 months before the date it is delivered to Buyer and must contain at a minimum the information required by Section 82.157, Texas Property Code.
   (Check one box only):
   ☐ (1) Buyer has received the Certificate.

   ☐ (3) Buyer has received Seller's affidavit that Seller requested information from the Association concerning its financial condition as required by the Texas Property Code, and that the Association did not provide a Certificate or information required in the Certificate. Buyer and Seller agree to waive the requirement to furnish the Certificate.

3. **SALES PRICE:**
   A. Cash portion of Sales Price payable by Buyer at closing.................. $_____
   B. Sum of all financing described below (excluding any loan funding fee or mortgage insurance premium).. $_____
   C. Sales Price (Sum of A and B)... $_____

Initialed for identification by Buyer_____ _____ and Seller _____ _____   TREC NO. 30-7

54

32-2 Condominium Resale Certificate (amended June 2008)

- Paragraph N changed to conform to 37-3

- Signature block

    o Changed to conform to 37-3

    o "E-mail ____" is added to the signature block

    o Buyer and Seller initials are removed at the bottom of the first page

    o Buyer signature line is removed

    o "Date ____" is moved above the line before "Mailing Address ____"

PROMULGATED BY THE TEXAS REAL ESTATE COMMISSION (TREC)   06-30-08

CONDOMINIUM RESALE CERTIFICATE
(Section 82.157, Texas Property Code)

Condominium Certificate concerning Condominium Unit _____, in Building _____, of _____
_____,a condominium project, located at _____
_____(Address), City of _____,
County of _____, Texas, on behalf of the condominium owners' association
(the Association) by the Association's governing body (the Board).

A. The Declaration ☐does ☐does not contain a right of first refusal or other restraint that restricts the right to transfer the Unit. If a right of first refusal or other restraint exists, see Section _____of the Declaration.

B. The periodic common expense assessment for the Unit is $_____ per _____.

C. There ☐ is ☐is not a common expense or special assessment due and unpaid by the Seller to the Association. The total unpaid amount is $_____ and is for _____.

D. Other amounts ☐are ☐are not payable by Seller to the Association. The total unpaid amount is $_____and is for _____.

E. Capital expenditures approved by the Association for the next 12 months are $_____.

F. Reserves for capital expenditures are $_____:of this amount $_____ has been designated for_____.

G. The current operating budget of the Association is attached.

H. The amount of unsatisfied judgments against the Association is $ _____.

I. There ☐are ☐are not any suits pending against the Association. The nature of the suits is _____

J. The Association ☐does ☐does not provide insurance coverage for the benefit of unit owners as per the attached summary from the Association's insurance agent.

K. The Board ☐has ☐has no knowledge of alterations or improvements to the Unit or to the limited common elements assigned to the Unit or any portion of the project that violate any provision of the Declaration, by-laws or rules of the Association. Known violations are:_____
_____

L. The Board ☐has ☐has not received notice from a governmental authority concerning violations of health or building codes with respect to the Unit, the limited common elements assigned to the Unit, or any other portion of the condominium project. Notices received are: ____
_____

M. The remaining term of any leasehold estate that affects the condominium is _____ and the provisions governing an extension or a renewal of the lease are: _____
_____
_____

N. The Association's managing agent is _____
                                                                                        (Name of Agent)

_____
                          (Mailing Address)

_____   _____
     (Telephone Number)   (Fax Number)

_____
E-mail Address

TREC NO. 32-2

55

33-1 Addendum for Coastal Area Property (amended April 2007)

The amendments to TREC No. 33-1, Addendum for Coastal Area Property, make non-substantive conforming changes consistent with current forms.

PROMULGATED BY THE TEXAS REAL ESTATE COMMISSION (TREC)   04-23-07

ADDENDUM FOR
COASTAL AREA PROPERTY
(SECTION 33.135, TEXAS NATURAL RESOURCES CODE)

TO CONTRACT CONCERNING THE PROPERTY AT

_____
(Address of Property)

NOTICE REGARDING COASTAL AREA PROPERTY

1. The real property described in and subject to this contract adjoins and shares a common boundary with the tidally influenced submerged lands of the state. The boundary is subject to change and can be determined accurately only by a survey on the ground made by a licensed state land surveyor in accordance with the original grant from the sovereign. The owner of the property described in this contract may gain or lose portions of the tract because of changes in the boundary.

2. The seller, transferor, or grantor has no knowledge of any prior fill as it relates to the property described in and subject to this contract except:_____
_____
_____.

3. State law prohibits the use, encumbrance, construction, or placing of any structure in, on, or over state-owned submerged lands below the applicable tide line, without proper permission.

4. The purchaser or grantee is hereby advised to seek the advice of an attorney or other qualified person as to the legal nature and effect of the facts set forth in this notice on the property described in and subject to this contract. Information regarding the location of the applicable tide line as to the property described in and subject to this contract may be obtained from the surveying division of the General Land Office in Austin.

_____   _____
Buyer   Seller

_____   _____
Buyer   Seller

This form has been approved by the Texas Real Estate Commission for use with similarly approved or promulgated contract forms. Such approval relates to this form only. TREC forms are intended for use only by trained real estate licensees. No representation is made as to the legal validity or adequacy of any provision in any specific transactions. It is not suitable for complex transactions. Texas Real Estate Commission, P.O. Box 12188, Austin, TX 78711-2188, 1-800-250-8732 or (512) 459-6544 (http://www.trec.state.tx.us) TREC No. 33-1. This form replaces TREC No. 33-0.

TREC No. 33-1

56

34-3 Addendum for Property Located Seaward of the Gulf Intracoastal Waterway (amended December 2007)

The addendum was revised to reflect changes that were made to the disclosure under House Bill 2819, 80th Legislature, R.S. (2007).

PROMULGATED BY THE TEXAS REAL ESTATE COMMISSION (TREC)   12-10-07

ADDENDUM FOR
PROPERTY LOCATED SEAWARD OF THE
GULF INTRACOASTAL WATERWAY
(SECTION 61.025, TEXAS NATURAL RESOURCES CODE)

TO CONTRACT CONCERNING THE PROPERTY AT

_____
(Address of Property)

DISCLOSURE NOTICE CONCERNING LEGAL AND ECONOMIC RISKS OF PURCHASING COASTAL REAL PROPERTY NEAR A BEACH

WARNING: THE FOLLOWING NOTICE OF POTENTIAL RISKS OF ECONOMIC LOSS TO YOU AS THE PURCHASER OF COASTAL REAL PROPERTY IS REQUIRED BY STATE LAW.

- READ THIS NOTICE CAREFULLY. DO NOT SIGN THIS CONTRACT UNTIL YOU FULLY UNDERSTAND THE RISKS YOU ARE ASSUMING.
- BY PURCHASING THIS PROPERTY, YOU MAY BE ASSUMING ECONOMIC RISKS OVER AND ABOVE THE RISKS INVOLVED IN PURCHASING INLAND REAL PROPERTY.
- IF YOU OWN A STRUCTURE LOCATED ON COASTAL REAL PROPERTY NEAR A GULF COAST BEACH, IT MAY COME TO BE LOCATED ON THE PUBLIC BEACH BECAUSE OF COASTAL EROSION AND STORM EVENTS.
- AS THE OWNER OF A STRUCTURE LOCATED ON THE PUBLIC BEACH, YOU COULD BE SUED BY THE STATE OF TEXAS AND ORDERED TO REMOVE THE STRUCTURE.
- THE COSTS OF REMOVING A STRUCTURE FROM THE PUBLIC BEACH AND ANY OTHER ECONOMIC LOSS INCURRED BECAUSE OF A REMOVAL ORDER WOULD BE SOLELY YOUR RESPONSIBILITY.

The real property described in this contract is located seaward of the Gulf Intracoastal Waterway to its southernmost point and then seaward of the longitudinal line also known as 97 degrees, 12', 19" which runs southerly to the international boundary from the intersection of the centerline of the Gulf Intracoastal Waterway and the Brownsville Ship Channel. If the property is in close proximity to a beach fronting the Gulf of Mexico, the purchaser is hereby advised that the public has acquired a right of use or easement to or over the area of any public beach by prescription, dedication, or presumption, or has retained a right by virtue of continuous right in the public since time immemorial, as recognized in law and custom.

The extreme seaward boundary of natural vegetation that spreads continuously inland customarily marks the landward boundary of the public easement. If there is no clearly marked natural vegetation line, the landward boundary of the easement is as provided by Sections 61.016 and 61.017, Natural Resources Code.

Much of the Gulf of Mexico coastline is eroding at rates of more than five feet per year. Erosion rates for all Texas Gulf property subject to the open beaches act are available from the Texas General Land Office.

State law prohibits any obstruction, barrier, restraint, or interference with the use of the public easement, including the placement of structures seaward of the landward boundary of the easement. OWNERS OF STRUCTURES ERECTED SEAWARD OF THE VEGETATION LINE (OR OTHER APPLICABLE EASEMENT BOUNDARY) OR THAT BECOME SEAWARD OF THE VEGETATION LINE AS A RESULT OF PROCESSES SUCH AS SHORELINE EROSION ARE SUBJECT TO A LAWSUIT BY THE STATE OF TEXAS TO REMOVE THE STRUCTURES.

The purchaser is hereby notified that the purchaser should: (1) determine the rate of shoreline erosion in the vicinity of the real property; and (2) seek the advice of an attorney or other qualified person before executing this contract or instrument of conveyance as to the relevance of these statutes and facts to the value of the property the purchaser is hereby purchasing or contracting to purchase.

_____   _____
Buyer   Seller

_____   _____
Buyer   Seller

This form has been approved by the Texas Real Estate Commission for use with similarly approved or promulgated contract forms. Such approval relates to this form only. TREC forms are intended for use only by trained real estate licensees. No representation is made as to the legal validity or adequacy of any provision in any specific transactions. It is not suitable for complex transactions. Texas Real Estate Commission, P.O. Box 12188, Austin, TX 78711-2188, 1-800-250-8732 or (512) 459-6544 (http://www.trec.state.tx.us) TREC No. 34-3. This form replaces TREC No. 34-2.

TREC No. 34-3

57

36-5 Addendum for Property Subject to Mandatory Membership in a Property Owners' Association (amended June 2008)

- Title of the form is changed to conform to §5.012, Texas Property Code

- The term "mandatory" is added before "membership"

- The term "property" is substituted for "mandatory" to describe a "Property Owners' Association"

- The term "owners" is deleted from Paragraph B and the last paragraph

PROMULGATED BY THE TEXAS REAL ESTATE COMMISSION (TREC)   06-30-08

ADDENDUM FOR PROPERTY SUBJECT TO MANDATORY MEMBERSHIP IN A PROPERTY OWNERS' ASSOCIATION
(NOT FOR USE WITH CONDOMINIUMS)
ADDENDUM TO CONTRACT CONCERNING THE PROPERTY AT

_____

(Street Address and City)

_____

(Name of Property Owners' Association)

A. SUBDIVISION INFORMATION: "Subdivision Information" means: (i) the restrictions applying to the subdivision, (ii) the bylaws and rules of the Property Owners' Association (Association), and (iii) a resale certificate, all of which comply with Section 207.003 of the Texas Property Code. (Check only one box):

☐ 1. Within _____ days after the effective date of the contract, Seller shall at Seller's expense deliver the Subdivision Information to Buyer. If Buyer does not receive the Subdivision Information, Buyer may terminate the contract at any time prior to closing and the earnest money will be refunded to Buyer. If Seller delivers the Subdivision Information, Buyer may terminate the contract for any reason within 7 days after Buyer receives the Subdivision Information or prior to closing, whichever first occurs, and the earnest money will be refunded to Buyer.

☐ 2. Buyer has received and approved the Subdivision Information before signing the contract.

☐ 3. Buyer does not require delivery of the Subdivision Information.

If Seller becomes aware of any material changes in the Subdivision Information, Seller shall promptly give notice to Buyer. Buyer may terminate the contract prior to closing by giving written notice to Seller if: (i) any of the Subdivision Information provided was not true; or (ii) any material adverse change in the Subdivision Information occurs prior to closing, and the earnest money will be refunded to Buyer.

B. FEES: Buyer shall pay any Association fees resulting from the transfer of the Property not to exceed $_____ and Seller shall pay any excess.

NOTICE TO BUYER REGARDING REPAIRS BY THE ASSOCIATION: The Association may have the sole responsibility to make certain repairs to the Property. If you are concerned about the condition of any part of the Property which the Association is required to repair, you should not sign the contract unless you are satisfied that the Association will make the desired repairs.

_____   _____
Buyer   Seller

_____   _____
Buyer   Seller

The form of this addendum has been approved by the Texas Real Estate Commission for use only with similarly approved or promulgated forms of contracts. Such approval relates to this contract form only. TREC forms are intended for use only by trained real estate licensees. No representation is made as to the legal validity or adequacy of any provision in any specific transactions. It is not intended for complex transactions. Texas Real Estate Commission, P.O. Box 12188, Austin, TX 78711-2188, 1-800-250-8732 or (512) 459-6544 (http://www.trec.state.tx.us) TREC No. 36-5. This form replaces TREC No. 36-4.

TREC NO. 36-5

58

37-3 Subdivision Information, Including Resale Certificate for Property Subject to Mandatory Membership in a Property Owners' Association (amended June 2008)

- The title of the form is changed to conform to §5.012, Texas Property Code

- The parenthetical below the title is amended to read "Chapter 207, Texas Property Code"

- "Property owner's association" is defined as "Association" in the first paragraph and conforming changes are made in the rest of the form

- Buyer and Seller initials are moved at the bottom of the first page

- Another line is added near the end of the form for the name of the person signing the form

- The term "Print" is added before "Name" on page 2

PROMULGATED BY THE TEXAS REAL ESTATE COMMISSION (TREC)   06-30-08

SUBDIVISION INFORMATION, INCLUDING
RESALE CERTIFICATE FOR PROPERTY SUBJECT TO
MANDATORY MEMBERSHIP IN A PROPERTY OWNERS' ASSOCIATION
(Chapter 207, Texas Property Code)

(NOT FOR USE WITH CONDOMINIUMS)

Resale Certificate concerning the Property (including any common areas assigned to the Property) located at _____ (Street Address), City of _____, County of _____, Texas, prepared by the property owners' association (Association).

A. The Property ☐is ☐ is not subject to a right of first refusal or other restraint contained in the restrictions or restrictive covenants that restricts the owner's right to transfer the owner's property.

B. The current regular assessment for the Property is $_____ per _____.

C. A special assessment for the Property due after the date the resale certificate was prepared is $_____ payable as follows_____.

D. The total of all amounts due and unpaid to the Association that are attributable to the Property is $_____.

E. The capital expenditures approved by the Association for its current fiscal year are $_____.

F. The amount of reserves for capital expenditures is $_____.

G. Unsatisfied judgments against the Association total $_____.

H. There ☐ are ☐ are not any suits pending against the Association. The style and cause number of each pending suit is: _____

I. The Association's board ☐has actual knowledge ☐has no actual knowledge of conditions on the Property in violation of the restrictions applying to the subdivision or the bylaws or rules of the Association. Known violations are: _____

J. The Association ☐has ☐has not received notice from any governmental authority regarding health or building code violations with respect to the Property or any common areas or common facilities owned or leased by the Association. A summary or copy of each notice is attached.

K. The Association fees resulting from the transfer of the Property are $_____, payable to _____

TREC NO. 37-3

59

38-2 Notice of Buyer's Termination of Conract
(amended June 2008)

The termination notice is modified to serve as an all-purpose Buyer's notice of termination to be used to notify the Seller that

- The contract is terminated under Paragraph 23

- Buyer cannot obtain financing approval

- Property does not satisfy the lenders' underwriting requirements for the loan

- Buyer elects to terminate under Paragraph A of the Addendum for Property subject to Mandatory Membership in a Property Owners' Association

- Buyer elects to terminate under Paragraph 7B(2) of the contract

- Buyer is terminating pursuant to a specific paragraph in the contract or addendum to be identified in the form

06-30-08

PROMULGATED BY THE TEXAS REAL ESTATE COMMISSION (TREC)

NOTICE OF BUYER'S TERMINATION OF CONTRACT

CONCERNING THE CONTRACT FOR THE SALE OF THE PROPERTY AT

_____
(Street Address and City)

BETWEEN THE UNDERSIGNED BUYER AND_____

_____ (SELLER)

Buyer notifies Seller that the contract is terminated pursuant to the following:

☐(1) the unrestricted right of Buyer to terminate the contract under Paragraph 23 of the contract.

☐(2) Buyer cannot obtain Financing Approval in accordance with the Third Party Financing Condition Addendum to the contract.

☐(3) the Property does not satisfy the lenders' underwriting requirements for the loan under Paragraph 4A(1) of the contract.

☐(4) Buyer elects to terminate under Paragraph A of the Addendum for Property Subject to Mandatory Membership in a Property Owners' Association.

☐(5) Buyer elects to terminate under Paragraph 7B(2) of the contract relating to the Seller's Disclosure Notice.

☐(6) Other (identify the paragraph number of contract or the addendum): _____

_____

_____

_____

NOTE: Release of the earnest money is governed by the terms of the contract.

_____   _____   _____   _____
Buyer   Date   Buyer   Date

This form has been approved by the Texas Real Estate Commission for use with similarly approved or promulgated contract forms. Such approval relates to this form only. TREC forms are intended for use only by trained real estate licensees. No representation is made as to the legal validity or adequacy of any provision in any specific transactions. It is not suitable for complex transactions. Texas Real Estate Commission, P.O. Box 12188, Austin, TX 78711-2188, 1-800-250-8732 or (512) 459-6544 (http://www.trec.state.tx.us) TREC No. 38-2. This form replaces TREC No. 38-1.

60

TREC No.38-2

40-3 Third Party Financing Addendum (amended December 2007)

- On page 2 of the addendum, a reference to having HUD form 92564-CN signed and dated by the buyer was removed as the form no longer has a signature line

- The title and reference to "Texas Veterans Housing Assistance Program Loan" was changed in paragraph B to "Texas Veterans Loan" because other types of loans are offered by the Texas Veterans Land Board

12-10-07

PROMULGATED BY THE TEXAS REAL ESTATE COMMISSION (TREC)

THIRD PARTY FINANCING CONDITION ADDENDUM
TO CONTRACT CONCERNING THE PROPERTY AT

_____

(Street Address and City)

Buyer shall apply promptly for all financing described below and make every reasonable effort to obtain approval for the financing (Financing Approval). Buyer shall furnish all information and documents required by lender for Financing Approval. Financing Approval will be deemed to have been obtained when (1) the terms of the loan(s) described below are available and (2) lender determines that Buyer has satisfied all of lender's financial requirements (those items relating to Buyer's assets, income and credit history). If Buyer cannot obtain Financing Approval, Buyer may give written notice to Seller within ____ days after the effective date of this contract and this contract will terminate and the earnest money will be refunded to Buyer. If Buyer does not give such notice within the time required, this contract will no longer be subject to Financing Approval. Time is of the essence for this paragraph and strict compliance with the time for performance is required.

NOTE: Financing Approval does not include approval of lender's underwriting requirements for the Property, as specified in Paragraph 4.A.(1) of the contract.

Each note must be secured by vendor's and deed of trust liens.

CHECK APPLICABLE BOXES:

☐ A. CONVENTIONAL FINANCING:

    ☐ (1) A first mortgage loan in the principal amount of $_____ (excluding any financed PMI premium), due in full in _____ year(s), with interest not to exceed _____% per annum for the first _____year(s) of the loan with Loan Fees (loan origination, discount, buy-down, and commitment fees) not to exceed _____% of the loan.

    ☐ (2) A second mortgage loan in the principal amount of $_____(excluding any financed PMI premium), due in full in _____year(s), with interest not to exceed _____% per annum for the first _____year(s) of the loan with Loan Fees (loan origination, discount, buy-down, and commitment fees) not to exceed _____% of the loan.

☐ B. TEXAS VETERANS LOAN: A loan(s) from the Texas Veterans Land Board of $_____ for a period in the total amount of _____years at the interest rate established by the Texas Veterans Land Board.

☐ C. FHA INSURED FINANCING: A Section _____ FHA insured loan of not less than $_____ (excluding any financed MIP), amortizable monthly for not less than _____years, with interest not to exceed _____% per annum for the first _____year(s) of the loan with Loan Fees (loan origination, discount, buy-down, and commitment fees) not to exceed _____ % of the loan. As required by HUD-FHA, if FHA valuation is unknown, "It is expressly agreed that, notwithstanding any other provision of this contract, the purchaser (Buyer) shall not be obligated to complete the purchase of the Property described herein or to incur any penalty by forfeiture of earnest money deposits or otherwise unless the purchaser (Buyer) has been given in accordance with HUD/FHA or VA requirements a written statement issued by the Federal Housing Commissioner, Department of Veterans Affairs, or a Direct Endorsement Lender setting forth the appraised value of the Property of not less than $_____. The purchaser (Buyer) shall have the privilege and option of proceeding with consummation of the contract without regard to the amount of the

Initialed for identification by Buyer____ ____ and Seller____ ____   TREC NO. 40-3

61

41-1 Loan Assumption Addendum (amended April 2007)

The amendments to TREC No. 41-1, Loan Assumption Addendum, make non-substantive conforming changes consistent with current forms.

PROMULGATED BY THE TEXAS REAL ESTATE COMMISSION (TREC)　　04-23-07

LOAN ASSUMPTION ADDENDUM
TO CONTRACT CONCERNING THE PROPERTY AT

_____

(Address of Property)

A. CREDIT DOCUMENTATION. To establish Buyer's creditworthiness, Buyer shall deliver to Seller within_____days after the effective date of this contract ❑ credit report ❑ verification of employment, including salary ❑ verification of funds on deposit in financial institutions ❑ current financial statement and ❑ _____.
Buyer hereby authorizes any credit reporting agency to furnish copies of Buyer's credit reports to Seller at Buyer's sole expense.

B. CREDIT APPROVAL. If the credit documentation described in Paragraph A is not delivered within the specified time, Seller may terminate this contract by notice to Buyer within 7 days after expiration of the time for delivery, and the earnest money will be paid to Seller. If the credit documentation is timely delivered, and Seller determines in Seller's sole discretion that Buyer's credit is unacceptable, Seller may terminate this contract by notice to Buyer within 7 days after expiration of the time for delivery and the earnest money will be refunded to Buyer. If Seller does not terminate this contract within the time specified, Seller will be deemed to have approved Buyer's creditworthiness.

C. ASSUMPTION. Buyer's assumption of an existing note includes all obligations imposed by the deed of trust securing the note.
❑ (1) The unpaid principal balance of a first lien promissory note payable to_____
_____which unpaid balance at closing will be $ _____.
The total current monthly payment including principal, interest and any reserve deposits is $ _____. Buyer's initial payment will be the first payment due after closing.

❑ (2) The unpaid principal balance of a second lien promissory note payable to _____
_____which unpaid balance at closing will be $ _____.
The total current monthly payment including principal, interest and any reserve deposits is $ _____. Buyer's initial payment will be the first payment due after closing.

If the unpaid principal balance of any assumed loan as of the Closing Date varies from the loan balance stated above, the ❑ cash payable at closing ❑ Sales Price will be adjusted by the amount of any variance. If the total principal balance of all assumed loans varies in an amount greater than $500 at closing, either party may terminate this contract and the earnest money will be refunded to Buyer unless the other party elects to pay the excess of the variance.

D. LOAN ASSUMPTION TERMS. Buyer may terminate this contract and the earnest money will be refunded to Buyer if the noteholder requires:

(1) payment of an assumption fee in excess of $ _____in C(1) or $ _____in C(2) and Seller declines to pay such excess, or

(2) an increase in the interest rate to more than _____% in C(1) or_____% in C(2), or

(3) any other modification of the loan documents.

E. CONSENT BY NOTEHOLDER. If the noteholder fails to consent to the assumption of the loan, either Seller or Buyer may terminate this contract by notice to the other party and the earnest money will be refunded to the Buyer.

F. SELLER'S LIENS. Unless Seller is released from liability on any assumed note, a vendor's lien and deed of trust to secure assumption will be required. The vendor's lien will automatically be

Initialed for identification by Buyer_____ and Seller_____　　　　TREC NO. 41-1

62

43-0 Addendum Containing Required Notices Under §5.016, §420.001, §420.002, Texas Property Code (amended December 2007)

The new addendum contains disclosures required by House Bill 1038, 80th Legislature, R.S. (2007) in cases where the seller may be subject to or exempt from requirements of Title 16, Texas Property Code, regarding registration with the Texas Residential Construction Commission

PROMULGATED BY THE TEXAS REAL ESTATE COMMISSION (TREC)   12-10-2007

ADDENDUM CONTAINING REQUIRED NOTICES
UNDER §5.016, §420.001 AND §420.002,
TEXAS PROPERTY CODE

TO CONTRACT CONCERNING THE PROPERTY AT

_____
(Address of Property)

❑ A. NOTICE OF NONAPPLICABILITY OF CERTAIN WARRANTIES AND BUILDING AND PERFORMANCE STANDARDS.

The property that is subject to this contract is exempt from Title 16, Property Code, including the provisions of that title that provide statutory warranties and building and performance standards.

❑ B. NOTICE TO BUYER REQUIRED BY SECTION 420.001, TEXAS PROPERTY CODE.

STATE LAW REQUIRES THAT A PERSON HOLD A CERTIFICATE OF REGISTRATION FROM THE TEXAS RESIDENTIAL CONSTRUCTION COMMISSION IF THE PERSON CONTRACTS TO CONSTRUCT A NEW HOME OR IF THE PERSON CONTRACTS TO CONSTRUCT A MATERIAL IMPROVEMENT TO AN EXISTING HOME OR CERTAIN IMPROVEMENTS TO THE INTERIOR OF AN EXISTING HOME AND THE TOTAL COST OF THE IMPROVEMENTS IS $10,000 OR MORE (INCLUDING LABOR AND MATERIALS).

YOU MAY CONTACT THE TEXAS RESIDENTIAL CONSTRUCTION COMMISSION AT 1-877-651-8722 TO FIND OUT WHETHER THE BUILDER HAS A VALID CERTIFICATE OF REGISTRATION. THE COMMISSION HAS INFORMATION AVAILABLE ON THE HISTORY OF BUILDERS, INCLUDING SUSPENSIONS, REVOCATIONS, COMPLAINTS, AND RESOLUTION OF COMPLAINTS.

THIS CONTRACT IS SUBJECT TO CHAPTER 426, TEXAS PROPERTY CODE. THE PROVISIONS OF THAT CHAPTER GOVERN THE PROCESS THAT MUST BE FOLLOWED IN THE EVENT A DISPUTE ARISES OUT OF AN ALLEGED CONSTRUCTION DEFECT. IF YOU HAVE A COMPLAINT CONCERNING A CONSTRUCTION DEFECT YOU MAY CONTACT THE TEXAS RESIDENTIAL CONSTRUCTION COMMISSION AT THE TOLL-FREE TELEPHONE NUMBER TO LEARN HOW TO PROCEED UNDER THE STATE-SPONSORED INSPECTION AND DISPUTE RESOLUTION PROCESS.

❑ C. INFORMATION REQUIRED BY SECTION 420.002, TEXAS PROPERTY CODE.

Name of Builder: _____

Certificate of Registration Number: _____

_____   _____
Buyer   Seller

_____   _____
Buyer   Seller

This form has been approved by the Texas Real Estate Commission for use with similarly approved or promulgated contract forms. Such approval relates to this form only. TREC forms are intended for use only by trained real estate licensees. No representation is made as to the legal validity or adequacy of any provision in any specific transaction. It is not suitable for complex transactions. Texas Real Estate Commission, P.O. Box 12188, Austin, TX 78711-2188, 1-800-250-8732 or (512) 459-6544 (http://www.trec.state.tx.us) TREC No. 43-0.

TREC No. 43-0

63

References

ADA & Architectural Barriers	www.usdoj.gov/crt/ada/adahom1.htm www.hud.gov/offices/fheo/FHLaws/index.cfm
Appraiser Regulation	www.talcb.state.tx.us
Environmental Quality	www.tceq.state.tx.us
Insurance Regulation	www.tdi.state.tx.us
Licensee Lookup	www.trec.state.tx.us
Regulatory Issues	www.trec.state.tx.us
Real Estate Publications (foreclosure procedures, property owner's rights, homestead protections, water code and conservation districts, landlord and tenants guidelines)	www.recenter.tamu.edu

Associations

CCIM Institute	www.ccim.com
National Association of Real Estate Brokers	www.nareb.com
Texas Association of REALTORS®	www.texasrealtors.com

64

TEXAS REAL ESTATE COMMISSION
P.O. Box 12188
Austin, TX 78711-2188
800-250-TREC
http://www.trec.state.tx.us

REAL ESTATE CENTER
Texas A&M University
2115 TAMU
College Station, TX 77843-2115
979-845-2031
http://recenter.tamu.edu

Administrator

TIMOTHY K. IRVINE

Director

GARY MALER

Commissioners

JOHN S. WALTON, JR., CHAIRMAN
Lubbock
JOHN D. ECKSTRUM, VICE CHAIRMAN
Conroe
TOM C. MESA, JR., SECRETARY
Pasadena
TROY C. ALLEY, JR.
Arlington
ADRIAN A. ARRIAGA
McAllen
MARY FRANCES BURLESON
Dallas
ROBERT C. DAY
Jacksonville
BILL FLORES
Houston
ELIZABETH LEAL
El Paso

Advisory Committee

DAVID E. DALZELL, CHAIRMAN
Abilene
D. MARC McDOUGAL, VICE CHAIRMAN
Lubbock
JAMES M. BOYD
Houston
CATARINA G. CRON
Houston
JOHN D. ECKSTRUM
Conroe
Ex-Officio representing
the Texas Real Estate Commission
TOM H. GANN
Lufkin
JACQUELYN K. HAWKINS
Austin
BARBARA A. RUSSELL
Denton
DOUGLAS A. SCHWARTZ
El Paso
RONALD C. WAKEFIELD
San Antonio

Ethics

Pre-Assessment Evaluation

Please answer the following questions.

1.   It is now a requirement that each real estate inspector or active real estate broker licensed by the Texas Real Estate Commission must display Consumer Information Form 1-1 prominently in each place of business that the broker or inspector maintains.

      True   False

2.   The Association of REALTORS® and other trade associations may receive complaints and refer them to a hearing panel, which may take disciplinary action as long as it does not include a fine.

      True   False

3.   If a listing agent has a substantive dialogue with a buyer who is represented by another licensed broker, the Information About Brokerage Services Form is still required.

      True   False

4.   If a broker receives more than one offer, all offers must be presented to the seller unless otherwise instructed by the seller and no offer has a priority of presentation over another.

      True   False

5.   A 2005 amendment to the Real Estate License Act requires that a broker who represents both a buyer and seller must agree to act as an intermediary.
      True   False

Texas Real Estate Commission Ethics MCE

Edition 3.0

Prepared By

Compiled and Edited
by Denise Whisenant

September 2007

Acknowledgments

MCE Advisory Committee

Jan Agee, Arlington, TX

Loretta Dehay, Austin, TX

Louise Hull, Victoria, TX

Chuck Jacobus, Bellaire, TX

Larry Jokl, Brownsville, TX

Kathleen McKenzie-Owen, Pipe Creek, TX

Tom Morgan, Austin, TX

Minor Peeples, Corpus Christi, TX

Ron Walker, Austin, TX

Avis Wukasch, Georgetown, TX

Real Estate Center Staff

Gary W. Maler, Director

Denise Whisenant, Education Coordinator

David S. Jones, Communications Director

Nancy McQuistion, Associate Editor

Kammy Baumann, Assistant Editor

Robert P. Beals II, Art Director

JP Beato III, Graphics Designer

Brian Pope, Associate Editor

Foreword

In cooperation with the Texas Real Estate Commission, the Real Estate Center at Texas A&M University developed this real estate ethics curriculum with the assistance of an advisory committee of active licensees, attorneys and education providers. Real estate licensees are encouraged to acquire additional information and to take courses in specific, applicable topics.

This curriculum has been developed using information from publications, presentations and general research. The information is believed to be reliable, but it cannot be guaranteed insofar as it is applied to any particular individual or situation. The laws discussed in this curriculum have been excerpted, summarized or abbreviated. For a complete understanding and discussion, consult a full version of any pertinent law. This curriculum contains information that can change periodically. This curriculum is presented with the understanding that the authors and instructors are not engaged in rendering legal, accounting or other professional advice. The services of a competent professional with suitable expertise should be sought.

The authors, presenters, advisory committee, Real Estate Center and Texas Real Estate Commission disclaim any liability, loss or risk personal or otherwise, incurred as a consequence directly or indirectly from the use and application of any of the information contained in these materials or the teaching lectures and media presentations given in connection with these materials.

When using this course for three hours of Ethics MCE credit as required by the Texas Real Estate Commission, the student course manual must be reproduced and used in its entirety, without omission or alteration.

Contents

1

Canons of Professional Ethics

 Title 22 of the Texas Administrative Code (TAC), Chapter 531 includes five canons of professional ethics and conduct. The canons apply to real estate licensees and are included in the rules of the Texas Real Estate Commission (TREC). Acting as a fiduciary, the real estate licensee must exercise a standard of duty and care when representing a client in a real estate transaction. The licensee must subordinate his or her own interest to the client's interest. The canons also support the Federal Fair Housing Act in forbidding discrimination in real estate activities. These canons are similar in content to general business ethics and common law agency principles from a variety of sources including case law, statutory law and the REALTOR® Code of Ethics. The five canons are:

Fidelity (22 TAC 531.1)

A licensee represents the interests of the agent's client. The agent, in performing duties to the client, must

- ☑ make his or her position clear to all parties concerned in a real estate transaction;
- ☑ treat other parties to a transaction fairly;
- ☑ be faithful and observant to the trust placed in the agent;
- ☑ perform his or her duties scrupulously and meticulously; and
- ☑ place no personal interest above the interest of his or her client.

Integrity (22 TAC 531.2)

A licensee

- ☑ has a special obligation to perform his or her responsibilities; and
- ☑ uses caution to avoid misrepresentation by acts of commission or omission.

Notes

> The duties of fidelity, integrity, and competency are aspirational goals expressed in the preambles to the Code of Ethics of the National Association of REALTORS® and the Code of Ethics of the CCIM Institute (Certified Commercial Investment Member).
>
> The Code of Ethics of the National Association of Real Estate Brokers (the Realtists) imposes a duty on Realtists to protect the public against misrepresentation, unethical practices, or fraud in their practices (Part I, §3).

1

Competency (22 TAC 531.3)

A licensee should

- ☑ be knowledgeable as a real estate practitioner;

- ☑ be informed on market conditions that affect the real estate business;

- ☑ continue his or her education in the intricacies involved in marketing real estate for others;

- ☑ stay informed about national, state and local issues and developments in the real estate industry; and

- ☑ exercise judgment and skill in the performance of his or her work.

Consumer Information Form 1-1 (22 TAC 531.18)

Each real estate inspector or active real estate broker licensed by the Texas Real Estate Commission must display Consumer Information Form 1-1 prominently in each place of business that the broker or inspector maintains.

Discriminatory Practices (22 TAC 531.19)

No real estate licensee shall inquire about, respond to or facilitate inquiries about or make a disclosure, which indicates or is intended to indicate any preference, limitation or discrimination based on protected classes.

Protected classes include race, color, religion, sex, national origin, ancestry, familial status, or handicap of an owner, previous or current occupant, potential purchaser, lessor or potential lessee of real property.

A handicapped individual includes a person who had, may have had, has or may have AIDS, HIV-related illnesses or HIV infection as defined by the Centers for Disease Control of the U.S. Public Health Service.

TREC Complaints

A person may file a complaint with TREC against a real estate licensee if the person believes the licensee violated the Real Estate License Act. Assuming that the commission has jurisdiction over the complaint, the commission will typically investigate the allegations by interviewing the parties and witnesses and gathering relevant information. After review of the information, TREC's enforcement division will notify the licensee if it intends to initiate disciplinary proceedings against the licensee. After a hearing or other settlement procedure, the

Notes

2

commission will render a decision. If the evidence establishes a violation of the Real Estate License Act, the commission may impose disciplinary action which may include:

- ☑ a reprimand;
- ☑ suspension of the license;
- ☑ revocation of the license;
- ☑ a fine;
- ☑ probation; or
- ☑ any combination of the foregoing.

Commission Investigations

The commission is required to maintain a system to promptly and efficiently act on complaints filed with it and must maintain a file on each complaint. The commission must also ensure that it gives priority to the investigation of complaints filed by a consumer and any enforcement case resulting from the consumer complaint. The commission is required to assign priorities and investigate complaints using a risk-based approach based on the degree of potential harm to the consumer, potential for immediate harm to a consumer, overall severity of the allegations and the complaint, number of license holders potentially involved in the complaint, previous complaint history of the license holder, and the number of potential violations in the complaint.

In addition to suspension and revocation, the commission may order a licensee to pay a refund to a consumer as provided in an agreement resulting from an informal settlement conference, or an enforcement order, in addition to imposing an administrative penalty or other sanctions.

The commission is required to adopt procedures governing informal disposition of the contested case, which, if utilized, may expedite disciplinary matters and avoid formal hearings. These informal dispositions must provide the complainant and the license holder the opportunity to be heard. They require the presence of a public member of the commission for a case involving a consumer complaint, and at least two staff members of the commission with experience in the regulatory area that is the subject of the proceeding.

In consumer cases involving more serious allegations, the commission has some authority to take immediate, temporary action. In such a case, a disciplinary panel consisting of three commission members determines whether a person's license to practice should be temporarily suspended. If the disciplinary panel determines from the information that a person licensed to practice would constitute a continuing threat to the public welfare by continuing to practice, the panel must temporarily suspend that person's license.

Notes

3

Association Complaints

The Association of REALTORS®, the Realtist Organization and other trade associations receive complaints alleging ethics violations against their members. Such complaints may be directed to the local association to which the member belongs. Typically, a grievance panel will conduct an initial review to determine if the complaint alleges a violation of the organization's code of ethics. Additionally, the grievance panel will determine if the matter is appropriate for review by its organization given its specific rules. After the grievance panel's review, a hearing may be called. The hearing panel, made up of peers, hears the testimony and presentation of evidence. The hearing panel will decide if any violation of the association's code of ethics occurred. The hearing panel may order disciplinary action against the respondent, which may include:

- ☑ a reprimand;
- ☑ fine;
- ☑ probation;
- ☑ suspension of membership;
- ☑ revocation of membership;
- ☑ or any combination of the foregoing.

The panels advise the parties of any rights to appeal the decision.

NAR's Code of Ethics and the CCIM Code of Ethics prohibit their members from the following:

- ☑ denying equal professional services to any person on the basis of protected class;
- ☑ being a party to any agreement or plan to discriminate on the basis of protected classes;
- ☑ discriminating in their employment practices on the basis of protected classes;
- ☑ volunteering information regarding racial, religious, or ethnic composition of any neighborhood;
- ☑ engaging in any activity that may result in panic selling; and
- ☑ printing or distributing material that indicates any preference or limitation or discrimination based on a protected class (Art. 10).

CCIM members may provide demographic information when involved in the sale or lease in commercial property if the information is needed to complete the transaction and is obtained from a recognized, reliable, independent, and impartial source (SP10-3).

Part I, §2 of the Realtist Code of Ethics provides that a Realtist should never be instrumental in establishing, reinforcing or extending restrictions that limit the use or occupancy of property to any racial, religious or national origin groups.

Notes

4

2

Agency Relationships

Agency relationships can be confusing, not only to buyers and sellers, but to brokers and their agents, as well. Increasing your understanding of this important concept will greatly aid you and your clients in future transactions. It is important to keep in mind the difference between a customer and a client.

☑ Customer — a person(s) who is unrepresented by an agent but may receive information and assistance from a licensee (for example, a listing broker who assists a buyer who is not represented)

☑ Client — a person(s) whom the agent has agreed to represent

Fiduciary Duties

A fiduciary is a person who has a high duty of care for another person, the client. The law requires the fiduciary to place the client's interest ahead of his or her interest. When a licensee begins to provide agency services to a party, or a party believes that such services are being provided, the fiduciary relationship begins.

Fiduciary relationships are common and can involve attorneys, trustees, investment brokers and real estate agents, among others. The principal, or client, is the person with whom the licensee has a fiduciary relationship. Although the licensee's duty is to act in the principal's interest, the licensee owes a duty of honesty and fairness to all parties in the transaction.

Information About Brokerage Services and Agency Disclosure

At the first substantive dialogue with a client or prospect, always provide the Information About Brokerage Services form, which is a written statement containing the statutory information relating to brokerage services. The statute permits the Information About Brokerage Services to appear in any format as long as it is in at least ten-point type (1101.558(e)).

Notes

The duty to treat other parties to a transaction honestly is also found in Article 1 of the NAR Code of Ethics and the CCIM Code Ethics, and is expressed as a theme in the Realtist Code of Ethics.

The duty to disclose who the agent represents at the first contact with the other party in the transaction or the other party's agent is also expressed in NAR's and CCIM's Codes of Ethics (SP 16-10, 11, & 12).

5

The commission publishes a form entitled Information About Brokerage Services that most licensees use to comply with the statute.

A substantive dialogue is a meeting or written communication that involves a substantive discussion relating to specific real property. A substantive dialogue does not include a dialogue at an open house or a meeting after the time of the contract. The Information About Brokerage Services form is not required if the transaction is a residential lease for one year or less and a sale is not being considered. For example, a face-to-face meeting with a prospective client in which you are discussing properties is a substantive dialogue. Any written correspondence (including e-mail or other electronic means) about specific properties constitutes a substantive dialogue. A telephone conversation by itself may not constitute a meeting that would require providing the form, but any written follow-up or face-to-face meeting would require that the client receive the form. However, a telephone conversation could, arguably, be classified as a meeting at which a substantive dialogue occurs.

The *Information About Brokerage Services* form is not required if the licensee is meeting with a party represented by another licensee. For example, if you are the listing broker and happen to meet a buyer you know is represented by a buyer's agent, you do not need to provide the form.

The form published by the commission provides for signatures. The signatures are not required by statute; however, it is prudent to request acknowledgement of the principal's receipt of the form.

Disclosure of Agency Representation

Keep in mind that the Information About Brokerage Services form only informs parties as to the potential representation and does not disclose the licensee's agency or representation. A licensee *representing a party* is required to disclose such representation at the first contact with *another party* to the transaction or *another licensee* who represents another party to the transaction. This agency disclosure may be oral or in writing. For example, when making an appointment with a listing agent or seller to show a property, a buyer's agent must disclose that he or she represents the buyer. This could be accomplished by stating that you represent a buyer interested in the property. Other examples include when the

☑ listing agent meets a prospect at an open house; or

☑ listing agent meets a prospect at the listed property.

When making appointments through a centralized showing service, the disclosure is not required to the service.

Notes

The NAR and CCIM Codes of Ethics require the member to advise their clients of any potential for the member to represent more than one party in the transaction. This communication is required at the time a listing or buyer representation agreement is signed (SP 1-12 & 13).

6

Intermediary Brokerage Relationship Services

Intermediary status was created by statute in 1996 to acknowledge that a broker may be in the position of assisting two principals involved in the same transaction. A broker who represents the buyer and the seller in the same transaction must act as an intermediary. An intermediary is a broker who is employed to negotiate a transaction between parties and, for that purpose, may act as an agent of the parties. For a broker to negotiate a transaction for two principals as an intermediary, the broker first must obtain written permission from the parties to act in such capacity, and the agreement must state the source of any expected compensation.

When entering into an agreement with a principal, the agreement may address whether the intermediary relationship is a possibility. To authorize the possibility of an intermediary relationship in a listing agreement or buyer representation agreement, the statute requires that the

☑ agreement be in writing and that the following be in bold print:

☑ intermediary may not disclose that the seller will accept a price less than the asking price, unless authorized in writing to do so by the seller;

☑ intermediary may not disclose that the buyer will pay a price greater than the price submitted in a written offer, unless authorized in writing to do so by the buyer;

☑ intermediary may not disclose confidential information, unless authorized in writing to disclose the information, or required to do so by the Texas Real Estate License Act, or a court order or if the information materially relates to the condition of the property;

☑ intermediary may not treat a party dishonestly; and that the intermediary may not violate the Real Estate License Act.

Note: The foregoing are requirements under Section 1101.651(d) of the Real Estate License Act.

The intermediary may appoint different associated licensees to communicate with and carry out instructions of the respective parties. The appointment of associated licensees requires the written consent of the parties and written notification of appointments to the parties. The appointed licensees must still comply with the requirements listed above.

Each appointed licensee may provide opinions and advice to his or her respective party. The intermediary is required to treat both parties fairly and impartially. The appointed licensees are not subject to the intermediary's duty of impartiality.

Notes

Brokers or firms will have specific company policies in place that address whether the firm authorizes the intermediary relationship, whether appointments will be made, how appointments are to be made, and other procedures that must be followed. Each licensee should be familiar with his or her company's policies and procedures. If the licensee questions whether the company's policies are in compliance with the Real Estate License Act, the licensee should address such questions to his or her broker.

7

If appointments are made:

1. there must be a written authorization from both parties for the broker to act as an intermediary (this may be done in the written buyer representation agreement and the written listing agreement);

2. the intermediary may not appoint himself or herself to either party;

3. the intermediary cannot make appointments to one party without also making appointments to the other party;

4. the intermediary must give a written notice to each principal that appointments have been made and identify the respective appointees to the principals; and

5. the appointees must keep confidential information confidential.

An intermediary is not required to make appointments in every transaction. There should be clear company policies regarding appointments.

Example 1. Agent A lists a shopping center. Agent B, working for the same company, comes in with a buyer. In this example, the broker's policy in such a situation is to appoint Associate A to the seller and Associate B to the buyer. In this case, the intermediary (broker) does not

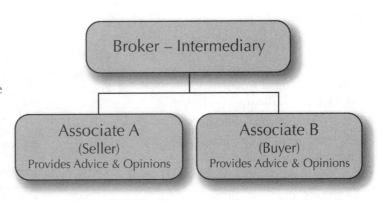

provide any opinions or advice to either party during negotiations. Each associate may provide opinions and advice during negotiations to the parties to whom each is appointed. The intermediary (broker) and the appointed associates remain obligated to comply with the items under §1101.651(d).

Notes

All associates in a brokerage act in the role of an intermediary except for those associates who are appointed to the parties.

8

Example 2. Assume the same facts as Example 1, except now the broker's policy is that he does not make appointments. In this example, the associates may not provide opinions or advice during negotiations to the party(s) each is servicing. The associates may facilitate the transaction and assist the parties as neutral service providers.

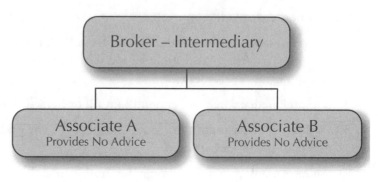

Example 3. In a multiagent brokerage, Associate A brings in both the buyer and seller. The Real Estate License Act permits the broker to select an appropriate course of action in this example.

Alternative 1—The intermediary may choose to make no appointments, in which case the intermediary (broker) and Associate A may not provide opinions or advice to either party during negotiations and remain obligated to comply with the items under §1101.651(d). Associate A and the intermediary may process or facilitate the transaction.

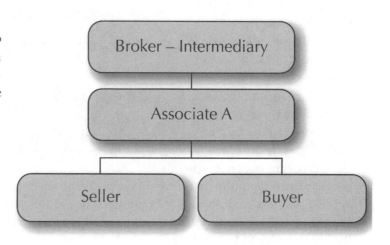

Notes

9

Alternative 2—The intermediary may choose to reassign one or both of the parties to another agent. In the following example, the buyer is reassigned to Associate B. The intermediary (broker) does not provide any opinions or advice to either party during negotiations. Each associate may provide opinions and

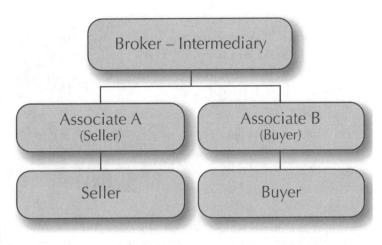

advice during negotiations to the parties to whom each is appointed. The intermediary (broker) and the appointed associates remain obligated to comply with the items under §1101.651(d). The broker must have written consent for appointments. The issue of compensation is a matter of the brokerage's policy and is an internal concern.

Example 4. What if the broker is a solo practitioner? May the solo practitioner act as an intermediary? Yes, but the solo practioner cannot make appointments of associated licensees. The intermediary (broker) does not provide any opinions or advice to either party dur-

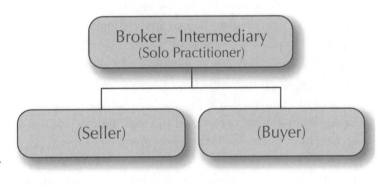

ing negotiations and remains obligated to comply with the items under §1101.651(d). *No appointments are possible.* The intermediary may process or facilitate the transaction.

NAR's and CCIM's Codes of Ethics prohibit members from selling or acquiring an interest in real estate for themselves, their immediate families, members of their firms, or entities in which they have an ownership interest without making their true position known (Art. 4). Such disclosures must be in writing before signing a contract (SP 4-1). Part I, §9 of the Realtist Code of Ethics requires the Realtist to disclose if he or she has a personal interest in the property being purchased.

NAR's and CCIM's Codes of Ethics prohibit the member from receiving any commission, rebate or profit on expenditures without the client's knowledge and consent (Art. 6). Any referral fees received for referring a person to a service provide must be disclosed to the client or customer to whom the recommendation is made.

The prohibition against receiving compensation from more than one party without the knowledge and consent of all parties is also found in Article 7 of NAR's and CCIM's Codes of Ethics and in Part I, §6 of the Realtist Code of Ethics.

The prohibition against interfering with the agency relationship of another broker is also found in Article 16 of NAR's and CCIM's Code of Ethics and Part II, §7 of the Realtist Code of Ethics.

Notes

10

Example 5. When a broker owns a small brokerage and actively lists and sells property, may the broker appoint himself or herself to one of the parties?

The broker shall not appoint himself or herself to one of the parties because the broker would be in two different roles. The broker may choose to make no appointments, and the broker and Associate B would not provide opinions or advice during negotiations. Each could process or facilitate the transaction. Alternatively, the broker could reassign the seller to another agent in the example above and make appointments.

Example 6. A broker orally agrees to represent a buyer. The buyer now wants to buy one of the broker's listings. The broker must get a written consent from both buyer and seller to act as an intermediary before proceeding and the written consent must comply with statutory requirements (Sec. 1101.559). One practical solution is to have a written buyer representation agreement containing the consent for the broker to act as an intermediary.

What happens if the buyer does not agree to give written consent to act as an intermediary? The agent must advise the buyer that he or she is no longer represented and that fiduciary duties are owed to the seller under the listing agreement.

A related question is: "I have a listing and an unrepresented buyer wants to make an offer. Must I act as an intermediatry?" No. A broker representing one party (client) to a transaction in which the other party is unrepresented (customer) is not an intermediary. One may assist the buyer and represent the seller in this example. Agents should check with their brokers about this situation as many companies have policies addressing this and other situations.

Notes

11

Subagency

"Subagent" means a license holder who represents a principal through cooperation with and consent of a broker representing the principal. The subagent is not sponsored by or associated with the principal's broker. Subagency is less common today than in previous years. It would commonly occur when a buyer was not represented, but utilized the services of a broker who sold or leased to the buyer a property that was listed by another brokerage firm. It is akin to the contractor subcontractor relationship. The

subagent acts for the listing broker and, therefore, indirectly for the seller's interest. While a subagent is considered an agent of the principal, the subagent should obtain the consent of the listing agent before attempting to negotiate directly with the principal. Any broker who acts as a subagent should exercise caution so that the buyer is aware of the relationship and is not confused.

Conflicts of Interest

☑ When buying, selling or leasing property on his or her account, the licensee must disclose in writing that he or she is a licensee.

☑ The licensee may not use his or her expertise to the disadvantage of the other party.

☑ The licensee may not act in the dual capacity as an agent and undisclosed principal in the transaction.

☑ The licensee must exercise extreme care when purchasing property either currently or recently listed by his or her broker.

☑ A mortgage broker may not act as a mortgage broker and a real estate licensee in the same transaction without knowledge and written consent from the mortgage applicant.

☑ If you receive a commission, rebate or fee from a service provider, you must obtain your principal's consent and you must also disclose to the person being referred to the service provider that you are receiving the commission, rebate or fee.

☑ The licensee may not receive compensation (money, trips, bonus bucks) from more than one party without the knowledge and consent of all parties to the transaction.

Notes

12

☑ The licensee may not interfere with the exclusive agency relationship of another broker.

☑ If the licensee represents two buyers who are making offers on the same property, the licensee should obtain the consent of both buyers to represent competing buyers.

Conflicts Arising in Early Termination of Agency

The agency relationship is a highly personal relationship. It requires continuing consent of the principal and the agent. Agency may be terminated at any time by either party; however, an early termination without cause may expose the terminating party to liability under the agency agreement. If an agent continues to offer the property for sale without the consent of the principal, it constitutes a violation of the Real Estate License Act. Upon receipt of a notice of termination from a principal, the agent should cease acting as the principal's agent. A listing agent should cease all advertising. For example, remove signs, remove MLS listing, remove information from web site, etc.

If a principal approaches a licensee and informs the licensee that the principal is subject to an existing exclusive agency relationship with another broker, the licensee should not provide any services until confirmation that the prior agency relationship has been terminated. The licensee should not interfere with an existing exclusive agency relationship under any circumstances. For example, the licensee should not suggest to the principal how the existing agency relationship should be terminated.

Notes

13

3
Offers

Minimum Services

Commission regulations have addressed this issue in a number of ways.

Under 22 TAC §535.156. The licensee

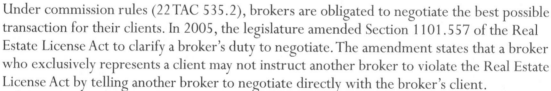

- ☑ has an obligation to submit all offers.

- ☑ must convey all known information that will affect the principal's decision to make,
accept or reject offers.

- ☑ must deal fairly and honestly with all parties, but he or she owes a duty of fidelity to his or her principal.

- ☑ has an affirmative duty to keep the principal informed, at all times, of significant information applicable to the transaction.

- ☑ The licensee has a duty to convey accurate information.

Under commission rules (22 TAC 535.2), brokers are obligated to negotiate the best possible transaction for their clients. In 2005, the legislature amended Section 1101.557 of the Real Estate License Act to clarify a broker's duty to negotiate. The amendment states that a broker who exclusively represents a client may not instruct another broker to violate the Real Estate License Act by telling another broker to negotiate directly with the broker's client.

Section 1101.652(b) (22) of the act provides that a broker may not negotiate a transaction directly with a principal in the transaction if the broker knows that the principal is subject to an exclusive agency relationship with another broker. The amendment to Section 1101.557 provides that the mere delivery of an offer by one broker to a client of another broker does not violate Section 1101.652(b)(22) if the delivery is made with the consent of the client's broker and the client's broker receives a copy of the offer. Section 1101.557 also provides that the broker who exclusively represents a client must, at a minimum,

Notes

15

1. answer the client's questions if there are any about the offer or issues related to the offer;

2. keep the client informed of material information; and

3. present offers to or from the parties.

For example, a listing broker may NOT instruct a buyer's broker to negotiate directly with the seller. Instead, he or she may request the buyer's broker deliver an offer to the seller. If the buyer's broker delivers the offer to the seller at the listing broker's request, the buyer's broker must send a copy of the offer to the listing broker and may not engage in any other activity with the seller that constitutes a negotiation. All the buyer's broker may do is perform the administrative task of delivering the offer to the seller. If the listing broker receives an offer, the listing broker must inform the seller that an offer has been received. The listing broker may not withhold any material information from the client. A buyer's broker might refuse to deliver the offer to the seller and, instead, might send the offer to the listing broker. The listing broker would then be required under law to inform the seller that the offer has been submitted. Regardless of whether the buyer's broker delivers the offer to the seller at the listing broker's request or delivers it to the listing broker, the seller should receive the offer promptly and the listing broker should be aware that an offer has been made.

> TAR publishes Form 1504 "Notice from Buyer Agent to Seller" to address this situation.

If the seller wishes to make a counter-offer to the buyer's broker, the listing broker is obligated to communicate the offer to the buyer's broker. A sophisticated seller who needs little or no assistance from the listing agent might prepare a counter-offer and either (a) send it to the listing broker who may do nothing more than deliver it to the buyer's broker or (b) deliver it to the buyer's broker and send a copy of the listing broker. In either case, the listing broker is aware that negotiations are taking place and stands ready to assist the seller if necessary.

If the seller wants to engage in oral negotiations with the buyer or buyer's broker, the buyer's broker should not engage in such discussions unless the listing broker is present (either in person or phone or otherwise). Any subsequent offer back from the buyer to the seller should be communicated under this same procedure.

Section 1101.557 also addresses a few technical questions related to property managers, builders and governmental sealed bid procedures. If a property manager has the authority to

Notes

16

bind the owner to a lease, the property manager is considered to be the party in the transaction. The property manager does not need to communicate the offers to the owner if the property manager has the authority to enter into the lease and make such decisions for the owner.

If the seller is a builder, the buyer's broker may ask the builder's employee or sales representative about specific forms or contractual terms the builder may require. These inquiries do not violate the Real Estate License Act. The delivery of any offer to the builder should follow the same procedures as outlined previously. If the buyer's broker is assisting the buyer in bidding on a HUD- or VA-foreclosed property and the government requires that such bids be submitted through a sealed process, the buyer's broker does not have to deliver a copy of the offer to the listing broker.

Presentation of Multiple Offers

If a broker receives more than one offer, all offers must be presented to the seller unless instructed otherwise by the seller. No offer has a priority of presentation over another. The broker should submit all offers promptly. For example, if a licensee receives a written offer at 9 a.m. and presents it to the seller and then receives a second offer at 3 p.m. (before the seller has accepted the first offer), the licensee has the duty to submit the later offer to the seller for his or her consideration.

In the same example, if the agent representing the second buyer is aware that multiple offers have been received, the listing agent should notify the agent representing the first buyer that multiple offers have been received. The same would be true regardless of the number of offers. The listing agent should keep the terms and conditions confidential so as not to give one buyer a significant negotiating advantage over another. A broker is obligated to place his client's interest first and is also obligated to treat other parties in the transaction honestly and fairly.

A contract for the sale of real estate must be in writing, signed by the parties to be charged with performance, in order to be enforceable. The agents, therefore, should take care to make no representations as to acceptance of an offer until all parties have signed and communicated acceptance.

> **NAR Standard of Practice 1-15**
>
> Realtors®, in response to inquiries from buyers or cooperating brokers shall, with the sellers' approval, disclose the existence of offers on the property. Where disclosure is authorized, Realtors® shall also disclose whether offers were obtained by the listing licensee, another licensee in the listing firm, or by a cooperating broker. (Adopted 1/03, Amended 1/06)

Notes

17

Seller's Acceptance

The seller has the option of accepting or rejecting all offers, including a full-price offer. A seller should not counter multiple offers. If multiple buyers were to accept the seller's counteroffer, the seller potentially could be bound to sell the property to different buyers. The seller could:

☑ reject all the offers and invite the prospects to submit better offers;

☑ accept one offer and reject the other(s);

☑ make a counteroffer to one prospect (reject others or not respond to the others);

☑ reject all offers; or

☑ do nothing.

A seller is not bound to accept any offer, even at full price. In refusing a full-price offer, the seller may be obligated to pay a fee to the listing broker.

Licensees should recognize that two or more offers are rarely identical, even if they offer the same price. Significant distinctions usually can be made based on the various contingencies contained in most contracts — date of possession, ability of the buyer to secure a particular level of financing on certain terms and so on. The documentation of the decision-making process should support the seller's choice as the one most likely to reach closing with the fewest difficulties.

Revocation of Offers/Counteroffers

A buyer or seller may revoke any offer or counteroffer prior to acceptance by the other party.

Effective Date

TREC-promulgated contract forms instruct the broker to fill in the date of final acceptance as the effective date. Final acceptance occurs on the date that the person receiving the offer communicates acceptance to the person making the offer. Acceptance must be unequivocal.

4

Disclosure Requirements

Texas Real Estate License Act

Under the Texas Real Estate License Act, the commission may suspend or revoke a license or take disciplinary action against a licensee, if a licensee fails to:

- ☑ disclose to a potential purchaser any latent structural defect or any other defect known to the licensee;

- ☑ disclose to all parties which party he or she represents;

- ☑ disclose to all parties that he or she is receiving compensation from more than one party, if applicable;

- ☑ disclose to principal the licensee's acceptance, receipt or charge of a commission, rebate or direct profit on expenditures made for the principal;

- ☑ disclose that the licensee is a principal in a transaction, if applicable;

- ☑ provide copies of any document in a real estate transaction upon request to the person who signed that document;

- ☑ advise a purchaser in writing before closing a transaction that the purchaser should have an attorney review an abstract of title or obtain an owner's policy of title insurance;

- ☑ disclose the party that the licensee represents at the time of first contact with another party to the transaction (or that party's broker); and

NAR's and CCIM's Codes of Ethics prohibit members from selling or acquiring an interest in real estate for themselves, their immediate families, members of their firms, or entities in which they have an ownership interest without making their true position known (Art. 4). Such disclosures must be in writing before signing a contract (SP 4-1). Part I, §9 of the Realtist Code of Ethics requires the Realtist to disclose if he or she has a personal interest in the property being purchased.

NAR's and CCIM's Codes of Ethics prohibit members from exaggerating, misrepresenting, or concealing pertinent facts relating to the property or the transaction (Art. 2). Part I, §3 of the Realtist Code of Ethics requires the member to offer properties without exaggeration, concealment, or misleading information.

The duty to disclose who the agent represents at the first contact with the other party in the transaction or the other party's agent is also expressed in NAR's and CCIM's Codes of Ethics (SP 16-10, 11, & 12).

The prohibition against receiving compensation from more than one party without the knowledge and consent of all parties is also found in Article 7 of NAR's and CCIM's Codes of Ethics and in Part I, §6 of the Realtist Code of Ethics.

Notes

19

☑ provide the Information About Brokerage Services form at the first substantive dialogue with a party to the transaction unless that party is represented by another
licensee.

Under other statutes or common law, a licensee might also face civil liability for failure to
disclose. The licensee does not have a duty to inspect the property.

Deceptive Trade Practices Act

Brokers who violate the Deceptive Trade Practices – Consumer Protection Act (DTPA)
often do so by failing to disclose to their principals information of which they have actual
knowledge or by affirming misrepresentations, regardless of whether the brokers had actual
knowledge that these representations were false or incorrect. Among other things, the DTPA
prohibits brokers from representing that:

☑ goods or services have characters, uses or benefits that they do not;

☑ goods or services are of a particular standard, quality or grade that they are not;

☑ an agreement confers rights,
remedies or obligations that
it does not;

☑ salespersons, representatives
or agents have authority to
negotiate the final terms of
a transaction when they do
not;

☑ a guarantee or warranty confers rights or remedies that it
does not; and

> A party to a real estate transaction may sue the broker
> for violation of the DTPA. The DTPA now applies
> only to real estate transactions of $500,000 and less
> or transactions relating to the principal's homestead.
> In transactions between $100,000 and $500,000, the
> DTPA can be waived if the contract is negotiated by
> independent legal counsel and does not involve a
> homestead. Similar causes of action may be alleged
> under §27.01, Business and Commerce Code, which
> does not have limitations on the amount of recovery.

☑ work or services have been performed when they have not.

The act also requires that brokers disclose, at the time of the transaction, information that
was known concerning goods or services if the failure to disclose was intended to induce
consumers into a transaction they would not have entered had the information been disclosed.

> NAR's and CCIM's Codes of Ethics prohibit the member
> from receiving any commission, rebate, or profit on expen-
> ditures without the client's knowledge and consent (Art. 6).
> Any referral fees received for referring a person to a service
> provide must be disclosed to the client or customer to whom
> the recommendation is made.

Notes

20

5

Advertising

Truthfulness in advertising is the most fundamental concept in all applicable statutory law, rules and regulations. The laws allow brokerage firms to advertise and promote their services and special expertise, as long as those advertisements are truthful.

Section 1101.652(b) (23) of the Real Estate License Act authorizes TREC to take disciplinary action against a licensee who is responsible for an advertisement (in any media) that is likely to deceive the public or that in any manner tends to create a misleading impression, or one that fails to identify the advertiser as a licensed real estate broker or agent.

To ensure compliance, a broker who is familiar with the rules should review all marketing materials and advertising copy. Questionable marketing materials should be submitted to the broker's legal counsel for review and approval.

If a broker starts or stops using an assumed name, 22 TAC§535.154 requires the broker to notify TREC.

An advertisement (such as classified ads, websites, print advertising and e-mail), placed by a licensee must include an additional designation such as "agent," "broker" or a trade association name which serves clearly to identify the advertiser as a real estate agent.

Some licensees use inducements in their advertising, such as offering a free market analysis, a free home evaluation or similar enticements. This kind of advertising is permissible. However, the terms related to the availability of the offered product or service should be detailed carefully. Hidden "hooks," (when an offered service is not free) can render promotional material misleading and deceptive.

Marketing Listed Properties

According to 22 TAC §535.156(d), a licensee has a duty to convey accurate information to members of the public with whom he or she deals. In addition, 22 TAC §535.154 addresses the following specifics:

☑ Before advertising any property, a licensee must have the consent of the owner or the owner's authorized agent. The consent may be obtained in the written listing agreement or other appropriate agreement signed by the owner.

Notes

Article 12 of NAR's and CCIM's Codes of Ethics require members to: (1) present a true picture in their advertisements; and (2) disclose their professional status (broker, REALTOR®, etc.). The advertising of inducements is permitted if the advertisements clearly state any conditions required to obtain the inducement (SP 12-3). Advertisements of listed property must disclose the firm's name (SP 12-5).

21

☑ Listings may be taken only in the broker's name and not in a salesperson's name.

☑ All advertising must include information identifying the advertiser as either a broker or salesperson.

☑ The salesperson's name is not required in advertisements, but the broker's name must be included.

☑ In no case shall a broker or salesperson place an advertisement which in any way implies that the salesperson is the person responsible for the operation of a real estate brokerage.

☑ Written consent of the owner is required to place a sign on the property.

Regulation Z

Regulation Z, which was issued after Congress passed the Truth in Lending Act, generally covers advertisements for residential property only and does not govern loans primarily for commercial, investment or agriculture purposes. Regulation Z applies regularly to banks, mortgage companies and other arrangers of credit. Brokers who advertise credit terms are subject to Regulation Z as well.

There are three major disclosure requirements in advertising residential mortgage loans:

1. If an advertisement includes information about loan terms, those terms must actually be available to a qualified borrower.

2. If an advertisement states a rate of finance charge (defined as interest, points and loan fees), the advertisement must use the words "annual percentage rate" (APR). The advertisement must state the APR, and, if the finance charge can increase over the terms of the loan, the ad must disclose that fact.

3. Additional disclosure is triggered if an advertisement contains any of the following: the amount or percentage of any down payment, the number of payments or term of the repayment period, the amount of any regular installment payment on the loan or the amount of any finance charges. If any of these triggers appears in the advertisement, all of the following information must be disclosed in the advertisement:

   • amount of percentage of the down payment (e.g., $5,000 down, 10 percent down or zero down);

   • terms of repayment ($650 per month for 30 years);

Notes

22

- annual percentage rate (the interest rate); and

- whether the rate may be increased at a later date.

The mere mention of the APR alone will not trigger these additional disclosure requirements. If specific information is mentioned in the advertisement, such as $150,000 assumable note at 7.25 percent APR, the disclosure requirements are triggered, and the advertisement must contain all of the above information. The safest practice is to mention only the APR in the advertisement and suggest that prospects call for further information.

Fair Housing Laws (applicable to residential and commercial transactions)

Advertising also is governed by guidelines issued by the U.S. Department of Housing and Urban Development (HUD) pursuant to Section 804(c) of the Federal Fair Housing Act (the Act). Section 804(c) prohibits advertisements that state a preference, limitation or discrimination based on race, color, religion, sex, handicap, familial status or national origin. The act applies to publishers, as well as to the party placing the advertisement. Brokers should be extremely careful about loosely worded ads that may inadvertently imply a limitation or preference with respect to a protected class. HUD regulations also require diversity among the models in advertising photography.

Prohibited Words and Phrases

Racial and Ethnic Terms

The use of words describing current or potential residents, the neighbors or the neighborhood in racial or ethnic terms may constitute a violation of the Fair Housing Act and the Real Estate License Act. HUD has published a list of words and phrases that should never be used including "white private home," "Hispanic resident," "Oriental neighborhood," or "predominantly African-American schools."

Religious Preference

Advertisements must not contain any explicit preferences or limitations concerning religion. However, the advertisement may describe amenities without stating a preference, such as "apartment complex with chapel" or "kosher meals available." If the legal name of the entity

Notes

23

contains a religious reference, such as "Methodist Village Apartments," the advertisement should include a disclaimer stating that the owner-lessor does not discriminate.

Gender Preference

Advertisements must contain no explicit reference for the gender of the renter. One exception is for shared living spaces. Accordingly, a female advertiser may advertise, "female roommate wanted." Other common phrases permissible in advertising include "bachelor apartment" or "mother-in-law suite". These phrases are commonly used as physical descriptions of the available premises.

Disablilities

Advertisements must not discriminate or exclude persons with disabilities. Descriptions of properties as well as of services and amenities are permissible — such as "jogging trails," "great view". It is also permissible to describe conduct required of potential tenants. Advertising for "nonsmoking" or "sober" tenants does not violate the Act.

Familial Status

Advertisements must not contain limitations on the number or age of children or express a preference for adults, couples or single persons. There is an exemption for developments that qualify as housing for older persons in one of two ways. The first is housing intended for and occupied solely by persons 62 years of age or older. The second is housing intended for occupancy by at least one person at least 55 years of age or older per unit. Occupancy standards (the number of residents per bedroom) may apply and are adopted by statute or ordinance.

Misrepresentations in Advertising

The courts have interpreted the DTPA in a manner that creates liabilities for innocent misrepresentation or misstatement of fact as well as for negligent or intentional acts. The act makes brokers particularly vulnerable to claims if they rely upon information furnished to them by homeowners if: (1) such information is not verified or (2) the agent does not disclose the source of the information and state that the agent has no reason to believe it to be inaccurate.

Accurately describing the characteristics and qualities of a property will greatly reduce the likelihood of claims against the broker. Brokers should make a serious effort to keep current

Notes

24

with applicable laws since liabilities, penalties and sanctions can be substantial, including possible suspension or revocation of a license.

Square Footage in Advertising

Mistakes in the square footage of a property are one of the most frequent grounds for claims against brokers. There is no uniform or standard method for calculating square footage. Many brokers rely on data from the central appraisal district; however, that is no guarantee of accuracy. Many properties have additions or converted garages, porches or patios that are not reflected in the appraisal district's data. Always quote the source of the measurements being used. If there are multiple sources with different measurements, provide all sources.

Internet Advertising

Generally, an Internet website is considered an advertisement. The Internet is a medium where merchants, professionals, vendors and others place information designed to gain public attention and solicit and attract business. Each page on a broker's Internet site is considered a separate advertisement. A licensee must disclose his or her status as a broker or salesperson on each page. Disclosure at the top or bottom of each page declaring that all persons and firms named in this advertisement are licensed brokers or salespersons is permitted. While e-mail is a vehicle of communication through which business is conducted, it may also be considered an advertisement.

Internet Advertising Checklist

- ☑ Review for misleading statements
- ☑ Include name of firm or broker
- ☑ Name of salesperson's broker
- ☑ Identify license status of salesperson
- ☑ Disclose licensee's ownership in property
- ☑ Have authority to publish ad
- ☑ Correct price quote
- ☑ No contingencies for free services
- ☑ Conditions for any inducements

Removing a Listing From a Website

The Real Estate License Act prohibits any misleading or false advertisements. If a real estate licensee advertises listings on the Internet and fails to remove the listings within a reasonable time after the listing sells, the licensee could be accused of misrepresenting the status of available property in his or her advertisement.

Notes

25

Listing Services

Most Multiple Listing Services (MLS) in Texas have rules and regulations related to the display of MLS data on a MLS participant's website (known as IDX or IDL rules). Typically, by participating in the MLS, the participant authorizes other participants to display information about the participant's listings on their websites provided that they are in compliance with the MLS's IDX or IDL rules. Similar rules may apply to commercial MLSs (CMLS) or commercial information exchanges (CIEs).

Brokers who participate in MLSs, CMLSs, or CIEs should be aware of the IDX or IDL rules, opt-out procedures under such rules and how to comply with such rules when displaying listings of other participants. *Brokers who are not participants in such services may not advertise or display information about another broker's listing without consent from the listing broker.* The display or advertisement of another broker's listing, whether through IDX or IDL or otherwise, may not create any type of misleading impression (for example, implying that the person causing the advertisement to be published is the listing broker).

Notes

26

6

Dispute Resolution

Mediation

Texas statutes define a mediation resolution procedure as a forum before an impartial person (the mediator) designed to facilitate communication between parties and to promote reconciliation, settlement or understanding but *does not make decisions or give awards.* In a successful mediation, the parties agree on a settlement in writing which then becomes binding on both parties. Mediators are neither judges nor arbitrators. They are neutral facilitators in establishing dialogue among the parties to reach a settlement. A mediator may not impose his or her judgment on the issues.

The mediator need not be an attorney or hold any special license or credential, but should possess some knowledge of the subject matter, the outcome of prior cases involving the controversy and recoveries for similar matters in local courts. Although the mediator should remain neutral, his or her expertise may provide valuable guidelines for settlement.

There are numerous mediation service providers, such as county supported mediation services, private mediators, university law schools and REALTOR® Associations. Contact your county or district court clerk for a list of mediators in your area.

In 1987 mediation became one of the five statutorily recognized Alternative Dispute Resolution (ADR) procedures in Chapter 154 of the Texas Civil Practices and Remedies Code. Many Texas judges require court-ordered mediation before hearing a case. The Real Estate Center at Texas A&M University surveyed practitioners to determine how often mediation is used to settle real estate disputes. Researchers found that mediation was used to settle a high percentage of disputes.

Notes

27

Arbitration

Texas statutes define arbitration as a forum where parties and counsel present their positions before an impartial third party *who renders a specific award.* The parties must agree in writing to arbitrate a dispute. There are numerous arbitration providers, such as the American Arbitration Association, private attorneys, private arbitrators and REALTOR® Associations. Typically the arbitration procedure calls for a complaint or petition to be filed describing the dispute. The respondent will be given the opportunity to respond. A hearing is convened at which the parties present evidence and make arguments. The arbitrator(s) renders an award. The prevailing party may seek to enforce the award as a judgment by requesting that a court of law do so. Arbitration awards may be appealed on procedural or due process grounds.

Notes

28

7

TREC Disciplinary Case Studies

Forged Report

Facts

A salesperson assisted his clients in choosing a residential property for purchase and beginning the mortgage loan process. After receiving an appraisal report, the lender requested that a structural engineer inspect the garage floor. The salesperson engaged a professional engineer to inspect the garage floor. The engineer submitted a letter to the salesperson indicating the garage floor would have no adverse impact on the integrity of the house foundation. The letter included the statement, "The cracked slab in the garage can be replaced, repaired with epoxy or over-poured with a new concrete topping." Before forwarding the letter to the lender, the salesperson deleted the sentence referring to repair or replacement of the cracked slab in the garage without the knowledge or consent of the engineer.

After reviewing the engineer's letter, the lender requested an additional engineer's report concerning separations in the brick veneer of the property, a condition which had been noted in the appraisal report. The engineer could not evaluate this problem with another visual inspection of the property and the buyers were unable to pay for the second engineer's report.

The salesperson altered the date of the original engineer's letter in order to give the appearance that it referred to a subsequent inspection and added language indicating that no correction was recommended. The salesperson sent the altered copy to the lender with the intention that it be accepted as a genuine copy of the engineer's letter. The loan was approved. Subsequently, the lender required the original letter, and the salesperson was forced to reveal his actions in creating altered copies of the letter.

Notes

29

Conclusion

The salesperson engaged in conduct which constitutes dishonest dealings, bad faith, or untrustworthiness. The salesperson is also guilty of continued and flagrant misrepresentation.

Disciplinary Action

The salesperson's license was revoked.

Allowance? What allowance?

Facts

A salesperson assisted his clients in executing a sales contract for a residential property. A few days later, the parties executed an amendment to the contract requiring the seller, at seller's cost, to make certain repairs and for the seller to pay the buyer $1,000 at closing so that the buyer could complete other repairs (the repair allowance). The salesperson instructed his office to submit the executed amendment to the title company; however, he failed to follow through to determine if his instructions had been completed. The amendment was not submitted to the title company.

The buyers sold and closed their present residential property and on the same date closed on the new residential property. The repair allowance for the new property was not reflected on any closing documents. Although the buyers became aware of this fact immediately prior to signing the closing documents, they chose not to delay closing because they would be left without a residence to move into for an unknown period. Also, the salesperson assured the buyers he had confirmation of a fax of the amendment to the title company sent prior to closing, and he assured the buyers the matter could be resolved after closing. After closing the salesperson made an unsuccessful demand upon the seller to submit the repair allowance to the buyers. The salesperson then paid the buyers $1,000 for repairs to the property.

Conclusions

The salesperson acted negligently or incompetently in performing his duties as a licensee.

Disciplinary Action

The salesperson was formally reprimanded for his actions.

Notes

30

A Listing Without End

Facts

A broker completed a listing agreement for owners of a residential property. The agreement, which was between a corporation (for which the broker was a principal) and the sellers, contained a term of three months. The broker negotiated a sales contract between a buyer and the sellers. After the escrow agent acknowledged receipt of the contract and earnest money, the broker requested that the escrow agent disburse the commission to the unlicensed corporation for which she was principal. The buyer later terminated the contract, and the seller released the earnest money back to the buyer. The seller then terminated the listing agreement, which had already expired. The broker continued to market the property, stating to the seller's attorney that the seller did not properly terminate the listing agreement. The broker continued to market the property for another year without authorization.

Conclusions

The broker acted negligently or incompetently in performing an act for which a person is required to hold a real estate license. The salesperson marketed real property without the knowledge and consent of the owner of the property or the owner's authorized agent. The broker also committed a violation by attempting to have an unlicensed person (the corporation) act as a license holder.

Disciplinary Action

The broker's license was suspended for a period of six months. The suspension was fully probated for one year subject to the following terms and conditions:

The broker comply with Chapter 1101, Texas Occupations Code and the Rules of the Texas Real Estate Commission;

1. the broker fully cooperate with the enforcement division of the commission in completing its investigation of any complaints against her;

2. that on a date specified by the commission, the broker provide the commission's director of enforcement evidence of completion of thirty classroom hours in an agency law course and that these hours are in addition to the MCE hours required for the broker's next license renewal; and

3. the broker not engage any unlicensed person, including any corporation or LLC, in any brokerage activity.

Notes

4. the broker pay an administrative penalty of $3,000 to the Texas Real Estate Commission.

Friendly Repairs

Facts

A salesperson had been working with friends to find suitable property to purchase. The salesperson suggested that her friends purchase her own home, which was in need of repair. The salesperson agreed to pay for necessary repairs.

Because the buyer could not obtain financing, the buyer's father agreed to purchase the property. At the time the offer was drafted, the salesperson did not discuss having an inspection performed, and no option was included in the contract and no repairs were agreed upon by the salesperson and the buyer's father. In the contract the box under "Broker Information and Ratification of Fee" that was checked specified that the broker was representing the seller and buyer as an intermediary. The salesperson was a principal in the transaction and the buyer's father never authorized Intermediary Brokerage in writing. The contract was executed and the sale of property to the buyer's father closed.

After closing, the salesperson delayed the completion of the repairs promised to the buyer. The repairs were eventually completed. The salesperson believed that the buyer's father understood her position as both a licensee and the seller of the property. She also believed that the buyer's father understood that she was not representing him in the sale of the property. The salesperson believed that she did not indicate she was acting as an intermediary and did not intend to check the box on contract form. The salesperson believed that because of their friendship, all parties to the contract agreed to dispense with any formal agreement for repairs.

Conclusions

The salesperson's acts and omissions constitute engaging in misrepresentation, dishonesty, or fraud when selling real property in the license holder's own name.

Disciplinary Action

The salesperson was formally reprimanded and ordered to pay an administrative penalty of $500 to the Texas Real Estate Commission.

Notes

32

Commingling

Facts

A broker maintained an escrow account for the monies held in trust for others, including security deposits and rents collected from the properties managed by the brokerage company. On several occasions the broker used funds from the escrow account for operations of the brokerage and for the expenses of another owner. Over a three-month period, several property owners filed complaints with TREC alleging that they had terminated their property management agreements with the broker and that the broker had not remitted to them any security deposits or rents due to them. Sometime after the complaints were filed with TREC, each owner received their security deposits from the brokerage. The broker replaced all funds that had been improperly withdrawn from the escrow account.

Additionally, the broker, who was the designated officer for a corporation that held a real estate broker license, failed to notify the commission that the corporation used a business name.

Conclusions

The broker acted negligently or incompetently in performing an act for which a person is required to hold a real estate license. The broker commingled money that belonged to another person with the broker's own money.

Disciplinary Action

The broker's license was suspended for six months. The suspension was probated subject to the following terms and conditions:

1. the broker will comply with Chapter 1101, Texas Occupations Code and the Rules of the Texas Real Estate Commission;

2. the broker will fully cooperate with the enforcement division of the commission in completing its investigation;

3. the broker will complete 30 classroom hours in a property management course by a specified date in addition to the MCE hours required for the next renewal of the broker's license; and

4. the broker will not engage in any type of property management services on or before the specified date mentioned above.

Notes

33

Cheated Widow

Facts

A broker executed a contract in his own name to sell a property to a buyer. The broker did not reveal to the buyer that he was a licensed real estate broker acting on his own behalf. The buyer paid the broker $2,000 as earnest money. Two weeks later the buyer paid an additional $18,000 to complete the $20,000 down payment on the sales price of $55,000. The broker provided seller financing of the $35,000 balance by promissory note from the buyer to the broker.

Although the buyer was ready and willing, the broker indicated to her that there were some problems preventing his presence at closing and that he would close at some indefinite future date. The broker continued to delay closing; however, he permitted the buyer to take possession of the property, and she commenced making regular monthly payments to him. The broker also requested the buyer give him funds for tax and insurance payments for the property for 2 ½ calendar years.

The broker then obtained a mortgage on the property. The mortgage company foreclosed on the property for nonpayment by the broker. The buyer filed a complaint with the commission regarding the financial losses and loss of the purchase of the property. The commission requested the broker furnish information and documents for inspection in connection with the complaint. The broker did not respond to the request.

Conclusions

The broker contracted to sell real property to a buyer and was guilty of engaging in misrepresentation or dishonest or fraudulent action when selling real property in his own name. The broker was guilty of failing or refusing on demand to produce a document, book, or record in his possession concerning a real estate transaction conducted by him for inspection by the commission.

Disciplinary Action

The broker's license was revoked. In addition, a district court ordered the commission to pay the buyer $50,000 from the Real Estate Recovery Trust Account toward satisfaction of a judgment against the broker.

Notes

34

Appendix

Disclosure of Agency and Intermediary Practice

1. Q: How is a typical intermediary relationship created, and how does it operate?

A: At the first substantive dialogue with a seller or a prospective buyer, the salespersons or brokers associated with a firm provide the parties with a copy of the statutory information about agency required by TRELA. The statutory information would include an explanation of the intermediary relationship.

The brokerage firm negotiates a written listing contract with a seller and a written buyer representation agreement with a buyer. In those documents, the respective parties authorize the broker to act as an intermediary and to appoint associated licensees to work with the parties in the event the buyer wishes to purchase a property listed with the firm. At this point, the broker and associated licensees will be still functioning as exclusive agents of the individual parties. The listing contract and buyer representation agreement must contain the broker's obligations set. [TRELA Section 1101.651(d)]

When it becomes evident the buyer represented by the firm wishes to purchase property listed with the firm, the intermediary status comes into play, and the intermediary may appoint different associates to work with the parties. The intermediary notifies both parties in writing of the appointments of licensees to work with the parties. The associates provide advice and opinions to their respective parties during negotiations, and the intermediary broker is careful not to favor one party over the other in any action taken by the intermediary.

Notes

35

2. Q: What is an intermediary?

A: An intermediary is a broker who negotiates the transaction between the parties subject to the representation provisions of the Act. The intermediary may, with the written consent of the parties, appoint two licensees associated with the intermediary to work with and advise the party to whom they have been appointed.

3. Q: Is dual agency authorized by the representation provisions?

A: Effective September 1, 2005, a licensee may not represent both parties as a dual agent under revisions to the Act [S.B. 810 79th Legislature (2005)]. "A broker must agree to act as an intermediary under this subchapter if the broker agrees to represent in a transaction" a buyer or tenant, and a seller or landlord. Occupations Code Section 1101.561(b)]. Because a broker must act as an intermediary under this new provision, a licensee cannot act as a dual agent.

To the extent a dual agency relationship is created by accident or otherwise, a licensee must resolve the matter by complying with the notice and consent requirements of the representation provisions to act as an intermediary or by representing one of the parties only and working with the other party as a customer.

4. Q: When must the broker act as an intermediary?

A: If the broker and associates are going to continue working with parties they have been representing under listing contracts or buyer representation agreements, the intermediary role is the only way to handle "in-house" transactions, providing both parties the same level of service.

5. Q: If a salesperson or associated broker lists a property and have also been working with a prospective buyer under a representation agreement, how can the salesperson or associated broker sell this listing under the representation provisions?

A: There are three alternatives for the brokerage firm and the parties to consider:

1. The firm, acting through the salesperson or associated broker, can represent one of the parties and work with the other party as a customer rather than as a client. This probably means working with the buyer as a customer and terminating the buyer representation agreement.

2. If the firm has obtained permission in writing from both parties to be an intermediary and to appoint licensees to work with the parties, the salesperson or associated broker can be appointed by the intermediary to work with one of the

parties. Another licensee has to be appointed to work with the other party under this alternative. The law does not permit an intermediary to appoint the same licensee to work with both parties.

3. If the firm has obtained permission in writing from both parties to be an intermediary, but does not appoint different associates to work with the parties, the salesperson or broker associate can function as a representative of the firm. Because the firm is an intermediary, the salesperson and associated broker would be subject to the requirement not to act so as to favor one party over the other.

6. Q: If a salesperson may provide services to a party under the representation provisions without being appointed, why would a broker want to appoint a salesperson to work with a party?

A: Appointment following the procedures set out in the representation provisions permits the salesperson to provide a higher level of service. The appointed salesperson may provide advice and opinions to the party to whom the salesperson is assigned and is not subject to the intermediary's statutory duty of not acting so as to favor one party over the other.

7. Q: Is an intermediary an agent?

A: Yes, but the duties and obligations of an intermediary are different than for exclusive, or single, agents.

8. Q: What are the duties and obligations of an intermediary?

A: The representation provisions require the intermediary to obtain written consent from both parties to act as an intermediary. A written listing agreement to represent a seller/landlord or a written buyer/tenant representation agreement, which contains authorization for the broker to act as an intermediary between the parties, is sufficient for the purposes of the representation provisions. The agreement must set forth, in conspicuous bold or underlined print, the broker's obligations under Section 1101.651(d), and the agreement must state who will pay the broker.

If the intermediary is to appoint associated licensees to work with the parties, the intermediary must obtain written permission from both parties and give written notice of the appointments to each party. The intermediary is required to treat the parties fairly and honestly and to comply with TRELA. The intermediary is prohibited from acting so as to favor one party over the other. The intermediary may not reveal confidential information obtained from one party without the written instructions of that party, unless disclosure of that information is required by TRELA,

Notes

court order or the information materially relates to the condition of the property. The intermediary and any associated licensees appointed by the intermediary are prohibited from disclosing without written authorization that the seller will accept a price less than the asking price or that the buyer will pay a price greater than the price submitted in a written offer.

9. Q: **Can salespersons act as intermediaries?**

    A: Only a broker can contract with the parties to act as an intermediary between them.

    In that sense, only a broker can be an intermediary. If, however, the broker intermediary does not appoint associated licensees to work with the parties in a transaction, any salesperson or broker associates of the intermediary who function in that transaction would be required to act just as the intermediary does, not favoring one party over the other.

10. Q: **Can there be two intermediaries in the same transaction?**

    A: No.

11. Q: **Can a broker representing only the buyer be an intermediary?**

    A: Ordinarily, no; the listing broker will be the intermediary. In the case of a FSBO or other seller who is not already represented by a broker, the broker representing the buyer can secure the consent of both parties to act as an intermediary.

12. Q: **May an intermediary appoint a subagent in another firm to work with one of the parties?**

    A: Subagency is still permitted under the law, but a subagent in another firm cannot be appointed as one of the intermediary's associated licensees under the representation provisions of the Act.

13. Q: **May the same salesperson be appointed by the intermediary to work with both parties in the same transaction?**

    A: No; the law requires the intermediary to appoint different associated licensees to work with each party.

14. Q: **May more than one associated licensee be appointed by the intermediary to work with the same party?**

    A: Yes.

Notes

15. Q: **What is the difference between an appointed licensee working with a party and a licensee associated with the intermediary who has not been appointed to work with one party?**

A: During negotiations, the appointed licensee may advise the person to whom the licensee has been appointed. An associated licensee who has not been appointed must act in the same manner as the intermediary, that is, not giving opinions and advice and not favoring one party over the other.

16. Q: **Who decides whether a broker will act as intermediary, the broker or the parties?**

A: Initially, the broker, in determining the policy of the firm. If the broker does not wish to act as an intermediary, nothing requires the broker to do so. If the broker's policy is to offer services as an intermediary, both parties must authorize the broker in writing before the broker may act as in intermediary or appoint licensees to work with each of the parties.

17. Q: **When must the intermediary appoint the licensees associated with the intermediary to work with the parties?**

A: This is a judgment call for the intermediary. If appointments are going to be made, they should be made before the buyer begins to receive advice and opinions from an associated licensee in connection with the property listed with the broker. If the broker appoints the associates at the time the listing contract and buyer representation agreements are signed, it should be clear that the appointments are effective only when the intermediary relationship arises. The intermediary relationship does not exist until the parties who have authorized it are beginning to deal with each other in a proposed real estate transaction; for example, the buyer begins to negotiate to purchase the seller's property. Prior to the creation of the intermediary relationship, the broker will typically be acting as an exclusive agent of each party. It is important to remember that both parties must be notified in writing of both appointments. If, for example, the listing agent is "appointed" at the time the listing is taken, care must be taken to ensure that the buyer is ultimately also given written notice of the appointment. When a buyer client begins to show interest in a property listed with the firm and both parties have authorized the intermediary relationship, the seller must be notified in writing as to which associate has been appointed to work with the buyer.

Notes

39

18. Q: Can the intermediary delegate to another person the authority to appoint licensees associated with the intermediary?

A: The intermediary may delegate to another licensee the authority to appoint associated licensees. If the intermediary authorizes another licensee to appoint associated licensees to work with the parties, however, that person must not appoint himself or herself as one of the associated licensees, as this would be an improper combination of the different functions of intermediary and associated licensee. It is also important to remember that there will be a single intermediary even if another licensee has been authorized to make appointments.

19. Q: May a broker act as a dual agent?

A: A broker may not act as a dual agent under Occupations Code Section 1101.561(b), which provides that "a broker must agree to act as an intermediary under this subchapter if the broker agrees to represent in a transaction" a buyer or tenant, and a seller or landlord.

20. Q: What are the agency disclosure requirements for real estate licensees?

A: To disclose their representation of a party upon the first contact with a party or a licensee representing another party.

21. Q: Is disclosure of agency required to be in writing?

A: The disclosure may be oral or in writing.

22. Q: Are licensees required to provide parties with written information relating to agency?

A: Yes. The representation provisions require licensees to provide the parties with a copy of a written statement, the content of which is specified in the statute. The form of the statement may be varied, so long as the text of the statement is in at least 10-point type.

23. Q: Are there exceptions when the statutory statement is not required?

A: Yes. The statement must be provided when the first substantive dialogue occurs between a party and the licensee if the discussion occurs with respect to specific real property. The statement is not required for either of the following:

- a transaction that is a residential lease no longer than one year and no sale is being considered; or
- a meeting with a party represented by another licensee.

Notes

40

24. Q: **Are the disclosure and statutory information requirements applicable to commercial transactions, new home sales, farm and ranch sales or transactions other than residential sales?**

   A: Except as noted previously, the requirements are applicable to all real estate transactions. Licensees dealing with landlords and tenants are permitted by the law to modify their versions of the statutory statement to use the terms "landlord" and "tenant" in place of the terms "seller" and "buyer."

25. Q: **What are the penalties for licensees who fail to comply with the representation provisions?**

   A: Failure to comply is a violation of TRELA, punishable by reprimand, by suspension or revocation of a license, or by an administrative penalty (fine).

26. Q: **Do the representation provisions prohibit or permit disclosed dual agency?**

   A: The representation provisions prohibit disclosed dual agency.

27. Q: **Is the licensee required under any circumstance, to provide the "written statement" to buyer prospects at properties held open for prospective buyers?**

   A: An encounter at an open house is not a meeting for the purposes of the representation provisions. A licensee would not be required to provide the statutory statement at the open house. At the first substantive dialogue thereafter with the buyer regarding a specific property and during which substantive discussions occur, the licensee will be required to provide the statement.

28. Q: **When acting as an appointed licensee, what "agency" limitations does the licensee have when communicating with a buyer/tenant or seller/landlord that an agent representing one party only does not have?**

   A: The appointed licensee may not, except as permitted by Section 1101.651(d) of TRELA, disclose to either party confidential information received from the other party. A licensee representing one party is not be prohibited from revealing confidential information to the licensee's principal. If the information is material to the principal's decision, a licensee is required to reveal the information to the principal.

Notes

41

29. **Q: If a buyer's agent is required to disclose that licensee's agency status to a listing broker when setting up an appointment showing, must the listing broker also disclose to the buyer's agent that the listing broker represents the seller?**

   A: Yes, on the first contact with the licensee representing the buyer.

30. **Q: Does the TREC encourage brokerage companies to act for more than one party in the same transaction?**

   A: No.

31. **Q: Must the intermediary broker furnish written notice to each party to a transaction when the broker designates the appointed licensees?**

   A: Yes.

32. **Q: How is a property "showing" different from a proposed transaction? May an associate show property listed with the associate's broker while representing the buyer without first being appointed by the intermediary, and if so, why?**

   A: Yes. Only showing property does not require the associate to be appointed, because it does not require the licensee to give advice or opinions (only an appointed associate may offer opinions or advice to a party). If no appointments will be made, of course, the associate will be working with the party and will not be authorized to provide opinions or advice.

33. **Q: Does TREC recommend licensees provide a written disclosure of agency?**

   A: It is the licensee's choice as to whether disclosure is in writing or oral, just as it is the licensee's choice as to whether proof of disclosure will be easy or difficult.

34. **Q: Our company policy requires all buyers and sellers to agree to the intermediary practice before beginning to work with them. Does the law permit a broker employment agreement to specify this practice only?**

   A: If by "broker employment agreement" you mean a listing contract or buyer representation agreement, yes.

Notes

42

35. Q: **What are the differences between the duties provided to the seller or landlord by the intermediary broker and the duties provided to the buyer or tenant by the appointed licensee?**

A: The intermediary and the appointed licensees do not provide duties; they perform services under certain duties imposed by the law. The intermediary is authorized to negotiate a transaction between the parties but not to give advice or opinions to them in negotiations. The appointed licensee may provide advice or opinions to the party to which the licensee has been appointed. Both intermediary and appointed licensee are obligated to treat the parties honestly and are prohibited from revealing confidential information or other information addressed in Section 1101.651(d) of TRELA.

36. Q: **Must each party's identity be revealed to the other party before an intermediary transaction can occur?**

A: Yes. If associates are going to be appointed by the intermediary, the law provides that the appointments be made by giving written notice to both parties. To give notice, the intermediary must identify the party and the associate(s) appointed to that party. The law does not require notice if no appointments are going to be made. The law provides that the listing contract and buyer representation agreement are sufficient to establish the written consent of the party if the obligations of the broker under Section 1101.651(d) are set forth in conspicuous bold or underlined print.

37. Q: **As a listing agent, I hold open houses. If a buyer prospect enters who desires to purchase the property at that time, can I represent that buyer and, if so, must my broker designate me as an appointed licensee and provide the parties with written notice before I prepare the purchase offer?**

A: As a representative of the seller, you are be obligated to disclose your representation to the buyer at the first contact. The disclosure may be in writing or oral. As an associate of the listing broker, you can enter into a buyer representation agreement for your broker to act as an intermediary in a transaction involving this buyer and the owner of the property.

If the owner has similarly authorized the broker to act as an intermediary, it will depend on the firm's policy whether appointments are to be made. If appointments are not going to be made, you may proceed in the transaction as an unappointed licensee with a duty of not favoring one party over the other. If appointments are going to be made, the parties must both be notified in writing before you may provide opinions or advice to the buyer in negotiations.

Notes

43

38. Q: I have a salesperson's license through a broker, and I also have a licensed assistant. Can that assistant be an appointed licensee under me as an intermediary?

A: Your broker, not you, will be the intermediary. The intermediary may appoint a licensed associate to work with a party. If the licensed assistant is an associate of the broker, the licensed assistant can be appointed by the intermediary to work with one of the parties. If the licensed assistant is not an associate of the broker, the licensed assistant cannot be appointed. Note: If the licensed assistant is licensed as a salesperson, the licensed assistant must be sponsored by, and acting for, a broker to be authorized to perform any act for which a real estate license is required. If the licensed assistant is sponsored by a broker who is not associated with the intermediary, the licensed assistant would not be considered an associate of the intermediary, either.

39. Q: I am a listing agent and a buyer prospect wants to buy the property I have listed. How can I sell my own listing?

A: See the three alternatives discussed in question five. You can alter the agency relationships and only represent one party, you can be appointed to work with one party and another associate could be appointed to work with the other party, or no appointments may be made, or you can work with the parties being careful not to favor one over the other or provide advice or opinions to them.

40. Q: Must the respective appointed licensees each provide an opinion of value to the respective buyer prospect and seller prospect?

A: At the time a property is listed, the licensee is obligated to advise the owner as to the licensee's opinion of the market value of the property. Once appointments have been made, the appointed associates are permitted, but not required, to provide the party to whom they have been appointed with opinions and advice during negotiations.

41. Q: How can the intermediary broker advise the seller or buyer on value, escrow deposit amount, repair expenses or interest rates?

A: When the listing contract or buyer representation agreement is prepared, and no intermediary status yet exists, the broker may advise the parties generally on such matters. Offers from or to parties not represented by the intermediary's firm may have educated the parties on these matters. Once the intermediary status has been created, however, the intermediary broker may not express opinions or give advice

Notes

44

during negotiations. Information about such matters, which does not constitute an opinion or advice may be supplied in response to questions.

For example, the intermediary can tell the buyer what the prevailing interest rate is without expressing an opinion or giving advice. The seller's question about the amount of earnest money can be answered with the factual answer that in the broker's experience, the amount of the earnest money is usually $1,500 to $2,000, depending on the amount of the sales price. If the buyer asks what amount of money should be in the offer, the intermediary can respond with the factual statement that in the intermediary's experience, those offers closest to the listing price tend to be accepted by the seller. The intermediary also can refer the party to an attorney, accountant, loan officer or other professional for advice.

42. **Q: I was the listing agent for a property that did not sell but was listed by another broker after the expiration of my agreement. I now have a buyer client who wants to see that same property. Must the new broker, or my broker, designate me as an appointed licensee, or how may I otherwise act?**

A: Assuming an agreement with the listing broker as regards cooperation and compensation, you may represent the buyer as an exclusive agent. You cannot be appointed by the intermediary because you are not an associate of the listing broker, and from the facts described, no intermediary status is going to arise. Confidential information obtained from the seller when you were acting as the seller's agent, of course, could not be disclosed to your new client, the buyer.

43. **Q: How is the intermediary broker responsible for the actions of appointed licensees when a difference of opinion of property value estimates is provided?**

A: Brokers are responsible for the actions of their salespersons under TRELA. Opinions of property values may be different and yet not indicative of error or mistake by the salespersons. If a salesperson makes an error or mistake, the sponsoring broker is responsible to the public and to TREC under Section 1101.803 of TRELA.

44. **Q: Although both the buyer and the seller initially consented to the intermediary broker practice at the time each signed a broker employment agreement, must each party consent again to a specific transaction to ensure there are not potential conflicts?**

A: TRELA does not require a second written consent. TRELA does require written notice of any appointments, and the written notice would probably cause any objection

Notes

45

to be resolved at that point. A broker is not be prohibited from obtaining a second consent as a business practice, so that potential conflicts are identified and resolved. The sales contract, of course, typically identifies the parties and shows the intermediary relationship if the broker completes the "Broker Identification and Ratification of Fee" at the end of the TREC contract form.

45. Q: In the absence of the appointed licensees, can the intermediary broker actually negotiate a purchase offer between the parties?

A: Yes. See the answer to question eight relating to the duties of an intermediary.

46. Q: May a licensee include the statutory statement in a listing agreement or buyer representation agreement, either in the text of the agreement or as an exhibit?

A: Yes, but the licensee should provide the prospective party with a separate copy of the statutory statement as soon as is practicable at their first substantive dialogue.

Notes

46

TEXAS REAL ESTATE COMMISSION
Box 12188
Austin, TX 78711-2188
800-250-TREC
www.trec.state.tx.us

Administrator

TIMOTHY K. IRVINE

Commissioners

JOHN S. WALTON, JR., CHAIRMAN
Lubbock
JOHN D. ECKSTRUM, VICE CHAIRMAN
Conroe
TOM C. MESA, JR., SECRETARY
Pasadena
TROY C. ALLEY, JR.
Arlington
ADRIAN A. ARRIAGA
McAllen
MARY FRANCES BURLESON
Dallas
ROBERT C. DAY
Jacksonville
BILL FLORES
Houston
ELIZABETH LEAL
El Paso

REAL ESTATE CENTER
Texas A&M University
2115 TAMU
College Station, TX 77843-2115
979-845-2031
http://recenter.tamu.edu

Director

GARY MALER

Advisory Committee

DAVID E. DALZELL, CHAIRMAN
Abilene
D. MARC McDOUGAL, VICE CHAIRMAN
Lubbock
JAMES M. BOYD
Houston
CATARINA G. CRON
Houston
JOHN D. ECKSTRUM
Conroe
Ex-Officio representing
the Texas Real Estate Commission
TOM H. GANN
Lufkin
JACQUELYN K. HAWKINS
Austin
BARBARA A. RUSSELL
Denton
DOUGLAS A. SCHWARTZ
El Paso
RONALD C. WAKEFIELD
San Antonio

End of Required MCE Ethics Material... What Follows Is: MORE Intriguing Updates and Fun, Hot Information!

More on Intermediary Status

An intermediary is defined under the Texas Real Estate License Act as:

> "a broker who is employed to negotiate a transaction between the parties... and for that purpose may be an agent to the parties to the transaction."

Please note that, in most cases, the sponsoring broker (the intermediary broker) will act as an intermediary.

The Appointment Process

If a real estate broker obtains the consent of the parties to act as an intermediary, the broker may (it is not required) appoint, by providing written notice to the parties, one or more licensees associated with the broker to communicate with and carry out instructions of one party and one or more other licensees associated with the broker to communicate with and carry out instructions of the other party or parties. The parties must consent and authorize the broker to make the appointment, which may be set out in the listing agreement.

There are no guidelines in the statute for one-broker offices. Can they be intermediaries? Yes, the definitions say they are, but they cannot:

- go through the appointment process, or

- give advice or opinions.

During negotiations, only an appointed licensee may provide opinions and advice to the party to whom the licensee is appointed.

Remember that the Texas Real Estate Commission has taken the position that an intermediary broker may *not* appoint himself as an agent for either party. Therefore, a working sponsoring broker, even though it is that broker's listing, must appoint other agents to represent the parties in the transaction.

The statute also provides that the duties of a licensee acting as an intermediary supersede or are in lieu of the licensee's duties under common law or any other law; however, no duties are defined under the statute other than the above-referenced five duties (which are really no different than those required of a dual agent, discussed previously). Presumably, a licensee could be both a dual agent and an intermediary the way the statute is currently written. Depending on the appointment process, an intermediary may become an unappointed intermediary, or undisclosed dual agent!

In effect, one may say that the intermediary status is nothing more than the old dual agency, but allowing the broker to "opt out" of the agency relationship altogether. The duties and responsibilities of an intermediary are very similar, if not the same, as the dual agent under the previous statute. If the sponsoring broker is an intermediary, however, an appointed licensee *can give advice and opinions*, which is more service than could be provided as a dual agent. The intermediary broker is not allowed to give advice and opinions. TAR revised 12 forms for use by its members to conform to the new intermediary status. Summarized, the intermediary "checklist" should work as follows:

- Provide the required written information about brokerage services to any party you are working with (or to a party that is not represented) at your first substantive dialogue meeting. (It would be prudent to have it executed; note form Information About Brokerage Services.);

- When engaging employment either as a buyer's representative or as a listing broker, the listing broker should be sure that, when utilizing the TAR Form No. 1101, that Box 10.B.(1) is checked. When representing the buyer utilizing TAR Form 1501, box 9.A.(1) should be checked. Remember, *there must be a written agreement by both parties to be an intermediary.*

Commercial brokers who are TAR members can use TAR Forms 1301 and 1502.

- Inform everyone else in the transaction (parties and licensees) whom you represent at first contact. (While the statute doesn't require this disclosure to be in writing, it is good business practice.);

- If the real estate firm (and your employment contract) authorizes an intermediary relationship, the agent should:

- remind parties that the firm will act as an intermediary when an in-house sale is apparent (see TAR Form 1409, discussed next);

- the firm should choose whether or not to *make appointments* of *both* associated licensees at the time the in-house sale becomes apparent; and

- if appointments are made, *provide written notice* to the parties (TAR Form 1409 could be used for this).

In the intermediary situation, the complications of presentation that we have under the single-agency concept don't arise, as both parties have agreed and consented to the intermediary status.

The Notification Form

There is always a potential for conflict. The law has always emphasized "informed" consent. TREC has the approved agency information form; and when the intermediary relationship arises, TAR has created a form that can be utilized by its members. These forms reeducate the seller and/or buyer at the time that the intermediary status arises, reminding them of the terms of their respective employment agreements, and that the intermediary relationship has, in fact, arisen. See TAR Form 1409, page 330.

Note with particular concern the third paragraph of the Notification of Intermediary Relationship form. This is a very important paragraph. In the event that both parties have agreed to intermediary status in their representation employment agreements, and the intermediary status actually arises later (the following month), the real estate licensee now reintroduces that intermediary status issue to both parties. In a typical arm's length transaction, it should present no problems.

The concern, however, is if there is a "special" relationship with one of the parties. How does the other party react? For instance, the intermediary status relationship arises and it is later discovered that the buyer is not only the real estate broker's wife, but is also a board-certified real estate lawyer/investor who is coming in to "lowball" the offer. Will the seller feel that the agent can treat him impartially and fairly? If the situation is reversed, the buyer's representative is showing a home to the buyer, and it turns out that the home is the broker's home, does the buyer feel that the broker can be impartial to the buyer? In either circumstance, the principal will have to make the decision. If the principal doesn't feel he can be treated impartially because of the peculiar circumstance, it is suggested that the real estate broker allow the buyer or seller to terminate the employment relationship rather than create an irreconcilable conflict between the broker and the principal.

The rules of the Texas Real Estate Commission require disclosure by the licensee engaging in a real estate transaction on his or her own behalf, but also require disclosure if the licensee is working on behalf of the business entity in which the licensee is more than a 10% owner, or on behalf of a licensee's spouse, parent, or child. See TAC 535.144(b).

One might explain it this way:

The Texas Real Estate License Act has created three "window periods" that a licensee will go through to create intermediary status.

The first window period is the exclusive agency wherein the licensee has an exclusive right to sell and an exclusive buyer's representation agreement. During this phase, there is a 100 percent fiduciary duty and a 100 percent disclosure to the principal that the agent represents.

The second window period is that time when the buyer and the seller, both represented by the same broker, are going into the same transaction. When this potential conflict arises, the licensee is an unappointed intermediary until the intermediary process has been completed. This is *not* discussed in the Information About Brokerage Services form.

The third window period is when the buyer and seller have been notified and have accepted the notification that they now have an agent who represents them. At that point, the appointed agent can give advice and opinions. Presumably, during the second window period (as a dual agent), the agent cannot give advice and opinions. Is it a 100 percent fiduciary to both? Probably not. What percentage would you fill in? Is a whole fee being charged for less than 100 percent fiduciary duty? Hmm.

From a liability standpoint, the trick seems to be to keep with the second window period as narrowly as possible (i.e., as soon as the potential for conflict arises, the agent diligently pursues the intermediary appointments).

The following chart may help visualize this issue.

1st WINDOW PERIOD		2nd WINDOW PERIOD		3rd WINDOW PERIOD
Exclusive Buyer/Tenant and Exclusive Seller/Tenant Representation ——— 100% Fiduciary Duty to Each Can give advice and opinions	uh oh! →	Buyer/Tenant and Seller/Landlord both Represented by Same Broker Want to Do a Deal ——— Unappointed Intermediary No advice or opinions Get consent from parties?	"may" appoint agent to represent both parties → no appointment ↓ what is an unappointed intermediary?	Seller and Buyer Notified of Intermediary Status Can give advice and opinions ? % Fiduciary Duty

It does leave this lingering question: If the broker is defined as an "intermediary" but doesn't go through the appointment process, what is the broker's status? An intermediary without appointment? A dual agent? Is there a difference?

Difficult Questions! Consider the Following:

1. Does a party have to consent to the particular licensee who is appointed to represent them? What if the sponsoring broker (intermediary) appoints a licensee to work with a party and they don't get along? Presumably, they could simply appoint another licensee if there is one in that broker's office. What if the sponsoring broker isn't available when the appointment needs to be made?

2. Can the broker refuse to appoint? The listing agent who has met a new prospect may not want to split the commission. Sound like dual agency? What if a party wants advice?

3. Should the sponsoring broker inform the parties that the intermediary appointments are not made and that the parties shouldn't expect advice? Does it then create a dual agency? Hmm. The statute clearly doesn't require it, but it may be prudent to do so.

4. What is the liability of a sponsoring broker who has appointed one agent to represent the buyer and another to represent the seller (the statute doesn't allow the broker to appoint the same agent for both parties), and the agents give conflicting advice? For instance, the seller's agent advises, "Don't take the offer; it is worth far more than that!" Meanwhile, the buyer's agent advises the buyer, "They are asking for too much, so it isn't worth it." Did the seller obtain the services bargained for under the listing agreement?

5. What is the sponsoring broker's role if the appointed agent asks the sponsoring broker for advice?

6. Can an intermediary appoint a licensed assistant as an agent? It would be illogical to do so. The assistant may be under the control of another licensee.

7. Can the intermediary appoint spouses to different sides? It is probably not a good idea. The income is community property.

8. Can the intermediary appoint a 30-year experienced agent to represent one party, and then appoint a new 30-minute inexperienced agent to represent the other party?

One important thought on this issue: The intermediary must comply with all aspects of the statute in order to take advantage of its benefits. If any of the requirements are not met, it seems that the intermediary status almost certainly converts to unappointed intermediary status. If an appointed agent resigns or dies, it will also create an unappointed intermediary status. One cannot be too careful.

Pertinent Cases Interpreting Provisions of the License Act

There have been a number of cases over the last few years that have discussed determination of brokerage capacity and the TREC-promulgated forms (discussed later) under the Real Estate License Act. Although some of these cases are older, they still make good law and good discussion topics. Some are commercial, some residential ... it all applies!

Commercial

In one of those rare cases upholding an exemption under Section 3 of the License Act, *Collins v. Beste*, 840 S.W.2d 788 (Tex. App. –Ft. Worth, 1992, writ den.), the owner of the property (Collins) hired Beste to provide leasing and marketing services for Collins' properties. Later, Collins fired Beste. Beste sued, Collins defended, alleging that his compensation was actually a suit for brokerage commissions, and that he was entitled to be paid. Collins defended, alleging that Beste did not have a broker's license and therefore was not entitled to get a commission. The court upheld the Section 3 exemption, noting that an employee of an owner of property does not have to be licensed to lease property for the owner, but the exemption does not apply to purchases. Therefore, the employee was able to pursue his cause of action for the commission even though he was not licensed.

Another Texas case that points out a very interesting part of agency law is *Centex Corp. v. Dalton*, 840 S.W.2d 952 (Tex., 1992). In this case, the broker made a transaction involving savings and loans (S&Ls). Centex Corp. wanted to buy a package of failed S&Ls and agreed to pay the broker $750,000 to put the deal together. In the meantime, the governmental regulation was passed that made such payments in transactions illegal. Therefore, the broker was not due his commission. This is one of those rare cases where an agency relationship was terminated because of supervening illegality.

Residential

In *NRC, Inc. v. Huddleston*, 886 S.W.2d 526 (Tex. App. –Austin, 1994), Huddleston was a contractor who built homes for speculative resale. Huddleston signed a contract with the McGinleys for a $130,000 sale with a commission payable to NRC, Inc. Huddleston gave the McGinleys an extension to obtain financing. After the extension had expired, Huddleston negotiated with a second purchaser, Dallmann (no real estate broker was involved in the second sale). The Dallmann contract was for $153,000. When NRC (the broker) learned of the Dallmann contract, the agent threatened Huddleston that if he went through with the Dallmann sale, the agent would see to it that Huddleston would never sell another piece of property in that subdivision.

It was then determined that NRC never deposited the $2,000 escrow check from the first transaction, violating the well-established rule set by the Texas Real Estate Commission concerning an agent not depositing an escrow check. Ultimately, Huddleston lost the sale to the Dallmanns and eventually lost the subject property to foreclosure. The Trial Court entered judgment for Huddleston against NRC for actual damages, $23,042, and exemplary damages of $50,000 for NRC's breach of fiduciary duty. The court noted that "a fiduciary owes to its principal a strict duty of good faith and candor, as well as full disclosure respecting matters affecting the principal's interests, and that there is a general prohibition against the fiduciary's using the relationship to the benefit of his personal interest." The court affirmed the portion of actual and punitive damages for NRC's breach of fiduciary duty.

Commercial

In *Texas Builders et al. v. Keller*, 928 S.W.2d 479 (Tex., 1996), the Texas Supreme Court reverted to the old traditional rule that a real estate licensee cannot recover for a breach of contract if there is no written agreement that satisfies the Texas Real Estate License Act. The court stuck to the traditional theory that "the writing must furnish, either within itself or by reference to some other existing document, the means or data by which the real estate at issue may be identified." The sufficiency of the description is the same that is necessary to satisfy the Statutes of Frauds (to identify the property with reasonable certainty).

In addressing the fraud claim, the court held that even if Texas Builders committed fraud, Keller couldn't circumvent the requirements of the Texas Real Estate License Act by claiming the lost commission as damages for fraud.

This creates an interesting question as a buyer's broker. It is often impossible to determine the identity of the property to be purchased at the time the Buyer's Representation Agreement is signed. How, then, can a buyer's broker maintain an action for commission? There is at least some authority from a lower court that, under these circumstances, this legal description is not necessary. (See *LA & N Interest, Inc. v. Fish*, 864 S.W. 2d 745 (Tex. App. Houston [14th Dist.], 1993, no writ.) The only other alternative would be to insert the legal description at a later date, when the property is identified. That may be a good idea.

In *Trammel Crow Company No. 60, et al. v. William Jefferson Harkinson*, 944 S.W. 2d. 631 (Tex., 1997), a tenant authorized the broker to act as its exclusive representative in locating rental space. The broker found suitable space in Dallas. The owners told the broker that they would pay 4.5 percent cash commission to the broker and sent the broker a commission agreement, which the broker redrafted and sent back to the owners to execute. The owners never signed it.

The tenant ultimately negotiated with the owners, going around their tenant representative agreement, apparently assuming they would get cheaper rent. The owners paid their in-house broker a commission, but refused to pay the tenant's broker a commission, alleging that there was no agreement in writing, and therefore no right to a commission.

The court noted that the exclusive representation agreement did not specify a commission to be payable by the buyer, but only indicated that the commission would be paid by the seller. Therefore, it was not a commission agreement. With no agreement in writing, the broker lost his right to pursue the commission. The broker also alleged tortious interference by the broker who did receive the commission, alleging that he interfered with the rights of the broker who represented the buyer. The court held that he could not sue for tortious interference if it was merely a claim for a commission, and specifically disapproved the prior Texas case of *LA & N Interests v. Fish supra*, to the extent that it permitted a claim for tortious interference.

There was a well-reasoned dissent, relying on contract principals of tortious interference and violations of Section 15(a)(6)(N) of the Real Estate License Act by the broker who did receive the commission. The clear import of the case, however, is that if one is to be a buyer's broker: (1) they need to get a commission agreement in writing and signed by the person who is supposed to pay the commission, or (2) be sure an alternative commission is to be paid by the buyer in the event the seller refuses to pay a commission. Unfortunately, in many circumstances the buyer is not going to support the buyer's broker who pursues his commission if the buyer thinks he is going to get a cheaper deal without the commission. It is a tough lesson to learn.

In *WesTex Abilene Associates, L.P. v. Franco*, 3 S.W.3d 45 (Tex.App. Eastland, 1999), Southard negotiated a lease of a large building between WesTex's predecessor as Landlord and General Dynamics as Tenant. The lease was for an initial 5-year term, with two 5-year renewal options. WesTex acquired the building, along with the General Dynamics lease, and amended the lease a few times to increase the space and the rent. WesTex signed a listing agreement with Southard that stated, among other things, that Southard would be entitled to a commission on any renewals of the General Dynamics' lease. This agreement was later terminated by a written agreement in which Southard's right to a commission on the renewal of the General Dynamics' lease was preserved.

General Dynamics expressed an interest in renewing the lease for the full 5 years, but the company was subsequently bought by Lockheed, which had a policy of not renewing for more than a year at a time. The lease was not renewed for the full 5-year term, but only for a year, initially, then on a month-to-month basis. WesTex refused to pay Southard's leasing commission.

Southard sued WesTex for the commissions and sued Loeb for its tortious interference with the General Dynamics' renewal option. The trial court found for Southard on both claims and awarded damages against both WesTex and Loeb.

A tortious interference with contract claim can be brought only against a third party who interferes with a contract. Here, Loeb was not really a third party. It owned the general partner of WesTex and was the managing agent for WesTex. Thus, it could not tortiously interfere with the contract with General Dynamics.

WesTex, however, was liable for the leasing commission on Lockheed's renewal of the General Dynamics' lease. WesTex took the disingenuous position that the commission was due only if General Dynamics renewed the lease and that the lease was actually renewed, not by General Dynamics, but by Lockheed. The court noted that Lockheed was clearly the successor in interest to General Dynamics under the lease, and that its status as tenant under the lease was confirmed by WesTex in an estoppel agreement it gave Lockheed.

Residential

In *Frady v. May*, 23 S.W.3d 558 (Tex. App.–Ft. Worth, 2000), on August 31, 1996, the Fradys listed their farm with May, agreeing to pay May a 6 percent commission in the event he was able to procure a ready, willing, and able buyer during the listing term. The listing expired on March 1, 1997. After the listing expired, May and Frady discussed renewing and extending the listing agreement, but a new listing agreement was never signed. In May 1997, another realtor contacted May, ultimately resulting in an Earnest Money Contract that was to close on August 1, 1997. The Earnest Money Contract contained a commission agreement providing for the payment to be made of 6 percent "on the closing of the sale." The transaction did not close. On September 15, 1997, the same buyer signed a second Earnest Money Contract with the Fradys, which did not provide for the payment of the commission to May. May filed suit to recover his commission. The Fradys defended, saying that the contract that provided for the commission was terminated by its own terms and that the commission was not payable until "on the closing of the sale," which sale was never completed.

The court held that the agreement was not contingent on closing the sale under the Earnest Money Contract, noting that the broker effects a sale and is entitled to a commission if the seller may enforce specific performance of the contract. The court additionally held that the provision "on the closing of the sale" simply fixed payments of May's commission upon the transfer of equitable title of the property, and not on the closing of the first Earnest Money Contract. The court noted that if an enforceable contract results between a buyer and a seller, the seller necessarily accepts the buyer's readiness, willingness, and ability to perform in the absence of a special agreement to the contract.

Commercial

In *American Garment Properties, Inc. v. CB Richard Ellis-El Paso, L.L.C.*, 155 S.W.3d 431 (Tex. App.–El Paso, 2004) (discussed in Chapter 1), a real estate brokerage firm brought action against a seller of a building for alleged failure to pay the full amount of the real estate commission. The obligation to pay the commission was contained in both the agency agreement and the purchase agreement. The agency agreement specified that the owner would pay the real estate broker 6 percent commission on the purchase price if the procuring agent represented the purchaser. The agency agreement contained a merger clause, providing that their agreement could only be modified by a writing signed by the parties. The owner refused to pay the full commission at the closing, alleging that the broker had verbally agreed to lower the commission in order to make the sale.

The broker filed a summary judgment motion that was granted on the basis of the statute of frauds: an agreement that is in writing cannot be orally modified. There is an exception, and that is when the modification does not materially affect the obligations of the underlying agreement. The court held that an oral modification asserted in this case (changing the commission amount) was "material," and violated the statute of frauds.

Residential

In *Ebby Halliday Real Estate, Inc. v. Murnan*, 916 S.W.2d 585 (Tex. App.–Ft. Worth, 1996), the trial court held the sponsoring broker liable for damages, but not the sales agent! (Hmm.) The jury found that the real estate licensee handling the transaction did not cause any damage to the plaintiffs, nor did the agent engage in any false, misleading, deceptive, or unconscionable act that produced damage to the plaintiffs. This court held that because the licensee was the only Ebby Halliday agent who had contact with the plaintiff, the sponsoring broker, Ebby Halliday, could not be held liable for any misconduct or damages. The court reasoned that if the agent did not engage in any misconduct, you couldn't impute misconduct to a sponsoring broker who had no other contact with the plaintiff.

Commercial

In *Perl v. Patrizi*, 20 S.W. 3d 76 (Tex. App.–Texarkana, 2000), Joe Perl was a real estate agent who handled an agreement giving himself 6 percent commission on the income or lease payments of Patrizi's restaurant sold or leased to Post Oak Grill, L.L.C., which operated a restaurant in Houston. The agreement was signed by Tommy Patrizi on behalf of the corporation. The corporation became insolvent, and the property was later leased to a newly created entity Post Oak Grill, L.L.C.-Beaumont. Perl thought he was entitled to a commission and sued the current owners of the property, lienholders who had foreclosed, but were members of the family.

The court focused on whether or not the listing document was an enforceable contract. The court noted that Section 15(a)(6)(G) provided that the commission may suspend or revoke a real estate agent's license when it has been determined that the licensee has been guilty of failing to specify a definite termination date of their employment contract. The court further noted a Real Estate Commission Rule (Section 535.148) that also requires that the licensee's employment contract have a definite termination date. The court noted that the listing agreement clearly did not meet the requirements of the rule or the statute. The court held that by applying the legislature's stated definition of the terms of the agreement, the failure to provide a termination date is a failure to meet a condition precedent in the contract and therefore "by statutory fiat" is unenforceable.

There is a very good dissent in the case. Notice that Section 15 of the Texas Real Estate License Act "subjects the real estate broker or salesperson to sanctions involving his or her real estate licensee," but contains no language to void a listing contract. Similarly, nothing cited in the rules cited by the majority of the court suggests that it would void a contract, and it was never intended to negate all real estate contract listings if the ending date is not contained in the contract.

BUT WAIT!...

In *Northborough v. Cushman & Wakefield of Texas, Inc.*, 162 S.W.3d 816 (Tex App. –Houston [14th Dist.] 2005), a real estate brokerage firm brought a cause of action against an owner of an office building contending it was due brokerage commissions under an agreement reached with the building's previous owner. The facts in this case are somewhat complicated. The original owner was Alliance. It ultimately sold the property to Northborough. Alliance entered into an agreement to pay commissions with Cushman & Wakefield. Those agreements were specifically assumed by Northborough as a part of the sale transaction between Alliance and Northborough.

The primary commission that was agreed to be paid involved a tenant (Texaco) or any of its affiliates, or subsidiaries. The schedule of commissions provided that, if the lease was renewed or extended, or if a tenant leased additional space, the building owner would pay an additional commission to Cushman. Texaco assigned its office lease to Star Enterprises, which was a joint venture of Texaco, who ultimately assigned its interest to Equiva, also a joint venture of Texaco, and it was the renewal of Equiva's lease that became the basis for charging the commission.

The owner alleged two primary defenses. The first is that the Cushman commission agreement was void because it lacks a definite termination date in violation of the Texas Real Estate License Act. The second was that the final lease to Equiva was a "new arrangement" that superseded the Star lease and extinguished Northborough's obligations to pay the commissions (it was not extended and renewed).

The court quickly rejected the building owner's argument that express terminations is statutory required as a prelude to recovery of the commission. Specifically citing *Perl v. Patrizi*, the court "declined to follow" *Perl* because: (1) the section relied on under the *Perl* court has nothing to do with the enforceability of a broker's commission agreement, it relates solely to the suspension or revocation of a broker's real estate license; and (2) nothing in the section of the Real Estate License Act (1101.652) references the broker's ability to maintain a cause of action. The court acknowledged that it disagreed with the *Perl* decision and held exactly the opposite way of the *Perl* court.

In dealing with the extension and renewal provisions of the commission agreement, the court noted that even though the space involved different parties and an agent did not participate in the negotiations, there was no evidence to suggest that the lease was ever cancelled and that, in fact, Equiva assumed Star's position in the Star lease through an Assignment and Amendment of Lease. The court affirmed a lower court's summary judgment in favor of Cushman & Wakefield.

In *Swor v. Tapp Furniture Company*, 146 S.W.3d 778 (Tex. App. –Texarkana, 2004), a broker sued a seller to recover a fee for finding a buyer to purchase a funeral home business. The sale included all the assets of the business including the real estate. He alleged that there was an oral agreement for a "finder's fee" between the broker and seller. The court construed the definition of finder's fee as applying to real estate brokerage and therefore is addressed under the Texas Real Estate License Act. In reviewing the provisions of the Texas Real Estate License Act, the court noted that it was undisputed that there was no written agreement (as required by TRELA) and the plaintiff was not a licensed real estate broker (as required by TRELA). It's the same old story, whatever you call it, it's a commission. If it deals in real estate, it must comply with the Texas Real Estate License Act.

BBQ Blues Texas, Ltd. v. Affiliated Business Brokers, Inc., 183 S.W. 3d 543 (Tex. App. – Dallas, 2006, pet. denied). In this case, the business owners brought an action for declaratory judgment as to the enforceability of an oral agreement to pay business brokers a commission. The brokers filed a counterclaim alleging breach of contract, quantum meruit, promissory establin, and attorney fees. This is a classic conflict of selling of business and whether or not there is enough real estate in the transaction to bring the transaction into the Texas Occupations Code, which requires a written employment agreement in order to sue for a commission. Here the Court held that there was an oral commission agreement that did not contemplate the transfer of real estate even though the buyers of the business assumed an existing lease. The core reason was that the business could have been sold without the transfer of the lease, and therefore the real estate transaction was not a significant part of the transaction.

The Court seemed to give a lot of emphasis to the fact that the jury found that the sale of the business did not contemplate a transfer of the lease. Therefore, the Court held that the oral commission agreement for the sale of the business is enforceable because the jury found that the commission agreement did not involve the transfer of the real estate lease in Round Rock, Texas.

Additional Perspectives in the Law of Agency in Texas

Although this topic is old in many ways, new changes are always on the horizon. This discussion will include the basics (for review), then expand to the new ideas.

Texas has developed extensive laws and regulations for real estate brokers and salespersons. The theory generally espoused by these regulations is that a real estate licensee is ultimately responsible to the public and occupies a status in the law with recognized privileges and responsibilities. Texas requires its real estate license applicants to be competent, honest, trustworthy, and of good character. Those dealing with a licensed broker should naturally be able to assume that he or she possesses the requisites of an honest, ethical person.

The controlling Texas statute is the Texas Real Estate License Act. It applies to all persons who engage in the real estate business, and its stated legislative intent is to avoid fraud on the public by requiring a license of someone who deals in real estate. The real estate licensees are also held to be responsible to the Real Estate Commission, as well as to members of the public, and real estate agents are generally presumed to be experts who have been tested and found to be such. In most circumstances, a real estate broker represents the owner of the real estate and is hired by that owner and given the limited authority to market the owner's real estate. To market the property, the licensee's relationship with the owner is one of a special agent, not as a general agent, and the licensee does not have the authority to bind his principal, nor create liability for his principal, unless the agent's acts are specifically authorized by the principal, or are later ratified by the principal. In the simplest of situations, the duty of care of the licensee to his principal is simply to obtain the highest price then obtainable in his efforts to sell the property.

The creation of the agency relationship, however, is not that simple. It creates a duty between a licensee and seller called a fiduciary duty. The fiduciary duty, as defined in Texas, consists of four basic duties of care: performance, reasonable care, accounting, and loyalty. Of these duties of care, loyalty deserves the most emphasis, consisting primarily of two basic obligations: (1) putting the interest of the principal above that of his own, and (2) full disclosure to his principal of everything the agent knows. The agent must disclose all material facts known to the agent. It should also be a full, fair, and timely disclosure that might affect the principal's rights or influence his decision making. A "material fact" is one that a reasonable person might expect to attach importance to when making a choice of action.

Creation of the Agency Relationship

The agency relationship is created by the principal and agent in one of three ways: (1) actual authority, (2) ostensible authority, and (3) ratification.

Actual Authority

Agency by actual authority is an agreement between the principal and agent (usually a listing agreement or representation letter) and is generally governed by the law of contracts. There must be some exercise of control by the principal over the agent for the agency relationship to exist. You may recall that Texas has an absolute requirement that this contract be in writing in order for the real estate agent to sue for his commission.

Ostensible Authority

Agency by ostensible authority is an agency created because a third party thinks the agency relationship exists. This occurs when the conduct on the part of the principal leads a reasonably prudent purchaser to believe that the agent had the authority that he purports to exercise. In these situations, the agency relationship is created and all the fiduciary rights and liabilities of the agency relationship arise. The whole theory of ostensible authority creates the awkward situation where a principal and agency relationship is created, all fiduciary rights and liabilities exist, but the real estate agent does not have the right to sue for his commission if the contract is breached.

Texas courts have also further refined the theory of ostensible authority and due agency by "apparent authority" or agency by "estoppel." Agency by estoppel requires two elements:

1. The principal must have held the agent out in other instances, or in the particular transaction, as possessing authority sufficient to embrace the particular act in question, or he must have knowingly acquiesced in the agent's assertion of requisite authority.

2. The person dealing with the agent must have relied on the conduct of the principal to his prejudice.

Agency by apparent authority is based on estoppel and arises from:

- the principal knowingly permitting an agent to hold himself out as having the requisite authority; or

- the principal may, by lack of ordinary care, clothe the agent with indicia of authority as to lead a reasonably prudent person to believe that he actually has such authority.

The agency relationship can be created for either principal. Although Texas has no specific case in point, this theory has been applied in other states to create an agency for the purchaser. Texas courts have used ostensible authority to create an agency for the seller; see

Wilson v. Donze, 692 S.W.2d 734 (Tex. App.–Ft. Worth, 1985). The same theory can be used to create an agency for the buyer.

Ratification

The creation of the agency by ratification occurs when a principal, although he originally had no knowledge of the unauthorized acts of his agent, retains the benefits of the transaction after he acquires full knowledge of it. The agency relationship is confirmed when the principal discovers the completion of the transaction but fails to repudiate the consummation of that transaction after learning of the agent's agreement.

The problem, generally stated, is that an agent can become an agent, or a principal may create an agency relationship, without either of them knowing it, or without any formal written document. When this occurs, all fiduciary duties, rights, and liabilities create unanticipated causes of action and significant liability problems. One of the more disturbing elements of the creation of the agency relationship is *when* the relationship is created. There is some authority that the relationship is created as soon as the confidence and trust is present in the transaction between the principal and the agent. These confidences can be exchanged in the earliest stages of negotiating the listing agreement. Courts have even held that a real estate broker had liability to his principal because he had failed to disclose pertinent portions of his listing agreement. One Texas case has even held that the agency relationship arose even when the principal rejected the agency initially. *Wilson v. Donze, supra*, at 737.

Purchaser Representation: The Shift of Fiduciary Duty

It has long been recognized under Texas law that a real estate agent can represent the purchaser.

Buyer's brokerage is a common topic in real estate seminars and is often touted as a solution to the dual agency/intermediary conflict of interest. It gives the buyer representation, which some people feel the buyer is entitled to, or needs, in many circumstances. Buyer brokerage may even ease the duty of a listing broker. Recall *Kubinsky v. Van Zandt Realtors, supra*, when the court seemed to indicate that a listing broker was relieved of liability when the buyer hired his own inspector *and* broker. In cases of office building leasing and more sophisticated commercial property acquisitions, parties frequently seek the assistance of a real estate broker to represent them in making prudent purchases when they lack the expertise to do their own investigations.

A difficulty arises, however, when the seller of the property may not recognize, or is misled by, the fiduciary duty of the broker that represents the purchaser. The seller must be careful not to misplace trust or confidential information because the broker is then required to disclose all of this information to the purchaser instead of the seller. One state Supreme Court (Colorado) has held that buyer representation should never be the presumption and that real estate brokers should always represent the sellers unless there is a written contract to the contrary. It would be presumed that while being a buyer's broker, there must be immediate disclosure to the seller. This shifts the entire agency theory in the opposite direction of our traditional seller representation. See *Tatum v. Preston Carter Company, supra*, and *Stortroen v. Beneficial Finance Company of Colorado*, 736 P.2d 391 (Colo., 1987). To complicate matters further, there is little case law on buyer's brokerage and little comfort in projecting potential outcomes of these more unusual fact situations. In an effort to facilitate buyer representation, the Texas Association of REALTORS® has published a Buyer Representation Agreement. Great care should be taken when using it and a Realtor proposing to represent purchasers should read it very carefully to determine the shift in rights that is anticipated because of its use.

Buyer brokerage has gained wide acceptance. There is a growing niche in the agency marketplace as consumers move into a new area, a relocation company wants to utilize the services of a buyer's broker, or a first-time buyer wants advice. They perceive it as both beneficial and a cost-saving measure when a broker represents the best interest of the buyer. When representing a seller, a real estate agent and his resulting fiduciary duty focuses on the marketing of the product for the benefit of the owner. This involves "getting the highest price in the marketplace," maintaining the confidentiality of information, and trying to effect a sale within the shortest period of time for the benefit of the seller. This is the same focus of the traditional MLS subagency concept for cooperating brokers. There is a concern that most real estate agents have never been trained to be a buyer's broker. Historically, the MLS system and most state laws on agency encouraged agents to be trained as seller's brokers or cooperating brokers.

The buyer's broker, however, has a different focus. The emphasis in buyer's brokerage is to help the buyer (1) make informed decisions, (2) obtain the desired product, (3) get a fair price, and (4) have the buyer's circumstances considered utmost. This emphasis would apparently include getting the lowest price in the marketplace, or a "good deal" for the buyer, to facilitate resale or investment potential (a main reason why relocation companies are concerned about buyer's brokerage) and finding a "safe" purchase of a product without latent defects. There is also a shift of focus against effecting the sale of the property, as the buyer's broker is more concerned with a satisfactory purchase for the buyer's benefit rather than just making a sale. This may create a conflict between the seller's and buyer's brokers, as the end result may end up being the same, but the means of achieving the sale may be somewhat different. The buyer's broker may be expected to be more protective of the buyer (the primary focus) rather than effecting the sale (the main focus of the listing broker).

Procedures

Need for Advice

It is argued that consumers, particularly as purchasers, want and need advice in making important decisions. Buyer's brokerage may be the easiest answer to this consumer request, as it does not create unexpected (and misunderstood) complications that may arise through dual agency or intermediary status. The procedures for a buyer's broker for identifying property may significantly differ from those of a seller's broker. The buyer's broker might pursue property not on the market and should have a significant knowledge of the "for sale by owner" (FSBO) market, Web sites, and other sources for potential sales that are not in the traditional MLS listing. In representing the buyer, the agent will also perform other services, such as:

- providing an extensive comparative market analysis for the market that the buyer is attempting to locate in, pointing out factors in market trends and historical appreciation (or depreciation) factors in the neighborhood;

- making a special effort to be sure that offers are presented to owners;

- having studies available concerning inspections, financing, environmental hazards in special hazard areas, such as flood-prone areas, earthquake zones, fault lines, etc.; and

- making special provisions for a walk-through prior to closing.

Initial Interview

It has been suggested that in representing buyers, one should take as much care in interviewing and counseling the buyer as a listing agent typically does in preparing for the initial listing appointments. This may include a "buyer's kit," which would contain community information, standard documentation for real estate transactions, financing information, and inspection information. The better part of the counseling session probably would be devoted to determining the buyer's wants and needs for the product. In developing a priority list for determining the buyer's needs, the buyer's financial qualifications should also be examined in depth to determine the amount of down payment, closing costs, and debt service that the buyer can handle. Many buyer's brokers use a buyer information checklist for the buyer to sign, acknowledging that the buyer has received all of this information.

Earning the Commitment

It is also important that the buyer's broker develop a relationship with the client to be sure that the broker is protected as the client looks for property. Brokers have often discovered that when operating as a cooperating broker (under the subagency rules), it may be very difficult to keep the buyer's commitment and loyalty, particularly when it comes to compensation. A prudent agent should ultimately complete the initial consultation by having the buyer(s) execute a Buyer's Representation Agreement. A more professional attitude and approach by the buyer's broker may result in better commitment and rapport so that the broker's efforts don't go uncompensated.

Very simple questions may avoid this problem, such as: "How long have you been looking?", "Have you seen anything you liked?", "Have you talked with or seen homes with any other agents?", "What price range have you been looking in?", and maybe the all-time most important one, "Is one of your relatives or friends a real estate agent?"

As a buyer's broker, different skill levels are also required:

- **Presenting Yourself** as a buyer's broker, determining the buyer's special needs and preferences, developing rapport, commitment, and requiring an exclusive agency agreement;

- **Showing Property** utilizing agency disclosures, pointing out negatives about the property, and gathering facts about the subject property and neighborhood, and matching the buyer to types of available properties;

- **Writing and Negotiating the Offer**, using the proper forms, determining the existence of restrictions and the ability of the buyer to qualify for the loan, and informing the buyer of the types of loans available;

- **Exercising Due Diligence** on issues such as the general neighborhood reputation, application of deed restrictions, zoning requirements, surveys, market data, available warranty programs, and homeowners' association disclosures;

- **Resolving Closing** issues, such as reviewing settlement statements, buyer's walk-through, moving reminder checklists, switching utilities, homeowner's insurance, and timely funding; and

- **Following Up,** such as offering food and cold drinks during the move-in, making phone calls after the closing to determine the client's comfort with their new home, and possibly paying for rekeying the premises (a real "feel good" opportunity) to help the buyers feel more secure with their new home.

Buyer Brokerage Issues

The growing number of buyer-broker agents has created interesting buyer agency issues:

- If the real estate broker takes listings, should he allow his sales agents to become buyer's brokers and create a dual agency, or elect intermediary status? If so, does that particular agent have to be excluded from sales meetings when confidential information about the listings is being discussed? If the buyer's broker agent overhears that a seller is "desperate" in office conversation, does this encourage him to work against the brokerage company in forcing a lower sales price, because he now knows confidential information?

- We know that the buyer agent needs to utilize the new Agency Disclosure procedures, which are discussed later. If the listing broker, relying on traditional MLS subagency theories, discloses information to a buyer's broker before his status is disclosed, does it create a breach of fiduciary duty? The 1995 revisions to the Texas Real Estate License Act tell us that a buyer's broker should disclose (at least verbally) his status upon introduction to the listing agent or seller. The earliest disclosure keeps the buyer's broker in compliance with the Real Estate Commission regulations and eliminates the potential for disclosure of confidential information early in the transaction.

- Should the listing broker ask if a buyer is represented by a buyer's broker? A recent case in Houston finds the listing broker and the seller sued by a buyer's broker because the buyer went directly to the listing broker without disclosing to the listing broker that he was represented by a buyer's broker. The transaction was closed without the benefit or involvement of the buyer's broker. Logic tells us that the buyer's broker should be suing the buyer, not the listing broker or the seller. Unfortunately, lawsuits don't work that way. Plaintiffs sue everyone in sight! Therefore, a prudent listing broker may want to inquire as to whether or not the buyer is represented by a buyer's broker and document his file before becoming involved in a transaction with the buyer.

- Another problem exists as to duty of care of the real estate brokers when they are representing the buyer, because the buyer is relying on the agent for good advice and buying in a particular area. Does the buyer's broker have the duty of care to assist in inspections, look for potential hazards, and negotiate the best deal possible for his buyer? The broker, under this theory, is not representing a person in the traditional sale. The broker is finding a product for the buyer. This duty of care has really been poorly defined by the courts, although the *Tatum* case does create some duty. A well-reasoned case out of Maryland held that a buyer's agent had the fiduciary duty to discover and disclose the existence of restrictions and declarations of record against the property prohibiting the buyer's anticipated business use. *Lewis v. Long & Foster Real Estate, Inc.*, 584 A.2d 1325 (M.D. Ct. Spec. App., 1991). In the commercial environment, there have been two huge recoveries against commercial real estate brokers who had listings on office buildings. When a large tenant began seeking space in the area, the broker also represented the tenant. Predictably, the landlord sued the broker for not "steering" the tenant into the space on which the broker had a listing. In both cases, the recoveries were substantial against the listing broker for breach of fiduciary duty. A California case has held that a buyer's broker has the fiduciary duty to confirm that the property meets with the client's standards or should disclose that no such investigation has been made. *Salhutdin v. Valley of California, Inc.*, 29 Cal. Rptr. 2d 463 (Cal. App., 1994). An Iowa case required the broker to attempt to change the restrictions! *Bazol v. Rhines*, 600 N.W. 2b 327 (Iowa App., 1999).

If the buyer requests a "peaceful" house, the buyer's broker better deliver it! In *Wyrick v. Tillman & Tillman Realty, Inc.* (No. 03-00- 00061-CV, Tex. App.–Austin, 2001), a buyer brought a cause of action against Tillman Realty who acted as the buyer's agent for the purchase of property in New Braunfels. The purchaser anticipated moving to New Braunfels and requested that Tillman represent her. He agreed to represent her solely as a buyer's agent. The buyer explained that she was moving away from San Antonio to escape the city life, noise, and traffic. Tillman showed her a home and said it was in a quiet and safe neighborhood. Due to an illness, she only visited New Braunfels twice before the closing date and did not move in for several months. Near the end of her first month of occupancy (September 1996), the buyer discovered that the railroad right-of-way was near the house and a meat processing plant was a block away.

In 1988, the railroad temporarily discontinued the use of the railway for train traffic, but the railroad retained the right to reopen the right-of-way to rail traffic and did so in November 1998. The broker admitted that he knew the ongoing issues of the right-of-way and knew that it had not been resolved when he found the house for the buyer. It was further noted that the meat processing plant discharged fumes and odors and created a high volume of traffic from the trucks going to and from the plant. The broker alleged that: (1) he had no duty to disclose facts not known to the real estate agent, (2) there is no duty to disclose facts regarding other properties, and (3) the buyer is deemed to have relied on her own investigation. The trial court granted a summary judgment for the broker.

The buyer appealed, alleging that the broker had a duty to disclose these two facts because they materially affected her property. The broker told the buyer that the neighborhood in which the house was located was then, and historically had been, a quiet and safe neighborhood. The broker defended by saying the statements were true at the time they were made (1996) but that there was no guarantee they would be true in the future. **The court relied on the Canons of Professional Ethics and Conduct of the Texas Real Estate Commission in defining a fiduciary relationship and confirmed that a broker's contract of employment calls for the utmost good faith on the part of the broker, that he is bound to disclose to his principal all material facts within his knowledge affecting the transaction.** The court held that a buyer's agent has a duty to perform his work in a competent, skillful, and professional manner and to disclose all material facts that have a bearing on the decision to purchase and that, viewed in the context of the contract between the broker and his client, would have an effect on the client's satisfaction of the property. The court confirmed the fact that the broker already knew of the existence of the railroad right-of-way and meat processing plant.

As for the buyer's duty to inspect the property, the court held that the evidence tended to show that the railroad tracks were difficult to discover and that her visits to the house were in the evening when it was often dark. Therefore, she may not have been aware of the railroad right-of-way or the meat processing plant. The summary judgment was reversed, and the case was remanded for further proceedings. We may hear more about this case in the future.

It's a seller's market. The buyer's agent says, "It's not worth it, let's hold our offer at a lower price." Another buyer steps in and offers $5,000 more. The seller accepts it. Does the first buyer have a cause of action against the broker because he lost the deal? Is it merely opinion and exempt from the DTPA?

Procuring Cause

Buyer's brokers create a much more complicated issue involving procuring cause, which has caused considerable unrest in the real estate brokerage community. Some prospects may visit a property one or more times and spend a great deal of the listing broker's time asking questions and getting information. Before submitting an offer, however, the prospect goes to a buyer's broker and requests his assistance and advice in preparing a contract before presentation to the owner's agent. Who was the procuring cause? Although the listing agent may feel that they were the procuring cause, the buyer is likely to support the buyer's broker's position because the buyer chose to retain the services of that buyer's broker in presenting the offer. In the age of e-mail, the Internet, and highly informed consumers, there is an argument that buyers want and need representation. Once a consumer has sought and obtained a buyer's broker's advice, conceptually, the buyer's broker may become the procuring cause when the contract is signed and presented to the listing broker.

Is Non-Agency the Answer?

Colorado was one of the first states to establish "non-agency" where a state's Real Estate License Act does not presume agency in real estate transactions.

In *Hoff & Leigh, Inc. v. Byler*, 62 P.3d 1077 (Col. App. 2002), an owner agreed to pay a real estate brokerage firm a commission if the broker "procured a purchaser for [defendant's] property... which results in the sale of the property." The parties agree that the broker would be a "transaction broker." When the broker procured a buyer for the property, the owner refused to pay the commission, alleging that insufficiencies in the broker's performance warranted forfeiture of the commission. The trial court found in favor of the broker and awarded the commission.

The appeal centered on the statutory duties imposed on transaction brokers under Colorado law, but it has wide implications on whether similar legislation has been enacted by other states. The court noted that the Colorado statute was a significant departure from the traditional common law view of agency relationships in real estate transactions and that the Colorado Act recognized a non-agent real estate professional (the transaction broker). The court noted that the transaction broker is not an agent for either party (which is presumed under Colorado law) "absent a written agency agreement or a subagency relationship." The court noted that while a real estate broker acting as agent owes a fiduciary duty to his or her principal, a transaction broker is not in a fiduciary relationship with either party to a real estate transaction. Under Colorado law, the duties of a transaction broker include (1) presenting offers and counteroffers in a timely manner, (2) advising the parties and keeping them informed, (3) accounting for money and property received, (4) assisting the parties in complying with contractual terms and conditions, and (5) disclosing certain information. In what may be a key issue, the court noted that the Colorado Real Estate License Act does not prescribe a remedy for nonperformance of these obligations. Therefore, even it was violated and the duties were not performed. Forfeiture of the commission was not a remedy for nonperformance based on the fact that the agent was not a fiduciary. The court further noted, however, that the defendant would have a remedy for any out-of-pocket expenses accrued as a result of the broker's inaction, but found that the seller never asserted such a claim.

This case may support the theory that a transaction broker can be legally upheld, but it creates confusion over what happens if the broker breaches his or her "duty" as outlined in the License Act. If a real estate license act does not regulate the industry for violations of statutory duties, what is it regulating?

In *Stearns vs. McGuire*, 2005 WL 3036538 (10th Cir. 2005), there was a similar result:

In October 2001, Purchasers asked Broker to locate an investment property in Boulder, Colorado, for Purchasers to buy. Purchasers and Broker were long-time friends. In December 2001, Broker approached the owner of an apartment complex and stated that he may have some interested buyers for the apartment complex. Soon thereafter, Broker faxed to Seller a Contract to Buy and Sell Real Estate signed by Purchasers ("Contract One"). At the end of Contract One, and after Purchasers' signature, Broker checked boxes to indicate that he was the Seller's agent and a dual-agent with regard to this transaction. Seller submitted a counterproposal to Contract One and Broker thereafter faxed a revised Contract to Buy and Sell Real Estate signed by Purchasers ("Contract Two"). Contract Two gave Broker a 4 percent commission and indicated, at the bottom after the signature block, that Broker was Seller's agent for purposes of this transaction. Seller executed Contract Two.

Seller later refused to close on the sale of the apartment complex, citing Broker's failure to disclose pertinent information about the (1) Boulder market or the property and (2) Broker's failure to disclose his relationship with Purchasers. Seller was out of town and had not been to Boulder for a number of years. The relationship with Purchasers was a deep friendship dating from childhood, in addition to prior representation of Purchasers in six deals. Ultimately Purchasers brought a specific performance action and Seller settled by closing.

Broker sued Seller for his commission. Seller answered and asserted a variety of affirmative defenses, including breach of fiduciary duty, and also counterclaims for breach of fiduciary duty, negligence, negligent misrepresentation, and fraud.

The United States District Court for the District of Colorado dismissed Seller's breach of fiduciary duty claim and estoppel affirmative defenses on summary judgment. Seller appealed.

The Tenth Circuit affirmed the district court's decision and held that Broker acted as a transaction broker and not Seller's agent because there was no written agreement between Broker and Seller, despite the language at the bottom of Contract Two stating Broker was Seller's agent. The Tenth Circuit held that Contract Two did not contain a true manifestation of Seller's consent for Broker to serve as his agent, because the Seller's signature appeared *before* the declaration of agency relationship.

Apparently, under Colorado law agents don't have any duties, can do "nuthin," and can even get paid for it. **Does the industry want this lack of professionalism? Why would we need licensure?**

These cases may support the theory that a transaction broker can be legally upheld, but it creates confusion over what happens if the broker breaches his or her "duty" as outlined in the License Act. If a real estate license act does not regulate the industry for violations of statutory duties, what is it regulating?

Additional Legal Update and Hot Topics

Pre-Assessment Evaluation

Please answer the following questions.

1. The promulgated contracts now have seven "Title Notices" in paragraph 6E.

    True   False

2. When a TREC-promulgated form is not available for a specific situation, a TAR (Texas Association of REALTORS®) form must be used.

    True   False

3. A party to a DTPA suit may compel mediation if the motion is filed within 90 days.

    True   False

4. Texas has a new state pledge.

    True   False

5. An incorrect Seller's Disclosure Statement of Property Condition might constitute a Deceptive Trade Practice Act violation.

    True   False

Most Important Update!

Please note the new Texas pledge:

"Honor the Texas flag; I pledge allegiance to thee, Texas, one state under God, one and indivisible."

(effective June 15, 2007).

Texas Contracts

The following Real Estate Commission forms are currently promulgated for use by all real estate licensees, and their use is required in all transactions to which the form is applicable.

1. TREC 9-7 Unimproved Property Contract
2. TREC 20-8 One-to-Four Family Residential Contract (Resale)
3. TREC 23-8 New Home Contract (Incomplete Construction)
4. TREC 24-8 New Home Contract (Completed Construction)
5. TREC 25-6 Farm and Ranch Contract
6. TREC 30-7 Residential Condominium Contract (Resale)

Addendums for the above-referenced forms are also promulgated and required for use by licensees in all transactions in which the form is applicable:

1. TREC 10-5 Addendum for Sale of Other Property by Buyer
2. TREC 11-6 Addendum for "Back-Up" Contract
3. TREC 12-2 Seller's Release of Liability and VA Restoration of Entitlement
4. TREC 15-4 Seller's Temporary Residential Lease
5. TREC 16-4 Buyer's Temporary Residential Lease
6. TREC 26-5 Seller Financing Addendum
7. TREC 28-1 Environmental Assessment, Threatened or Endangered Species, and Wetlands Addendum
8. TREC 32-2 Condominium Resale Certificate
9. TREC 33-1 Notice for Coastal Area Property
10. TREC 34-3 Addendum for Property Located Seaward of the Gulf Intercoastal Waterway
11. TREC 36-5 Addendum for Property Subject to Mandatory Membership in an Owners' Association
12. TREC 37-3 Resale Certificate for Property Subject to Mandatory Membership in an Owners' Association
13. TREC 38-2 Notice of Termination of Contract

14. TREC 39-6 Amendment to Contract
15. TREC Consumer Information Form
16. TREC OP-C Notice to Prospective Buyer
17. TREC 40-3 Third-Party Financing Condition Addendum
18. TREC 41-1 Loan Assumption Addendum
19. TREC 43-0 Addendum Containing Required Notices under §5.016, §420.001, and §420.002, Texas Property Code
20. TREC 44-0 Addendum for Reservation of Oil, Gas, and Other Minerals
21. TREC 45-0 Short Sale Addendum

Other forms are also currently promulgated by the Texas Real Estate Commission:

1. TREC OP-H Seller's Disclosure of Property Condition
2. TREC OP-I Texas Real Estate Consumer Notice Concerning Recognized Hazards
3. TREC OP-K Information About Brokerage Services
4. TREC OP-L Lead-Based Paint Addendum

A few of the most commonly used forms are printed at the back of this text. All of the current forms are available at the Texas Real Estate Commission's Web site and can be downloaded at no cost. Its Web site is http://www.trec.state.tx.us. A licensee should visit this Web site frequently, as TREC uses it to update all of their rules and regulations, forms, and other pertinent consumer information. Put it on your "favorite places" list on your computer, and visit it often.

Computerized Forms

The Texas Real Estate Commission regulations provide that computer-driven printers can print forms, provided these guidelines are followed:

- The computer file or program containing the form text must not allow the end user direct access to the text of the form and may only permit the user to insert language in blanks in these forms.

- Typefaces or fonts must appear to be identical to those used by the Commission in printed forms of the particular form.

- The text and number of pages must be identical to that used by the Commission in printed proofs of the particular form.

- The spacing, length of blanks, borders, and placement of text on the page must appear to be identical to that used by the Commission in printed proofs of the form.

- The name and address of the person or firm responsible for developing the software program must be legibly printed below the border at the bottom of each page in no less than six-point type and no larger than ten-point type.
- The text of the form must be obtained from a proof of the form bearing a control number assigned by the Commission.

The control number of each proof must appear on all forms reproduced from the proof and may be reproduced with only the following changes or additions:

- The business name or logo of a broker, organization, or printer may appear at the top of the form outside the border.

- The broker's name may be inserted in any blank provided for that purpose.

Practicing Law

The Texas Real Estate Commission requires all licensees to use promulgated forms, when appropriate, in all real estate transactions. There are common questions and concerns that merit emphasis. Although this provision may seem too basic to review, please understand that the Texas Real Estate Commission takes a very strong position against the concept of brokers practicing law.

Please note the existing provision of the Texas Real Estate License Act regarding the practice of law:

Sec. 1101.654. A license granted under the provisions of this Act shall be suspended or revoked by the commission on proof that the licensee, not being licensed and authorized to practice law in this state for a consideration, reward, pecuniary benefit, present or anticipated, direct or indirect, or in connection with or as a part of his employment, agency, fiduciary relationship as a licensee, *drew* a deed, note, deed of trust, will, or other *written instrument that may* transfer or *anywise affect the title to or an interest in land*, except as provided in the subsections below, or *advised or counseled* a person as to the validity or *legal sufficiency of an instrument* or as to the validity of title to real estate.

(b) Notwithstanding the provisions of this Act or any other law, the completion of contract forms which bind the sale, exchange, option, lease, or rental of any interest in real property by a real estate broker or salesperson incident to the performance of the acts of a broker as defined by this article does not constitute the unauthorized or illegal practice of law in this state, *provided the forms have been promulgated for use by the Texas Real Estate Commission* for the particular kind of transaction involved, or the *forms have been prepared by an attorney-at-law licensed by this state and approved by said attorney for the particular kind of transaction involved*, or the forms have been *prepared by the property owner* or prepared by an attorney *and required by the property owner*.

Note that the provisions only allow a broker to use:
- the promulgated forms

- forms prepared by an attorney for the particular kind of transaction involved

- forms prepared by the property owner or prepared by an attorney and required by the property owner

Use of any other form will be practicing law without a license. If you are in doubt, call the Texas Real Estate Commission. Adaptation of a form to "make it fit" to a transaction is also a violation.

Another word of caution: When filling in the blanks or the special provisions of the promulgated form, if any information is inserted that could be construed to be legal advice or affecting the legal rights of the party, it will probably be construed as practicing law. The insertions in these areas of the contract are for business provisions only. If there is a concern as to filling in the blanks or the legality of certain special provisions, it is probably more prudent for the licensee to have the owner fill in the blank or special provision in the owner's own handwriting so it cannot be construed as the broker practicing law without a license.

Pertinent Provisions

There are general rules that apply to the interpretation of the promulgated contract forms that are commonly asked. It should be noted here that there are brokers who may not use TREC-promulgated contracts often, such as commercial real estate brokers who feel the discussion of TREC contracts may be inapplicable to them. It should be pointed out that the provisions of the TREC earnest money contracts are encountered in many commercial contracts, so discussion of each of these issues is pertinent to all real estate brokers, commercial as well as residential. In addition, TAR has introduced a number of forms that are drafted for the use of REALTOR® members that, in many cases, are very practical documents to use in a broker's practice in conjunction with the contracts. A copy of the new TREC Form 20-8 is shown on page 139 for reference.

Contingencies

It should be noted that all of the Texas Real Estate Commission-promulgated forms provide for two basic contingencies:

- Buyer's approval of title and survey.

- Buyer's ability to obtain financing.

It should be noted that the contracts, even though they contain specific performance provisions, are not binding earnest money contracts until these two contingencies have been satisfied. Therefore, the buyer is not bound to performance until the two contingencies can be removed from the contract. Technically, these contingencies are called "conditions precedent to buyer's performance."

Specific Paragraphs

Paragraph 1. Parties. This provision was revised in 2008 to make it very clear that the only parties to the contract are the buyer and the seller. The broker is not a party to the contract; the title company is not a party to the contract; only the buyer and seller are.

Paragraph 2. Property. In the most recent revision, Paragraph 2 was changed to make the definition of "property" clearer. Paragraph 2.B. identifies those items that are permanently installed and built in are labeled "improvements." Those items that are less likely to be attached to the real estate but are peculiarly adapted to the real estate in most circumstances are set out in Paragraph 2.C. and labeled "accessories." Paragraph 2.D., labeled "exclusions," provides a specific space to exclude those things that will not transfer with title to the real estate *and must be removed prior to delivery of possession.* If additional items are to be included, they must be set out in Paragraph 11. This paragraph of the contract will always change as lifestyles change.

Paragraph 4. Financing. This paragraph was significantly changed in the latest revision. Note that it provides three choices:

1. Third-Party Financing
2. Assumption
3. Seller Financing

Rather than including all of the financing provisions in the body of the contract, it now refers to the applicable addenda, which can be attached to the contract. This paragraph was recently reformatted to clarify that the contract is made subject to the lender's approval of the property (which is a contingency that continues until closing). Section 4(A)(2) is the contingency that applies only to the buyer's creditworthiness and financing approval. This contingency does have a time limit as set out in the third-party financing addendum, discussed later. If Box 4(A)(2)(b) is checked, there is no need to attach any financing condition addendum.

Paragraph 5. Earnest Money. In Paragraph 5, there is a specific provision for the buyers providing earnest money upon execution of the contract by all parties. Note, however, that the new contract states that if the earnest money is not deposited (e.g., a bad check), the buyer shall be in default, triggering the provisions of Paragraph 15. A prudent practice, however, is to request that the buyer provide a cashier's or certified check to prevent the "bouncing check" issue.

Paragraph 6. Title. The new contract provides boxes to determine who should pay for the owner's policy of title insurance. Traditionally, the seller has paid in most counties, and most listing agreements provide that the seller will pay for the title insurance. So, as a practical matter, the seller agrees to pay pursuant to the listing agreement. The contracts give us a choice! This may help if the buyer's employer pays for all closing costs, as the buyer might be able to bargain for a better sales price. Paragraph 6 also contains a significant change in the most recent revision. Note that Paragraph 6.A.(8) allows the buyer at buyer's expense to have the exception as to "discrepancies, conflicts, shortages in area for boundary lines, encroachments or protrusions, or overlapping of improvements" amended to read only "shortages in area." This provision has been commonly used in commercial contract forms, although this is the first time it has been utilized in the residential forms. The issue presented is a rather complex one, and now real estate licensees will have to become very familiar with this issue because many buyers, particularly those from out of state, might ask about this provision.

The initial issue involves title insurance coverage. The standard owner's policy of title insurance has an exception for "discrepancies, conflicts, shortages in area for boundary lines, encroachments or protrusions, or overlapping of improvements," which means that the buyer does not have title insurance coverage for most minor encroachment issues (e.g., fences, garage eaves, deck encroachments onto power line easements, roof encroachments over building lines, and misaligned driveways). Many buyers are surprised when they acquire their properties that this coverage is not provided, but the coverage traditionally has not been available under title insurance policies in Texas unless the buyer pays an additional premium (currently 5 percent of the existing title premiums on residential policies, and 15 percent on commercial policies) and provides the title insurer with a staked, on-the-ground survey. In most cases, this could mean a considerable additional expense. The old contract form did not deal with who would pay this expense or whether or not this insurance coverage was available. This new revision to the contract form clearly makes it available at the buyer's expense. As a practical matter, the title insurance company will then review the survey to determine whether there are any conflicts or encroachments. If these conflicts exist, the title insurance company may except to a specific encroachment or choose to insure against enforcement of any third party's rights regarding that encroachment by express insurance coverage. That is, the title insurance company can agree to insure against the enforcement of an easement right removal of an encroachment or protrusion so that the buyer can rest assured that he has "clear" title. If there is a complaint about any of the conflicts or encroachments, the title insurance company will defend them against that enforcement by another party.

If a licensee represents a buyer, they may want to pay particular attention to this new provision. Many buyers tend to be extremely picky, and they are firmly convinced that they do not have good title if there is a 3-inch encroachment of a pool deck into a power line right-of-way. The fact is that they don't have good title if this exists, but, as we just previously discussed, the title insurance company can insure against any damages as a result of the encroachment. Some buyers, however, will worry about their ability to sell the property in the future with this encumbrance and will choose not to purchase. For the first time, this new revision in the contract helps an agent and his buyer focus on alternatives available if this condition exists.

The contract also provides that the title company does not have to deliver the commitment until 20 days after the title company receives a copy of the contract and specifies the seller's authorization for the title company to deliver the commitments and all related documents, and that they are to be delivered at the buyer's address shown on the contract. If the commitment is not delivered in a timely manner, the delivery is automatically extended for up to 15 days. In smaller counties where title companies have a more difficult time getting the commitments out, this is a tremendous relief and eliminates the problem of where to send the documents to the buyer. It puts an additional duty on the broker, however, to be sure to fill in the buyer's address at the end of the contract.

Title commitment not delivered in a timely manner? That may be a real problem! In *Humphrey v. Camelot Retirement Community*, 893 S.W.2d 55 (Tex. App.–Corpus Christi, 1994), the plaintiff sued the defendant to recover earnest money that was paid to the defendant for the purchase of a new home. The contract required that within 30 days of the date the contract was executed, the defendant "shall cause to be furnished to purchaser a standard Commitment for Owner Policy of Title Insurance." The defendant did not cause the title commitment to be furnished within 30 days required by the contract. In its failure to comply with this provision, the seller breached the contract, and the court considered that a breach that "would go to the essence of the contract" allowing for a rescission of the contract, return of the earnest money, and damages in the amount of $13,750. This court felt that delivery of the title commitment was critical!

Paragraph 6.C. has been changed significantly. Either party may provide the survey, or an old survey may be used if it is acceptable to the title company or buyer's lender. Buyer and seller must agree, however, how many days they can produce the survey, which is out of the control of both parties. A good suggestion may be to utilize the maximum number of days (the day prior to closing?) so that the buyer and seller aren't in default because of a slow surveyor. **Note another problem: If the seller checks box (1) and can't find the survey, it may constitute a misrepresentation. Be sure the survey is available before making this choice.** This paragraph has also been recently revised to require the seller to provide the Residential Real Property Affidavit promulgated by the Texas Department of Insurance. If the seller does not provide the survey in a timely manner, the buyer may obtain one at the seller's expense no later than 3 days prior to the closing date.

Paragraph 6.D. has now been amended to provide that the buyer have a fixed time to object to the commitment, exception documents, and survey. Therefore, the buyer's objection period does not begin until he has received all three documents. Buyer's failure to object within the time allowed constitutes a waiver of buyer's right to object. Nevertheless, that outside date is now the same for all three contingencies (commitment, exception documents, and survey).

Note that the contracts now have seven "Title Notices" in Paragraph 6E. The first notice advises the buyer to have an abstract of title covering the property examined by an attorney of buyer's selection or should be furnished with or obtain a title policy. This automatically provides for a licensee's compliance with Section 1101.555 of the Texas Real Estate License Act. The second disclosure concerns mandatory owners' association membership and whether or not the buyer is required to be a member of a property owners' association in his subdivision. The third notice provides for a required notice if the property is located in a municipal utility district. This is a specific notice required by the Texas Water Code regarding the additional ad valorem taxation, which is imposed on the property as a result of being located in a municipal utility district. The fourth notice gives the buyer a specific notice as required by the Texas Natural Resources Code if the property abuts highly influenced waters of this state. The fifth notice is a notification that the property may be subject to annexation as provided under the Texas Property Code. The sixth notice is a required notice that the seller of property located in a certificated service area of the utility service provider must give to a buyer. The seventh notice is a statutory required notice that a seller of a property in a public improvement district (often referred to as a PID), which cautions the buyer that a PID may make special assessments against the property located in the PID.

Paragraph 7. Property Condition. Paragraph 7.A. provides an absolute right for the buyer to have inspections and access to utility by an inspector "licensed by TREC or otherwise permitted by law to make such inspections." This may prevent the "setup" of an uncle or cousin doing a bad inspection to create a better negotiating position for the buyer. However, it does allow for a qualified engineer who is permitted by law to make such inspections, but not licensed as an inspector, to perform these inspections. Please note that this new paragraph also provides for reinspection after the repairs have been made. *Paragraph 7.A. does not make inspections or reinspections a contingency.* However, if the property does have significant defects, the buyer may have a cause of action against the seller for misrepresentation or failure to disclose those defects. You may notice also that the seller is required to permit the buyer and buyer's agents access to the property at reasonable times. **The buyer has the right to a walk-through any time prior to closing, so long as it is at a reasonable time.**

Paragraph 7.C. confirms the seller's obligation to comply with the Lead-Based Paint Disclosure. There is a box to check as to whether or not the disclosure is attached.

Federal law does not require the addendum for property constructed after January 1, 1978, property sold at foreclosure, the sale of a zero bedroom dwelling with a sleeping unit that is not separated from the living area, and housing for the elderly or disabled where children under age 6 are not expected to reside.

A clarification has been provided in Paragraph 7.D. In the old Paragraph 7.D, licensees, buyers, and sellers were often inserting into the blank spaces things that were not anticipated, such as "subject to inspection" and other vague comments that could render the contract unenforceable. Paragraph 7.D was revised to require that one of two boxes be checked. The first box deals with the property "in its present condition." We have had several appellate cases that indicate Paragraph 7.D.(1) will be construed as an "as is" provision. See *Larsen v. Langford*, 41 S.W. 3d 245 (Tex. App.–Waco, 2001).

If box 7.D.(2) is checked, it means the buyer has noticed a specific item on the property (broken trapeze in the master bedroom) that needs to be repaired and specifies the repair and/or treatment that must be completed prior to closing. In theory, this creates a shift of the burden, where the buyer is agreeing to take the property either "as is" or only after the seller has made the specific repairs. So it is up to the buyer to carry out inspections during the option period.

What if a defect is discovered during the option period? At this point, the buyer has to make a choice: (1) exercise his right to terminate as set out in Paragraph 23, using TREC Form No. 38-2, or (2) propose an amendment to the contract, using TREC Form 39-6. Now the seller has the choice of either agreeing to the repairs or running the risk that the buyer will terminate the contract if the seller does not agree to the amendment.

Paragraph 7.E. provides for lender-required repairs and provides that the buyer can terminate the contract if the lender-required repairs exceed 5 percent of the sales price. If lender-required repairs are not made, the loan won't be approved, and the buyer may avoid performance by exercising the financing contingency set out in Paragraph 4, provided the buyer terminates in a timely manner. If the repair does not exceed 5 percent, what happens? As a practical matter, the buyer can't get the loan, so the deal is over, i.e., you probably can't successfully sue the buyer who can't get financing because of the condition of the house, and the seller may have liability for failure to disclose the defect.

Paragraph 7.F. provides for completion of repairs and treatments, and additionally provides that the repairs and treatments must be performed by persons who regularly provide such services, hopefully eliminating "Uncle Elmo the Handyman" from making these repairs. There is also a provision for all transferable warranties to be transferred to the buyer, at the buyer's expense.

There is an important change in this provision in the most recent revision to the contract form. Note that if the seller fails to complete any agreed-upon repairs prior to the closing date, the buyer has the right to do so and receive reimbursement from the seller at closing. This apparently is without regard to the expense, and it seems to give the buyer the unilateral right to do any repairs that are "agreed to." It also allows the closing date to be extended up to 15 days to complete those repairs and treatments. There is a practical problem to this. What if the seller won't let the buyer in to make the repairs? This may have created another area for conflict in the contract rather than resolving disputes.

Paragraph 8. Broker's Fees. Note that broker's fees under Paragraph 8 in the promulgated contract forms are nothing more than a ratification of the existence of an agreement. This refers the buyer, seller, or broker back to the original agreement to pay the commission and/or to pursue any legal remedies.

Paragraph 9. Closing. This paragraph was significantly changed, and the most recent revisions note that they still contain a 7-day extension or an automatic 7-day extension after the objection to title and survey have been assured. *There is no automatic extension to complete lender's closing requirements.* The paragraph is also more specific about items to be provided at the closing. Paragraph 9.B.(2) now provides an agreement by the buyer to provide good funds acceptable to the escrow agent at closing (not contained in the previous contract form). Note that this paragraph now contains the notice to the buyer that the seller may continue to show the property, and receive and negotiate back-up offers. This was previously in Paragraph 6 of the old form.

Paragraph 10. Possession. There is a revision in the new form that allows buyer possession of the property either (i) upon closing and funding or (ii) according to the temporary residential lease (this provision is clearer than it was in the old form). There is still no definition for what "funding" means, whether the buyer funds, or the lender funds, or if both elements of funding will be required. Often a buyer will fund his proceeds at closing, but the lender's funding may be delayed. Does the buyer still get possession in this circumstance? The contract simply does not address it.

Note that this paragraph requires the use of a TREC Temporary Lease form or an "at sufferance relationship" is created between the parties. The paragraph does not distinguish one day's occupancy versus one year's occupancy, so long as it is "temporary." Remember that this is a TREC-required form and must be utilized if it applies to your situation.

Paragraph 11. Special Provisions. Note that under Special Provisions (the infamous Paragraph 11) agents need to be very, very careful not to insert any items that may constitute the practice of law or refer to nonpromulgated forms not specifically required by the principal or his attorney.

Real estate brokers are not allowed to alter the terms of the contract, only to "fill in the blanks" of the TREC-promulgated forms. Contingencies for performance inserted into Paragraph 11 of the TREC contracts are for the insertion of business details, nothing more. Any changes to the form have to be at the direction of the principal and not at the instigation or direction of the broker; otherwise, it constitutes the practice of law. No contingency should be inserted in Paragraph 11 unless specifically directed by the principal. Even then, it is smart to have the principal write it in.

Another concern should be noted. If a contingency is truly superfluous, such as "this contract is contingent upon the approval of buyer's attorney" without further specification, it probably makes the contract a mere option (the seller can't sue for specific performance because the buyer always has an "out"). If the earnest money is also refundable, there may be no contract at all, as there is no consideration for the option. See *Culbertson v. Brodsky*, 788 S.W.2d 156 (Tex. App.–Ft. Worth, 1990).

Paragraph 12. Sales Expenses. There were some important changes to this paragraph in the most recent (2003) revisions. The most significant change, however, involved Paragraph 12.A.(1)(b), which provides for the seller to pay any additional expenses that the buyer is prohibited by FHA or VA from paying. Because there is only one contract form, this paragraph provides for certain notice items for FHA and VA that are included and do not require the use of separate contract forms. What if the amount exceeds the seller's limit? The seller has a contingency, too. Paragraph 12.B. requires the buyer to pay PMI, FHA, and VA fees.

Paragraph 14. Casualty Loss. This provision has come under additional scrutiny in recent years because of flooding damage in Houston and tornado damage in northern parts of the state. If the property is damaged or destroyed by fire or other casualty after the contract date, the seller is required to restore the property to its previous condition as soon as reasonably possible. If the seller fails to do so (due to factors beyond seller's control), the buyer has three options: (1) he can terminate the contract and receive a refund of his earnest money, (2) he can extend the time for performance up to 15 days, or (3) he can accept the property in its damaged condition with an assignment of the insurance proceeds. There is now a new provision for the seller to pay the deductible on the insurance policy.

Paragraph 15. Default. Note that in Paragraph 6.B. the *seller* (not the real estate agent or the title company) is required to deliver to the buyer within 20 days after the effective date of the contract, a commitment for title insurance and at buyer's expense, legible copies of restrictive covenants and documents evidencing exceptions in the Commitment, other than the standard printed exceptions. If the Commitment is not delivered in a timely manner, this Default paragraph gives the buyer the option to terminate the contract.

These two paragraphs have given title companies great concern over their ability to: (1) produce the Commitment in a timely manner, and (2) pay for the cost of all copies, with no explanation as to how the buyer is supposed to pay the title company (e.g., upon receipt, at closing, or C.O.D.). In some cases, the title company may not be able to deliver copies of title exceptions within 20 days (probates, out-of-state bankruptcies, heirship proceedings in a foreign country, etc.). In that event, Paragraph 6.B. allows for an automatic extension. If the Commitment is still not delivered within the 35 days, this paragraph gives the buyer the right to terminate the contract if the failure to deliver the Commitment in a timely manner is through no fault of the seller.

It should also be specifically noted that when a broker attempts to alter the Default paragraph (Paragraph 15), the seller can lose the ability to sue the buyer for specific performances by striking out the "specific performance" provisions. The contract may then become an option contract, which is performable purely at the option of the buyer. This not only materially alters the performance obligations under the contract, but also eliminates the broker's ability to sue for a commission unless the transaction closed. It may be no contract at all. See *Culbertson v. Brodsky supra*.

Paragraph 16. Mediation. Paragraph 16 provides that it is the policy of the state of Texas to encourage resolution of disputes under the contract through mediation and provides a choice for agreed mediation, eliminating the need for the Mediation Addendum with this form. Many licensees have been concerned that the buyer and seller are forced to discuss disputes even before the contract is signed. The fact is, however, that mediation resolves many disputes without having to resort to litigation, hiring lawyers, and expensive court proceedings. As most earnest money disputes involve minor differences, mediation forces the parties into a discussion of the dispute. This is less time consuming, less costly, and an easier way to resolve disputes in most circumstances. As a practical matter, most earnest money contract disputes do not involve large amounts of money, and a court will order mediation anyway.

Paragraph 17 was revised in response to a lawsuit that denied a broker's right to get attorney's fees. See *Williamson v. Guynes*, 2005 WL 675512 (Tex. App. Waco, 2005). Frequently, a broker may be a defendant in a lawsuit, win the lawsuit, and still have to bear the cost of defense, which can be substantial. This paragraph was revised to provide that, in addition to the buyer or seller, the listing broker, other broker, or escrow agent who prevails in any legal proceedings is entitled to recover reasonable attorney fees and all costs incurred. This provision now poses a risk to the plaintiff in some lawsuits. If the plaintiff fails to prove his or her case, and the broker or the title company prevails, the defendant may be awarded attorney fees and costs, to be paid by the plaintiff.

Paragraph 18. Escrow. This paragraph was changed significantly in the new form. It no longer requires the signature of the broker to disburse the earnest money. In addition, if one party makes a demand for the earnest money, the escrow agent is required to give notice of that demand to the other party. If the other party doesn't respond within 15 days, the escrow agent can go ahead and disburse the earnest money to the party demanding it. This should help "clear out" a lot of escrow accounts when parties cannot be reached for response. Note that a new paragraph, 18.D., was added to provide that if a party wrongfully refuses or wrongfully fails to sign a release, the party entitled to the earnest money is also entitled to liquidated damages of three times the amount of the earnest money, plus attorneys' fees and court costs.

Paragraph 20. Federal Tax Requirement. There is specific reference to foreign parties as sellers of the property and amounts of currency in connection with the real estate closing. It should be pointed out that a foreign party has specific tax requirements that put the burden on the buyer to withhold taxes for the Internal Revenue Service. Although this is not a common problem in residential transactions, foreign sellers in commercial transactions can create unique problems. These sorts of issues should be resolved early in the transaction rather than at the closing table. The same is true of cash. Federal law prohibits the deposit of large amounts of cash in the bank without justifiable reason. Title companies are therefore very reluctant to close transactions where cash or other forms of consideration (e.g., jewels) may be involved. A wise broker may want to caution parties to a real estate transaction not to engage in cash transactions, which are outside of the normal business practice. Use wired funds, cashier's checks, or certified checks, and closings will go much more smoothly.

Paragraph 21. Notices. This is a new provision put in the body of the contract to provide notices to the seller and the buyer. This is more effective than putting it at the end of the contract (past the signatures). It now makes it part of the body of the contract, and it must be filled in. This was a detail often overlooked by licensees. Putting it in the body of the contract will make that omission much less likely.

Paragraph 22. Addenda. Paragraph 22 now lists all promulgated addenda. It should be reemphasized that a nonpromulgated addendum must be prepared by an attorney or the principal because it is not an official TREC-promulgated form.

Paragraph 23. Option to Terminate. This paragraph provides an option to terminate the contract for any reason whatsoever during the option period. Note that this paragraph was recently revised to provide that the option fee can be paid within two days after the effective date of the contact, although the consideration can be "nominal." If no dollar amount is stated as the option fee or if the buyer fails to pay the option fee within the time prescribed, the buyer loses his right to terminate. Note that in this paragraph, time is of the essence, but this provision is applicable to this paragraph only.

This new paragraph is somewhat unique. It gives the buyer (in consideration for the payment of the option fee) the right to terminate the contract within the specified number of days. Note that if the blanks of this contract are not filled in, the buyer does not have the termination option; or if, for whatever reason, the buyer has not paid the option fee, there is no right to terminate and the buyer and seller have a binding contract for the sale of their real estate. Therefore, if the seller does not receive the option fee (or the check bounces) or the contract blanks are not filled in, *this is a binding earnest money contract on both parties, subject to the conditions of the agreement*. Note that the right of termination is within the stated number of days after the *effective date* of the contract.

The burden is on the buyer to give notice of the termination within the time specified, and there is a choice as to whether or not the option fee will be credited to the sales price at closing. The appropriate form has been promulgated by TREC as Form No. 38-1. If the buyer fails to give the notice, the right to terminate is waived. Buyer's agents, mark your calendars!

The size of the option fee is always negotiable, and it is always prudent to negotiate an option period long enough to allow for inspections and to obtain costs for repairs.

BUT. . .if the buyer finds that the need for extensive repairs exists, the buyer should give notice of termination in a timely manner, or amend the Earnest Money Contract, utilizing the TREC Amendment Form (No. 39-6). This new amendment form is discussed later in this chapter.

Paragraph 24. Consult an attorney. This is a new addition to the contract forms providing for the address, telephone, and facsimile numbers for the respective parties' attorneys. As you may recall, the old form required you to "squeeze" everything into one line.

Note also that there is a new provision at the end of the contract for the seller's receipt of the option money (if Paragraph 23 is utilized).

Third-Party Financing Addendum. This recently revised addendum makes the financing contingency much clearer than what was provided in the old contract. Note that Paragraph 4 of the contract provides for two different contingencies; one is whether or not the property (the condition of the house, or appraised value) satisfies the lender's underwriting requirements, notwithstanding the buyer's ability to qualify for the loan. There is no time limit on this contingency; so if a lender determines on the day of closing that the property doesn't satisfy the lender's underwriting requirements, this contingency has not been satisfied. The buyer has an "out" until the day of closing, depending on the lender's underwriting requirements. There is also a provision (Paragraph 4.A.[2]) that eliminates the buyer's contingency for financing. Presumably, if Box 4.A.(2) is checked, the buyer either has the cash to close or has guaranteed financing already in place. It might be construed as a representation to the seller of the buyer's financial ability to close. If you cannot qualify for a loan after making this representation, does it become a deceptive trade practice? This may create an unexpected liability for a buyer. If there is a financing contingency, the contract requires the use of the new Third-Party Financing Condition Addendum. Note that this Addendum creates contingencies for conventional financing, Texas Veterans Housing Assistance Program Loans, FHA financing, and VA guaranteed financing. The form provides that the borrower must *make every reasonable* effort to obtain financing approval, including but not limited to, furnishing all information and documents required by the lender. Financing approval is obtained when the terms of the described loan are available and the lender determines that the buyer has satisfied all of the lender's financial requirements. Note also that if the buyer doesn't give written notice to the seller to exercise his financing contingency, the contingency is automatically removed!

The most recent amendment to this form also clarifies that financing approval of the buyer does not include the approval of lender's underwriting requirements for the property, as specified in Paragraph 4.A.1.

Assumption. If the buyer is going to assume the loan, the contract now requires the utilization of the Loan Assumption Addendum, which, again, is similar to what is contained in the existing contract form. Note that it gives the seller the right to approve buyer's credit (rather than the lender). As in prior contract forms, if the assumed loan varies in an amount greater than $350 at closing, either party may terminate the contract, and the earnest money will be refunded to the buyer unless the other party elects to eliminate the excess by an appropriate adjustment at the closing. There are also contingencies involved in any assumption fee that may be required by the lender. If there is an existing escrow account, the escrow account is required to be transferred to the buyer without any deficiency and the buyer is to reimburse the seller for the amount of the transferred account at closing.

Seller Financing Addendum. This form was revised in 2006 to include common provisions for note payments and an interest rate. New provisions for seller's consent to a subsequent conveyance by the buyer and continued liability for the buyer if the buyer is not specifically released from liability in the subsequent conveyance were also added. There are requirements for credit documentation and credit approval, and it gives the buyer the right to prepay the promissory note holder in part at any time without penalty. It also has automatic provisions for late payment fees along with the payment provisions that are required in the promissory note. The addendum also has specific choices for the terms of the Deed of Trust regarding property transfers (due-on-transfer clauses) and tax and insurance escrows, so that the seller can be assured that the taxes and insurance are current and paid on time each year.

Addendum for "Back-Up" Contract. This was revised in 2007, and is for use in the fairly common situation where a buyer (Buyer 2) will choose to execute a contract with the seller to buy the property in the event an existing contract (with Buyer 1) should terminate. Note that Paragraph B puts the burden on the seller to notify the buyer on a specific date that the previous contract has terminated. If the seller does not notify the buyer, the contract (back-up contract with Buyer 2) automatically terminates. This addendum gives the buyer no rights other than to create a contract in the event of termination of the prior contract. A real estate licensee should be seriously cautioned not to attempt to encourage the termination of contract number 1. This may be construed as tortious interference of a contract, and the licensee may be subject to license revocation or suspension for this kind of conduct as a direct violation of Section 1101.652(6)(21) of the Texas Real Estate License Act (even if the second offer is higher than the first). It should be understood that the first contract is a binding and enforceable contract and any attempt to interfere with the (parties) performance may result in severe legal consequences.

This form provides for the parties' obligations under the "back-up" contract. The buyer is required to deposit any earnest money and option fee as provided in the "back-up" contract, but is not otherwise obligated to perform during the contingency period. The addendum now also addresses the time for the buyer to give notice of termination if the buyer exercises the option to terminate under Paragraph 23 of the contract (Buyer 1).

This creates complicating situations. Two things can happen: (1) the seller can notify the buyer that the previous contract is terminated; or (2) the buyer would need to notify the seller that the buyer terminates the back-up contract. TAR has prepared two forms to address this situation. TAR-1912 Paragraph B provides a form for the seller's notice to buyer that the previous contract is terminated. This satisfies Paragraph B of the Back-up Addendum and confirms the Seller Notification. Note that Paragraph C of the Back-up Addendum automatically terminates the contract if the seller does not notify the buyer. Notwithstanding the language, TAR has another form (TAR-1913) where the buyer acknowledges that the notification has not taken place and confirms the termination of the back-up contract. Although this may seem unnecessary, it is always good business practice to have the buyer acknowledge the termination to the seller to avoid the risk that the seller may attempt to "activate" the contract a few days later. A well-documented file of confirming documentation is always an asset should problems arise.

Addendum for Sale of Other Property by Buyer. This form was revised in 2007, and is another fairly common situation where a buyer needs to sell his house before he can commit to the actual purchase of the house that is the subject of this contract. *If your buyer has not closed on the sale of a prior home, you must use this addendum unless your buyer can confirm the ability to purchase without the sale of the prior home.* Please note that the seller may continue to show the property and consider other offers from buyers. There is in many realtor systems a special provision in MLS for this situation where the property is "under contract," but is still "on the market." Note Paragraph C. If a seller "accepts" a written offer to purchase the property (presumably this second contract will have a "back-up" addendum), the seller notifies the buyer and the buyer must remove the contingency specified in this addendum. If the buyer fails to do so, the back-up contract is terminated. Note that the buyer may only waive the contingency by notifying the seller of the waiver and depositing $_____

with the escrow agent. There is no requirement that dollars be inserted in this blank, but it is presumed that some additional funds would be deposited to show the increased commitment of the buyer. Note that if the buyer removes the contingency, there can be no financial contingency as set out in Paragraph E.

Not unexpectedly, complications arise here. To simplify these issues, TAR has also addressed the addendum under TAR Forms TAR-1912 and TAR-1913. Under Paragraph A, it acknowledges that the seller has accepted another written offer to purchase the property (again, presuming it would have a "back-up" provision). TAR Form 1912 acknowledges that the buyer must notify the seller no later than the time required under the addendum to waive the contingency and deposit the required additional earnest money. In TAR Form 1913, Paragraph A, the buyer acknowledges waiving the contingency and deposits the additional earnest money or executes his alternative of terminating the contract and refunding the earnest money. Please remember that in order to use these forms, you must be a member of the Texas Association of REALTORS®.

Addendum for Property Subject to Mandatory Membership in an Owners' Association. Logically, it's fair to provide the buyer this notice so he is not surprised with additional expenses after he moves into the property.

Subdivision Information, Including Resale Certificate for Property Subject to Mandatory Membership in an Owners' Association. This form was revised in 1999 to comply with new state legislation that requires homeowners' associations to provide certain information to purchasers. This "Subdivision Information," if not received by the buyer, gives the buyer the right to terminate the contract at any time prior to closing. After the seller delivers the Subdivision Information, the buyer has the right to terminate the contract for any reason within 7 days after the buyer receives the Subdivision Information, or prior to closing, whichever occurs first.

Addendum for Seller's Disclosure of Information on Lead-Based Paint and Lead-Based Paint Hazards. This new addendum is to comply with the federal lead-based paint disclosure statute discussed in Chapter 2. Note that there are convenient boxes for both buyer and seller to check, and this addendum presumably keeps all parties (including brokers) in compliance with the new federal law.

Buyer's and Seller's Temporary Residential Lease. These forms are new for 2006 and required for use. Note that Paragraph 4 specifies that rentals shall be paid per day. There is no longer a provision for monthly rental payment. This presumes the "temporary" nature of the residential lease. Please note also that this is required in the event it applies to your transaction. A licensee should not presume that another form would be acceptable, because these forms were specified for those particular transactions. Occupancy by the buyer (prior to closing) or seller (after the closing) without these temporary leases presumes a tenancy at sufferance, which means neither party has rights, other than to dispossess the tenant or terminate the relationship. The new revisions emphasize "residential" rather than "single family" to clarify that duplexes and quadplexes were also included. There is also a new emphasis on property insurance (note Paragraph 16).

Amendment. This new, revised Amendment form (TREC 39-6) is for an accommodation to the parties to change the terms of their contract after it has been signed and the conditions have changed. Please note that there are now nine (a) boxes to check concerning the amendments. There is also a required additional option fee, and the buyer waives his rights to terminate under Paragraph 23 of the TREC form. If the parties choose to amend the contract for any other reason, there is no provision for that (e.g., change possession dates or other special provisions). In those situations, an attorney or the principals themselves should draft the amendment. Otherwise, a licensee may run the risk of practicing law without a license.

Notice of Termination of Contract. (TREC 38-2–see page 139). In accordance with Paragraph 23 of the contract, this is the official notice that the buyer must give in order to terminate his rights under the option provisions. There is a common problem in utilizing this notice of termination. If the seller is currently considering whether or not to amend the contract (using the new Amendment form), but does not respond in a timely manner, the buyer may be bound by the terms of the contract if he hasn't exercised his Notice of Termination in a timely manner. Particularly buyer's brokers, mark your calendar carefully to make sure that the buyer's obligation to send this Notice of Termination is done.

Effective Date

Note that the "broker" is required to fill in the date of final acceptance and the parties' addresses to the contract. This is extremely important! The Effective Date keys all the time requirements in the contract. The "broker" should note that if the contract is tendered to the title company 5 or more days after the Effective Date stated in the contract, it substantially alters the title company's ability to issue the title commitment, as well as all the other contingencies under the contract. This may create a significant liability for brokers who fail to fill in these items properly as required by the contract.

New Addenda!

There are two new addenda that have been approved by the Real Estate Commission, due to current changes in the marketplace.

The first is a Short Sale Addendum, which provides for the contingency of a sale of the property at a price below the current mortgage balance. It provides that the seller should obtain the lien holder's consent, or refund the earnest money in the event the lien holder's consent is not obtained.

The second is the Addendum for Reservation of Oil, Gas, and Other Minerals. The price of oil and new technology has made oil, gas, and other minerals available in paying quantities in new areas of the state. Many of these areas are under existing subdivisions. This makes mineral rights a new bargaining chip for sellers and buyers. The problem is that this is a complicated legal issue. Most residential real estate agents are not prepared to deal with these issues. This addendum only deals with very fundamental issues of ownership and waiver of surface rights, and warns all parties to seek legal counsel before signing the contract. Note the new addenda in the appendix.

Homestead Issues

Almost all Texans are familiar with the traditional homestead exemptions and the protection from forced sale of a homestead by the owner's creditors. Likewise, there has always been an absolute prohibition against mortgaging the equity in one's homestead. The basic rule is that the homestead cannot be encumbered by any increase of debt over those traditionally allowed lien rights. Texas has recognized two types of homesteads, either urban or rural. The urban homestead can consist of two homesteads, a business and residential, which are construed together as one homestead under Texas law.

The lien rights that have been determined to be foreclosable against homesteads in Texas are:

- purchase money mortgage.

- home improvements, when those improvements have been properly contracted for in writing by husband and wife (or single homestead claimant, if there is no marriage) *prior* to *any* work being done.

- taxes.

- homeowners' association maintenance fund liens, if they have been reserved in the deed restrictions.

In 1995, we expanded the list of liens that are foreclosable against homesteads to include Internal Revenue Service liens, which are the debt of both spouses, general federal tax liens, and owelty liens.

Then in 1997, we were blessed with home equity liens and reverse mortgages. It is still changing!

Home Equity Liens

The new constitutional amendment has consumer-friendly protections that are mandatory and still make Texas homestead protection unique. The requirements are as follows:

Voluntary Lien. The lien can only be created under a written agreement under the consent of each owner and each owner's spouse. Section 50(a)(6)(A).

Loan to Value Cap. The amount of the equity loan plus the total of all other debt against the homestead property cannot exceed 80 percent of the market value of the property on the date the loan is closed. Section 50(a)(6)(B).

It doesn't look like a 125 percent loan is valid!

Nonrecourse Loans. All loans will be nonrecourse (i.e., no personal liability for the homeowner beyond the homestead property) unless the homeowner obtained the loan through actual fraud. Section 50(a)(6)(C).

You can't get sued for a deficiency!

Judicial Foreclosure. A lender must file suit and obtain a judgment ordering foreclosure of the lien securing the equity loan. Section 50(a)(6)(D). The Texas Supreme Court has promulgated rules of civil procedure for expedited foreclosure proceedings for equity loans.

Fees. Loan fees (not including interest) are capped at 3 percent of the loan amount. This prohibits the owner or the owner's spouse from paying fees to any person necessary to originate, evaluate, maintain, record, insure, or service the extension of credit that exceeds, in the aggregate, 3 percent of the original principal amount of the extension of credit. Section 50(a)(6)(E).

Can lenders pay these expenses, and then add them to the loan amount? Hmm.

Lines of Credit. An equity loan may be in the form of an open-end account (i.e., line of credit).

Prepayment Penalty. Prepayment penalties are prohibited. Section 50(a)(6)(G).

Additional Collateral. A lender may not require any property other than the homestead property as collateral for an equity loan. Section 50(a)(6)(H). With the new 10-acre urban exemption, this problem has little effect on most home sites.

Agricultural Property Exemption. Property with an "agricultural use" exemption cannot be used as collateral for an equity loan unless the property is primarily used for the production of milk. Section 50(a)(6)(I).

Decrease in Market Value. Lender may not demand payment on an equity loan if there is a decrease in the market value of the homestead property. Section 50(a)(6)(J).

One Debt. The debt secured by the homestead at the time the extension of credit is made must be the only debt, except for other permitted encumbrances. Enumerated under subsections (a)(1)-(a)(5). Section 50(a)(6)(K).

Substantially Equal Payments/Full Interest Amortization. An equity loan must be repaid in substantially equal monthly payments that fully amortize the interest owed. Section 50(a)(6)(L).

Cooling Off Period. An equity loan cannot be closed until at least 12 days after the later: (1) of the date that the borrower applies for the loan; (2) or the date the lender provides the borrower a copy of the notice prescribed in the Constitution. Presumably, the most efficient procedure would be to have the loan application coupled with the notice (shown on Exhibit B). Section 50(a)(6)(M).

Location of Closing. An equity loan cannot be closed in a borrower's home; closing must occur in the office of a lender, a title company, or an attorney. Section 50(a)(6)(N).

Cross Default. A lender may not demand payment on an equity loan because of a default on another debt. Section 50(a)(6)(Q)(i).

Authorized Lenders. Equity loans can be made only by certain authorized lenders:

- A bank, savings and loan association, savings bank, or credit union doing business under the laws of this state or the United States.

- A federally chartered instrumentality or a person approved as a mortgagee by the United States government to make federally insured loans.

- A person licensed to make regulated loans as provided by statute of this state (presumably any lender that is a regulated lender licensed by the Consumer Credit Commissioner under the Texas Credit Code). See Chapter 3(a) of the Texas Credit Code.

- A person who sold the homestead to a current owner and provided all or part of the financing for the purchase.

- A person who is related to the homestead property owner within the second degree of affinity or consanguinity.

See Section 50(a)(6)(P). Note the following conditions:

- The proceeds can't be used to repay another debt except a debt secured by the homestead.

- There can be no assignment of wages as security.

- The owner may not sign the instrument if substantive terms of agreement are left to be filled in.
- The owner may not sign a confession of judgment or power of attorney to the lender or to a third person to confess judgment or to appear for the owner in any judicial proceeding.

- The lender must provide the owner of the homestead a copy of all documents signed by the owner related to the extension of credit.

- The instruments must contain a disclosure that the extension of credit is the type of credit defined by Article XVI, Section 50(a)(6), Texas Constitution.

- Upon final payment the lender is required to cancel and return the promissory note to the owner of the homestead, then give the owner, in recordable form, a release of the lien securing the extension of credit or a copy of an endorsement and assignment of the lien to a lender that is refinancing the extension of credit.

- There must be a provision that any owner or spouse may, within 3 days after the extension of credit is made, rescind the extension of credit without penalty or charge.

- The owner of the homestead and the lender must sign a written acknowledgment as to the fair market value of the homestead on the date the extension of credit is made.

- The lender or any holder of the note for the extension of credit shall forfeit all principal and interest to the extension of credit if the lender or holder fails to comply with lender's or holder's obligations under the extensions of credit within 60 days after the lender or holder is notified by the borrower of the lender's failure to comply.

This last provision may have diluted homestead protections significantly. Texas has a long history of strict enforcement of homestead protection. However, in interpreting the above provision (allowing the lender a reasonable time for failure to correct the defect) the Texas Supreme Court was very liberal in allowing lenders to correct defects. *Doody v. Ameriquest Mortgage Company* 49 S.W.3d 342 (Tex. 2001). See also *Doody v. Ameriquest Mortgage Corp.*, 242 F 3rd 286, at 289.

See Section 50(a)(6)(Q).

Anti-Flipping Provision. An equity loan cannot be refinanced more frequently than once a year. Section 50(a)(6)(M)(ii).

Anti-Redlining Provision. Any lender found by a federal regulatory agency to have engaged in "redlining" is prohibited from making equity loans. Section 50(a)(6)(P).

The 2003 Legislature passed a new joint resolution recommending an amendment to the Texas Constitution to allow refinancing of a debt secured by a homestead for extensions of home equity loans or reverse mortgages. This permits refinancing of a home equity loan with a reverse mortgage.

Home Improvement Loans

Another constitutional amendment modifies Section 50(a)(5) to provide a valid lien for work and material used in constructing *new* improvements thereon, if contracted for in writing, or work and material used to repair or renovate existing improvements thereon, if:

- The work and materials are contracted for in writing with the consent of both spouses.

- The contract for work and materials is not executed by the owner or the owner's spouse before the fifth day after the owner makes written application for any extension of credit for the work and materials, unless due to an emergency affecting health and safety.

- The contract for work and materials provides that the owner may rescind the contract without penalty or charge within 3 days after the execution of the contract with all the parties.

- The contract for the work and materials is executed by the owner and the owner's spouse:
  o at the office of the third-party lender making an extension of credit for the work and materials;
  o is an attorney at law; or
  o a title company.

In *Spradlin v. Jim Walter Homes, Inc.*, 34 S.W.3d 578 (Tex., 2000), Spradlin contracted with Jim Walter to build him a new house on homestead property. Spradlin later contended that Jim Walter's mechanics' lien on the house and property was invalid and unenforceable because Jim Walter failed to comply with the newly enacted constitutional provisions Article XVI, §50(a)(5)(A)-(D). Jim Walter sued, claiming those new constitutional provisions didn't apply to the construction of new improvements thereon, if contracted for in writing, or work and materials used to repair or renovate existing improvements thereon, if certain other things are done.

Spradlin argued that the "other things" had to be done for a new construction as well as for repair of existing construction. Jim Walter said they didn't. The court invoked the rule of construction known as the "doctrine of the last antecedent" in agreeing with Jim Walter. Under that doctrine, a qualifying phrase must be confined to the words and phrases immediately preceding it to which it may be applied without impairing the meaning of the sentence. All of this is supposed to be done with regard for the meaning of the language read as a whole.

The court applied the doctrine to the phrase "if contracted for in writing" and held that it modified only the new construction aspect. Likewise, all the other requirements modified only the repair aspects.

Spradlin argued that this construction removes the statutory requirements of the Property Code that sets forth the requirements for a lien on a homestead. The court disagreed. The statutory lien provisions still exist and are not repealed—only the constitutional lien is changed.

Reverse Mortgage Loans

A third constitutional amendment provides for reverse mortgages. Reverse mortgages have been available in a number of states since the mid-1970s. They work like conventional mortgages except in reverse; they pay the homeowner in regular installments (or as a line of credit one can draw down as needed) over a number of years. The loan balance of a reverse mortgage grows larger over time because the loan principal increases (as interest and other charges also accrue) each month on the total funds advanced from the mortgage company. When the homeowner leaves the home, the balance becomes due and payable, but the obligation to repay the loan is limited to the market value of the home. Effectively without recourse, the lender cannot require repayment from assets other than the home. In general, the reverse mortgage permits the borrower to retain homeownership and doesn't require repayment as long as the borrower remains in the home.

Texas law defines "reverse mortgage" as an extension of credit:

- that is secured by a voluntary lien on homestead property created by a written agreement with the consent of each owner and each owner's spouse.

- that is made to a person who is or whose spouse is 62 years or older.

- that is made without recourse for personal liability against each owner and the spouse of each owner.

- under which advances are provided to a borrower based on the equity in a borrower's homestead.

- that does not permit the lender to reduce the amount or number of advances because of an adjustment in the interest rate if periodic advances are to be made.

- that requires no payment of principal or interest until:
  o all borrowers have died.
  o the homestead property securing the loan is sold or otherwise transferred.
  o all borrowers cease occupying the homestead property for a period of longer than 12 consecutive months without prior written approval from the lender.
  o the borrower:
    - defaults on an obligation specified in the loan documents to repair and maintain, pay taxes and assessments on, or insure the homestead property.
    - commits actual fraud in connection with the loan.
    - fails to maintain the priority of the lender's lien on the homestead property, after the lender gives notice to the borrower, by promptly discharging any lien that has priority or may obtain priority over the lender's lien within 10 days after the date the borrower receives the notice, unless the borrower takes one of the following three actions: (1) He or she agrees in writing to the payment of the obligation secured by the lien in a manner acceptable to the lender; (2) He or she contests in good faith the lien by, or defends against enforcement of the lien in, legal proceedings so as to prevent the enforcement of the lien or forfeiture of any part of the homestead property; or (3) He or she secures from the holder of the lien an agreement satisfactory to the lender subordinating the lien to all amounts secured by the lender's lien on the homestead property.

- that provides that if the lender fails to make loan advances as required in the loan documents and if the lender fails to cure the default as required in the loan documents after notice from the borrower, the lender forfeits all principal and interest of the reverse mortgage, provided, however, that this subdivision does not apply when a governmental agency or instrumentality takes an assignment of the loan in order to cure the default.

- that is not made unless the owner of the homestead attests in writing that the owner received counseling regarding the advisability and availability of reverse mortgages and other financial alternatives.

- that requires the lender, at the time the loan is made, to disclose to the borrower by written notice the specific provisions contained in Subdivision (6) of this subsection under which the borrower is required to repay the loan.

- that does not permit the lender to commence foreclosure until the lender gives notice to the borrower, in the manner provided for a notice by mail related to the foreclosure of liens under Subsection (a) (6) of this section, that a ground for foreclosure exists and gives the borrower at least 30 days, or at (6) (D) (iii) of this subsection, to:
  o remedy the condition creating the ground for foreclosure.
  o pay the debt secured by the homestead property from proceeds of the sale of the homestead property by the borrower or from any other sources.
  o convey the homestead property to the lender by a deed in lieu of foreclosure.
  o that is secured by a lien that may be foreclosed upon only by a court order, if the foreclosure is for a ground other than a ground stated by Subdivision (6) (A) or (B) of this subsection.

The advances made on a reverse mortgage loan under which more than one advance is made must be made according to the terms established by the loan documents by one or more of the following methods:

- at regular intervals.

- at regular intervals in which the amounts advanced may be reduced, for one or more advances, at the request of the borrower.

- or at any time by the lender, on behalf of the borrower, if the borrower fails to pay on time any of the following that the borrower is obligated to pay under the loan documents to the extent necessary to protect the lender's interest in or the value of the homestead property:
  o taxes.
  o insurance.
  o costs of repairs and maintenance performed by a person or company that is not an employee of the lender or a person or company that directly or indirectly controls, is controlled by, or is under common control with the lender.
  o assessments levied against the homestead property.
  o any lien that has, or may obtain, priority over the lender's lien as it is established in the loan documents.

A reverse mortgage may provide for an interest rate that is fixed or adjustable and may also provide for interest that is contingent on appreciation in the fair market value of the homestead property. Although payment of principal or interest shall not be required under a reverse mortgage until the entire loan becomes due and payable, interest may accrue and be compounded during the term of the loan as provided by the reverse mortgage loan agreement.

The borrower either can receive the proceeds as a lump sum payment at closing or can arrange equal monthly payments over the loan term. It can also be a line of credit loan, discussed in Chapter 4 of the Law Update section of the book. The loan balance increases rather than decreases over the term of the loan. The term of the reverse mortgage most likely will be indefinite. The loan comes due when the borrower no longer needs that home as a residence. This generally occurs when the borrower dies, permanently moves to a health-care facility, or moves in with their children!

A reverse mortgage can also be used to buy a home. Fannie Mae's HomeKeeper for Purchase Program allows a person over the age of 62 to purchase a home financed with a reverse mortgage. The purchase requires a substantial down payment, but there are no monthly mortgage payments as long as the homeowner remains in the house. The payments are considered loan proceeds, not income, and therefore, are not taxable.

Borrowers must receive counseling on the conditions and appropriateness of the loan to their needs and situations. Whereas Texas law now allows a home equity lien to be refinanced by a reverse mortgage, the reverse mortgage cannot take the form of a line of credit.

Who Needs a Reverse Mortgage?

Most who plan on living in their present home for as long as they are able can reap significant benefits from these types of loans, which could mean the difference between a comfortable existence or living on a very tight budget. When the borrower dies, the heirs can always pay off the loan but it may result in a much smaller amount of equity being passed to one's heirs.

Although this may be an excellent estate-planning vehicle, one should always consult experts in estate planning and retirement for making this kind of a loan.

Mobile Homes

The last amendment to our homestead protection was voted into law on November 6, 2001. It added a new vendor's lien that can be incorporated into the loan documents to allow for financing on manufactured housing and mobile homes. Traditionally, when one financed mobile homes, the lien attached to the house before it became part of the real estate. Once the mobile home or manufactured home became attached to the real estate, could they get financing as purchase money mortgage? The simple answer was no. This new constitutional amendment allows that lien to become part of the real estate and a valid lien against the real estate. Another good move for homestead protection.

Bigger Urban Homestead

The 1999 Legislature, subject to approval by the voters, increased the homestead exemption in the urban environment to "not more than 10 acres." (It used to be 1 acre.) The statute now also requires that the lot(s) be contiguous (not a previous requirement).

The Legislature also attempted to define urban homestead, again, as property:

- located within the limits of a municipality or extraterritorial jurisdiction, or a plat in subdivision; and

- served by police protection, paid or volunteer fire protection, and at least three of the following services provided by a municipality or under contract to a municipality: electric; natural gas; sewer; storm sewer; and water.

Apparently it worked. The Fifth Circuit Court of Appeals in *Rush Truck Centers v. Bouchie* 324 F.3rd 780 (5th Cir. 2003), held that under the well-known canon of "inclusio unius est exclusio alterius," the legislature intentionally excluded all other factors from the rural/urban determination and, therefore, this new statute is the exclusive vehicle for distinguishing between rural and urban homesteads.

Another recent case has held that the property will be classified as urban, even if the city services were available to the property but not utilized by the homestead claimant. *Smith v. Hennington* 249 S.W. 3d 600, 604 (Tex. App.–Eastland 2008).

Judgment Liens

This remains a hot topic! Recall that we passed a new statute to address this issue (see Chapter 1). A good Texas case has given us some comfort in the fact that judgment liens do not attach to homesteads. In *Tarrant Bank v. Miller*, 833 S.W.2d 666 (Tex. App.–Eastland, 1992, writ denied), the homeowner sued for slander of title when the bank refused to honor the homeowner's request for a partial release of its lien. The bank had obtained a judgment against the homeowner that stopped the sale of the homeowner's homestead. The bank acknowledged the lien was unenforceable, but would not sign a release. The homeowner sued and recovered substantial damages for slander of title. This provides an excellent incentive for lien holders to release their judgment liens or be subject to a substantial damage claim in the event the sale of property is lost because of title problems.

A similar result was reached in the federal courts in *In re Henderson*, 18 F.3d 1305 (5th Cir., 1994), wherein the creditor argued that because the judgment lien did not attach, it could not create a cloud on title, and therefore, no liability should arise for the creditor who refuses to release the judgment against the homestead. The court held that because the defendant refused to release the lien on the plaintiffs' homestead, the title company refused to issue an owner's title policy, and the plaintiffs were unable to complete the sale of their home. The court noted that the decision in *Tarrant Bank* demonstrated that the judicial lien does impair the homestead exemption in a very real and practical sense. The court held that as a matter of federal law, the judgment lien creates a cloud on the title to the homestead, making it difficult, if not impossible, to obtain title insurance. It therefore "impairs" title to the property.

In a partial response to the *Tarrant Bank* case, the 1993 legislature provided another method of releasing judgment liens. The problem existed because if a person declared bankruptcy, his debts might be discharged, but the liens of record in the county in which the property was located would not be released except under specific circumstances defined under the Bankruptcy Code. Unfortunately, an awful lot of people who went through bankruptcy didn't realize the clouds on title weren't released and subsequently were stopped at the closing table because of these liens. We amended the Property Code in 1993, however, to provide that if an abstract of judgment or judgment lien is recorded before September 1, 1993, a judgment or judgment lien may be discharged from his debts under the Federal Bankruptcy Law. If the judgment or judgment lien is recorded on or after September 1, 1993, a judgment is discharged and the abstract of judgment or judgment lien is cancelled and released without further action in any court, and may not be enforced if the lien is against real property owned by the debtor before a petition for debtor relief was filed under Federal Bankruptcy Law and the debt or obligation evidenced by the judgment is discharged in the bankruptcy.

Does this mean automatic damages? Citing *Tarrant Bank*, the Texas Attorney General determined that a cloud on title results from two factors:

1. the recording and indexing of the abstract.

2. the lack of conclusive determination that the debtor's property is homestead.

The Attorney General opined that any judgment creditor's knowledge of the judgment debtor's homestead right does not constitute knowledge that the judgment lien is forever inapplicable to the homestead, nor does the creditor's refusal to release the potential lien created by the abstract of judgment constitute a claim that the creditor has a present lien on the homestead property. The Attorney General further suggested that a release of a judgment lien against the homestead should be expressly conditioned upon the closing of the specific contemplated sale of the property, and stating that the release shall be void in the event the judgment debtor ever again acquires an interest in the property, and that provisions on the face of the release of lien should include: (1) expressly conditioning the release; and (2) stating that the release shall be void in the event the debtor ever reacquires an interest in the property. See *Opinion No. DM-366 (1995)*. See also *Cadle Company v. Harvey*, 46 S.W.3d 282 (Tex. App.–Ft. Worth, 2001). The Fifth Circuit recently addressed the lien priority issue again in *United States v. Johnson*, 160 F.3d 1061 (5th Cir.–1998). Johnson continuously claimed his property was homestead and resided in it except during a period of incarceration for a 1989 criminal conviction. A judgment was obtained against him on December 24, 1986, and the abstract of judgment was recorded in Travis County. Johnson subsequently conveyed a one-half interest in the property (under an option to purchase) to Property Trading, Inc., on August 3, 1989. Property Trading, Inc., did not record the deed until October 28, 1992. The question in the case was whether or not that one-half interest conveyed was free and clear of the judgment lien. The judgment creditor alleged that the judgment lien attached to the undivided one-half interest conveyed to Property Trading, Inc., during the period between the conveyance and the recordation. The Fifth Circuit recited long-standing Texas homestead law, overruling one prior inconsistent Texas Court of Appeals case. Judgment liens do not normally attach to homestead property in Texas. Because the property was uncontestedly Johnson's homestead at the time he conveyed the one-half interest, Property Trading, Inc., took title free and clear of the judgment lien.

In another recent homestead case, a seller got a judgment lien against him, and his property was in excess of the homestead limit (one and one-half acres when, in 1999, the homestead limit was one acre). The court noted that the constitutional amendment expanding the homestead from one acre to ten acres in an urban environment was effective on January 1, 2000. The court noted that the lien was valid because it was filed before January 1, 2000, but that the creditor could not execute on it because the writ of execution was issued after January 1, 2000. *Wilcox v. Marriott*, 230 S.W. 3d 266 (Tex. App.-Beaumont, 2007).

New Bankruptcy Rules

The federal government recently passed new bankruptcy rules involving homestead exemptions that have a significant effect on bankruptcy protection under Texas law. When one declares bankruptcy, there is a choice of going under the federal laws or state laws. Texas laws have always been so protective that all claimants have opted for the Texas homestead protection. Some (particularly Congress) have seen this Texas Homestead Protection as unfair and overly protective, when compared to other states.

The new rules apply a federal homestead cap to a debtor claiming a homestead exemption under state laws. Under these new rules, a debtor may not exempt any interest that was acquired by the debtor during the 1,215 days preceding the date of the filing of the bankruptcy petition that exceeds the aggregate of $125,000 in value of real property that the debtor (or dependent of the debtor) claims as a homestead. 11 USC §522(p)(1). In effect, if one declares bankruptcy and has acquired a homestead within the last 1,215 days (roughly 3.3 years) the homestead claimant is limited to an exemption of only $125,000 in the homestead. It only applies to homesteads acquired, not an increase in equity in the home. *In re Blair* 334 B.R. 374 (Bankr. N.D. Tex. 2005).

The $125,000 homestead cap also applies if the court finds the debtor committed crimes involving a violation of the Federal Securities laws or any criminal act, intentional tort, or willful or reckless misconduct that causes serious physical injury or death to another individual in the preceding 5 years. 11 USC §522(q)(1)(B). This new penalty, however, does not apply if the debtor's homestead exemption is reasonably necessary for the support of the debtor or a dependent of the debtor. This seems to a spouse and children the right to full homestead protection, but there is no case law yet on how this provision will be interpreted.

Recent Homestead Cases

One of the first home equity loan cases was decided in *Rooms With a View v. Private National Mortgage Association, Inc.*, 7 S.W.3d 840 (Tex. App.–Austin, 1999, writ den.). In this case, a home remodeler was closing at the offices of a "title abstractor," although all the parties thought that it was a "title company." The lender declined to close the loan on the grounds that the abstract office is not a title company as required by Article 16 §50(a)(6) of the Texas Constitution. The contractor sued the lender, seeking a declaration that the constitutional amendment allowing for home equity loans was unconstitutional. The contractor's arguments were summarily rejected by the Appeals Court. A title company is a title company, not an abstracting company.

In another home equity case, *Tarver v. Sebring Capital Credit Corp.*, 69 S.W.3rd 708, (Tex. App.–Waco, 2002), the Court of Appeals held that discount points (commonly charged as an added compensation to the lender exchanged for a lower interest rate) are not "fees" that are to be included in the calculation of the 3 percent limitation on fees under the Texas Constitution.

In *National Union Fire Insurance Company of Pittsburgh v. Olson*, 920 S.W.2d 458 (Tex. App.–Austin, 1996), a decedent died testate survived by his adult son and a minor daughter. The minor daughter lived with her mother and had not lived with her father since her parents divorced. The decedent however, did contribute to the emotional and financial support of the minor child. The decedent's estate was insolvent and owed a large sum of money to National Union, who held two final judgments against the decedent in his estate. The homestead claimants alleged that under Texas law, the homestead passed to devisees free and clear of the creditor's claim, because the decedent had a minor child at the time of his death.

The court held that title to the homestead in an insolvent estate, where a constituent member of the family survives, descends to those entitled to inherit free and clear of claims of creditors to touch them. Determining whether the homestead property is exempt at the decedent's death turns upon whether the decedent is survived by a spouse, minor child, or an unmarried adult residing with the family.

The court further held that there is no requirement that the minor child reside with the decedent in order to be considered a constituent family member for purposes of asserting a homestead claim. The court further held that the exempt status of the homestead is not affected by a subsequent voluntary sale of the homestead property.

In re Preston, 233 B.R. 375 (Bkrtcy. E.D. Tex., 1999). TPC 41.001(a) states, "A homestead and one or more lots used for a place of burial of the dead are exempt from seizure...." Here, Preston, a single woman, claimed exemption in four burial plots valued at $2,000 each. The bankruptcy trustee objected to the exemptions.

The debtor claimed that the plain meaning of the statute was that "one or more" burial plots could be exempted. There is nothing in the statute limiting the number, although the statute before revision in 1985 limited the exemption to lots used for a single adult or family members. The court looked at the legislative intent in making the revision. Here, the legislature removed the "family" limitation from the statute because the definition of family was too restrictive and the legislature intended that an exemption be available for lots for people related to the claimant but not within the "dependency" and "support" ranges required by the court-created definition of family. Allowing exemptions for lots to benefit brothers and sisters seemed reasonable enough to the court, but expanding the statute to allow an unlimited number of exempt burial plots would be clearly contrary to the legislative intent: "The legislature had to have meant that one could claim as exempt the number of burial plots that are reasonable based on the facts and circumstances." 233 B.R. at 377.

In re Box, 340 B.R. 782 (S.D. Tex. 2005), the bankruptcy court considered a purported home equity loan that did not comply with the Texas Constitutional requirements for making such loans. Mr. Box had been a First State Bank (FSB) customer for over 15 years. The bank made several loans to Mr. Box's business and in August of 2003, Mr. Box liquidated his business to pay off his creditors. After the liquidation was complete, Mr. Box still owed FSB an unsecured debt of approximately $107,000.

FSB then approached Mr. Box about obtaining a home equity loan to secure the debt. Mr. Box reluctantly agreed. After executing a series of documents for the home equity loan containing recitals and affirmations that they "were not required to use the proceeds of the loan to repay another debt to the same lender," Mr. Box claimed he had never read the documents. The court found otherwise, and said that the intent of the parties was unambiguous and the intent of the parties was to make a home equity loan to collaterize the prior debt to FSB.

The court noted, however, that Mr. Box did not receive the funds. Instead, the proceeds of the home equity loan were applied to Box's preexisting debt to FSB. The court noted that the effect of the transaction was to collaterize the previously unsecured debt. Section §50(a)(6)(Q)(i) of the Texas Constitution states that "the owner of a homestead is not required to apply the proceeds of the extension of credit to repay another debt, except debt secured by the homestead or debt to another lender." The court held that the lender violated this constitutional requirement, notwithstanding the fact that the debtor signed various documents to the contrary. The court noted, "It is fundamental to Texas Homestead Law that an owner may not change the status of a homestead through false recitals or declarations." The court then concluded that because the lien did not meet the requirements set out in the Texas Constitution, the debt was only an unsecured extension of a credit.

In *Ortega vs. LPP Mortgage, Ltd.*, 160 S.W.3d 596 (Tex. App.–Corpus Christi 2005, writ den.), one partner and wife conveyed their homestead to a partnership to use as collateral for loan to facilitate a partnership obtaining an SBA loan. The court held that the conveyance and the lien were not valid. The Texas Constitution provides that any pretended sale of homestead involving a condition of defeasance was void and ineffective to pass legal title to the grantee. Likewise, any subsequent attempt by grantee to encumber legal title to the former homestead was ineffective to create a valid lien.

In a rather surprising result, at least one court has determined that homesteads can still be seized for violation of state drug laws. In *Lot 39, Section C, Northern Hills Subdivision, Grayson County, Texas v. The State of Texas* and cited as 85 S.W.3rd 429, (Tex. App. Eastland, 2002), the state brought a forfeiture proceeding pursuant to the Texas Code of Criminal Procedure to forfeit a parcel of real estate in Grayson County, Texas, which was the homestead of the defendant, Daniel Helm. Helm argued that the homestead exemption precluded the forfeiture of his residence.

The parties acknowledged that Helm processed methamphetamine at his house on two different occasions when search warrants were executed. Items used in the manufacture of methamphetamine were seized from within the residence. The court acknowledged that this case was one of "first impression" in Texas and there were few published opinions from Texas courts that indicate a homestead was forfeited pursuant to the Code of Criminal Procedure. The court held that it did not believe the homestead exemption could be construed to protect Helm's homestead from foreclosure in Texas, noting that the Constitution and statute indicate that the homesteads may not be seized or subjected to forced sales for the payment of the owner's debts or claims of creditors. The forfeiture of real property based upon the owners' use of the property to conduct criminal activity is not forfeiture for the payment of owners' debts and claims of creditors.

In *Norris v. Thomas*, 215 S.W.3d 851 (Tex. 2007), the Texas Supreme Court responded to an inquiry from the 5th Circuit Court of Appeals to determine whether or not a boat qualifies as a homestead under the Texas Constitution. After reviewing a long history of Texas homestead protection, the Texas Supreme Court held that the Constitution has long since been interpreted to mean that improvements to real property must include improvements to real property as contemplated by Article 16, Section 51 of the Constitution, and that there can be no homestead rights in personalty until it is annexed to the real estate, and even at that, it must be a permanent improvement.

The court analogized the situation to a house trailer, mounted on wheels and moved into the backyard of a residence. The Court noted that the house trailer was only a homestead because it was permanently attached to the real estate and set alongside the house, essentially becoming an extra room, and that house trailers without the characteristics of permanent fixture are not protected homesteads.

In this case, dock-based connections to utilities and plumbing are sufficient for a mobile home or house trailer, but the boat retains its independent, mobile character even when attached to the dock-based amenities, because of (1) its self-contained utility and plumbing systems and (2) its own propulsion. The Court further noted that the legislature is certainly free to put a proposed amendment before the Texas voters to include boats, since amending the Texas Constitution is no Sisyphean task. (Go look up Sisyphean and surprise your friends.)

Landlord and Tenant

Waiver of Implied Warranty of Fitness

Texas is the only state where the Supreme Court has provided for an implied warranty of suitability for commercial premises. The Texas Supreme Court has also held that "as Is" provisions are also enforceable. Which controls?

In *Gym-N-I Playgrounds, Inc. v. Snider*, 220 S.W.2d 905 (Tex. 2007), the case resolves a split in the lower appeals courts as to the meaning of Davidow and as to the application of the prudential doctrine on "as Is" clauses. In *Prudential Ins. Co. of Am. v. Jefferson Assocs. Ltd.*, 896 S.W.2d 156 (Tex. 1995), the Texas Supreme Court upheld the application of an "as Is" clause in a sale agreement of commercial property, holding that it demonstrated that the cause of any injury to the buyer as a consequence of defects in the premises arose due to the buyer's failure to identify the problems, rather than the seller's failure to disclose or remedy them.

The case construes the well-known holding in *Davidow v. Inwood North Professional Group-Phase I*, 747 S.W. 2d 373 (Tex. 1988). This case, based on some particularly good plaintiff's facts, concluded that commercial landlords in Texas implicitly warrant the suitability of their premises for a tenant's commercial purposes. The case involved a multi-tenant office building and a claim by a doctor occupying a relatively small portion of the building who suffered from significant structural and systems problems originating inside and outside of his leased area. The case mentioned the superior ability of a landlord to identify and remedy building problems. No court has followed Davidow, and, as the court notes here, at least four jurisdictions have rejected it expressly (Kansas, Nebraska, New Hampshire, and North Dakota).

The Davidow warranty was never as broad as the implied warranties of habitability recognized almost universally in residential leases. The court indicated that in determining whether there was a breach of the warranty, a court needed to consider: "the nature of the defect; its effect on tenant's use of the premises; the length of time the defect persisted; the age of the structure; the amount of the rent; the area in which the premises are located; whether the tenant waived the defects; and whether the defect resulted from any unusual or abnormal use by the tenant."

When the Texas Supreme Court, however, decided in Prudential that broad "as is" clauses would be recognized on freedom of contract grounds in commercial real estate sales, the stage was set for a broad reading of the lease waiver language.

The tenants in this case were long-time employees of the buildings and, in the words of the landlord, themselves "knew more about the building than anyone else." The City Code required that buildings containing combustible materials of certain kinds contain sprinkler systems, but the city inspector had not required sprinklers here, though he recommended them. Tenants were fully aware of this.

The tenants, leasing under a "hold over" clause following the end of an initial five-year term, suffered a fire that destroyed the premises. The insurer paid them for their business losses and then brought a claim against the landlord based upon various grounds, including implied warranty, and all predicated on the absence of a sprinkler system and claimed defective wiring.

But the insurers ran head on into the language of the lease dealing with waivers of warranties:

> "Tenant accepts the Premises 'as is.' Landlord has not made and does not make any representations as to the commercial suitability, physical condition, layout, footage, expenses, operation or any other matter affecting or relating to the premises and this agreement, except as herein specifically set forth or referred to and tenant hereby expressly acknowledges that no such representations have been made. Landlord makes no other warranties, express of implied, of merchantability, marketability, fitness or suitability for a particular purposes or otherwise, except as set forth herein, and implied warranties are expressly disclaimed and excluded."

The clause undoubtedly expresses the meaning that there is no implied warranty given under the lease, and does not do so in the context of transferring any repair responsibilities to the tenant. The court found the waiver enforceable, and found no implied warranty in the lease, thus resolving once and for all the enforceability of such waivers in Texas.

Misrepresentation

In *Prudential Ins. Co. of America v. Italian Cowboy Partners, Ltd.*, 2008 WL 2841848 (Tex. App. 7/24/08), the tenant was a successful and experienced restauranteur looking for a new location. The party commenced negotiations with the landlord to acquire a site in landlord's development. The negotiations continued for five months, and both sides were represented by counsel. The tenant's principals visited the site frequently.

After the lease was executed and tenant improvements commenced, the tenant's employees noticed an occasional sewage smell. The tenant complained to the landlord but completed the tenant improvements and opened for business. The landlord commenced efforts to resolve the problem of the intermittent sewage smell. Later, a guest at the restaurant informed the tenant that the prior restaurant located at that location had experienced the same problem and had never been able to correct it.

After further efforts to resolve the problem were unsuccessful, and after the landlord informed the tenant that the tenant would be responsible for any further remediation, tenant closed the restaurant, stopped paying rent, and sued for fraud, negligent misrepresentation, breach of quiet enjoyment, and constructive eviction. The landlord counterclaimed for damages. The trial court found for tenant and awarded damages in excess of $1 million, exemplary damages, and attorney's fees.

The appellate court reversed the decision.

The trial court had found that the landlord's agent, in representations endorsed by landlord, had stated as follows during negotiations:

a. The premises (although known to have been occupied by a prior restaurant) "was practically new and was problem-free."

b. No problems had been experienced with the premises by the prior tenant;

c. The building on the premises was a perfect restaurant site.

Although these might be construed as statements of opinion or "puffery," the trial court concluded that they were intended as statements of fact based upon the agent's experience in the industry and with the building.

The Court of Appeals assumed these findings were binding, but concluded that they meant nothing because the tenant, in the lease, had agreed that the landlord and the agents had not "made any representations or promises with respect to the Site, the Shopping Center or the Lease except as expressly set forth [in the lease]." The lease further contained an integration clause stating that this was the entire agreement of the parties.

Mitigation of Damages

Cole Chemical & Distributing, Inc. **v.** *Gowing*, 228 S.W.3d 684 (Tex.App.–Houston [14th Dist.] 2005, no pet.). The tenant became delinquent in his rent payments. After finding out that the tenant had moved out of its space, the landlord changed the locks on the space. There were disputes about the rent payments, and the landlord sued the tenant.

Four and a half months after the lockout, the parties reached an agreement to mitigate damages, which allowed the tenant to reoccupy the leased space for the remainder of the contract term. The landlord maintained its suit to recover unpaid rent and late fees in addition to attorneys' fees. The trial court found that the tenant had breached the lease, but awarded only the part of what the landlord claimed in damages based on its finding that the landlord had failed to make reasonable efforts to re-let the space during the lockout period and therefore failed to mitigate its damages.

Section 91.006(a) of the Property Code provides that "[a] landlord has a duty to mitigate damages if a tenant abandons the leased premises in violation of the lease." Though it is the landlord's duty to mitigate damages, the *tenant* has the burden of proving that the landlord has mitigated or failed to mitigate damages and the amount by which the landlord reduced or could have reduced its damages.

Landlord's "Agent"?

In *2616 South Loop L.L.C.* v. *Health Source Home Care, Inc.*, 201 S.W.3d 349 (Tex.App.–Hous. (14 Dist.) 2006, no pet.), the tenants leased office space in a building in Houston. Health Source contracted to lease a suite on the property through December 31, 2003, and Pinwatana contracted to lease space through January 3, 2008. Both leases identified Quad Atrium Realty as the lessor and contained provisions requiring that all notices to the lessor be sent to Quad Atrium Realty at its offices on the property. The leases were signed by D.H. Virani, who was identified in the leases as the property manager for Quad Atrium Realty. However, at the time the tenants signed their respective leases, the property was owned by Quad L.P.

South Loop later bought the property. The day after the sale, South Loop's property manager notified the Tenants that South Loop now owned the property, and informed the tenants that their "month-to-month" leases were terminated "effective immediately."

The tenants were also told they had 30 days to vacate the property unless they entered into new leases.

The primary issue involved was whether the leases, signed by Virani on Quad Atrium Realty, were validly executed.

The Statute of Conveyances requires that "a conveyance of an ... estate for more than one year, in land and tenements, must be in writing and must be subscribed and delivered by the conveyor or by the conveyor's agent authorized in writing." Property Code §5.021. Its contract law counterpart, the Statute of Frauds, requires a lease of real estate for a term longer than one year to be in writing and "signed by the person to be charged with the promise ... or by someone lawfully authorized to sign for him."

A lessor may validly lease property to another, despite the fact that the title to the property is in a third person, if the lessor lawfully possesses the property. In such a case, the lessee may enforce the lease against the lessor. But this does not necessarily mean that the lessee can enforce the lease against the property owner. Although the lessee may have had a subjective belief, in good faith, that the lessor was the owner or an agent of the owner, this is not enough to create an agency relationship between the lessor and the property owner that binds the owner to the lessor's agreement. In the absence of the owner's ratification of the lease or the lessor's actual or apparent authority to act on the owner's behalf, there is no basis on which to enforce the lease against the property owner.

Here, the tenants failed to produce any document in which Quad L.P. authorized Virani or Quad Atrium Realty to execute the leases on Quad L.P.'s behalf, arguing, instead, that it was obvious that when South Loop purchased the property, its purchase was subject to the existing leases of the property. But this contention presupposes that the leases were binding on the prior owner of the property, Quad L.P., and were conveyed to South Loop at the time of purchase. The tenants apparently presumed that Quad Atrium Realty had actual or apparent authority to execute the leases on behalf of Quad L.P. Alternatively, the tenants presumed Quad L.P. ratified the leases.

Actual authority includes both express and implied authority and usually denotes the authority a principal (1) intentionally confers upon an agent, (2) intentionally allows the agent to believe he or she possesses, or (3) by want of due care allows the agent to believe he or she possesses. Here, the tenants presented no evidence that Quad L.P. authorized Virani or Quad Atrium Realty—orally, in writing, or through a want of due care—to act as its agents. Thus, there is no support for the tenant's presumption that Quad Atrium Realty or Virani had actual authority to bind Quad L.P.

The essential elements required to establish apparent authority are (1) a reasonable belief in the agent's authority, (2) generated by some holding out or neglect of the principal, and

(3) justifiable reliance on the authority. A court may consider only the conduct of the principal leading a third party to believe that the agent has authority in determining whether an agent has apparent authority. The principal must have affirmatively held out the agent as possessing the authority or must have knowingly and voluntarily permitted the agent to act in an unauthorized manner. In this case, the tenants presented no evidence that Quad L.P. affirmatively represented that Quad Atrium Realty or Virani were its agents or that Quad L.P. knowingly and voluntarily permitted them to act in an unauthorized manner.

I guess you *really* need to confirm the identity *and* authority of the landlord!

Contract Issues

Installment Land Contracts

There was a massive change in the 2001 Legislature concerning installment land contracts. That statute expanded very tough requirements for these executory contracts, once applicable only to the colonias regions of the state, to all regions of the state. It applies only to transactions involving an executory contract for conveyance by a seller of real property used or to be used as the purchaser's residence or as a residence of a person related to a purchaser within the second degree of consanguinity or affinity.

The 2005 Legislature made additional efforts to protect consumers under these contracts for deed, while drastically limiting the causes of action against the seller under the contracts for deed created in the prior statute. This new statute provides that a purchaser under a contract for deed or other executory contract (discussed later) has the right to ask (1) any governing body approving plats whether or not a plat is required of the subject property; and (2) if it is required, whether or not it has been prepared and approved by the authority. This is an amendment to §212.0115(c) of the Local Government Code.

The prior statute imposed horrendous fees for violations. Apparently, there were attempts to get around the old executory contract (contract for deed) penalties for conveyance by utilizing leases with options to purchase. The new statute now says that an option to purchase real property that includes a residential lease agreement, or is combined or executed concurrently with a residential lease agreement, is considered an executory contract for conveyance of real property. If the term of the executory contract is 3 years or less, sections §5.063, §5.064, and §5.065 (notice for foreclosures and vendor's right to cure) apply. If a tenant exercises an option to purchase leased property under the above-described residential lease, Chapter 92 (Landlord and Tenant Relationships) no longer applies to the lease. This seems to waive any requirements to pay rent or other obligations under the landlord and tenant laws, unless the written document provides otherwise. In the executory contract, as redefined, the contract may not include a provision that forfeits an option fee or other option payment paid under the contract for late payment; or increases the purchase price, imposes a fee or charge of any type, or otherwise penalizes a purchaser leasing property with an option to buy the property for existing repairs, or in exercising any right under Chapter 92. Any provision of the executory contract that waives any of these provisions is void.

The penalties were changed dramatically. One may recall the two prior statutes, under certain conditions and time frames, provided for damages as high as $250 per day for each violation. The new statute puts the seller into two categories, one in which he does less than two transactions in a 12-month period, and one where the seller does more than two transactions in a 12-month period. If the seller does less than two transactions, and violates any of the provisions of the statute, he is liable to the purchaser for liquidated damages in the amount of $100 for each annual statement the seller fails to provide to the purchaser, and reasonable attorney's fees. If the seller conducts two or more transactions in a 12-month period, he has the existing liquidated damages in the amount of $250 a day, but not exceed the fair market value of the property.

NOW, GET THIS! A purchaser in an executory contract, at any time without paying penalties or charges of any kind, is entitled to convert the purchaser's interest in property under executory contract, into a recorded, legal title if the purchaser tends to the seller an amount of money equal to the balance of the total amount owed by the purchaser. The seller is then required to transfer to the purchaser recorded, legal title to the property.

If the purchaser delivers to the seller of property a promissory note that is equal in amount to the balance of the total amount owed by the purchaser to the seller under the contract (and the note contains the same interest rate, same due date, and same late fees) the seller is then required to execute a deed containing any warranties required by the contract and conveying to the purchaser a recorded, legal title to the property. The purchaser is then required to simultaneously execute a deed of trust that contains the same terms of the executory contract. To exercise this right, the purchaser tenders the documents to the seller on or before the tenth day after the date the seller receives a promissory note. The seller shall either deliver to the purchaser a written explanation that legally justifies why the seller refuses to convert the purchaser's interest into recorded, legal title, or communicate with the purchaser to schedule a mutually agreeable day and time to execute a deed and deed of trust. If the seller fails to do this, he is liable to the purchaser in the same manner and amount as the seller who violates section §5.079, which could be as high $250 to $500 per day. The statute goes on to provide that forms published by the Texas Real Estate Commission for this transaction constitute compliance with the statute; there are none of these forms published by the Texas Real Estate Commission!

If the property is platted improperly, the new statute gives the purchaser the right to cancel it, unless the seller promptly plats it in accordance with the Local Government Code.

The legislature also added a new provision, §5.085, which provides that a potential seller may not execute an executory contract with a potential purchaser if the seller does not own the property in fee simple, free from any liens or other encumbrances. The requirement does not apply to a lien or encumbrance that is: (1) placed on the property because of the conduct of the purchaser; (2) agreed to by the purchaser as a condition of a loan obtained to place improvements on the property; (3) placed on the property by the seller and prior to execution of the contract if the loan is used only for purchase of the property and the seller notifies the purchaser of the name, address, and phone number of the lienholder or servicer of the loan to the loan number and outstanding balance of the loan, the monthly payments due on the loan, and the due date of those payments, and a fourteen-point type notice that if the seller fails to make timely payments to the lender, the lienholder may attempt to collect the debt by foreclosing on the lien and selling the property at a foreclosure sale. The lien can attach only to the property sold to the purchaser and can never be larger than the amount of the total outstanding balance owed by the purchaser under the executory contract. The statute further requires that the lienholder cannot prohibit the property from being encumbered by an executory contract, *and* consents to verify the status of the loan on request to the purchaser and accept payments directly from the purchaser if the seller defaults on the loan. If the property is sold subject to the loan, the following provisions must be contained in the executory contract: (1) a covenant that obligates the seller to make timely payments on the loan and to give monthly statements to the purchaser reflecting the amount paid to the lienholder, the date the lienholder receives the payment, (2) a covenant that states that the seller has to notify the purchaser in writing if he ever receives a notice of default, and a third provision that says if the seller does not make timely payments, the purchaser may, without notice, curry deficiency and receive a credit of the 150 percent of any amount so paid to the lienholder. The violation of the fee, simple provisions or loan notification provisions, subjects the seller to violations of the Deceptive Trade Practices Act.

As a final note, the changes in the Property Code pursuant to executory contracts apply only to an executory contract those entered into on or after the effective date (September 1, 2005).

The statute before amendment provided that the seller is liable for a "penalty" for a seller's failure to deliver a deed after final payment. The last set of amendments changed the "penalty" to "liquidated damages" and now says that the seller is liable to the purchaser for those penalties.

Oral Earnest Money Contracts

In *Ratsavong v. Menevilay*, 176 S.W.3d 661 (Tex.App.—El Paso 2005, pet. denied), Ratsavong and Menevilay were Laotian immigrants who had known each other for a long time. Menevilay lived in California and came to visit Ratsavong and during the visit decided he wanted to move to Texas. Ratsavong said there was a house next to his and that if Menevilay was interested in buying, Ratsavong would allow him to use his credit to do so. At the time, Menevilay did not have the necessary credit to purchase a house, but it is customary in the Laotian culture for friends to lend each other their credit for the purchase of homes and vehicles; also, it was customary to not sign written contracts for such agreements. Ratsavong indicated to Menevilay that the house was being sold for $ 14,500 and that Menevilay would need to give him $2,000 down payment and that he would take care of everything else. According to Menevilay, Ratsavong entered into a contract for the purchase of the home, but the understanding was that Menevilay would make the payments and that the house was really his.

Menevilay testified that the house was not in good condition and that it needed many repairs. When he bought the house, he indicated the bathroom was not in a usable condition. Menevilay testified that he repaired the bathroom, and painted the exterior and interior of the house; he constructed a garage; he improved the sidewalk and added a concrete driveway to the garage; he replaced a door and windows; and he added a utility room for the washer and dryer. He paid for all the repairs and completed most of the work himself with the help of his wife. After a repair was completed, Ratsavong would often come over to see the improvement and stay for dinner to celebrate the accomplishment. Menevilay testified that he would talk to Ratsavong about some of the repairs because they were friends and that he did not get a building permit for any of the improvements.

In addition to making these repairs, he testified that he made the mortgage payments, and paid the insurance on the home and the property taxes for the entire time he was living at the house, up to the point where litigation over the title was considered. Once Menevilay finished paying the mortgage on the house, Ratsavong refused to transfer the deed to the Menevilay. Rather, Menevilay received a Notice to Vacate and Notice of Termination of Tenancy at Will from Ratsavong's attorney.

Among other arguments made by Ratsavong, he claimed any alleged contract with Menevilay was void because it did not comply with the Statute of Frauds. The Statute of Frauds exists to prevent fraud and perjury in certain kinds of transactions by requiring agreements to be set out in a writing signed by the parties.

The Texas Supreme Court held that "to relieve a parol sale of land from the operation of the Statute of Frauds, three things were necessary: (1) payment of the consideration, whether it be in money or services; (2) possession by the vendee; and (3) the making by the vendee of valuable and permanent improvements upon the land with the consent of the vendor; or, without such improvements, the presence of such facts as would make the transaction a fraud upon the purchaser if it were not enforced." Each of these three elements is indispensable, and they must all exist. The court reviewed the facts and determined that all three elements were satisfied.

Ratsavong also argued that Menevilay's claims were barred by the four-year statute of limitations. According to Ratsavong, the oral contract was entered into in 1994 but the lawsuit was not filed until October of 2002, not within the four-year statute of limitations for a breach of contract in Texas. Texas Civil Practice & Remedies Code § 16.051. A party asserting a breach of contract claim must sue not later than four years after the day the claim accrues. It is a well-settled law that a breach of contract claim accrues when the contract is breached or when the claimant has notice of facts sufficient to place him on notice of the breach.

Contracts and Deeds

In *Johnson v. Connor*, _____ S.W. 3d _____ (Tex. App. Tyler 2008), the Johnsons listed 40 acres of land they owned near White House in Smith County with a real estate agent, Elaine Burgess. Burgess showed the property to the Connors and later drew up a Farm and Ranch Contract on the printed form promulgated by the Texas Real Estate Commission. Under the RESERVATIONS provision, Burgess wrote, "None of the above are available to be conveyed." When the deed was prepared conveying the property, it contained language saying that all reservations and exceptions to conveyance and warranty were subject to all instruments of record. The deed went on to provide that the grantor "conveys to Grantee the property, together with all rights and appurtenances thereto, in anywise belonging, to have and to hold it to Grantee."

The Johnsons learned two years after closing that the Connors were receiving payments under an oil and gas lease and brought a suit against the Connors asking the trial court to reform the deed, because the deed did not reflect the provisions of the contract. The Johnsons argued that the sales contract stated that no minerals were to be conveyed, and thought they were signing a deed that reserved the minerals. The court decided that the history of cases support the presumption that the grantor intends to convey the tract to which he has title, and will pass all of the estate owned by the grantor at the time of the conveyance. In this case, the deed did not explicitly reserve the mineral rights.

The court held that the reservation in the contract that "none of the above are available to be conveyed" meant that the minerals were present and ready for use, on hand and accessible, which in the court's opinion was unambiguous. The court further noted:

> "The parties thus had different understandings about the mineral estate. The Johnsons believed the deed should contain a reservation clause reserving the minerals from the conveyance. The Connors believed the deed accurately reflected the status of the mineral title, since the contract only mentioned the minerals that were already reserved to record."

There was no mutual mistake, and the court upheld the summary judgment in favor of the Connors.

Was the real estate agent practicing law when she wrote in the reservation language?

Recording

Electronic Recording

The 2005 Legislature added a new Chapter 15 to the Property Code, called the Uniform Real Property Electronic Recording Act, which provides that an electronic document can be recorded in the Official Public Records of Real Property. The statute defines an electronic document as a document that is received by a county clerk in electronic form. It further defines electronic signature as an electronic sound, symbol, or process attached to or logically associated with a document, and executed or adopted by a person with the intent to sign the document.

The county clerk is authorized to receive, index, store, archive, and transmit electronic documents, as well as to provide access to, and for search and retrieval of documents and information by electronic means. They are also allowed to convert paper documents accepted for recording into electronic form and accept electronically any fee or tax that the county clerk is authorized to collect.

However, they may also continue to accept paper documents, and place entries for paper documents and electronic documents in the same index. The statute grants the authority to the Texas State Library and Archives Commission to adopt standards to implement this new statute.

While a few Texas counties are currently recording electronically, that number is certainly going to multiply over the next few years. This will provide a convenience that we can close electronically, transmit our documents to record electronically, and even pay the fee electronically. According to this statute, we would also be able to perform a limited search of documents of record, so an average person can locate and print documents from their computer.

Fair Housing

This is becoming a more difficult concept to discuss. The original Fair Housing statutes were passed to provide access to housing for all Americans. Their enforcement is now taking on a different focus to some federal agencies. They are using the Fair Housing Statutes as a sword rather than a shield, to punish rather than to protect. In addition, society has changed since the laws were initially passed in 1968. There is some indication that the pendulum may be swinging somewhat, as many appeals courts are beginning to encounter lawsuits that are somewhat abusive in an attempt to enforce Fair Housing laws.

The Fair Housing legislation is still the same, and is still very important. One cannot discriminate on the basis of race, color, creed, national origin, sex, familial status, and handicap status. Remember, the objective is to see that all Americans have the same right to housing. A real estate licensee is enabling that access and is critically important.

Marital Status

In *McCready v. Hoffius*, 593 N.W.2d 545 (Mich., 1999) vacating in part 586 N.W.2d 723 (Mich., 1998), defendants, a married couple, owned a residential property that they refused to rent to plaintiffs, two couples each consisting of an unmarried man and woman. Plaintiffs filed two separate actions in Circuit Court.

The Supreme Court stated that the question before it was whether the state's interest in providing equal access to housing to all regardless of their membership in prescribed categories supersedes defendants' religious rights. The court determined that the issue was complicated by the existence of an antiquated and rarely enforced statute prohibiting lewd and lascivious behavior. Let's think for a while: How does a sex change operation affect this? Can two men live together, but not a man and a woman? Hmm...

The court determined that the landlord's refusal to rent to the prospective tenants because their marital status was single was a discriminatory act. The court rejected the landlord's argument that they did not discriminate against plaintiffs because of their marital status, but rather refused to rent to them on the basis of their conduct. The court also stated that by protecting the prospective tenants' rights, it was not legitimizing criminal behavior. The statute prohibiting lewd and lascivious behavior does not prohibit cohabitation *per se*, and in this case, there was insufficient evidence that the prospective tenants intended to engage in lewd and lascivious behavior. Let's think for a while: How does a sex change operation affect this? Can two men live together, but not a man and a woman? Hmm.

Brokers: Duty to Disclose Diversity

In *Hannah v. Sibcy Cline Realtors*, 769 N.E.2d 403 (Ohio Ct. Ap. 2001), the court was asked to determine whether a real estate agent or a broker has the fiduciary duty to: (1) inform a client whether a neighborhood or community is ethically diverse, or (2) direct the client to sources to provide ethnic diversity information. The Hannahs had three school-age sons and were considering moving their family from Virginia to Cincinnati, Ohio. They contacted Sibcy Cline, a real estate brokerage company, explaining that they wanted a five-bedroom house in move-in condition and further specified that the house be located in an excellent school district in an ethnically diverse neighborhood. The broker sent the Hannahs a relocation packet that contained a guidebook, a map, and general brochures. While looking at prospective homes, the Hannahs constantly asked the broker if the areas in which the houses were located were ethnically diverse. The broker told them that she could not give them that information. However, she did imply that a neighborhood was diverse by stating that it "fit the Hannahs' criteria." The Hannahs asked where they could get information concerning ethnic diversity in schools and communities and asked what organization existed that Mrs. Hannah could contact regarding ethnically diverse neighborhoods. The Hannahs never received the requested information from the broker. The Hannahs contacted six schools using the telephone numbers supplied by the guidebooks received from the broker and asked the person contacted whether the school was racially diverse, stating that Mrs. Hannah did not want her child to be the only African-American in his class. Mrs. Hannah had also contacted a children's advocacy group in local N.A.A.C.P. and the Urban League, but did not receive any information about ethnic diversity. The Hannahs ultimately signed a contract in Milford. Mrs. Hannah contacted the principal at the school, who told her the school was ethnically diverse. The Hannahs moved into the neighborhood; they were "uncomfortable," and one of her sons was the only African-American child in the fourth grade. All three of her sons were called derogatory names and were taunted and hit at school and on the bus on a regular basis.

The broker had confirmed that she told the Hannahs she was precluded from disclosing racial diversity information concerning neighborhoods. She further stated that she directed Mrs. Hannah to the schools for information and provided the family with a copy of the *Cincinnati Magazine* School Guide, which contained diversity statistics regarding schools, with the relocation packet she sent them.

The trial court ruled that the Hannahs had failed to demonstrate that there was a duty for a real estate agent to inform the client whether a neighborhood was ethnically diverse or to direct the client to resources concerning this information. The Hannahs appealed. The Appeals Court noted that a real estate agent was normally instructed not to discuss the racial composition or diversity of an area. The reason for this cautious attitude is that such comments could be misconstrued so as to result in claims that an agent had violated the Fair Housing Act. The court noted that:

> Nowhere have we found that an agent or broker has the fiduciary duty to disclose such information. In fact, our reading has convinced us that, in order to avoid claims of unlawful steering in violation of the Fair Housing Act, it would not be in the best interests of an agent or broker to do so.

The court further noted that:

> Imposing a duty on real estate agents or brokers to give information about the ethnic makeup of a neighborhood, even for benign purposes such as those here, would prove detrimental to the goal of fair housing.

In its conclusion, the court noted that it was a court of law and its ability was limited to correcting legal wrongs, not social wrongs.

Fair Housing: Liability for Officers and Shareholders?

In *Holley v. Meyer*, 04 C.D.O.S. 9533, No 99-56611 (9th Cir. 10/26/04), 386 F.3d 1248 (2004), the case originated in a claim by a biracial couple and a builder that a real estate agent working for Triad Realty committed violations of the Federal Fair Housing Act in refusing to submit the buyers' offer to the builder for racially discriminatory reasons. Triad was owned by Meyer, who was also the designated supervising broker (known in Californiaspeak as the "designated officer") for the agency.

In *Meyer v. Holley*, 537 U.S. 280 (2003), the Supreme Court reversed and vacated a prior Ninth Circuit decision in this case and held, contrary to the Ninth Circuit's view, that liability would not lie against the owner/broker for the agent's actions on the basis that the duty to obey laws relating to racial discrimination under the FHA is nondelegable. The Supreme Court also found that Meyer could not be held liable as the designated officer/broker of Triad based solely on his duty to control the agent. The Supreme Court remanded, however, for further discussion of issues of California law relating to vicarious liability and (in the eyes of the Ninth Circuit at least) other liability theories. The Ninth Circuit here serves up a whole passel of such additional theories and remands for further proceedings at the District Court level to evaluate the facts relating to such theories.

With a little fancy footwork, the Ninth Circuit panel first determined that the plaintiffs preserved the claim that Meyer was liable under traditional state law vicarious liability theories even though they had pressed their original appeal based upon HUD regulations.

The court then held that certain special facts pertaining to Meyer's relationship to the agent in question raised significant issues of fact as to whether Meyer had delegated his duty to supervise agents in the office to the offending sales associate (who was in fact a senior sales associate in the office). This special theory of delegation arose because Meyer had not been personally present at the office on a regular basis, because he had elected to pursue other business ventures, and in fact, Meyer was anticipating that the agent in question would soon get a broker's license and undertake supervision of the office and ownership of Triad. In the interim, although Meyer was not present at the office, it worked pursuant to Meyer's license. The court noted that California law requires that an individual brokerage licensee have personal supervisory responsibility over sale associates, and that the corporation, even though licensed, cannot itself have that responsibility. As the offending agent was supervising the sales activities of another junior agent when the acts of discrimination occurred, the FHA violation was within the scope of the delegation, and Meyer therefore was liable under traditional agency principles.

The other two bases that the court posited for Meyer's liability for the acts of the offending sales associate are more generally applicable. First, the court recognized that liability might lie on the basis of negligent supervision. (Such a claim doesn't quite fit within the notion of "vicarious liability," but rather would appear to be a separate and independent tort. The court again uses fancy footwork in holding that the claim was preserved on appeal, although apparently not argued. But it also refers to the theory as one of "vicarious liability.") Certainly, if Meyer in fact had a duty to supervise and was not supervising while he was pursuing other business and leaving the office unsupervised by a properly licensed broker, this would appear to be a viable claim.

The third theory of liability posited by the court is the notion that Meyer would be liable for the acts of Triad's employees because he was the owner of Triad. Although Triad was a corporation, which would preclude individual liability, the court suggests that California law would recognize certain factors in this case that would support "piercing the corporate veil" to justify disregarding the employer's corporate status and impose liability directly on the corporate owner.

Here, the court states, the allegations in the complaint suggested that Meyer had "wide-ranging control" of Triad as its owner, president, and designated officer/supervising broker. The court further notes that Meyer did not always punctiliously observe corporate niceties. For instance, Meyer paid Triad's taxes pursuant to his own tax ID number instead of under Triad's. Furthermore, the corporation was thinly capitalized. That was enough for the court to remand for a determination on the issue of "piercing the corporate veil" and sticking Meyer with liability for all sales associate acts in violation of the Fair Housing Act. One problem for the plaintiffs on this theory is that, at the time of the FHA violations, Meyer may already have transferred ownership of Triad to the sale associate he was grooming to take over.

Child Predators

In *Doe v. Miller*, 405 F. 3d 700 (8th Cir. 2005), the court represents that this is a case of first impression in U.S. courts.

In 2002, in an effort to protect children in Iowa from the risk that convicted sex offenders may reoffend in locations close to their residences, the Iowa General Assembly passed, and the Governor of Iowa signed, a bill that prohibits a person convicted of certain sex offenses involving minors from residing within 2,000 feet of a school or a registered child care facility. The district court declared the statute unconstitutional on several grounds and enjoined the Attorney General of Iowa and the county attorneys in Iowa from enforcing the prohibition.

On appeal, the Eighth Circuit Court of Appeals panel reversed. The court ruled unanimously that the residency restriction is not unconstitutional on its face.

The statute defines "sex offender" to include only persons found guilty of sexual crimes involving minors. The statute was promptly challenged in a class action brought by persons affected by the statute for themselves, other similarly situated, and other convicted sex offenders who might plan to move to Iowa. In reaching its decision that the statute was unconstitutional, the trial court reviewed maps and heard testimony from a county attorney, and found that the restricted areas in many cities encompass the majority of the available housing in the city, thus leaving only limited areas within city limits available for sex offenders to establish a residence. In smaller towns, a single school or child care facility can cause all of the incorporated areas of the town to be off limits to sex offenders. The court found that unincorporated areas, small towns with no school or child care facility, and rural areas remained unrestricted, but that available housing in these areas is "not necessarily readily available."

The appellate court, reversing the district court, stated, more or less, that the fact that a person could find few places to reside in Iowa didn't mean that a person could not travel there:

> The Iowa statute imposes no obstacle to a sex offender's entry into Iowa, and it does not erect an "actual barrier to interstate movement."... There is "free ingress and regress to and from" Iowa for sex offenders, and the statute thus does not "directly impair the exercise of the right to free interstate movement." Nor does the Iowa statute violate principles of equality by treating nonresidents who visit Iowa any differently than current residents, or by discriminating against citizens of other States who wish to establish residence in Iowa. We think that to recognize a fundamental right to interstate travel in a situation that does not involve any of these circumstances would extend the doctrine beyond the Supreme Court's pronouncements in this area. That the statute may deter some out-of-state residents from traveling to Iowa because the prospects for a convenient and affordable residence are less promising than elsewhere does not implicate a fundamental right recognized by the Court's right to travel jurisprudence."

> The Iowa residency restriction does not prevent a sex offender from entering or leaving any part of the State, including areas within 2,000 feet of a school or child care facility, and it does not erect any actual barrier to intrastate movement. . . . The Does also urge that we recognize a fundamental right 'to live where you want.' This ambitious articulation of a proposed unenumerated right calls to mind the Supreme Court's caution that we should proceed with restraint in the area of substantive due process, because '[b]y extending constitutional protection to an asserted right or liberty interest, we, to a great extent, place the matter outside the arena of public debate and legislative action.'

Although the court acknowledged that there was some evidence that the statute would present a severe restriction on living accommodations for some individuals, the court concluded that the state's only burden was to show that this restriction was rationally consistent with the civil purpose of the enactment. The court cited evidence in the record that convicted sex offenders generally are not fully deterred by punishment and cannot be cured. Consequently, it was rationale for the state to protect its children by separating them as a class from places where children congregated.

Two dissenting judges concluded that the statute swept too broadly, and imposed a "banishment" result on persons who did not present the high level of threat to children that the statute was designed to address:

> There is no doubt a class of offenders that is at risk to reoffend and for whom such a restriction is reasonable. However, the restriction also applies to John Doe II, who pleaded guilty to third-degree sexual abuse for having consensual sex with a 15-year-old girl when he was 20 years old. The restriction applies to John Doe VII, who was convicted of statutory rape under Kansas law. His actions that gave rise to this conviction would not have been criminal in Iowa. The restriction applies also to John Doe XIV, who pleaded guilty to a serious misdemeanor charge in 1995 after he exposed himself at a party at which a 13-year-old girl was present. John Doe XIV was 19 at the time of his offense. The actions of these and other plaintiffs are serious, and, at least in most cases, illegal in this state. However, the severity of residency restriction, the fact that it is applied to all offenders identically, and the fact that it will be enforced for the rest of the offenders' lives, makes the residency restriction excessive.

Residential Lead-Based Paint Hazard Reduction Act of 1992

The final rule has been issued from the Environmental Protection Agency concerning lead-based paint disclosures. To facilitate compliance with the federal rules, the Texas Real Estate Broker-Lawyer Committee has developed a contract addendum for use with TREC-promulgated contract forms.

Newly enacted penalties can be severe. The EPA issued a guidance document clarifying its enforcement policy for violations of federal disclosure requirements in January 1998. Under this policy, EPA establishes a procedure to issue a first-time violator a Notice of Noncompliance ("NON"), in lieu of a civil penalty, unless the violation is considered egregious (a child or pregnant woman "put at risk").

The penalties are set up in two stages: the Gravity-Based stage and the Adjustment stage. The Gravity-Based Penalty stage can reach an upper limit of $11,000 per violation. The Adjustment stage adjusts the Gravity-Based Penalty stage up or down, based on various factors (the violator's ability to pay, history of prior violations, degree of culpability, and whether or not the violator qualifies as a "small business").

Each requirement of the disclosure is separate from the others and penalties will be assessed on each violation; therefore, a landlord with ten apartments who fails to distribute a pamphlet and also fails to disclose lead-based paint could be liable for twenty violations, each carrying a potential $11,000 penalty!

INTERESTING NOTE! A housing group calling itself the National Multi-Housing Council is dedicating a portion of its legislative agenda to fight new proposals concerning lead-based paint, apparently contending that little, if any, good has come from the laws already on the books. The organization noted that the problem of childhood lead poisoning was well on its way out long before the disclosures were mandated in 1996. According to the Centers for Disease Control and Prevention, the presence of elevated lead levels in the general population decreased 94 percent between 1988 and 1994. The incidence of lead poisoning has dropped even more dramatically, with just 0.4 percent of young children reported as having lead poisoning.

What caused the lead poisoning to drop? The organization notes that the decline in blood levels through the 1990s was the result of eliminating lead from most gasoline products, lead solder from food and beverage cans and water supply pipes, and limits on the emission of lead from industrial facilities. The organization notes, "Regulations on housing providers embody a costly and cumbersome regulatory approach that increases the cost of and threatens the supply of affordable housing and has little impact on the overall incidence of childhood lead poisoning" (*Real Estate Intelligence Report*, Spring 2000).

Lead-Based Paint Disclosure (RLPHRA)—Actual Damages

In *McCready v. Main Street Trust, Inc.* (2008), the case involved a dispute in regard to McCready's purchase of a two-story building constructed in the late 1800s, which was being used as office space. Plaintiffs' son used the property as both office space and living quarters after the sale.

McCready alleged violation of the Residential Lead-Based Paint Hazard Reduction Act ("RLPHRA") due to defendants' failure to provide a lead-based paint disclosure at any time prior to or following the sale of the property. Defendants admitted that a disclosure was not provided, reasoning that because the property was listed as commercial real estate, the RLPHRA did not require such a disclosure.

The Plaintiffs admitted that no lead-based paint had actually been discovered on the premises and that they had not had an inspection done to determine whether or not lead-based paint existed on the premises. As such, plaintiffs did not incur any expenses in lead-based paint removal or cleanup.

However, plaintiffs pursued a claim under the RLPHRA enjoining the defendants to deliver all required disclosures and seeking damages to compensate for any costs that may be incurred in the abatement of lead-based paint hazards, as well as costs and attorney fees. Plaintiffs also argued that until the defendants provided them with the required disclosures, they were not obligated to purchase under the real estate contract executed five years earlier.

The court granted a summary judgment for defendants, finding that plaintiffs' arguments lacked merit. Under the RLPHRA, nondisclosure itself does not affect the validity of a contract for sale [42 U.S.C. Sect. 4852(c)]. Therefore, the contract cannot be void for failure to make necessary disclosures.

In addressing the damages claim, the court stated that the RLPHRA allows a private plaintiff to recover compensatory damages for costs actually incurred by a plaintiff. In this case a damage recovery was not available because plaintiffs had not incurred any expenses. They had not made an effort to discover or remedy conditions of lead-based paint on the property. As such, plaintiffs were not a "prevailing party," and were therefore not entitled to costs associated with the litigation.

Mold Development?!

A study by the Institute of Medicine (an entity of the National Academy of Sciences, which is chartered by Congress) has concluded that mold does not cause cancer, fatigue, gastrointestinal problems, or neurological disorders, as many had believed in the past. The Institute of Medicine study found that there are many factors in indoor environments that can intermingle to produce allergic reactions, but that the mold alone cannot be held responsible for causing such severe illnesses. Note report dated June 1, 2004, in www.GlobeSt.com.

New Foreclosure Procedures

The 2007 Legislature created the following new foreclosure procedures:

> If the courthouse or county clerk's office is closed because of inclement weather, natural disaster, or other acts of God, the foreclosure notice to be posted at the courthouse may be posted or filed up to 48 hours after the courthouse or county

clerk's office reopens for business. If the foreclosure sale is going to be held at some place other than the courthouse (within a reasonable proximity of the county courthouse), a sale may not be held at that location before the 90th day after the designation of the new location is recorded in the real property records.

The new law also provides that a trustee may not be held to the obligations of the fiduciary of the mortgagor or mortgagee. This is nothing new, case law has held this for some time, but it is now a new statute (see Section 51.0074 of the Texas Property Code).

There are also new procedures during the bidding process. The purchase price in a sale held by the trustee or substitute trustee is payable immediately upon acceptance of the bid by the trustee or substitute trustee.

Under prior court decisions, one could bid at the sale, and the trustee had to give the bidder 30 to 45 minutes to go get the cash (or cashier's check) and bring it to the trustee. This new procedure seems to indicate that the proceeds must be paid during the bidding process, and there will not be any excused delay for getting the funds.

Title Insurance

Closing Attorney's - Referral Fees

An exception has always existed in the Insurance Code for attorneys (usually in small counties) who examine titles or close transactions on behalf of a title company. They are commonly referred to as "approved attorneys" or "fee attorneys", and they would receive a portion of the premium for performing this function for the title companies, usually around forty percent of the premium. Today, some attorneys in larger metropolitan areas want to be a fee attorney so that they, too, can get a portion of the premium. The Texas Department of Insurance has recently published a commissioner's bulletin discussing these issues and classified these attorneys into two different categories. The first, described as "fee attorneys," includes attorneys who are licensed to act as escrow officers and close in the name of a title insurance company, or title agent pursuant to the Texas Insurance Code. The second, known variously by title practitioners as "outside closing attorneys," "approved attorneys" and "P-22 attorneys," includes attorneys who do not have a license to act as an escrow officer, and who close the transaction in the name of the law firm.

The first category of attorneys clearly comes under the Texas Department of Insurance rules and must comply with all the provisions of the Texas Insurance Code and related regulations promulgated by the Texas Department of Insurance; the second category, however, does not, as they are handling on behalf of the law firm rather than an insurance company. Not only do they not have to follow all the regulations, but they also can't perform a number of services which title insurance companies are allowed to perform because these attorneys are not regulated by the Department of Insurance.

Many consumers and real estate professionals do not understand the difference between these two categories. What is more discomforting is that these attorneys may be representing a party to the transaction as well as being the escrow officer, which creates a high potential for conflicts of interest.

This brings up another referral fee question, however. If a title company has escrow officers, why would they employ a closing attorney to close a transaction for them? Is it merely a referral fee to get the business? Referral fees are prohibited under the Insurance Code. The Texas Department of Insurance is currently looking into these issues with much greater scrutiny, as this practice has continued to expand into metropolitan areas of Texas.

The New EPA "All Appropriate Inquiry" Rule

In 2002, the Brownfields Revitalization and Environmental Restoration Act ("Brownfields Act") provided innocent landowner defense to CERCLA by defining the due diligence criteria that must be satisfied to provide an innocent landowner defense to CERCLA liability. The rule defining exactly what constitutes due diligence criteria was "all appropriate inquiries." Permanent standards were not published in November 2005 and became effective on **November 1, 2006**.

All appropriate inquiries as defined under CERCLA Section 105(35)(B) must include the results of an inquiry conducted by an environmental professional within **one year prior** to the date of the acquisition of the subject property, which takes into account the following items:

1. interviews with past and present owners, operators, and occupants.
2. evaluations of historical sources of information.
3. searches for recorded environmental cleanup liens.
4. reviews of federal, tribal, state, and local government records.
5. visual inspections of the facility and of adjoining properties.
6. the degree of the obviousness of the contamination and the ability to detect the contamination by appropriate investigation.
7. commonly known or reasonably ascertainable information about the property.

Items 1, 3, 4, and 5 must be updated within the **180 days of and prior to the date** of acquisition of the property, and must also include a declaration made by an environmental professional.

New rules specifically require the hiring of an environmental professional, defined as a person who meets specific education and experience requirements necessary to render a professional judgment. The environmental professional must develop opinions and conclusions about releases or threatened releases of hazardous substances concerning the subject property sufficient to satisfy certain objective and performance standards. Their inquiry should seek to reveal present and historical uses of the hazardous substances at the subject property and neighboring and adjoining properties, potentially harmful waste management and disposal practices, the presence of engineering and institutional controls, and current and past corrective actions and response actions and response activities undertaken to address past and ongoing releases of hazardous substances. They must also inquire as to the past uses of the subject property and past corrective actions associated with petroleum and petroleum products. How far back must they search? The environmental professional is entitled to rely on professional judgment as to how far back in time it is necessary to search these historical records to trace past uses of the property.

As the inquiry relates to federal, state, tribal, and local government records, the review includes searching for records in databases pertaining to nearby and adjoining properties as well as records concerning the subject property. There is no distance from the boundary that is specified by the rules, and may be modified and the judgment of the environmental professional to accounts for such factors as development and geological conditions. For commercial real estate brokers, this is a significant change. In many cases, there were pending sales that had to have second environmental inquiries because the contract wasn't closed by November 1, 2006, therefore a new inquiry had to be maintained after November 1, 2006, to comply with the new rules.

There's an interesting question: What if the adjoining land owners won't allow inquiries? In these situations, the environmental professional may inspect the property by other means, including aerial imagery.

It reminds me of the environmental professional who was pulled from the tree. He suffered severe damage because wood particles were wedged into his body as a result of the extrication. He went to the hospital for treatment, and the surgeon responded that he couldn't remove natural forestry products from sensitive locations without EPA approval, and therefore couldn't help.

Mortgage Fraud

There is hardly a more pervasive problem in lending today than of mortgage fraud. It almost always involves a conspiracy between a loan originator and an appraiser. Additional conspirators can include a buyer's broker (it can also be the mortgage broker), a title company, and the seller's real estate agent. An additional conspirator could be the purchaser of the loan in the secondary market who is encouraging loan originators to make loans as fast as possible so they can be sold to investors in the secondary market. Many of these loans are sold with very little due diligence as to the quality of the borrower or credit scores. Let's talk about the potential fact situations.

The Fact Situations

While not illegal on their face, "flip" closings have been blamed for a number of mortgage fraud transactions in which the title company was allegedly complicit, resulting in fines in the millions of dollars against various underwriters throughout the United States levied both by the Department of Housing and Urban Development and by the States' Department of Insurance. One cannot be too careful to note the "red flags," which can turn a seemingly simple transaction into active mortgage fraud against a lender:

The "Flip"

In a "flip" transaction, it is usually the use of a straw man established in the middle of the transaction. For instance, in an A to B to C transaction, B would be a mere nominee (phony company) who is buying at a low price from a legitimate seller, but selling it at a much higher price to a buyer, either legitimate or another straw man. The fraud involved is a phony appraisal that reflects property value much higher than its real sales price, and a loan application to a lender loaning far more than what the property is worth. The problem is that the sale from B to C has to close before the sale from A to B so that funds are available to pay A. For instance, if it is a $400,000 initial sales price, and a $600,000 conveyance from B to C, the lender has to fund on the $600,000 in order to get to $400,000 to pay A. The straw man (B) nets the $200,000. Under most computer programs the transaction is caught because you can't close the second transaction until the first transaction is closed (B is not in title yet). In an effort to appease the greed, however, the escrow officer may override the program or use no program at all (filling out the closing documents by hand). In this case, it's difficult to defend if a lender discovers the fraud. The escrow officer has to step out of standard office procedure in order to complete the transactions. If the A to B transaction closes at one title company, and the B to C transaction closes at another, it may be easier to juggle the timing, but the "conspiracy" net grows!

The Old Switch

In this mortgage fraud, the buyer and seller agree to change the sales price in the contract and the seller kicks money back to the buyer at the closing. In this scenario, the house is sold for $400,000 and appraised for $600,000; the buyer then returns to the seller and asks that they increase the sales price to $600,000 so he can get the higher loan and pocket the difference. The seller then has to agree to kick back the excess proceeds to the buyer either in cash or through a "soft second lien," which will never be repaid. Once again, we have a lender making a loan for more than the property is worth, putting money in the buyer's pocket and destroying the loan-to-value ratio that the lender had anticipated. The problem with this scenario is that the seller is happy to do it and the real estate broker too is happy to do it, because the seller ultimately gets his agreed sales price and doesn't care that the buyer profits in the transaction. In addition to this, the seller and the broker make their sale! The buyer never makes one mortgage payment and moves on to his next transaction.

The Contractor's Scheme

In this scenario, the buyer is supposedly going to do a substantial amount of improvements to the property; he gets a bid from a contractor (a straw company) and then pays that contractor at closing… who turns out to be the buyer. Using the same example, it's a $400,000 purchase, a $200,000 home improvement and the loan is based on the inflated $600,000. There is no construction loan! The deal is closed and funded, the contractor turns out to be a front for the buyer, and no improvements are ever made. Again, the buyer never makes one mortgage payment, puts the money in his pocket, and moves on to the next transaction.

The Ultimate Lie

In this scenario, there is a borrower who simply lies to the lender. At the closing, the lender provides his loan application that may include income tax returns, W-2s, paycheck stubs, and a number of other back-up documents for the borrower's application. The problem is when the loan application information (submitted by the borrower earlier in the loan application process) turns out to be completely false, and if the title company doesn't properly check picture identifications, or confirm signatures of the applicant and their spouse. It could be aiding and abetting the fraudulent loan application process.

The Innocent "Investor"

A smart mortgage broker encourages uninformed, first-time investors to invest in a home. He will set up the mortgage plan; he will get them a good price (often buying homes in bulk from a builder with a low sales volume) and help the new investor "get rich quick" by investing in real estate. Many of these investors are foreign and easily duped by a glib-tongued mortgage broker who is licensed by the state and can apparently be trusted. The broker even pays buyer $1,000.00, then sets up a "flip" transaction where the broker takes the money out of the middle, and sets up a loan for the new investor who can't really afford to make the monthly payments. He often promises to lease the property and manage it for the investor in order to make it an easy closing. After closing, when no tenants are obtained, the buyer determines that the loan broker made a significant amount of money on the transaction, and the investor can't afford to make the monthly payments when no tenant can be found. The investor has been duped, but is personally liable for a significant mortgage loan.

"Trust Me"

In this scam, elderly or uninformed homeowners may be facing a foreclosure and, once again, are desperate for relief. In this fraud, the investor requests that the homeowner place the land in a trust with the investor (or investor's lackey) as a trustee, which gives them complete control over the ownership of the property. The owner may maintain a "beneficial" interest, or they may assign their beneficial interest to another investor in the trust. In almost every case, an investor third then takes complete control of the property, and the homeowner is not really aware of the impact of signing these odd-looking documents. In the homeowner's mind, it has not triggered the "due on transfer" clause of their mortgage, and they trust the smooth-talking investor. After the homeowner can no longer pay the investor, keep up their lease payments, or whatever their relationship happens to be, the investor simply informs the homeowner that they no longer own the property and he is free to resell it at a profit, although he is happy to inform them that he has "saved their credit."

Believe it or not, there are seminars that teach people how to do this scam. Similar to the "Flip" scam, the entire transaction may be technically legal, with paperwork in apple pie order, but the homeowner is duped with a wink and a nod.

Who's Liable?

The fraud is typically uncovered when the buyer refuses to make any payments (or doesn't make one payment!) and the lender pursues foreclosure. If the lender is an investor, he may look to the loan originator as the fraudulent party for selling him a loan that the loan originator knew was a bad (or maybe non-existent) applicant. There is usually a pattern to these fraudulent transactions, and they can almost always be tied to a loan originator working in concert with an appraiser. The appraiser, however, only gives an opinion of value and therefore it is hard to find liability with the appraiser, provided his opinion can be justified.

The real estate brokers may have some potential liability, particularly if the buyer's representative is also the loan broker. This tends to lead to conflicts of interest wherein a real estate broker loses as a sale (and his share of the commission) if the buyer does not qualify for the loan. In situations where there is excess money being funded back to the buyer at the closing, there is a concern that both buyer's broker and the seller's broker may have some liability if they "turn a blind eye" to an obvious fraud being committed on the lender because of over-inflated appraisals, suggested contract prices, or false debtor information. By the way, these issues are being criminally prosecuted as well as civilly prosecuted in the courts today.

The title company seems to be in the middle of everything! While the title company tends to be a disinterested third party, they are present when the closing takes place, and when the instructions from the lender are tendered and the parties sign the documents. Remember though that as a disinterested third party they cannot take sides in representing one party against another and courts have held that the traditionally fiduciary escrow duties are somewhat limited to the instructions of the parties because the title company necessarily serves two conflicting parties. One bad case has arisen, however, *Home Loan Corporation v. Texas American Title Company*, 191 S.W.3d 728 (Tex. App. -Houston [14th Dist.], writ applied for) wherein the Court held that the title company was a fiduciary to all parties of the transaction and had a 100 percent duty of disclosure to all parties of the transaction. While this case seems to be very troublesome, and is currently on appeal to the Supreme Court, it may have a significant on how title companies handle escrows in the future.

Note the following list of "Red Flags":

- Investors making offers of significantly above asking price, particularly on property that has been on the market for a long time.

- Investor/buyer/mortgage officers telling buyers that they can acquire appraisals in excess of the sales price.

- Investors claiming property as their primary principal residence, which is to be owner occupied.

- Investors and/or sellers receiving excess sales proceeds after acquiring the property.

- Use of for-sale-by-owner transactions to circumvent the use of real estate professionals.

- Use of inexperienced or unsupervised licensees.

- Undisclosed concessions at the closing table.

- Not knowing the source or actual amount of the buyer's down payment, inflated appraisals, false information about the borrower's credit, and undisclosed rebates to an unknown third party.

- Secret second mortgages, earnest money deposits paid outside of closing.

- Double contracting," closing the sale on one tract while closing the loan on the second, higher priced contract.

When any of the foregoing become apparent, the advice is easy: get out of the transaction. If you are an escrow officer, don't close the transaction. While one may forego a commission or a title insurance premium, it is a lot cheaper than what may be a cost of defense at a later date.

Closings can be complicated. Buyers, sellers, and even real estate agents often misunderstand how many issues are handled at closing. Good escrow officers require a lot of communication skills, accounting skills, and ability to stay cool in a frequently difficult environment where buyers and sellers don't know each other. The lender or agent may be forcing some issues. Then there are the title problems! It is not a business for sissies.

Texas Deceptive Trade Practices Act:
Nothing New, Just to Refresh You. It's Still the Law!

At one time, virtually every lawsuit brought against a real estate broker in Texas included some cause of action under the Texas Deceptive Trade Practices Act. Tort reform has helped to change this a little.

Any consumer can maintain a deceptive trade practices action for one of the following violations designated in Section 17.50 if it is a **producing cause** of damages:

- the use or employment by any person of a false, misleading, or deceptive act or practice that is specifically enumerated in the subdivision of Subsection (b) of Section 17.46 of this subchapter (certain of these specific provisions will be discussed later).

- breach of an express or implied warranty.

- any unconscionable action or course of action by any person.

- the use or employment by any person of an act or practice in violation of Article 21.21, Texas Insurance Code, as amended.

A producing cause requires proof of: (1) actual causation and fact, (2) the fact that but for the defendant's conduct the plaintiff's injury would not have occurred, and (3) the act or omission being a substantial factor in bringing about injury, and thus, liability should be imposed. The plaintiff only has to show producing cause and does not have to show that the harm was foreseeable. Section 17.50 was amended in 1995 to provide for "**economic**" damages rather than "actual" damages, or damages for mental anguish. The amount of economic damages is found by the trier of fact (jury, or judge, if there is no jury). If the trier of fact finds that the conduct of the defendant was committed "**knowingly,**" the consumer may also recover damages for mental anguish, as found by the trier of fact, and the trier of fact may award not more than three times the amount of economic damages; or if the trier of fact finds the conduct was committed "**intentionally,**" the consumer may recover damages for mental anguish, as found by the trier of fact, and the trier of fact may award not more than three times the amount of damages for mental anguish and economic damages.

"Intentionally" is actual awareness, or flagrant disregard of prudent and fair business practices.

"Economic damages" means compensatory damages for pecuniary loss, including costs of repair and replacement. The term does not include exemplary damages or damages for physical pain and mental anguish, loss of consortium, disfigurement, physical impairment, or loss of companionship and society.

"Knowingly" means actual awareness of a falsity, deception, or unfairness of an act or practice giving rise to the consumer's claim or, in an action brought under a breach of an express or implied warranty as provided in Section 17.50, actual awareness of the act or practice constituting the breach of warranty, but actual awareness may be inferred where objective manifestations indicate the person acted with actual awareness.

These new amendments are part of our new tort reform, limiting the overwhelming damages that were in the old statute.

Definitions

As you may recall, there are certain key definitions that apply to real estate brokers under the Texas Deceptive Trade Practices Act:

- "Goods" are defined as tangible chattels or **real property** purchased for lease or use (Section 17.45[1]).

- "Services" means work, labor, or services purchased or leased for purchase, including services furnished in connection with the sale or repair of goods (Section 17.45[2]).

- "Consumer" means an individual, partnership, corporation, or governmental entity that seeks or acquires by purchase or lease any goods or services (Section 17.45[4]).

- "Unconscionable action or course of action" means an act or practice that, to a consumer's detriment, takes advantage of the lack of knowledge, ability, experience, or capacity of a person to a grossly unfair degree.

Other Important Provisions

Section 17.42 Waivers

The 1995 Legislature made major changes in the DTPA as it pertained to waivers. A waiver is now valid and enforceable if: (1) the waiver is in writing and is signed by the consumer; (2) the consumer is not in a significantly disparate bargaining position; and (3) the consumer is represented by legal counsel in seeking or requiring the goods and services. Section 17.42(a)(1).

The waiver is not effective if the consumer's legal counsel is directly or indirectly identified, suggested, or selected by a defendant or an agent of the defendant.

To be effective, the waiver must be: (1) conspicuous and in boldface of at least ten points in size; and (2) identified by the heading "Waiver of Consumer Rights," or words of similar meaning and in substantially the following form:

> <u>Waiver of Consumer Rights</u>
> "I waive my rights under the Deceptive Trade Practices-Consumer Protection Act, Section 17.41 et seq., Business & Commerce Code, a law that gives consumers special rights and protections. After consultation with an attorney of my selection, I voluntarily consent to this waiver."

Unlike the old statute, it does not require the signature of the consumer's attorney.

Section 17.44

This subchapter states that the DTPA shall be liberally construed and applied to promote its underlying purposes, which are to protect consumers against false, misleading, and deceptive business practices, unconscionable action, and breaches of warranty and to provide effective and economical procedures to secure such protection.

Section 17.49 Prohibited Claims

Section 17.49 prohibits a claim for damages based on the rendering of a professional service, the essence of which is the providing of advice, judgment, opinion, or similar professional skill. **This exemption may apply to real estate brokers as a very broad exemption, if the courts consider real estate brokerage a "professional service." The exemption does not apply, however, to: (1) an express misrepresentation of the material fact; (2) an unconscionable action or course of action, the failure to disclose information and violation of §17.46(b)(24); or (3) a breach of an express warranty that cannot be characterized as advice, judgment, or opinion. See §17.49(c). Note that the Texas Statute on Professional Corporations does not list real estate licensees as "professionals."** A recent Supreme Court case in Idaho used these criteria to disclaim a real estate agent's "professional" status. *Sumpter v. Holland Realty, Inc.*, 93 P.3d 680 (Idaho, 2004).

Recall Chapter 2. The statute prohibits a claim for damages, under Section 17.49(f) of the DTPA, for a claim arising out of a written contract, if the contract relates to a transaction involving total consideration by the consumer of more than $100,000 if the consumer is represented by legal counsel and the contract does not involve the consumer's residence. Similarly, the act also exempts claims arising from a transaction, a project, or a set of transactions relating to the same project, involving total consideration by the consumer of more than $500,000, other than a cause of action involving a consumer's residence, even if the consumer is not represented by a legal counsel.

"The Laundry List"

We previously discussed the application of Section 17.46(b) as a violation of the DTPA. There are twenty-six specific violations enumerated in 17.46. Many of these are specifically applicable to the real estate brokerage business and will be emphasized here.

- Representing that goods are original or new if they are deteriorated, reconditioned, reclaimed, used, or secondhand. Sec. 17.46(b)(5).

- Representing that goods or services are of a particular standard, quality, or grade, or that goods are of a particular style or model, if they are of another. Sec. 17.46(b)(7).

- Disparaging the goods, services, or business of another by false or misleading representations of facts. Sec. 17.46(b)(8).

- Making false or misleading statements of fact concerning the reason for, existence of, or amount of price reductions. Sec. 17.46(b)(11).

- Representing that an agreement confers or involves rights, remedies, or obligations that it does not have or involve or that are prohibited by law. Sec. 17.46(b)(12).

- Knowingly making false or misleading statements of fact concerning the need for parts, replacement, or repair service. Sec. 17.46(b)(13).

- Misrepresenting the authority of the salesperson, representative, or agent to negotiate the final term of a consumer transaction. Sec. 17.46(b)(14).

- Representing that work or services have been performed on or parts replaced in goods when the work or services were not performed or the parts not replaced. Sec. 17.46(b)(21).

- The failure to disclose information concerning goods or services that was known at the time of the transaction, if such failure to disclose such information was intended to induce the consumer into a transaction into which the consumer would not have entered had the information been disclosed. Sec. 17.46(b)(24).

This last "laundry list" item is tough. Unlike affirmative misrepresentations, where the law imposes a duty on the seller to know whether an affirmative statement is true, this duty does not arise when the seller fails to reveal information about which he does not know. To prove a DTPA action for failure to disclose information concerning goods or services, plaintiffs must show that the information: (1) was known at the time of the transaction, (2) was intended to induce the plaintiffs into a transaction, and (3) had it been disclosed, would have caused the plaintiffs to not enter into the transaction. There is no duty of disclosure under the DTPA if a defendant fails to disclose material facts and merely should have known. *Kessler v. Fanning* (953 S.W. 2d 515, 521, Tex. App.–Fort Worth, 1997).

Although the court cannot suspend a broker's license under the DTPA, there are a number of pertinent corresponding provisions of the Real Estate License Act that provide that a licensee can have his or her license revoked or suspended for:

- making a material misrepresentation, or failing to disclose to a potential purchaser any latent structural defect or any other defect known to the broker or salesperson. A latent structural defect and other defects do not refer to trivial or insignificant defects but refer to those defects that would be a significant factor to a reasonable and prudent purchaser in making a decision to purchase, Section 15(a)(6)(A).

- soliciting, selling, or offering for sale real property under a scheme or program that constitutes a lottery or deceptive practice, Section 15(a)(6)(I).

- pursuing a continued and flagrant course of misrepresentation or making a false promise through agents, salesperson, advertising, or otherwise, Section 15(a)(6)(C).

- failing to make clear, to all parties to a transaction, which party he is acting for, or receiving compensation from more than one party except with full knowledge and consent of all parties, Section 15(a)(6)(D).

- inducing or attempting to induce a party to a contract of sale or lease to break the contract for the purpose of substituting in lieu thereof a new contract, Section 15(a)(6)(M).

- guaranteeing, authorizing, or permitting a person to guarantee that future profits will result from a resale of real property, Section 15(a)(6)(K).

- acting in the dual capacity of broker and undisclosed principal in a transaction, Section 15(a)(6)(J).

- accepting, receiving, or charging an undisclosed commission, rebate, or direct profit on expenditures made for a principal, Section 15(a)(6)(H).

Unconscionable Action or Course of Action

This portion of the statute has been interpreted as meaning "taking advantage of the consumer's lack of knowledge to a grossly unfair degree," which seems to be tailor-made for suing brokers because of their superior knowledge of the marketplace, and would be particularly applicable to brokers when they are acting in their capacities as principal when dealing with a consumer who is held to a much lower duty of care. Note *Chastain v. Koonce* and *Wyatt v. Petrila*, discussed later in this chapter.

Brokerage Cases Interpreting the DTPA

Under the Deceptive Trade Practices Act, the consumer has been held to have a duty of care of being ignorant, unthinking, and credulous, *Spradling v. Williams*, 566 S.W. 561 (Tex., 1978). Brokers have been held to provide services of an expert who has been tested and found to be such, *Holloman v. Denson*, 640 S.W.2d 417 (Tex. Civ. App.–Waco, 1982). The result is sometimes referred to as "disparity in bargaining position," and a real estate licensee should not take advantage of those who are less qualified. This poses an interesting question: Can a real estate licensee be held liable for selling a house for too high a price? What if it is his or her own house? (Particularly if there is a failure to disclose information.) Some discussion was given to this in the case of *Wyatt v. Petrila*, 752 S.W.2d 683 (Tex. App. –Corpus Christi, 1988), wherein there is a lengthy discussion involving gross disparity between value received and consideration paid as an unconscionable action under the DTPA. In that case, a disparity of $50,000 in a house costing $625,000 was not considered to be "gross," as a matter of law.

There has never been much concern over whether or not the seller could sue the broker for misrepresentation of services either for sale or management of the property, *Lerma v. Brecheisen*, 602 S.W.2d 318 (Tex. Civ. App.–Waco, 1980). *Henry S. Miller Management Corp. v. Houston State Associates*, 792 S.W.2d 128 (Tex. App.–Houston [1st Dist.], 1990).

In *Cameron v. Terrell & Garrett, Inc.*, 618 S.W.2d 535 (Tex., 1981), the Texas Supreme Court held that the purchaser could sue the broker for misrepresentation in calculating the square footage of a house.

New case concerning square footage!

Although not a deceptive trade practices case, *Trenholm v. Ratcliff*, 646 S.W.2d 927 (Tex., 1983) wiped out any defense of a broker maintaining "mere opinion" as a defense. This may be particularly true when one of the parties has superior knowledge to the other or superior access to information. Representations as to matters not equally open to parties are legally statements of fact and not opinions. *Robertson v. United New Mexico Bank at Roswell*, 14 F.3d 1076 (5th Cir., 1994).

In *Pleasant v. Bradford*, 2008 Westlaw 2544814 (Tex. App. 6/26/08), a listing broker listed a house for sale and prepared an MLS sheet that disclosed the square footage of the house as approximately 1850 sq. ft. She obtained this information from the local county assessor. It was the custom to put square footage information in MLS listings, although not required. It was also the custom to reveal in the listing the source of the information, e.g., "per Bell County Assessor's Office." But in this case, allegedly because of a scrivener's error by an employee of the broker's office, this qualification did not appear next to the square footage information on this particular MLS sheet. The computerized MLS listing automatically computed a "per square footage" price that was part of the information on the sheet.

The buyers looked at the house with a selling broker, and in one way or another got the selling broker's MLS listing sheet, which was also not an unusual event. The buyers maintained at trial that they were attracted to the house because, although it needed repair, its price was substantially lower per square foot than that of other houses in the neighborhood.

Because the sellers were anxious to close the deal and because buyers could not get a loan until they received confirmation of the husband's residency contract at a local hospital, the parties executed a contract that permitted the buyers to occupy the home on a rental basis before closing, during which time they did substantial repairs and renovation. When they did get the confirmation and applied for a loan, however, the bank appraisal indicated (accurately, unfortunately) that the house was in fact 1571 square feet. Buyers closed on the house and sued broker for the difference between the value of the house at its true size and the value of the house at the size represented. A jury found for the buyers and awarded them the difference of about $2,500. Plus, the buyers got attorney's fees. The broker appealed.

The court of appeals affirmed. The broker first argued on appeal that buyers had not relied on the broker's representation because there was evidence that buyers had indeed checked the assessment department's Web site on their own and saw the (erroneous) square footage report. The court conceded that indeed there was Texas authority that said that there must be evidence of reliance and that if a party, after receiving a misrepresentation, independently checks out the facts, there may be no factual link between the representation and the actual reliance. In this case, however, there was evidence that the buyers, encouraged by their broker, had gone to the Web site not to check the square footage but to look for any evidence of defects in the property so that they could understand why the per square foot price was so much less than other houses. They incidentally saw the square footage information, but the purpose of their checking the Web site was not to verify that information. Consequently, the jury could have found that they were still relying, at least in part, on the selling broker's representation.

The broker next pointed out that the buyers had signed a document provided by the selling broker, which contained the following statement:

> "The Buyer is advised to verify all information important to him/her and to ask the appropriate questions of the appropriate authorities himself/herself or through an attorney with respect to important issues such as ... size of structure ... Any statements with respect to problems or with respect to the availability or existence of any of these items which were made by the REALTOR and his/her associates were made based on information given to the REALTOR by the Seller/Owner and/or government agencies, and/or others, and there is no intention that the

Buyer rely on the statements of the REALTOR and his/her associates, and the Buyer is urged to confirm any such statements on his/her own.

Having read the foregoing disclaimer, I/we, the prospective Buyer(s), by my/our signature(s) below, state that I/we have not relied upon any statement given to me/us by the REALTOR and/or his/her associates with regard to the property, and my/our decision to make an offer on the property and to subsequently purchase the property is based on my/our independent decision with or without legal counsel."

The court ruled that it was a jury issue whether this constituted a statement that the buyers were not relying upon the "listing broker's" representations, as opposed to only the representations made by their selling broker. The court noted that the statement quoted above did not constitute a waiver of a right to make a claim or bring a lawsuit and at best could only be construed as an assertion of nonreliance. To this extent, the question was properly before the jury. The jury, of course, had found for the buyers on the point.

Ridco v. Sexton, 623 S.W.2d 792 (Tex. Civ. App.–Ft. Worth, 1981) wipes out any defense of mere puffing as a defense or cause of action under the act. There was a recent Texas case, however, that indicated that "mere puffing" was not a representation and therefore not actionable, *Autohaus, Inc., v. Aguilar*, 794 S.W.2d 459 (Tex. App.–Dallas, 1990). In that case, it was determined that "good" was only a general term of approval and the term "probably" is "relatively likely but not certain" and statements that are too general cannot be actionable. It should be noted that the Texas Supreme Court refused to hear the case but specifically did not approve or disapprove of the lower court's opinion. *Aguilar v. Autohaus, Inc.*, 800 S.W.2d 853 (Tex., 1991). Puffing is still a dangerous practice.

Kelley v. Texas Real Estate Commission, 671 S.W.2d 936 (Tex. Civ. App.–Houston, 1984) held a broker liable even though the misrepresentations were innocent and unknowing; a plaintiff is not required to prove a licensee's knowledge of the falsity of the misrepresentation. *Henry S. Miller v. Bynum*, 797 S.W.2d 51 (Tex. App.–Houston [1st Dist.], 1990). The new DTPA amendments may have made a big difference in these cases.

Ramsey v. Gordon, 567 S.W.2d 868 (Tex. Civ. App.–Waco, 1978) wipes out any defense of an agent claiming he is a principal in a transaction. *Weitzel v. Barnes*, 691 S.W.2d 598 (Tex., 1985) wipes out the defense of using "as is" in an earnest money contract, but the holding has been somewhat limited after the *Prudential* case, discussed later. See also *Wyatt v. Petrila*, discussed earlier.

Canada v. Kearns, 624 S.W.2d 755 (Tex. Civ. App.–Beaumont, 1981) held the broker liable for the misconduct of his or her agent even though the broker received no fee.
If the sponsoring broker is not sued, though, there's a different result. In *Miller v. Keyser*, 90 S.W.3d 712 (Tex., 2002), the court was determining whether an agent or a disclosed principal could be held liable for passing along false representation. The court held that,

because the DTPA allows a consumer to bring suit against "any person," the agent can be held personally liable for the misrepresentation he or she makes when acting within the scope of employment.

The case revolves around the sale of lots in Pearland, Texas, which backed up to Brazoria County's Drainage District, located on the back 20 feet of each lot. Each buyer knew that the drainage easement was on the lot, but the agent (salesperson) represented to the homeowners that the lots were oversized and that they were, in fact, larger than the lots of a competing builder in the subdivision. The homeowners paid a premium for these "oversized" lots. After their homes were built, the buyers received a letter from the Brazoria County Drainage District, telling them that all fences in the easement must be removed at the owner's expense. As a result, the homeowners sued. Through a series of procedural maneuvers, the only defendant left was the salesperson, Barry Keyser, who argued that a corporate agent couldn't be held personally liable for company misrepresentations (apparently assuming under Texas law that everything he did was on behalf of the corporation that held his license).

The court disagreed, noting that Keyser personally made the representations about the size of the lot and the location of the fence. He was the only person with whom the homeowners had any contact. Based on the plain language of the statute, Keyser was liable for his own DTPA violations.

Keyser then claimed that his misrepresentations were innocent (apparently relying on information given to him by the sponsoring broker). The court noted, however, that the DTPA does not require the consumer to prove that the employee acted knowingly or intentionally in order to create liability. Keyser was liable even if he did not know his representations were false or even if he did not intend to deceive anyone. The court held that the homeowners did have a right to seek indemnification from the employer and, therefore, could have sued the employer, brought into the case as part of their defense.

ECC Parkway Joint Venture v. Baldwin, 765 S.W.2d 504 (Tex. App.–Dallas, 1989) held that a broker's failure to disclose a height restriction on property supported a purchaser's cause of action against the broker for fraud, negligent misrepresentation, and breach of fiduciary duty as well as a violation of the Texas Deceptive Trade Practices Act. The course of action was upheld notwithstanding the deed restrictions being of record in the county courthouse and the purchaser accepting the deed subject to all restrictions of record in the county. The **failure to disclose** is a very difficult defense for brokers, as it often involves what the broker "should have known" but didn't disclose, as well as the actual failure to disclose. To prevail at trial, the plaintiffs must prove: (i) a failure to disclose information concerning goods or services; (ii) which was known at the time of the transaction; (iii) which was intended to induce them into the transaction; and (iv) that they would not have entered into the transaction if the information had been disclosed. *O'Hern v. Hogard*, 841 S.W.2d 135 (Tex.

App.–Houston [14th Dist.], 1992). The 1995 amendments to the Texas Real Estate License Act may give more relief in this area, however. *Haney v. Purcell Company, Inc.*, 770 S.W.2d 566 (Tex., 1989), although not a brokerage case, held a seller of real estate liable for failing to disclose that there was an unrecorded cemetery in the purchaser's backyard.

The criteria for a violation of the act appears to be found in circumstances where the knowledge of the agent, in conjunction with the consumer's relative ignorance, operates to make the slightest divergence from mere praise (by the agent) into representations of fact (as understood by the consumer). *ChryslerPlymouth City, Inc., v. Guerrero*, 620 S.W.2d 700 (Tex. App.–San Antonio, 1981).

In *Century 21 Page One Realty v. Naghad*, 760 S.W.2d 305 (Tex. App.–Texarkana, 1988) a broker listed "no known defects" in the listing agreement, and there was no other communication with the purchaser prior to the sale. The court held that both parties (the seller and broker) benefitted and both were jointly and severally liable because both parties benefitted from the misrepresentation.

Nix v. Born, 870 S.W.2d 635 (Tex. App.–El Paso, 1994) held that where the broker did not tell the seller that he had an interest in the partnership/buyer, the broker's fiduciary duty had been breached and upheld a jury award for lost profits and exemplary damages.

In *Chastain v. Koonce*, 700 S.W.2d 579 (Tex., 1985) the Texas Supreme Court also addressed criteria for "unconscionable action" or course of action under 17.45(5). It requires "taking advantage of a consumer's lack of knowledge to a grossly unfair degree, thus, requires a showing of intent, knowledge, or a conscious indifference" at the time the misrepresentation was made.

Sanchez v. Guerrero, 885 S.W.2d 487 (Tex. App.–El Paso, 1994) is a frightening case! The Guerreros saw a vacant house in El Paso, which was listed by Century 21 Casablanca Realty. The Guerreros executed an earnest money contract with $500 for earnest money. The deal was ultimately closed, making the Guerreros the owners of their "dream house." The same evening, the Guerreros saw a television news program about a woman who had been tried and acquitted of child molestation charges, which allegedly occurred in the Guerreros' new home. The Guerreros sued the real estate brokers, alleging that they knew that the woman had lived there and withheld the information from the appellees in an attempt to induce appellees to complete the transaction, and that this is a violation of the Texas Deceptive Trade Practices Act. The jury found that Sanchez (the broker) knowingly engaged in false, misleading, or deceptive acts or practices and that they knowingly engaged in the unconscionable action or course of action and that such action is a producing cause of damages to the Guerreros. The court discussed an excellent explanation of failure to disclose information under the DTPA and the unconscionability provisions of the DTPA. It ultimately held that the real estate broker took advantage of the Guerreros' lack of knowledge of real estate to a grossly unfair degree and supported mental anguish damages as being recoverable because the conduct was committed knowingly.

The jury awarded the Guerreros the sum of $120,000, which consisted of $20,000 for the closing costs and $100,000 for their mental anguish.

There were two distinctly different facts presented to the court. The purchaser alleged that he requested information about the prior ownership of the home (the title was currently held by the Veterans Administration). The real estate broker denied that particular conversation ever took place. However, the appeals courts have a very difficult time reversing a finding of the jury because they are the final arbiter of the facts.

In *Lefmark Management Company v. Old*, 946 S.W.2d 52 (Tex., 1997), a widow of a customer killed during an armed robbery of a shopping center store sued the store, the shopping center owners and managers, and the former property manager of the shopping center. The Texas Supreme Court reiterated the general rule that a landowner must use reasonable care to make the premises safe for the use of business and invitees. However, on the date of the indicated, Lefmark, as a previous manager, did not own, occupy, manage, possess, or otherwise have any control of the shopping center. The court held that a management company does not have a duty to disclose a dangerous condition to a subsequent management company.

Okay. This is a California case, but it gives "stigma" a whole new meaning. In *Shapiro v. Sutherland* (1998 WL 333914 [Cal. App. 2 Dist.]), a purchaser of residential property from a relocation management service sued the relocation service and the former owners who had sold the property, alleging fraudulent misrepresentation and material nondisclosure.

The prior owner had occupied the property for 15 years and was transferred to the new location. The company's relocation policy allowed the relocation company to purchase the property for a preestablished price. The homeowners entered into the home purchase agreement with the relocation company, which had purchased the property for $349,000. The owners executed the deed, which was signed and notarized, but left a blank as to the name of the grantee. The documents were then transferred to the relocation company. The owners executed the state-mandated disclosure form that included the following question: "Are you aware of any... (11) neighbor noise problems or other nuisances?" The homeowners responded "no."

The record reflected that the owners' next-door neighbors were, over a period of years, a source of disturbing noises and commotion. The owners had called the police on a number of occasions. The relocation company did not know of these matters.

The court here held that there was a common law duty of disclosure "where a seller knows the facts materially affecting the value or desirability of the property...and also knows such facts are not known to or within the reach of the diligent attention and observation of the buyer, the seller is under a duty to disclose them to the buyer," citing the earlier California case of *Alexander v. McKnight*, 7 Cal. App. 4th 973, 977 (1992). The court held that California law provides specific seller disclosure requirements. It contains questions concerning neighborhood noise problems, and should have been disclosed truthfully. In essence, the owner was held liable for failing to disclose a noisy neighbor. Does this mean that a noisy neighbor can stigmatize the neighborhood? Hopefully, the precedent in this case will be limited to California!

NUISANCE; diminished property value?

In *Smith v. Kansas Guest Service Co., et al*, 169 P. 3d 1052, real property owners brought a class action against the operator of a gas storage facility, asserting claims of negligence and nuisance and seeking injunctive relief and damages for diminished property values that resulted from an escape of natural gas from the facility. There was an explosion in downtown Hutchinson, Kansas, in January of 2001, and it was determined that escaped gas migrated underground through a porous geological formation and rose to the surface in Hutchinson through abandoned brine wells that were not properly plugged. After the source of the problem was identified, the leak was remedied.

The issue presented to the Kansas Supreme Court was whether or not a property owner can collect damages under either a negligence or a nuisance theory for a diminution in the property's market value caused by the stigma or market fear resulting from an accidental contamination, where the property owner has not proved either a physical injury to the property or an interference with the owner's use and enjoyment of the property. In holding that the owner could not, the court acknowledged that even though stigma damages may be recoverable, remote, speculative and conjectural damages are not to be considered. Having determined that there was no physical injury to the properties in question, the court's second focus was whether or not the landowners showed interference in the use and enjoyment of the property, and held that they did not. The court noted other jurisdictions holding the same way: Virginia, Arkansas, California, Kentucky, Mississippi, North Carolina, Pennsylvania, Utah, and Wyoming.

This case apparently follows the more traditional logic of legal history. What damage have you suffered because you are "afraid" of something that has happened or might happen, without showing a physical injury or an interference with the use or enjoyment of the property? These damages are very difficult to prove.

In *Smith v. Herco, Inc.*, 900 S.W.2d 852 (Tex. App.–Corpus Christi, 1995, writ denied), Smith purchased a townhouse for $64,000. Herco told Smith he would be deeded the unit "wall to wall" and gave Smith a warranty deed. When he attempted to resell the townhouse, he learned that one corner of the townhouse, indicating a portion of the interior, extended into the common area of the development. Smith could not obtain a deed from all the other townhouse owners. Therefore, he stopped making mortgage payments, and the townhouse eventually foreclosed.

Smith sued the seller and surveyor under DTPA and for breach of contract and warranties. The trial court found that both defendants had affirmatively misrepresented that the plaintiff would receive title to the entire unit. Specifically, the court held that the deed and statements that Smith would own all of the unit were false. Regardless of the reason, when a good real estate does not have the characteristics it is represented to have, or does not perform as represented, the injury to the consumer is the same.

The Court of Appeals affirmed the trial court judgment for $87,600 in damages, $30,016 in attorney's fees, and $87,890 in prejudgment interest. The damages represented $32,000 for loss in value of the unit and $57,600 for damage to the plaintiff's credit rating.

In *McFarland v. Associated Brokers*, 977 S.W.2d 427 (Tex. App.–Corpus Christi, 1998), the purchaser brought suit against the defendant (listing broker) for violations of the DTPA, negligence, and fraud. The purchaser had requested the inspection of the home prior to closing, which was performed by a real estate inspection company. The inspector neither discovered nor reported any major roof damage. On the same date as the inspection, however, the purchaser discovered water in the light fixture in the closet in the master bedroom, indicating there was a roof leak. The purchaser requested that the roof be repaired at the seller's expense with the assurance that the repair work would be guaranteed for at least 1 year.

Repairs were made by a contractor who assured the purchaser that the roof was in good shape and extended a 1-year warranty on the repairs. The purchaser closed the sale, moved into the house, and discovered that the roof was still leaking. The purchaser then brought suit against the listing broker for damages, alleging the broker's knowing concealment, nondisclosure of known defects, and the nondisclosure of false representations made by the sellers.

The broker defended by saying that the broker was not the cause of the damage, alleging that:

- a contract addendum eliminated their liability (it stated that the buyer had not relied upon any representations or statements made by the real estate agent).

- the inspection was performed by the buyer.

- the buyer discovered the leakage.

- the buyer had an agreement and warranty with the roof; therefore, the broker could not have been the cause of the damage. The trial court entered judgment in favor of the broker and awarded the broker $19,200 for legal services, plus additional amounts for appeal.

The Court of Appeals reversed the trial court, holding that an independent inspection was not, in and of itself, enough to constitute a new and independent basis for the purchase of the dwelling. The court seemed to infer that if the buyer had subsequently agreed to take the property "as is," then the case may have gone the other way. The case was then remanded to the trial court for a full trial on the merits.

Rosas v. *Hatz*, 147 S.W.3d 560 (Tex.App.–Waco, 2004, no pet.). While a broker has no duty to inspect the property and disclose all facts that might affect its value or desirability, one who knows all the facts and provides false information, or one who makes a partial disclosure and conveys a false impression, may be liable for negligent misrepresentation. Fraud and DTPA claims also require a false representation.

The Rosas' claim that the broker, Hatz, told Mrs. Rosas that the house had been "partially rewired" and the plumbing "replaced or redone" and that this constitutes an affirmative misrepresentation due to the wiring and plumbing problems discovered afterwards. Hatz's representation to Mrs. Rosas that the house had been rewired and the plumbing "redone" gives rise to a reasonable inference that any problems with the house had been fixed. This statement, in combination with the evidence that the seller's tenant told Hatz of a leak in the home, creates a fact issue as to whether Hatz's statements were affirmative representations of false information. Thus, there is more than a scintilla of evidence that Hatz made affirmative misrepresentations

Brokers; Can you represent two buyers?

In *Zuazua v. Tibbles*, 150 P.2d 361 (Mont. 2006), Stone, an agent of the Coldwell Banker agency, had on July 8 executed a form with Zuazua that identified Stone as a buyer's agent for Zuazua. Two days later, Zuazua authorized Stone to submit an offer on a property. Two days after that, Stone signed another buyer's agency agreement with Moritzky and submitted an offer on the same property on that same day. Even though two days had passed since the supposed presentation of the first offer, the seller testified that he evaluated both offers and accepted Moritzky's.

Zuazua sued in federal court, and the court referred to the Montana court the question of whether the Montana statute prohibits a buyer's agent from submitting two offers from two different clients on the same property.

The Montana Supreme Court, in a split decision, found that the requirement in the statute that the buyer's broker work "solely in the best interests of the buyer" was dispositive of the question, and it ignored other language, emphasized heavily by the three dissenters, that implicitly authorized buyer's brokers to submit offers from different brokers, subject to the injunction that the broker could not disclose to either client the terms of the other bid. The Montana Real Estate Commission had already issued rules permitting the submission of competing offers by the same agent. Both sides agreed that the statute did not expressly address the practice.

The Supreme Court limited its decision to the behavior of the individual agent and would have permitted the agent in question to designate (with client's consent) another agent in the same office to move forward on an offer. Indeed, one commentator on the case suggested that, if the result stands, agents might be well advised to designate different "submitters" for each of the buyers, so that the designated buyer's agent can maintain comfortable relations with both buyer clients after the issue is resolved. (Remember that the seller might reject both offers, leaving both clients still looking.)

In *Rivkin v Century 21 Teran Realty LLC*, 858 N.Y.S. 2d 55 (N.Y. 2008), a buyer was looking for a lakefront property in a certain area that had special meaning to him. He contacted Luborsky, an agent for Teran, a real estate broker, and got Internet information about a certain property listed for $100,000. He realized that this might be his dream property, and told Luborsky as much, authorizing Luborsky to make a verbal offer of $75,000 before he had even visited the property, but indicating that he would not be in a position to sign a contract until he had made such a visit. Luborsky contacted the listing broker and made the offer.

Three days later, the buyer visited the property and, although the improvements were, in his view, "tear down," the site was perfect, and he authorized Luborsky, on the agent's advice, to make a written offer of $75,000, expecting a counter offer or an invitation for final highest bids. He told Luborsky that he was willing to go to the asking price to get the property. He also signed an agency disclosure that stated, as required by New York law, that the "buyer's agent acts solely on behalf of the buyer" and has "without limitation, the following fiduciary duties to the buyer: reasonable care, undivided loyalty, confidentiality, full disclosure, obedience and a duty to account."

Over the weekend following, Luborsky told the buyer that other offers had been received, and the buyer indicated that he would go higher. So Luborsky agreed that he would contact the selling broker and ask whether a counteroffer or a "highest and best" solicitation would be forthcoming.

Unbeknownst to either buyer or Luborsky, another buyer, the Martins, were also interested in the property. The Martins had been working with another agent from Teran, Luborsky's office, and had submitted a full price unconditional offer on the property, which the sellers ultimately accepted, despite the buyer's and Lubrosky's attempts to communicate an unconditional overbid. The buyer made several direct contacts with one of the sellers, who consistently referred him to the selling broker, who ultimately informed the buyer that the property had in fact been sold through an offer from Teran, the buyer's own brokerage firm.

The buyer brought this lawsuit claiming that Teran and Luborsky and the other agent had all violated the exclusive fiduciary duty set forth in the disclosure and required by New York law.

This was apparently an issue of first impression since the law had been amended and the buyer brokers began to appear on the scene. The court concluded that the statute sometimes used the term "broker" and sometimes used the term "agent," and that the term "agent" referred only to an individual. It concluded that Luborsky owed an exclusive duty of loyalty to the buyer, and could not have acted on behalf of another client, but another agent in the office could represent a competing buyer:

> "An individual buyer's agent acting on behalf of multiple clients bidding on the same property cannot negotiate an optimal purchase price for all of them. The buyers' interest conflict; the agent's representation is inevitably compromised. But two buyer's agents simply affiliated with the same real estate brokerage firm and acting on behalf of different buyers bidding on the same property generally do not present comparable risks…they only earn commissions for sale to their own clients. As a result, in this situation the agents have every reason to negotiate in their clients' best interest."

The court also noted that a brokerage with an agency relationship with a seller would have the right to show other competing properties to potential buyers, even if those properties are listed for sale with the same brokerage firm, but suggested that a seller's agent would have a duty to disclose that it intended to do so.

Defenses Under the DTPA

Statutory Defenses

Section 17.506. There are several defenses to damages under the Deceptive Trade Practices Act. If the defendant can prove that before consummation of the transaction, he gave reasonable and timely notice to the plaintiff of the defendant's reliance on:

- written information relating to the particular goods and service in question obtained from official governmental records, if the written information was false or inadequate and the defendant did not know and could not reasonably have known of the falsity or inaccuracy of the information.

- written information relating to the particular goods or service in question obtained from another source if the information was false or inaccurate and the defendant did not know of the falsity or inaccuracy of the information.

- written information concerning a test required or prescribed by a government agency, if the information from the test was false or inaccurate and the defendant did not know and could not reasonably have known of the falsity or inaccuracy of the information.

Apparently the term "and could not reasonably have known of the falsity or inaccuracy" imposes upon the real estate broker this duty of care to at least investigate the information to determine whether or not it was true.

Section 17.505

Under the DTPA, a consumer must give the defendant a specific complaint and amount of actual damages at least 60 days prior to filing of the lawsuit. If the lawsuit is filed without the 60-day notice, the effect of filing the petition is the same as providing the written notice, as it gives the defendant 60 days from filing of the lawsuit to serve his defense.

The 1989 amendment changed 30 days to 60 days. It also provides that during that 60-day period the consumer has to give the defendant permission to inspect the product that is the source of the complaint. If the consumer fails to produce the product for inspection, his damages are limited.

- The notice required apparently does not have to meet any formal requirements as it is to purely "inform the seller of the consumer's complaint and thus therefore provide an opportunity for the parties to settle the matter without litigation." *North American Van Lines v. Bauerele*, 678 S.W.2d 229 (Tex. Civ. App.–Ft. Worth, 1984). The "specific complaint" can be relatively general in description. *Jim Walters Home, Inc., v. Valencia*, 690 S.W.2d 239 (Tex., 1985).

- The notice, however, must state a specific monetary amount of damages. *Sunshine Datsun v. Ramsey*, 687 S.W.2d 652 (Tex. Civ. App.–Amarillo, 1984).

- If the defendant gives a tender offer to settle the conflict within the time allowed, it is a defense to the potential treble damage exposure. DTPA Sec. 17.50(d). It should also be noted that any tendered offer made by the defendant during the 60 days must also include the attorney's fees in addition to the actual damages claimed by the plaintiff. *Cail v. Service Motors, Inc.*, 660 S.W.2d 814 (Tex., 1983). The 1989 amendment to the Deceptive Trade Practices Act also specifically prohibits any attempts to offer the settlement offer as evidence before a jury.

Section 17.5051 Compulsory Mediation

This section provides for compulsory mediation and offers of settlement through mediation. Under this new procedure, a party may, no later than the 90th day after the date of service of the pleading, file a motion to compel mediation in a dispute. After the motion is filed, the court must, no later than 30 days after the motion is filed, sign an order setting the time and place of the mediation. The mediation must be held within 30 days after the date the order is signed, unless the parties agree otherwise. A party, however, may not compel mediation if the amount of economic damages claimed is less than $15,000, unless the party seeking to compel the mediation agrees to pay the cost of the mediation. Offers made during the mediation are treated very similarly to those under §17.505.

Section 17.555

This provision extends indemnity and contributions under the act to encompass all possible damages under the act and can be considered a very effective defense under the rights to the fact situation. The statute provides that the defendant may seek contribution or indemnity from one whom, under statute law or at common law, may have liability for the damaging event of the consumer complaint. This would allow the defendant to implead the seller, property inspector, or other person who may be determined to have the ultimate liability. The statute also provides for the defendant to get reimbursement for reasonable attorney's fees and costs.

The 1995 Legislature also made an attempt to limit some of the licensee's liability through an amendment to the Texas Real Estate License Act. The act now provides the licensee is not liable for misrepresentation or concealment of material fact made by a party in a real estate transaction, or made by his subagent in a real estate transaction unless the licensee knew of the falsity of the misrepresentation or concealment and failed to disclose the licensee's knowledge of the falsity of the misrepresentation or concealment. *V.T.C.A. Occupations Code §1101.805*. This seems to impose an "actual knowledge" requirement on the broker and eliminates the ability to impute liability for what the broker "should have known." Note, however, that the new provisions do not diminish the real estate broker's liability for the broker's acts, nor the acts or admissions of the broker's salespersons.

Case Law Defenses

1. *Didn't say it.* One effective defense has been when the agent never made the representation, *Newsome v. Starkey*, 541 S.W.2d 468 (Tex. Civ. App.–Dallas, 1976); *Ozuna v. Delaney Realty*, 593 S.W.2d 797 (Tex. Civ. App.–El Paso, 1980, writ ref'd n.r.e.); *Stagner v. Friendswood Dev. Co., Inc.*, 620 S.W.2d 103 (Tex., 1981); *Micrea v. Cubilla Condominium Corp.*, 685 S.W.2d 755 (Tex. Civ. App.–Houston, 1985).

2. *Didn't know.* The courts will not hold an agent to the duty of care of failing to reveal information that he does not know, *Robinson v. Preston Chrysler Plymouth, Inc.,* 633 S.W.2d 500 (Tex., 1982). *Steptoe v. True, ante.* The real estate agent has also been held not liable when the plaintiff was not relying on the real estate agent's representations because of the plaintiff's own inspections of the property prior to acquisition, *Lone Star Machinery Corp. v. Frankel,* 564 S.W.2d 135 (Tex. Civ. App.–Beaumont, 1978). This defense may also apply to any consumer who hires his or her own inspector. *Pfeiffer v. Ebby Halliday,* 747 S.W.2d 887 (Tex. App.–Dallas, 1988).

3. *Not me.* If the broker is *not* a party to the earnest money contract, he will not be held responsible for his principal's default or misconduct. *Baxter & Swinford, Inc., v. Mercier,* 671 S.W.2d 139 (Tex. Civ. App.–Houston, 1984). As a general rule, the broker has no right, duty, or power to affect a principal's decision, and he has no duty except to forward information to the principal. *James Shore v. Thomas A. Sweeney & Associates,* 864 S.W.2d 182 (Tex. App.–Tyler, 1993).

4. *I told him.* If the seller discloses a defect and the buyer buys anyway, there may also be a defense. *Zak v. Parks,* 729 S.W.2d 875 (Tex. App.–Houston, 1987).

In *Cendant Mobility Services Corporation v. Falconer,* 135 S.W.3d 349 (Tex.App.–Texarkana 2004, no pet.). The Gregg County house purchased by Kenneth S. Falconer turned out to be a nightmare. Falconer purchased the house in 1999 through Cendant Mobility Services Corporation, a relocation firm selling the property for the prior owners, the Gunnelses. After the purchase, and a severe drought, Falconer began to see damage to interior and exterior walls and floors revealing serious and widespread structural flaws. Falconer sued Cendant, asserting causes of action for fraud and violation of the DTPA, claiming that Cendant failed to disclose that the house's foundation had shown evidence of substantial movement in the past and that Cendant provided only a portion of the relevant engineer's report for his review. The evidence reveals, however, that Falconer's initials appear on each page of the previous homeowner's real estate disclosure and an engineer's structural inspection report.

Despite Falconer's admission that he received and initialed at least those portions of the documents describing the foundation's condition, he nevertheless maintains that he was misled by Cendant's agent. He testified he would not necessarily characterize what she affirmatively told him about the house as a misrepresentation of the information available to her, but believed she misled him by selectively informing him of certain portions of the disclosures and reports, omitting the fact that substantial movement had taken place in the past. Instead, she reportedly pointed out from the seller's disclosure statement only that minor settlement had occurred in the past and then jumped forward to the last two sentences of the engineers' report, indicating that the foundation was stable, that the house was structurally sound, and that no additional repairs were warranted. In answer to the question: "Do you expect Cendant to sit down and read each—the contract through line by line with you?", he said: "If that's what it takes."

Despite Falconer's belief that Cendant's agent should have explained every detail of the contract, including any disclosures or attached reports, this is simply not the law. Even where there exists a fiduciary relationship—which did not exist here—there is no duty under the DTPA requiring sellers to orally disclose the contents of a written contract. The information provided in the seller's disclosure and the engineers' report was clear and unambiguous and subject to Falconer's review before signing. It is well settled that the parties to a contract have an obligation to protect themselves by reading what they sign. Unless there is some basis for finding fraud, the parties may not excuse themselves from the consequences of failing to meet that obligation. In this case, there was no evidence of fraud. The evidence was that he had everything in front of him and didn't read it. The failure of one party to read a contract, or any of the materials appertaining to it, however, does not equate with a failure of the other party to disclose the information contained within the four corners of that contract. Absent showing Cendant misrepresented the information disclosed in written form, Falconer was obligated to protect himself by reading the contract. He cannot now be excused from the consequences of failing to meet that obligation.

5. *Too vague. Autohaus v. Aguilar, supra*, held that a description of "good" was too general to be actionable, as was the statement that the consumers would "probably" have no problems with the item they were purchasing. Another recent case has also held that a "good house" that "had been repainted," a "roof put on," "new carpet," "a good buy," "a good value," "built on a good foundation," "a sound foundation," "in a good neighborhood," "house had been inspected," did not hold an agent liable for failing to disclose that there was a geological fault in the neighborhood when the broker had no knowledge of the fault. *Hagans v. Woodruff*, 830 S.W.2d 732 (Tex. App.–Houston [14th Dist.], 1992).

6. *Not my job.* In a very good case, the Court of Appeals held that §15(a)(6)(A) does *not* impose a duty on agents to inspect listed properties or to make an affirmative investigation for visible defects, *Kubinsky v. Van Zandt Realtors, et al.*, 811 S.W.2d 711 (Tex. App.–Ft. Worth, 1991, writ den.), particularly when the buyers retained their own agent *and* inspector in purchasing the home. Note a similar holding following the Kubinsky case in the Hagans' case, referenced earlier.

Another exception may be available when the circumstances and information from another source are correct, although the agent's information was incorrect, *Mikkelson v. Quail Valley Realty*, 641 P.2d 124 (Utah, 1982); or, that the principal still has the duty to read and understand his own contract, *Jones v. Maestas, supra*, but see *Phillips v. JCM, supra*; and *Wilkenson v. Smith, supra*.

In *Bartlett v. Schmidt*, 33 S.W.3d 35 (Tex. App.–Corpus Christi 2000, writ denied), Schmidt bought some land from sellers, who were represented by their broker, Bartlett. Schmidt wanted the property for use as a shipbuilding facility, where he intended to build ocean-going vessels. Pursuant to the contract, Schmidt was given a title commitment. The commitment showed some restrictive covenants that affected adjacent property, but that did not restrict commercial development on his property. The title company failed to show various amendments to the restrictions that, in fact, did prohibit commercial use of the property. Schmidt consulted with his lawyer and then bought the property. When he began laying the foundation for a shipbuilding enterprise, he was advised that the property had been annexed by the adjacent subdivision and was now limited to residential use only. Schmidt sued the seller, the broker, and the title company. The title company settled.

The trial court held that Bartlett was liable for fraud, negligent misrepresentation, and DTPA violations.

Both fraud and negligent misrepresentation require a showing of *reliance*. Here Bartlett argued that because Schmidt had consulted with his lawyer before buying the property, that consultation was an independent investigation that negates his claims. The decisions that support this notion are based on the notion that the buyer's decision to undertake a separate investigation indicates that he is not relying on representations about the property. Here, before he bought the property, Schmidt asked third parties to review conveyancing documents to be sure there were no restrictions on his intended use. He did this after he heard Bartlett's representations about the property. So the court held, relying on the third parties' representations, not on Bartlett's representations. Reliance on the title company's two external assessments of the feasibility of purchasing property was held to introduce a "new and independent" cause of the buyer's damages, thus negating the producing cause element of a DTPA claim. See also *Steptoe v. True*, 38 S.W.3d 213 (Tex. App.–Houston [14th Dist.], 2001).

7. *"As Is."* The *Prudential Insurance Company of America v. Jefferson Associates, Ltd.*, 896 S.W.2d 156 (Tex., 1995). In 1984, the Prudential Insurance Company of America sold a four-story office building in Austin, Texas, to F.B. Goldman, who later conveyed to Jefferson Associates, Ltd., a limited partnership of which Goldman was a partner. Goldman was an experienced investor and had bought and sold several large investment properties on an "as is" basis. Before bidding on the building, Goldman had it inspected by his maintenance supervisor, his property manager, and an independent professional engineering firm. Prudential's representative told Goldman that the building was "superb," "superfine," and "one of the finest little properties in the city of Austin." Goldman's original architects reviewed the specifications in 1987, some 3 years after the sale, and found nothing to indicate that the building contained asbestos. The building, however, had a fireproofing material called MonoKote® that contained asbestos. There was no evidence that Prudential actually knew that the Jefferson building contained asbestos before Goldman filed the lawsuit.

The contract to purchase the building contained the following provisions:

> As a material part of the consideration for this Agreement, seller and purchaser agree that purchaser is taking the Property "AS IS with any and all latent and patent defects and that there is no warranty by seller that the property is fit for a particular purpose. Purchaser acknowledges that it is not relying upon any representation, statement, or other assertion with respect to the property condition, but is relying upon its examination of the property. Purchaser takes the property under the express understanding that there are no express or implied warranties (except for limited warranties of title set forth in the closing documents). Provisions of this Section 15 shall survive the Closing;" and

- Purchaser hereby waives an action under the Texas Deceptive Trade Practices Act.

The Texas Supreme Court held that by agreeing to purchase something "as is," a buyer agrees to make his own appraisal of the property and to accept the risk that he may be wrong. The court noted that the sole cause of buyer's injury in said circumstances, by his own admission, is the buyer himself, as he has agreed to take the full risk of determining the value of the purchase. Rather than pay more, a buyer may choose to rely entirely upon his own determination of the condition and value of the purchase. In making this choice, he removes the possibility that the seller's conduct will cause this damage. The court qualified its holding, though, that the "as is" language is not determinative in every circumstance and would not apply if: (1) the buyer is induced to make a purchase because of fraudulent representation or concealment of information by the seller; (2) the buyer is impaired by the seller's conduct, such as obstructing an inspection; or (3) the "as is" clause is merely an incidental or "boilerplate" provision. In order for the "as is" clause to be enforceable, it must be an important basis of the bargain and apparently set out in some distinctive type style, such as ten-point type.

The court also noted that there was no evidence that Prudential actually knew of the asbestos and restated Texas law as it relates to Deceptive Trade Practices Act:

- a seller has no duty to disclose facts he does not know.

- a seller is not liable for failing to disclose what he only should have known.

- a seller is not liable for failing to disclose information he did not actually know.

Concerning the statements made by the Prudential representative, the court held that they were merely puffing and could not constitute fraud, unless the maker knew it was false when he made it or made it recklessly without knowledge of the truth. The court also noted that the problems of asbestos had been well known and publicly discussed for years when

Goldman bought the building, and, therefore, Goldman's agreement to buy the building "as is" precluded him from recovering damages against Prudential.

As to the Deceptive Trade Practices Act, the court noted that the "as is" provision does not violate the prohibition against consumer's waiver under the DTPA, noting that "Goldman's agreement does not say he cannot sue Prudential for violating the DTPA; it says he cannot win the suit. He cannot win because he has asserted facts which negate proof of causation required for recovery."

Justice Gonzales noted that the court "returns to reason by reinstating reliance as an essential part of producing cause in a DTPA claim premised on a representation."

Does this theory apply to home sellers and buyers? Probably so.

In *Smith v. Levine*, 911 S.W.2d 427 (Tex. App.–San Antonio, 1995), the Smiths leased a house to Mr. Grissom, who was interested in buying the house. Grissom hired an inspection company to do a foundation analysis. It reflected that the foundation was defective. Grissom discussed the report with Mr. Smith and offered to give him a copy in exchange for paying part of the fee. The seller refused, indicating that the report "would have no value to us." The Smiths later listed the house with a real estate agent and did not mention the defective foundation on the agent's questionnaire. After the listing agreement expired, the Smiths put the house on the market themselves, describing the house as being in "excellent" condition. When showing the house, the Smiths also assured the purchasers that visible cracks were superficial. The purchasers (Mitchells) hired an engineer to do a "walk through" inspection, which also indicated that the cracks were minor and superficial.

The Mitchells later listed the house with a REALTOR® who secured a contract with a new purchaser. This second purchaser hired the same inspector who did the original inspection showing the foundation as being defective. What a coincidence!

The jury found that the Smiths knowingly engaged in a "false, misleading, or deceptive act or practice," as well as "unconscionable acts or course of action," both of which were the producing cause of damages to the Mitchells. The court affirmed that the jury was entitled to find that the Smiths knew the foundation was defective because of the original inspection.

The earnest money contract also contained an "as is" provision. The court held, however, citing the Prudential case, that "as is" is not a defense to a cause of action where a party is induced to enter into the contract because of fraudulent misrepresentation or concealment of information by the seller.

The Prudential case seems to be an open door to provide "as is" as a defense under the Deceptive Trade Practices Act, shifting the burden to the buyer. Later cases have indicated that the "as is" language in the earnest money contract must be clear, not "boilerplate," and should be in bold, ten-point type to be sure the buyer or reader of the contract would not have overlooked the provision. For instance, one case has indicated that the "as is" provision should emphasize the buyer's sole reliance on his own inspection to preclude causation under the Deceptive Trade Practices Act. It is also helpful if the buyer has an attorney, which seems to reinforce the ability to use "as is" as a defense. See *Erwin v. Smiley*, 975 S.W.2d 335 (Tex. App.–Eastland, 1998).

In *Fletcher v. Edwards*, 26 S.W.3d 66 (Tex. App.–Waco, 2000), the Fletchers filed suit against Edwards alleging that Edwards (a real estate agent) represented to them that they could get a water connection to the lot that they ultimately purchased, when they could not obtain the necessary connection because of a lack of easements across an adjoining lot. The trial court prevented a summary judgment in favor of the broker, and the Fletchers appealed. The court noted the parties' dispute—whether Edwards affirmatively represented to them that the water was available to the lot or Edwards maintained that he never told the Fletchers the water service was available to the lot, but told the Fletchers that they needed to check with a water company. The Fletchers signed an "Acceptance of Title" agreement at closing that contained an "as is" clause. The Fletchers asserted that the "as is" clause was not applicable in DTPA cases. The court noted that in the earnest money contract the Fletchers contractually bound themselves to accept the property "in its present condition." The court held that this is an agreement to purchase the property "as is" (this is the standard language in the TREC Form, paragraph 7.D.2). The court noted that the "as is" negates the causation essential to recovery for DTPA. However, it does not bind a buyer who is induced to enter in the agreement because of fraudulent misrepresentation. The court went on to hold that the Fletchers could prevail under a common law fraud claim if they could show that Edwards recklessly made the alleged representations as positive assertions without knowledge of the truth.

The court affirmed the fact that the defendant was entitled to judgments as a matter of law on the claim for exemplary damages under the DTPA and common law because of the "as is" defense, but they reversed the trial court's holding as to fraudulent inducement.

In *Larsen v. Langford & Associates, Inc.*, 41 S.W.3rd 245 (Tex. App.–Waco, 2001), involves the second "as is" case out of the Waco Court of Appeals. A real estate broker (Larsen) and his wife, who had access to the Multiple Listing Service, were looking for a house in Corsicana, Texas. The house was described as historic, built in 1913, and needing work. The property was listed with Carlene Langford & Associates, Inc. The broker, representing himself, requested to see the home. No one from the Langford office accompanied the Larsens to the home. They ultimately entered into a residential Earnest Money Contract to purchase the home for $65,000 through an assumption of the seller's loan. Langford was the seller's broker. The buyer's broker represented himself. The buyers admitted learning of problems with the home before closing and also agreed to receiving a Seller's Disclosure Form before the closing and before signing the final inspection. The sellers did not fill out some parts of the Seller's Disclosure Form. The buyer, however, never requested that they complete the form.

After closing, the broker/buyer alleged common law fraud, negligent misrepresentation, and violations of the DTPA. The court noted that all four cases of action were predicated on the reliance of the buyer on a representation made by the seller or the seller's agent. The court further noted that the box 7.D.2 was checked, which indicated that the home was purchased "as is." The listing broker also prepared another document that was signed by the buyers at closing that included the following clauses:

> I/We have been advised by the named Realtor/Real Estate Company to make any and all inspections of the subject property either by myself or anyone that I wish to employ, such as a licensed real estate inspector.
>
> I have made all inspections or have had an employee of my choice to make them for me. I accept the property in its present condition and am satisfied with the inspections and any repairs that were required.
>
> Brokers and sales associates shall not be liable or responsible for any inspections or repairs pursuant to this Contract and Addendum even in an event of a problem that has been overlooked by any or all parties involved in this transaction.

The court noted that enforceability of the "as is" agreement is determined: (1) in light of the sophistication of the parties, (2) by the terms of the "as is" agreement, (3) by whether the "as is" clause is freely negotiated, (4) by whether it was an arm's length transaction, and (5) by whether there was a knowing misrepresentation or concealment of a known fact. The court noted that the transaction was conducted at arm's length and that both parties were similarly knowledgeable and sophisticated parties in the real estate business, *particularly in light of the fact that the buyer acted on his own behalf as a broker.* The court also noted that the "as is" language was found in two separate documents, the preprinted Earnest Money Contract and the Final Inspection and Disclosure Form. The court held that by signing both agreements, the Larsens (buyers) explicitly agreed that they would accept the property in its present condition without requiring any repairs by the seller, that they had made their own inspection, and that they would relinquish Langford of any liability for the repairs known or unknown by the seller. The relevant contract provisions were clearly unambiguously demonstrated. Because the Larsens agreed to rely solely upon themselves, their own inspections, or the inspectors they chose and because the agreement affirmatively negated the element of each claim that the Langfords' conduct caused them any harm, the court further found that there was no inducement for the buyer to buy the house based on representations made by the broker and that the "as is" language effectively waived their rights to prevail under an allegation under the Deceptive Trade Practices Act.

In *Cole v. Johnson,* 157 S.W. 3d 856 (Tex. App.–Ft. Worth, 2005), purchasers sued a seller for nondisclosure of certain information regarding the foundation of their home. At closing, the purchaser signed a document indicating that the sales price was being lowered $2,000 in lieu of foundation repairs, agreed that the sellers would be held harmless for any present or future repairs, and further agreed that the property was being purchased in an "as-is" condition. Other documents were provided to buyers at or prior to closing, totaling fifty-five pages of documentation relating to the foundation repairs. In the seller disclosure form, the seller represented that they were not aware of any undisclosed defective conditions, and that they were unaware of any current defective conditions to the drainage on the property. After the closing, there was a telephone conversation between the buyers and the sellers in which the seller indicated that the foundation work had failed. The buyers sued the seller based solely on this verbal allegation of nondisclosure.

The trial court awarded a summary judgment to the sellers, including attorney's fees. The court found that the purchasers were aware that there was no foundation warranty on the premises, they were aware that the property had an extensive history of foundation problems and foundation work. The court further found that they were aware that the foundation work had not cured the foundation problems because the foundation had continued to move and that there were numerous references in the reports given to the buyer that indicated there were continuing slab problems. The court noted the seller of a house is charged only with disclosing such material facts as to put a buyer exercising reasonable diligence on notice of a condition of the house, and that it was obvious, even to a layman, that the foundation had not corrected all of the problems and that they were ongoing at the time of the inspection reports that had been given to the buyer.

The court further noted that the use of the "as-is" provision is enforceable depending on the "totality of the circumstances" surrounding the agreement and that absent fraud, the "as-is" agreement is enforceable. The court found no fraud in this transaction at all.

Cherry v. McCall, 138 S.W.3d 35 (Tex.App.–San Antonio 2004, pet. pending). The Cherrys bought a home from the McCalls. After the Cherrys bought the home, they discovered a walled-in room in the basement. The room was filled with trash, including rusty plumbing fixtures, bathtubs, sinks, commodes, boards, pipes, rocks, and used building materials. The trash was damp and contaminated with mold.

The Cherrys brought a declaratory judgment action, seeking declaration that (1) the McCalls breached the contract, and (2) the walled-in room constitutes a mutual mistake justifying rescission. The McCalls answered by general denial. The McCalls also asserted the "as is" provision of the contract as an affirmative defense.

The Cherrys argue that the "as is" clause is unenforceable under the "totality of the circumstances" test set out by *Prudential*. The Cherrys do not allege that the McCalls fraudulently induced them to buy the house or concealed knowledge about the hidden room, nor do they allege that they were prevented from making their own inspection. Rather, they argue that their lack of sophistication, the fact that the "as is" provision was not negotiated but a standard boilerplate provision, the high price the Cherrys paid for the property, and the fact that the defect was hidden are all factors indicating that the "as is" clause is unenforceable under the "totality of the circumstances."

The court disagreed. While there is some evidence indicating that Mrs. Cherry, who had never handled the details of purchasing a home on her own before, was less sophisticated than the McCalls, who owned rental properties, there is no evidence that the Cherrys and the McCalls entered into the contract from unequal bargaining positions or that the transaction was not made at arm's length. Additionally, there is no evidence to support the Cherrys' argument that the "as is" provision was not freely negotiated. In fact, Mrs. Cherry confirmed in her deposition testimony that she "agreed to purchase the property in its current condition" and that she "accepted the risk" that the property might be deficient. Because the Cherrys contracted to accept the property "as is," they cannot, as a matter of law, prevail on their breach of contract claim.

In order to be entitled to a declaratory judgment that the contract was made under a mutual mistake, the Cherrys had to prove: (1) a mistake of fact, (2) held mutually by the parties, (3) which materially affects the agreed-upon exchange. Under section 154 of the Restatement (Second) of Contracts, however, a party bears the risk of mistake when the risk is allocated to him by agreement or when he knowingly treats his limited knowledge of the facts surrounding the mistake as sufficient. Here, the risk of mistake was allocated to the Cherrys by agreement when they contracted to accept property "in its current condition." Accordingly, their claim of mutual mistake fails as a matter of law.

The Cherrys argue, however, that the contract itself is invalid because a mutual mistake prevented the "meeting of the minds" necessary to the formation of a valid contract. Again, the court disagreed. Mrs. Cherry confirmed in her deposition testimony that she "agreed to purchase the property in its current condition" and that she "accepted the risk" that the property might be deficient. Thus, the evidence confirms that a meeting of the minds did take place, i.e., though neither party knew of the hidden room when it entered into the agreement, both parties agreed to place the risk of any unknown defects on the Cherrys.

There are exceptions to the "as is" rule. In *Kupchynsky v. Nardiello*, 230 S.W. 3d 685 (Tex. App.–Dallas, 2007), Nardiello sued Kupchynsky and FGH Homebuilders, Inc., in connection with construction defects on a house. FGH was the builder of the home, and George Kupchynsky was the vice president of the company, but lived in the house as his residence. He contracted to sell the house to Nardiello, who obtained home, foundation, and termite inspections while the contract was pending. The residence featured two tiled balconies, one in the front and the other in the back of the house. Nardiello closed the transaction, and approximately five months later, the back balcony began to leak in several places. Nardiello sued after discovering that the balconies had been leaking "for quite some time" and the galvanized metal pans in the balcony were rusted and had holes. Construction experts concluded during the trial that the home was not built in a good, workmanlike manner.

At trial, the jury found that the defendants engaged in false, misleading, or deceptive acts and further made a negligent misrepresentation on which the purchasers relied. Kupchynsky's defense was that the plaintiffs had gotten independent inspections, and therefore they could not have relied on his representation as a matter of law. The trial court found otherwise, however, noting that the buyer may have relied on an expert's opinion, but (1) they did not renegotiate the price based on that opinion, and (2) the plaintiffs followed the inspector's recommendation and questioned Kupchynsky about the moisture that had accumulated in the balcony. Therefore, they could not have relied on the inspector alone.

A more confusing part of the case is that there was an "as is" provision (Paragraph 7.D. of the standard TREC form), which the court held did not negate the cause of action as a matter of law and that it was not an "as is" provision, "given the totality of the circumstances and the nature of the transaction." This contradicts two other courts of appeals cases. There is a vigorous dissent that 7.D. was an "as is" provision, and was not an exception to the "as is" rule, if there was no fraud in the inducement on behalf of the seller of the property.

In another similar case a seller misrepresented the cash flow of an apartment project and the court considered it a fraudulent inducement and not subject to the "as is" defense. *San Antonio Properties, L.P. v. PSRA Investments, Inc.* (Tex. App.–San Antonio, 2008).

Licensed Real Estate Property Inspectors

The Real Estate License Act provides for a program of inspectors to inspect and report on the condition of real property. In the event an inspector engages in conduct that constitutes fraud, misrepresentation, deceit, or false pretenses, there are statutory procedures for recovering money from the Real Estate Inspection Recovery Fund. This also provides a "safe harbor" for real estate agents to refer the purchaser to a real property inspector, particularly as to the technical, mechanical defects in the property. It also gives the purchaser another party to rely on, rather than the representations of the real estate agent, particularly in light of the holding in *Ozuna*, *Kubinsky*, and *Stagner* cases.

There is some authority, however, that such recommendations may result in liability; see *Diversified Human Resources Group, Inc., v. PB-KBB, Inc.*, 671 S.W.2d 634 (Tex. Civ. App.–Houston, 1984).

Ooh. Interesting Issue!

In *Head v. U.S. Inspect DFW, Inc.*, 159 S.W.3d 731 (Tex. App.–Ft. Worth 2005, no pet.), a home purchaser brought action against a home inspector for breach of contract, reach of implied warranty, negligence, and breach of DTPA for failure to discover and disclose roof problems. Inspector defended DTPA claims by raising as affirmative defense the professional services exemption of Tex. Bus. Com. Code Ann. §17.49(c) precluding claims arising out of advice, judgment, opinion, or similar professional skill. The inspector stated in the report that the roof was "performing its intended function," but it was not a misrepresentation of fact, but an expression of professional opinion.

The court noted that the inspector's contract provided that inspection would be conducted by "licensed real estate inspector." The inspector was assisted in inspection of roof by an apprentice inspector. This was some evidence that the services provided were nonconforming with the express warranty given on who would conduct the inspection.

But wait! The inspection contract limited the liability of inspector for breach of contract or negligence to the contract price of inspection ($348.27). The court held that the homeowner and inspector were free to contractually limit liability in absence of controlling public policy precluding enforcement of the agreement. With many providers of inspection services available, there was no disparity of bargaining power between the parties that made the limitation unconscionable. In view of the small fee paid to the inspector for a visual inspection of house, there were legitimate commercial reasons for limiting liability.

Could brokers do the same thing??? Hmm.

Seller Disclosure Forms

Similar to the real estate inspectors, a defense can be created for the licensee if the seller disclosed the defects. The theory behind this is that if the purchaser knows of the defect but buys anyway, he may have lost his right to sue for damages. See *Zak v. Parks*, 729 S.W.2d 875 (Tex. App.–Houston, 1987); *Dubow v. Dragon*, 746 S.W.2d 857 (Tex. App.–Dallas, 1988); *Pfeiffer v. Ebby Halliday*, 747 S.W.2d 887 (Tex. App.–Dallas, 1988). This may be particularly true in light of the new statutory Seller's Disclosure Statement.

In 1993, the Texas Legislature added a new section to the Property Code that now requires the seller of residential real property, comprising not more than one dwelling unit, to give the purchaser of the property a written notice in a form.

The notice is to be completed with the best of the seller's knowledge and belief as of the date the notice is completed and signed. If the information required is unknown to the seller, the seller should indicate that fact on the notice and stay in compliance with the section. This probably does not mean, however, that the seller can be blind to an obvious defect and say he doesn't know. Disclosure of a defect is required for a broker under §1101.652(b)(3) & (4) of the License Act! **The statute does not apply** to any transfers:

- pursuant to a court order.

- by a trustee in bankruptcy.

- to a mortgagee by a mortgagor or successor in interest.

- by a mortgagee or a beneficiary under a deed of trust who has acquired the real property by sale conducted pursuant to a power of sale under a deed of trust or a sale pursuant to a court-ordered foreclosure or has acquired the real property by deed in lieu of foreclosure.

- by a fiduciary in the course of the administration of a decedent's estate, guardianship, conservatorship, or trust.

- from one co-owner to one or more other co-owners.

- made to a spouse or to a person or persons in the initial line of consanguinity of one or more of the transferors.

- between the spouses resulting from a decree of dissolution of marriage or a decree of legal separation or from a property settlement agreement incident to such a decree.

- to or from any governmental entity.

- of new residences of not more than one dwelling unit that have not previously been occupied for essential purposes.

- of real property where the value of any dwelling does not exceed 5 percent of the value of the property.

The notice must be delivered by the seller to the purchaser on or before the Effective Date of an executory contract (signing the Earnest Money Contract) binding the purchaser to purchase the property. Note that the broker is required to fill in the Effective Date on the TREC forms. If the contract is entered into without the seller providing this required notice, the purchaser may terminate the contract for any reason within 7 days (by the 6th day!) after receiving the notice. A new issue exists, however. What if the seller never delivers the notice? What if the disclosure form is given on the Effective Date but before buyers had a chance to review it—can the buyer then not revoke?

A provision of the new statute parallels a similar change in the Texas Real Estate License Act, that a seller or seller's agent (does it apply to a buyer's broker?) has no duty to make a disclosure or release information related to whether a death by natural causes, suicide, or accident unrelated to the condition of the property occurred on the property. Note that the Texas Real Estate License Act says that a licensee has no duty even to *inquire about* whether death occurred on the property under these circumstances. Presumably, a seller would not need to inquire! How would a licensee know that the death was exempt from disclosure, however, if the licensee didn't inquire? One may want to put the "death disclosure" on the seller's disclosure form so that the broker has no need to inquire.

Seller's Disclosures in the Courts

In *Kessler v. Fanning*, 953 S.W. 2d 515 (Tex. App.–Ft. Worth, 1997, no writ history to date) in connection with buying a house, the buyers received the required Property Condition Disclosure Statement. With respect to the questions on the statement about improper drainage or previous structure repairs, the sellers had answered "no." There appears to have been no other statements about drainage or structure made by the sellers. The buyers had the house inspected and detected no drainage problems during the inspection, even though it was raining at the time.

After moving into the house, the buyers noticed some real drainage problems. They sued the sellers, alleging DTPA violations.

The first question on appeal was whether any statement by the sellers was the producing cause of the Fannings' injury. In order to recover under the DTPA, the consumer must prove that the deceptive act was the producing cause of damages. The Fannings testified that, if they had known of the drainage problem, they would not have bought the house. The sellers claimed that the inspection of the property by the buyers was an intervening factor that broke the causal connection. The court held in favor of the buyers as to the issue of producing cause. The possibility of an independent investigation that might have uncovered fraud does not preclude recovery damages for fraudulent misrepresentations.

The second question was whether the statutorily required disclosure statement continued misrepresentations of fact or was merely a statement of opinion. The form stated that it was "not a substitute for inspections or warranties" and that it contained "representations made by the owner(s) based on owner's knowledge." The sellers claimed that these statements showed that the disclosures were merely statements of opinion or mere puffing, and not actionable misrepresentations. Whether a statement is opinion or not depends on (i) the specificity versus vagueness of the statement, (ii) the comparative knowledge of the parties, and (iii) whether the representation pertains to a past versus a future condition. The court held that the disclosure statement was not vague, was not based on equivalent knowledge by the parties, and pertained to past as opposed to future conditions. Thus, it did amount to a misrepresentation rather than merely a statement of opinion. Similarly, in *Blackstock v. Dudley*, 12 S.W.3d 131 (Tex. App.–Amarillo, 1999), a seller was sued for allegedly failing to disclose plumbing problems prior to the purchase. The home was inspected, but the court held that the plumbing defects were not, and because of their nature could not, have been discovered. The court noted that there is conflicting testimony as to what was actually said about the condition of the house. The jury resolved those conflicts in favor of the plaintiffs, and when the jury makes a decision, the court is highly unlikely to reverse that decision if there is even a scintilla of evidence that exists in support of the jury findings. That is the risk of the courthouse! In *Fernandez v. Schultz*, 15 S.W.3d 658 (Tex. App.–Dallas, 2000), Mr. Fernandez, a real estate agent, bought a house from HUD. He personally examined the property and purchased it on September 1, 1995. The real estate agent testified that he was familiar with the signs of termite infestation and denied seeing any evidence of termites in the house before he bought it. Fernandez remodeled the house, utilizing Mr. Nova, who testified that he noticed evidence of active termites and informed Fernandez about the termites, but Fernandez told him to continue his work making cosmetic repairs.

Fernandez offered the house for sale, gave the buyer (Schultz) a Seller's Disclosure of Property Condition dated October 29, 1995, which indicated that Fernandez had no knowledge of any active termites, termite damage, or previous termite treatment. Upon the Schultzes' inspection, they discovered evidence of previous termite treatment along the front porch. Fernandez agreed to have "spot" termite treatment done for the exterior of the house.

Following the purchase, the Schultzes discovered several swarms of termites inside their home and, ultimately, paid for full treatment by a different pest control company. Schultz sued under the Texas Deceptive Trade Practices Act alleging that Fernandez "knowingly" violated the DTPA. Fernandez defended by saying that there was a professional inspection, which relieves him from liability as a seller upon sale of the house, relying on *Dubow v. Dragon*. The court distinguished the holding in *Dubow*, however, noting that in *Dubow* the independent inspection resulted in a re-negotiation of the sales contract, relying on the professional opinions and quotes of their inspector. This was not the case here. The contract was never re-negotiated based in reliance on the inspection. Therefore, the seller still had liability for failing to disclose the termite problem.

There may be some relief in sight. In *Bynum v. Prudential Residential Services*, et al., 129 S.W.3rd 781 (Tex. App.–Houston [1st Dist.] 2003), parents sued on behalf of their children to hold various Prudential entities (relocation company), inspectors and sellers, alleging violations of the Deceptive Trade Practices Act. They alleged that the home was remodeled without getting building permits. The contract for sale to the Bynums included an "as is" clause. The court held that there was no evidence that Prudential had actual knowledge that the sellers had remodeled their home without the necessary permits and, therefore, the buyers were not entitled to have the "as is" clause set aside on grounds of fraudulent misrepresentation or concealment.

As it related to the Seller's Disclosure Form, the court held that the Homeowner's Disclosure Form, standing alone, is not evidence that the McNamaras knew that their Disclosure Statement to the Bynums was false. The McNamaras apparently did not know much about construction, did not inquire as to the necessity of building permits, so it did not follow that they had actual knowledge that permits were required to remodel their bathrooms. In upholding the "actual knowledge" standard, the court said that there was no evidence that the McNamaras actually knew that they had remodeled without the necessary permits. The court further noted long-standing Texas law that when a buyer purchases "as is," he is agreeing that there is no express or implied warranties and that the buyer is relying only on his own examination of the property.

An important issue was raised concerning the Homeowner's Disclosure Form. The court held that the law (Section 5.008 of the Property Code) requires only that the form be completed to the best of seller's belief at the time the Notice is completed and signed, and there was no duty to provide continuing updates as to matters within the form.

In *Sherman v. Elkowitz*, 130 S.W.3d 316 (Tex. App.–Houston [14th Dist.] 2004), the question posed for the court was whether the listing agent for the seller of the home could be liable for alleged misrepresentations and nondisclosures in a disclosure notice required by the legislature. In May of 1998, the Shermans purchased a home; Elkowitz acted as listing agent for the Shields and assisted them with the sale of the property to the Shermans. The Shields completed and provided to the Shermans a Seller's Disclosure Notice as required by Texas law, in which they just identified cracks in the driveway as a known defect needing repair and also disclosed a treatment for termites in 1990. The Shermans had the property inspected before agreeing to the purchase.

After purchasing the property, the Shermans discovered various defects in the property and eventually learned that the Shields (the sellers) had sued the previous owner for failing to disclose the same defects the Shermans had discovered. They then brought suit against the Shields claiming that the Shields and Elkowitz were required to disclose the alleged defects and the earlier lawsuit. In the trial court, the Shermans obtained a favorable judgment against the Shields, but the trial court handed a directed verdict for Elkowitz.

The disclosure notice was the same form provided by the Texas Association of REALTORS® that noted that the notice was not a substitute for inspections and was not a warranty. There is an additional notice in the disclosure that states that the broker has relied on the notice as true and correct and has no reason to believe that it is false. The Shermans placed emphasis on the statement that "there was no reason to believe it was false."

The court noted that the broker would have a duty to come forward *only* if he had any reason to believe that the seller's disclosures were false or inaccurate, and the notice makes it clear the disclosure is by the seller, not by the seller and the broker, and is merely statement of the broker's knowledge concerning the seller's disclosures. The court noted that the only way the broker could be held liable for the statement in the notice is if it were shown to be untrue.

There were two other issues: (1) that there was a defect that was corrected and not disclosed; and (2) the broker's duty to disclose the prior lawsuit. The court noted that repairing corrected defects does not prove their continued existence, therefore, one could logically conclude that there was no duty to disclose defects that had been repaired.

The court went on to hold that as a matter of law, brokers are not required to disclose prior lawsuits and that the disclosure only requires to a current lawsuit. That statutory form did not require disclosure of a lawsuit that was not pending.

Damages Under the DTPA

As previously discussed, the statutory damages recoverable under the Deceptive Trade Practices Act were changed in 1995 and now include:

- the amount of economic damages found by the trier of fact. In addition, the court may award two times that portion of the actual damages if it does not exceed $1,000. If the trier of fact finds that the conduct of the defendant was committed *knowingly*, the trier of fact may award no more than three times the amount of actual damages in excess of $1,000.

- an order adjoining such acts or failure of act.

- orders necessary to restore to any part of the suit any money or property, real or personal, which may have been acquired in violation of this subchapter.

- any other relief that the court deems proper, including the appointment of a receiver or the revocation of a license or certificate authorizing the person who engages in business in this state if the judgment has not been satisfied within 3 months of the date of final judgment. *The court may not revoke or suspend a license to do business in the state or appoint a receiver to take over the affairs of the person who has failed to satisfy judgment if the person is a licensee of or regulated by a state agency that has the statutory authority to revoke or suspend a license or to appoint a receiver or trustee.* [Emphasis added.] It has further been held that the treble damages must be found by the trier of the fact and is not an automatic award. *Martin v. McKee Realtors, Inc.*, 663 S.W.2d 446 (Tex., 1984).

A recent 1999 Amendment to the Texas Deceptive Trade Practices Act eliminates the requirement that attorney's fees be reasonable in relation to the amount of work expended.

Apparently, this opens the door now for the court to award contingency fees to plaintiffs rather than requiring fees to be "reasonable."

This case may greatly limit plaintiff's suits if the plaintiff's attorney is unwilling to settle for an hourly rate paid at the successful conclusion of the case. Contingency fees are still legal, but the ability to recover them from the defendant is now greatly limited.

Negligent Misrepresentation

Another cause of action beginning to permeate cases involving real estate brokers is negligent misrepresentation. When alleging negligent misrepresentation, the parties seeking the remedy must prove that: (i) a representation is made by the defendant in the course of his business for a transaction in which he has a pecuniary interest; (ii) the defendant provides "false information" for the guidance of others in their business; (iii) the defendant did not exercise reasonable care or competence in obtaining or communicating the information; and (iv) the plaintiff suffers pecuniary loss by justifiable reliance on the representation. *O'Hearn v. Hogard*, 1992 W.L. 324462 (Tex. App.–Houston [14th Dist.], 1992).

In the case of *Hagans v. Woodruff*, 830 S.W.2d 732 (Tex. App.–Houston [14th Dist.], 1992), the court, in reasoning similar to *Aguilar, supra*, held that the false information must be provided by the broker to the plaintiff but that general comments, such as the house was in a "good neighborhood," are not an all-encompassing negligent representation that no faults exist in the neighborhood.

Following the reasoning of the *Kubinsky, supra*, the court held that a broker has no legal duty to inspect listed property and disclose all facts that might affect its value or desirability. In this case, there was a fault line running through the neighborhood. Licensees should continue to be very cautious, however. The court in *Hagans* also followed the *Bynum* court's theory that any false representation tied to the broker creates a cause of action under the DTPA as well as for negligent misrepresentation. The key defense seems to be that the agent, after reasonable investigation, did not know that the information was "false."

Real Estate Recovery Fund

The plaintiff is also guaranteed solvency of any real estate licensee defendant under the Real Estate Recovery Fund. Any party that has been held to be an aggrieved party can recover for the wrongful act of real estate agents, *Texas Real Estate Commission v. Century 21 Security Realty, Inc.*, 598 S.W.2d 920 (Tex. Civ. App.–El Paso, 1980). The recovery fund is also liable for attorney's fees, *Texas Real Estate Commission v. Hood*, 617 S.W.2d 838 (Tex. Civ. App.–Eastland, 1981). Any valid claim for a recovery out of the fund may result in a suspension of the broker's or salesperson's license, and the license cannot be reinstated until he or she has repaid the recovery fund in full plus interest at the current legal rate. The recovery fund is limited to the aggregate of $50,000, including attorney's fees, in the same transaction or $100,000 against any one licensed real estate broker or salesperson. Only actual damages (not treble damages) may be recovered out of the fund. *State v. Pace*, 640 S.W.2d 432 (Tex. Civ. App.–Beaumont, 1982).

Regarding liability insurance, the Texas standard policy form for omissions and errors for real estate might *not* cover violations of the DTPA!! *St. Paul Ins. Co. v. Bonded Realty, Inc.*, 583 S.W.2d 619 (Tex., 1979). Another word of caution: Many insurance policies do *not* provide coverage for damages in excess of actual damages. This may mean that a real estate broker does not have insurance coverage for punitive damages, exemplary damages, or multiple damages under the Deceptive Trade Practices Act. Be sure to check your policy for this coverage.

Economic and Finance Update, Federal and State

Pre-Assessment Evaluation

Please answer the following questions.

1.   Fannie Mae and Freddie Mac have been taken over by the U.S. Treasury.

      True   False

2.   To avoid a foreclosure, a homeowner may deed the collateral property to the lender.

      True   False

3.   FHA emerged as a significant force in the mortgage market in the last year.

      True   False

4.   Federal law requires lenders to provide borrowers with an annual notice that they may cancel mortgage insurance coverage but leaves it up to the borrowers to request the cancellation.

      True   False

5.   If a Public Improvement District (PID) is to be established, it must be established by the city in which it resides.

      True   False

ECONOMIC UPDATE—Introduction

The field of real estate finance includes many related subjects. Similarly, there are many economic factors that affect real estate. However, this chapter is limited to key changes that have occurred over the past two to three years that have had an effect on Texas real estate licensees and the real estate market.

The Federal Reserve Bank provides financial and economic data in a publication commonly known as the Beige Book. This report is published eight times per year. Each Federal Reserve Bank gathers anecdotal information on current economic conditions in its District through reports from Bank and Branch directors and interviews with key business contacts, economists, market experts, and other sources. The Beige Book summarizes this information by District and sector. An overall summary of the twelve district reports is prepared by a designated Federal Reserve Bank on a rotating basis. The information given here is condensed from the report based on information collected before October 15, 2008.

To keep current with the information provided in this publication access either of these Web sites:

http://www.federalreserve.gov/FOMC/BeigeBook/2008/
http://www.federalreserve.gov/FOMC/BeigeBook/2009/

Reports indicated that economic activity weakened in September, 2008 across all 12 Federal Reserve Districts. Several Districts also noted that their contacts had become more pessimistic about the economic outlook.

Consumer spending decreased in most Districts, with declines reported in retailing, auto sales and tourism. Nearly all Districts commenting on nonfinancial service industries noted reduced activity. Manufacturing slowed in most Districts. Residential real estate markets remained weak, and commercial real estate activity slowed in many Districts.

Inflationary pressures moderated a bit in September, 2008. While several Districts noted continuing pass-through of earlier price increases for metals, food and energy, most indicated that cost pressures had eased. Labor market conditions weakened in most Districts, and wage pressures remained limited. Several Districts reported lower capital spending or reductions in capital spending plans due to the high level of uncertainty about the economic outlook or concerns over the availability of credit.

Consumer Spending and Tourism. Consumer spending was softer in nearly all Districts. Retail sales were reported to have weakened or declined in Philadelphia, Cleveland, Richmond, Atlanta, Chicago, Minneapolis, and Kansas City; Dallas and San Francisco cited weak or sluggish sales; and Boston and New York indicated that sales were mixed and moderately below plan sales, respectively.

Retailers cited these recent sales trends and concerns about credit availability as reasons for a weaker economic outlook, including a slow holiday season. Most Districts reporting on light vehicle sales saw declines, with several Districts pointing to reduced credit availability as a limiting factor for automobile sales. However, Kansas City, St. Louis, and Chicago noted that dealers offering incentive and discount programs had seen some positive effect on sales.

Business Spending. Hiring and capital spending varied across Districts. Labor market conditions weakened in most Districts. Boston, Chicago and Richmond cited reductions in hiring or hiring plans. Atlanta, Minneapolis, Kansas City, San Francisco and Dallas all noted some weakening in employment. However, the demand for skilled labor remained strong in several Districts, and Kansas City noted market tightness for minimum-wage jobs in leisure and hospitality.

Boston reported capital spending was mixed as firms were cautious about spending resources. Cleveland reported capital spending remained on plan but intentions to increase outlays have declined. Philadelphia indicated concerns over restrictions in access to credit were limiting future capital expenditures for some manufacturers. In contrast, Kansas City and Chicago reported that capital spending for producers of heavy machinery continued to be strong.

Nonfinancial Services. Nonfinancial service industries experienced weaker activity in most Districts. Several Districts reported that activity in real-estate and related industries such as legal and title services was weak. New York cited widespread deterioration in business conditions. Boston reported consulting firms were experiencing reduced demand for their services from a range of clients. Cleveland, St. Louis, and Dallas noted slower activity in the transportation industry; however, Dallas' slowdown was due mostly to temporary disruptions caused by Hurricane Ike.

Trucking contacts in Atlanta indicated declines in retail, automotive, and construction-related shipments, but increases in energy and farm products. Minneapolis reported continued strength in professional business services, while demand for professional business services was down in San Francisco and Philadelphia. Demand for health-care-related services was strong in Boston, Richmond, and Chicago but weaker in St. Louis and San Francisco.

Manufacturing. Manufacturing activity moved lower in most Districts, and contacts expressed heightened concern about the economic outlook. Several Districts noted that credit conditions were contributing to a high level of uncertainty on the part of contacts. Declines in manufacturing activity of varying degrees were reported in Boston, New York,

Cleveland, Richmond, Chicago, St. Louis, Kansas City, San Francisco, and Dallas. Atlanta reported that production remained at a low level, whereas Minneapolis described conditions as mixed and Philadelphia noted a slight increase in activity.

Activity in the automotive industry also continued to decline. Kansas City, Richmond, Philadelphia, and Chicago reported continued strength in exports. However, Atlanta indicated a decline in export orders, reversing a trend of the past several months. Energy-related manufacturers and heavy equipment manufacturers with ties to energy or agriculture continued to do well in most Districts. Dallas and Atlanta reported that Hurricanes Ike and Gustav disrupted oil production and refining, restricting the supply of petroleum and related products and leading to gasoline shortages in the Southeast and along the East Coast.

Real Estate and Construction. Residential real estate and construction activity weakened or remained low in all Districts. Housing activity was reported to have moved lower in Boston, New York, Philadelphia, Chicago, St. Louis, Minneapolis, Dallas, and San Francisco. Although still slow, residential markets showed some signs of stabilizing in Cleveland, Atlanta, and Kansas City. Several Districts noted continuing downward price pressures and an increasing supply of homes for sale due to rising foreclosures. However, the inventory of unsold homes was reported to have declined in areas of the Boston and Atlanta Districts as well as in Philadelphia and Cleveland. Tighter credit conditions were cited as a limiting factor for demand in several Districts. Most Districts reported commercial real estate and construction activity had slowed, with New York, San Francisco, and Dallas noting the sharpest declines.

Banking and Finance. Credit conditions tightened in all the Districts that reported on them. Bank lending was described as either stable or lower for both consumers and businesses. Cleveland, Kansas City, and San Francisco noted that loan quality had deteriorated. Credit standards were tightened, particularly for commercial and residential real estate loans, in several Districts. Several also indicated that lenders in their District had become more highly cautious and more conservative. Liquidity problems in interbank markets along with a higher cost of funds were reported in several Districts. As a result, Chicago reported that banks were increasingly utilizing alternative sources of funds like the discount window and the brokered CD market; and Kansas City noted that banks had become more cautious in their liquidity management.

Agriculture and Natural Resources. Agricultural conditions remained favorable in most of the Districts reporting on them. Corn and soybean harvests were somewhat behind schedule in Chicago, St. Louis, Minneapolis, and Kansas City. Heavier precipitation slowed the harvests in some Districts but aided agriculture in Atlanta, Chicago, St. Louis, and Dallas. Drought continued to be a problem in parts of the Atlanta District, and hurricanes damaged agriculture in parts of the Dallas District. Yield projections slipped since the summer, but were still expected to be near historical averages. Livestock producers faced tighter margins due to high feed costs and problems with feed availability in some Districts. Most agricultural product prices fell in September. Exports continued to boost agricultural demand, while domestic demand lagged for some commodities.

Conditions for the energy and mining sectors were positive, except for temporary damage to infrastructure from the recent hurricanes. Disruptions to offshore oil drilling in Dallas were not as extensive as they were after other recent major hurricanes. Drilling in the U.S. increased, especially for natural gas. Coal prices were stable, whereas oil and natural gas prices declined. Even so, energy operations looked to expand in Cleveland, Minneapolis, Kansas City, Dallas, and San Francisco. In addition, Minneapolis reported new mining activity.

Prices and Wages. Most Districts reported that cost pressures on prices had eased, although a number of Districts noted that the costs of energy, raw materials, food, and transportation remain elevated and margins were tight. Manufacturers in New York said that they plan selling price increases; but, with activity weakening, fewer other businesses anticipate price increases. Dallas noted that businesses facing softer demand plan to pass cost reductions on to customers, and Cleveland cited a decline in fuel surcharges as gasoline prices fell. Wage pressures across the 12 Districts remained limited outside of skilled labor positions that continue to experience high demand, such as the energy industry in Cleveland, Dallas, and Kansas City.

ELEVENTH DISTRICT—DALLAS

The Eleventh District economy slowed markedly in late August and September, 2008. Many businesses were affected by temporary production disruptions caused by Hurricanes Gustav and Ike. In addition, softer demand and increased uncertainty caused some firms to reduce investment and payrolls. Moreover, a number of contacts reported recent credit market developments had led them to reevaluate future plans amid slower growth nationally and internationally. Outlooks were more pessimistic than in the last survey, with respondents citing many "unknowns" on the horizon.

Prices. Reductions in energy and commodity prices eased cost pressures in many industries, and transportation expenses were less of a concern than in recent surveys. Fewer firms reported pass-throughs, although several were still trying to recoup earlier cost increases of the year. Some respondents in industries with soft demand noted recent cost reductions will be passed on to customers, and retailers were offering more favorable promotions. Construction contacts said high costs remain a major issue, but some expect costs to edge down as the number of projects ebb.

Crude oil prices fell from $115 per barrel in mid-August to below $100 by the first week of October. Natural gas prices also edged down, in part due to high inventory levels. Despite a brief spike during recent storms, the national average price of gasoline fell about 11 cents per gallon, and diesel about 24 cents, during the survey period. Contacts expect soft demand for petrochemicals to lead to weaker prices for ethylene and polyethylene in the coming weeks.

Labor Market. The labor market loosened slightly in the fall/winter of 2008 and wage pressures were mild. Although most District respondents said employment levels remained steady, there were reports of layoffs in several industries, including primary and fabricated metals, residential construction-related manufacturing, and auto dealers. Contacts said skilled financial employees were easier to come by, a result of mergers in the financial industry. Labor shortages are prevalent in the energy sector, and firms continue to steal workers from other industries. Some manufacturing respondents still reported difficulty finding workers with highly specialized skills. Staffing firms noted difficulty filling upper-level positions.

Manufacturing. Many Eleventh District manufacturers reported interruptions in business activity from Hurricanes Gustav and Ike. In addition, the credit market squeeze added uncertainty to company outlooks. Producers of residential construction products said new orders and shipments continued to fall due to worrisome conditions in housing markets. One company had laid off salaried workers for the first time in 20 years. Some respondents expressed concern over builders' ability to pay existing contracts with suppliers or renew lines of credit.

The current financial situation is reflected in a more cautious business environment, with the possibility of fewer orders from retailers for the upcoming holiday season. Food product manufacturers said sales were solid, although there were reports of temporary production cuts and export delays due to the storms. Specialized transportation equipment firms said activity remained stable despite demand disruptions from clients tied to the Houston Port.

Orders for paper products were mixed. Refinery production in Texas and Louisiana was severely disrupted by the back-to-back storms, as plants were forced to reduce output or shut down. Contacts say damage was light, and all refineries but one are operating or restarting production. Still, the storms left inventories at record lows, leading to spot gasoline shortages in the Southeast and on the East Coast.

Retail Sales. A combination of factors—weather disruptions, consumer uncertainty and financial concerns—led to mostly weak reports from retailers. Sales of consumer durables were down markedly according to contacts, and the back-to-school season did not provide the usual bump. Discounters continued to fare better than most. Respondents said food and gasoline sales remain the primary drivers, whereas sales of discretionary items are flat to down. Although the outlook had been rather pessimistic, outside of storm-damaged areas, sales were somewhat better in Texas than elsewhere in the country.

Services. Demand for temporary staffing remained steady, overall. Orders were strong for workers in light industrial manufacturing but had slowed for employees in software/web services. Contacts said orders were down for workers in financial services and auto manufacturing. Legal service activity continued to be concentrated in litigation and bankruptcy work. Respondents said demand for legal services to support real estate and financial transactions had declined sharply, but demand remained strong from the oil and gas sector. Several respondents in the transportation services sector noted considerable, although temporary, loss of business as a result of Hurricane Ike. Intermodal transportation contacts saw a rise in cargo volume as activity caught back up after the closing of the Port of Houston. Overall, respondents were thankful the port was closed for just one week, and suffered minimal damage. Railroad cargo volumes continued to decline. The storms reduced cargo volumes of chemicals and petroleum products, while construction material and motor vehicle volumes fell dramatically—which contacts attributed to weaker consumer demand.

Construction and Real Estate. Worsening problems in credit markets permeated construction and real estate markets in the Eleventh District. The pace of new and existing home sales continued to slow, as economic uncertainty kept many potential homebuyers on the sidelines. Those deciding to buy found it much tougher to get qualified. Contacts noted weakness in sales of higher-priced homes, as equity requirements and interest rates for jumbo loans have increased significantly. Although inventories remain much lower than in other parts of the country, one builder said foreclosures in Dallas are adding to the supply of moderate to higher-priced homes.

On a more positive note, realtors said relocations were spurring some demand, and values appear to be holding up overall. The outlook for the housing market remains extremely uncertain, but many noted the "bottom was in sight." Contacts said apartment leasing picked up in the third quarter, and rents were holding up in the face of national declines.

Commercial real estate respondents said leasing activity for office and industrial space declined sharply as businesses reevaluate plans in the face of current uncertainties. Sales of commercial properties continue to plummet, with one contact in the industrial market saying closings had "hit the wall."

Financial Services. Heightened caution was prevalent among financial services contacts, although most still expect the effects of the current situation to be less severe than in other districts. Lenders reportedly have become even more conservative since the last survey—highly scrutinizing borrowers and enforcing strict underwriting standards. According to some contacts, the cost of capital remains high, inducing lenders to widen loan interest-rate spreads. Very few commercial real estate deals are getting done, with only smaller, low-risk projects able to meet current standards.

Energy. U.S. drilling activity rose in recent weeks, with the average number of active rigs above 2,000 for the first time since 1985. More than half the rise was attributed to the Eleventh District. Activity continues to be focused on land-based unconventional natural gas, despite the fall in price to $7.50 per thousand cubic feet. Offshore oil drilling was disrupted by the Hurricanes Gustav and Ike, but damage was light compared to Katrina and Rita. While demand for oil has weakened, contacts say long-run prospects for the industry have not changed.

The Federal Reserve Bulletin

The *Federal Reserve Bulletin* was introduced in 1914 as a vehicle to present policy issues developed by the Federal Reserve Board. Throughout the years, the *Bulletin* has been viewed as a journal of record, serving to provide data generated by the Board back to the public. Authors from the Federal Reserve Boards' Research and Statistics, Monetary Affairs, International Finance, Banking Supervision and Regulation, Consumer and Community Affairs, Reserve Bank Operations, and Legal divisions contribute to the contents published in each issue. The *Bulletin* includes topical research articles, legal developments, Report on the Condition of the U.S. Banking Industry, and other general information.

The tables that appeared in the Financial and Business Statistics section of the Bulletin (1914–2003) are now published monthly as a separate print publication titled *Statistical Supplement to the Federal Reserve Bulletin*.

Since 2006, the *Bulletin* is published on the Board's public Web site on a continuing basis, as it becomes available. The quarterly paper version of the *Bulletin* is no longer published. However, the Board will print an annual compendium. To access the *Bulletin*, utilize the following link:

http://www.federalreserve.gov/pubs/bulletin/default.htm

Interested parties may subscribe to the "The Federal Reserve Board E-mail Notification Service." The e-mail notification service alerts subscribers to newly available testimonies, speeches, articles, and reports in the *Federal Reserve Bulletin* and the *Statistical Supplement to the Federal Reserve Bulletin*, and press releases and other items (Consumer Credit, Flow of Funds, Industrial Production and Capacity Utilization, and Senior Loan Officer Survey statistical releases). The message provides a brief description and a link to the recent posting.

Texas Employment and the Economy

Review of the Texas Economy

The Real Estate Center provides a monthly review of the Texas economy. The information given here is excerpted from the **"Monthly Review of the Texas Economy—October 2008," by AH Anari and Mark G. Dotzour.**

Texas continues to gain jobs despite more job losses for the nation. Texas' nonfarm employment rose 2.3 percent from September 2007 to September 2008 compared with a decrease of 0.4 percent for the United States. The state's seasonally adjusted unemployment rate rose from 4.3 percent in September 2007 to 5.1 percent in September 2008. Over the same period, the United States' seasonally adjusted unemployment rate rose from 4.7 percent to 6.1 percent.

A review of Table 1 shows the relative employment growth for Texas and the U.S. Texas had a positive employment growth of 2.3 percent over 2007, whereas the U.S. had a negative growth rate of –0.4 percent.

Table 1
Texas and U.S. Labor Markets

Nonfarm employment	Sept. 2008	Sept. 2007	Absolute	Change Percent
Texas	10,657,900	10,419,700	238,200	2.3
United States	137,476,000	138,075,000	–599,000	–0.4

Unemployment Rate	Actual Sept. 2008	Sept. 2007	Seasonally Adjusted Sept. 2008	Sept. 2007
Texas	5.2	4.3	5.1	4.3
United States	6.0	4.5	6.1	4.7

The Texas oil and gas industry's employment increased 8.4 percent from September 2007 to September 2008, and ranked first among Texas industries in employment growth rate. The average number of active rotary rigs increased from 839.6 in October 2007 to 929.8 in October 2008 according to Hughes Tool Co.

A study of Table 2 will indicate the growth rates for the state of Texas by category. Only two categories had negative growth rates, manufacturing and information.

Table 2
Texas Industries Ranked by Employment Growth Rate from Sept. 2007 to Sept. 2008

Rank	Industry	Sept. 2008	Sept. 2007	Change Absolute	Percent
1	Natural Resources & Mining	226,700	209,100	17,600	8.4
2	Professional & Business Services	1,363,700	1,306,200	57,500	6.4
3	Leisure & Hospitality	1,030,100	990,500	39,600	4.0
4	Construction	674,200	654,000	20,200	3.1
5	Education & Health Services	1,304,200	1,270,000	34,200	2.7
6	Trade	1,705,100	1,673.400	31,700	1.9
7	Government	1,750,800	1,723,900	26,900	1.6
7	Other Services	360,000	354,500	5,500	1.6
9	Financial Activities	655,000	645,400	9,600	1.5
10	Trans., Warehousing, Util.	441,000	435,300	5,700	1.3
11	Manufacturing	930,100	937,600	-7,500	-0.8
12	Information	217,000	219,800	-2,800	-1.3

Source: Texas Workforce Commission and Real Estate Center at Texas A&M Univ.

Financial activities (finance, insurance, real estate, rental, and leasing services) added 9,600 jobs to the state's economy from September 2007 to September 2008, an annual growth rate of 1.5 percent. In this industry, real estate, rental, and leasing added 5,900 jobs while finance and insurance gained 3,700 jobs.

Texas Metropolitan Statistical Areas

All Texas metro areas experienced positive employment growth rates from September 2007 to September 2008. Laredo ranked first in job creation followed by McAllen-Edinburg-Mission, Odessa, College Station-Bryan, Longview, and El Paso. The annual employment growth rate for Austin-Round Rock metro area and the Dallas-Piano-Irving metro area from September 2007 to September 2008 was 1.9 percent; the two metro areas ranked 12th in job creation.

The annual employment growth rate for the Fort Worth-Arlington metro area fell from 3 percent in October 2007 to 1.7 percent in September 2008. The area ranked 15th in job creation. Houston-Sugar Land-Baytown posted an annual growth rate of 2.2 percent from September 2007 to September 2008 and ranked 6th among the state's metro areas.

The employment growth rate for the San Antonio metro area from September 2007 to September 2008 was 2.1 percent, with the metro area ranking 8th in employment growth rate.

The state's actual unemployment rate in September 2008 was 5.2 percent. Petroplexes Midland and Odessa had the first and second lowest unemployment rates, followed by Amarillo, Lubbock, and Abilene.

The most recent reviews of the Texas economy are available to anyone accessing the Real Estate Center website. The URL for the Real Estate Center is http://recenter.tamu.edu/. Real estate licensees are encouraged to reference the economic reviews to stay current with the latest Texas statistics. It is vitally important in the current volatile financial milieu to stay informed of the latest economic situation.

Houston Housing Construction Slump

According to the Houston Chronicle, third-quarter 2008 figures reveal Houston-area home starts on the steepest decline in 20 years, caused by the credit squeeze, weak consumer confidence, and Hurricane Ike. Home starts in all price ranges fell in the quarter, with entry-level properties the hardest hit.

Builders started 6,733 homes from July through September 2008, according to Houston-based Metrostudy—29 percent fewer than during the same period in 2007. The research firm estimates between 26,000 and 28,000 homes will be built in the area by the end of 2008, just over half of the 50,000 home starts two years ago when the market peaked.

Ike's trail of destruction through the area put many builders a month behind on construction. This, coupled with the difficulty in securing loans for land, has contributed to the slowdown.

Texas Tops in Apartment Building

Three major Texas metros reign over M/PF YieldStar's list of top U.S. apartment-building markets. Dallas-Fort Worth was the number one market, with 20,585 apartment units currently under development. Houston was second on the list, with 16,282 apartments being developed. Austin came in third, with 13,366 apartments under development.

San Antonio Hotel Performance Strong

A Smith Travel Research study has ranked San Antonio's hotel performance near the top, nationally, largely because of convention-related bookings. These bookings grew by almost 8 percent in the fiscal year ending in September 2008 totaling 811,000 room reservations. Direct delegate expenditures from these conventions exceeded $564 million.

The study showed San Antonio as having the second-best growth in room demand, 5.1 percent, among the 17 cities it reviewed in the first eight months of 2008. San Antonio also achieved the second-best performance in occupancy rate, falling less than half a point between 2007 and 2008. Room revenue grew by 9.3 percent, more than all but three other cities.

Business Cycles and the Texas Housing Market

In an article in the July 2008 edition of *Tierra Grande* entitled "Good Times, Bad Times," Dr. Ali Anari discusses business cycles and their effect on Texas housing prices and sales. Dr. Anari is a research economist with the Real Estate Center at Texas A&M University.

In the article Dr. Anari states that modern business cycles in the United States, that is, business cycles after the Second World War, are characterized by long periods of expansion followed by short contraction periods. According to the business cycle dating committee of the National Bureau of Economic Research, the average postwar economic expansion period is 57 months while the average contraction period is 10 months. Slow growth rates and downturns in some sectors of the economy normally are offset by higher growth rates of output in the rest of the economy.

Business Cycle Defined

Dr. Anari defines the business cycle as consisting of recurring wave-like fluctuations in economic activity. All economic time series normally exhibit fluctuations, but a cycle occurs when the time series shows several periods of persistent increase (or decrease) followed by several periods of persistent decrease (or increase). An *expansion phase* is several periods of higher-than-average economic growth rates culminating in a *peak* growth rate. A *contraction phase* consists of multiple intervals of lower or negative growth rates ending in a *trough* (the point at which recovery begins).

Most discussions and issues related to business cycles focus on the growth rates of sales and prices of goods and services within a time series rather than the levels of these variables. A type of goods or services may have high sales and price levels, yet the growth rate of sales and prices may slow or even become negative for several periods. Economists and statisticians define an economic time series, such as home sales, as consisting of four components: a seasonal wave, secular trend, cyclical fluctuation, and irregular components.

Seasonal variations may be daily, weekly, monthly, or quarterly data. For example, Texas home sales are seasonal, with peak sales in June and the trough in January. A secular trend is the general tendency in a time series to increase or decrease over a long period as a result of population growth, technology, preferences, and other factors.
Cyclical fluctuations are the ups and downs that stray from long-term secular trends. These fluctuations are caused by changes in economic policy, technology, and preferences. Irregular or random shocks are unpredictable components of economic variables. Natural disasters such as tsunamis and man-made catastrophes such as 9/11 are examples of random shocks.

According to Henry George, a nineteenth-century U.S. economist, real estate variables (especially land speculation) are the main causes of economic downturns and boom-bust cycles. In all, there are more than 30 theories or explanations of the business cycle. For pragmatic market participants and business practitioners, the most important question regarding business cycles is, "What stage of the business cycle is my market in right now?"

Texas Residential Real Estate Cycles

Real estate business cycles are about cyclical fluctuations of quantities and prices of construction, sales, permits, and inventories of real estate properties. The Real Estate Center at Texas A&M University has an ongoing research program monitoring several Texas real estate business cycles. This research yielded the following information about Texas residential real estate cycles:

Home Sales Cycles

Home sales in Texas clearly show three distinct periods since 1992: a slow increase in homes sold, from an average of 15,820 residential units in January 2001 to 16,778 units in April 2003, followed by a period of rapid growth to 24,281 units in February 2007, and finally a cooling off period that began in March 2007 and ran through December 2007, during which homes sold fell to 22,620 units.

The next step in uncovering business cycles from the home sales data is computing the annual growth rates of the monthly moving averages of homes sold, that is, the percentage change in the monthly moving averages from January to January. No two cycles are the same. Each one is unique in duration and amplitude. Also, expansion phases are long, whereas contraction phases are short. The state's residential market is currently experiencing negative home sales growth rates.

Home Price Cycles

Average prices of homes sold in Texas also display seasonal variations with peak prices in June and a price trough in January. The 12-month moving average price of homes sold shows steady price growth rates during the last two decades. The state's residential market has experienced variable home price appreciation since 1992, but no price declines. The seasonally adjusted average price of homes sold rose from 4.1 percent in July 2007 to 4.8 percent in December 2007 despite the declining growth rates of homes sold over the same period.

Dr. Anari concludes that "the business cycle analysis of home sales and home prices reveals that Texas homeowners may continue to enjoy moderate home price appreciation. At the same time, it may be appropriate for Texas home builders to slow down new home construction projects."

Miscellaneous Texas Economic Reports

Foreign Buyers Active in Texas

Home purchases by Americans may be waning, but foreigners are finding the U.S. housing market, especially the Texas housing market, an enticing place to spend their money. Offshore purchasers are lured to the market by bargains and currency rate advantages. Additionally, as one-third of these buyers have historically bought with cash, the mortgage credit crunch is not a worry for them.

Texas ranks fourth in the country for foreign homebuyers, with about 7 percent of the total, behind Florida, California, and Arizona, according to a National Association of REALTORS® (NAR) survey. According to NAR Chief Economist Dr. Lawrence Yun, the real estate sold to foreign buyers in Texas tends to be modest-priced homes purchased by Mexicans in the border area for work-related reasons. More than 60 percent of the homes purchased by Mexicans are priced under $200,000.

Texas is second only to Florida as a destination for Latin American home purchasers. Almost a quarter of Texas' real estate agents say their international business has increased in the last five years.

Prices Near Military Bases Remain Strong

It seems as though lenders are more comfortable making loans to purchasers of homes near military bases. The Associated Press found that communities surrounding big bases fared better than national averages because of steady wartime employment, more moderate value increases, and less reckless lending than in many other boom areas. Some communities have even seen a rise in home prices.

They also found that higher home values pool around high veteran populations. Veterans receive loans more easily because of their guaranteed mortgage benefits through the Veterans Affairs Department and lower-than-average interest rates through the Texas Veterans Land Board. Their ability to secure a home keeps the housing demand higher, which allows the home prices around them to stay afloat.

For the 12 months ending September 2008, the average monthly median price in San Antonio was $151,500, up 1 percent from the same period in 2007, compared with a 9 percent decline nationwide for that period. San Antonio is home to Fort Sam Houston, Lackland Air Force Base, and Randolph Air Force Base.

In addition, Texas veterans are more likely to pay their mortgages on time. According to the Mortgage Bankers Association, of Texas homes purchased with VA-insured loans, 0.8 percent went into foreclosure in second-quarter 2008. This is about half the 1.44 percent overall statewide foreclosure rate and less than one-third of the 2.75 percent national foreclosure rate.

NAR Chief Economist Speaks in Houston

Dr. Lawrence Yun, chief economist for the National Association of REALTORS®, was in Houston on Friday, November 21, 2008, speaking to a group of bankers and REALTORS®. After his talk, he answered questions about the nation's housing woes and how Houston is different.

Here are excerpts from an interview with the Houston Chronicle:

"The Houston market is not undergoing the transition that other markets are. Home prices are still rising or stable. The typical median price at $150,000 shows there was never the excessive price boom, and hence there's no reasonable price decline. Furthermore, the local job market condition is very solid.

"The nation is already in a recession. Going into 2009, job losses for the country will continue for the first half of the year. Then in the second half I believe there will be some turnaround in the economy. Through all this I believe Houston will not really see net job cuts as a whole because Houston is a business-friendly environment, and consistently the Texas market outperforms in the sense of job creation compared to the rest of the country. Even with the lower oil prices, jobs will continue to be created in the Houston market.

"The last time we had a nationwide recession back in 2001, home sales actually picked up as jobs were being cut. That was due to improving affordability conditions. So, anytime there's a better incentive for people with jobs—and even in a recession 90 percent of the workforce do have jobs—they respond to incentives. Back in 2001, it was lower mortgage rates that drew buyers back into the market. This time around, rates are already low to begin with. I think there will be some stimulus measure from Washington to provide additional incentives to help home buyers."

Two Texas Cities Were Ranked in the Top Ten

Coldwell Banker, in keeping with the competitive spirit of the football season, has again ranked major college football towns by home affordability. Fort Worth, home of Texas Christian University, is ranked third on the company's College Home Price Comparison Index. The city has an average home price of $148,625. Houston, which boasts two major universities, Rice University and the University of Houston, came in sixth with an average home price of $158,412.

Almost making the top ten was Lubbock, home of Texas Tech University, which ranked 11th. The city has an average home price of $170,700.

Akron, Ohio (University of Akron), was the most affordable market, with its average price of $135,780. At the other end of the spectrum was Palo Alto, Calif. (Stanford University), with a $1.7 million average home price.

Housing Affordability Index (HAI)

The Housing Affordability Index (HAI) is the ratio of median family income to the income required to qualify for an 80 percent, fixed-rate mortgage to purchase a median-priced home. Texas continues to be a better value than the rest of the country when it comes to buying a home, according to the latest index numbers. Texas finished second-quarter 2008 with an HAI of 1.55. The United States' HAI was 1.27.

"Nationally, housing affordability has improved considerably as the overall median home price continues to descend from its record high in mid-2006," said Dr. Jim Gaines, research economist with the Real Estate Center at Texas A&M University." As the HAI figure suggests, Texas remains even more affordable despite the fact that home prices in the state increased modestly during the first half of the year (2008).

The Texas HAI has been updated on the Center's website. To view the index, use this URL:

http://recenter.tamu.edu/data/misc/afford1.html

An index for first-time homebuyers is also available. To view the index, use this URL:

http://recenter.tamu.edu/data/misc/afford2.html

FINANCE UPDATE

To say the least, 2008 was certainly an interesting year for the financial world. Some of the more interesting stories centered around Countrywide Mortgage, Bear Sterns, AIG, Merrill Lynch, Citigroup, Washington Mutual, Downey Savings and Loan, PFF Bank and Trust, IndyMac Bancorp, and the 158-year-old Lehman Brothers.

As of December 1, 2008, at least 22 U.S. banks had failed. This is the largest number of bank failures in a one-year period since 50 banks failed in 1993. Of the 22 failures, only one Texas bank had bit the dust. Franklin Bank of Houston was the sole Texas failure. There were five bank failures in California, three banks in Georgia, and two each in Missouri and Nevada.

Of course, the major stories involved the takeover of Fannie Mae and Freddie Mac by the U.S. Treasury. The Federal Housing Finance Agency (FHFA) Reform Act of 2008, referred to as the Regulatory Reform Act, was signed into law by President Bush on July 30, 2008, and became effective immediately thereafter. The Regulatory Reform Act established FHFA as an independent agency with general supervisory and regulatory authority over Fannie Mae, Freddie Mac, and the 12 Federal Home Loan Banks. FHFA assumed the duties of Fannie and Freddie's former regulators, the Office of Federal Housing Authority and the Department of Housing and Urban Development, with respect to safety, soundness, and mission oversight of the two agencies. HUD remains their regulator with respect to fair-lending matters.

On September 7, 2008, the Director of FHFA issued a statement that he had determined that the agencies could not continue to operate safely and soundly and fulfill their critical public mission without significant action to address FHFA's concerns, which were, principally, the folowing: safety and soundness concerns as they existed at that time, including capitalization; market conditions; financial performance and condition; the agency's inability to obtain funding according to normal practices and prices; and the critical importance of supporting the U.S. residential mortgage market.

Overview of Treasury Agreements With Regard to Fannie Mae and Freddie Mac

Senior Preferred Stock Purchase Agreement

The conservator, acting on behalf of the agencies, entered into a senior preferred stock agreement with Treasury on September 7, 2008. This agreement was amended and restated on September 26, 2008. Under the agreement, Treasury provided the agencies with its commitment to provide up to $100 billion in funding under specified conditions. The agreement requires Treasury, upon the request of the conservator, to provide funds to Fannie and Freddie after any quarter in which they have a negative net worth. In addition, the agreement requires Treasury, upon the request of the conservator, to provide funds if the conservator determines, at any time, that it will be mandated by law to appoint a receiver for the agencies unless they receive funds from Treasury under the commitment.

In exchange for Treasury's funding commitment, Treasury was issued, as an initial commitment fee, (1) one million shares of Variable Liquidation Preference Senior Preferred stock, Series 2008-2, referred to as the "senior preferred stock," and (2) a warrant to purchase, for a nominal price, shares of common stock equal to 79.9 percent of the total number of shares of common stock outstanding on a fully diluted basis at the time the warrant is exercised. No cash proceeds were received from Treasury as a result of issuing the senior preferred stock or the warrant.

Under terms of the senior preferred stock, Treasury is entitled to quarterly dividends of 10 percent per year (which increases to 12 percent per year if not paid timely and in cash) on the aggregate liquidation preference of the senior preferred stock. To the extent the agencies are required to draw on Treasury's funding commitment, the liquidation preference of the senior preferred stock will be increased by the amount of any funds received. The amounts payable for the senior preferred stock dividend could be substantial and have an adverse impact on the financial position and net worth of the agencies.

The senior preferred stock is senior in liquidation preference to the common stock and all other preferred stock of the agencies. In addition, beginning on March 31, 2010, the agencies are required to pay a quarterly commitment fee to Treasury, which fee will accrue from January 1, 2010. This fee is to be paid each quarter for as long as the senior preferred stock purchase agreement is in effect, even if no funds are requested from Treasury under the agreement.

The senior preferred stock purchase agreement includes significant restrictions on the ability of the agencies to manage their business, including limiting the amount of indebtedness that can be incurred to 110 percent of their aggregate indebtedness as of June 30, 2008, and capping the size of their mortgage portfolio. In addition, beginning in 2010, the agencies must decrease the size of their mortgage portfolio at the rate of 10 percent per year until it reaches $250 billion.

Depending on the pace of future mortgage liquidations, the agencies may need to reduce or eliminate purchases of mortgage assets or sell mortgage assets to achieve this reduction. In addition, while the senior preferred stock is outstanding, the agencies are prohibited from paying dividends (other than on the senior preferred stock) or issuing equity securities without Treasury's consent. The terms of the senior preferred stock purchase agreement and warrant make it unlikely that the agencies will be able to obtain equity from private sources.

The senior preferred stock purchase agreement has an indefinite term and can terminate only in very limited circumstances, which do not include the end of the conservatorship. The agreement therefore could continue after the conservatorship ends. Treasury has the right to exercise the warrant, in whole or in part, at any time on or before September 7, 2028.

Treasury Credit Facility

On September 19, 2008, Fannie and Freddie entered into a lending agreement with Treasury pursuant to which Treasury established a new secured lending credit facility that is available until December 31, 2009, as a liquidity backstop. This is referred to as the "Treasury credit facility." In order to borrow pursuant to the Treasury credit facility, the agencies are required to post collateral in the form of Fannie Mae's or Freddie Mac's mortgage-backed securities (MBS) to secure all borrowings under the facility. The terms of any borrowings under the credit facility, including the interest rate payable on the loan and the amount of collateral provided as security for the loan, will be determined by Treasury. Treasury is not obligated under the credit facility to make any loans.

The Secondary Mortgage Market

The trend toward pools and trusts contributing most of the mortgage money continues. Fannie Mae and Freddie Mac alone own or guarantee 51 percent of the country's single-family mortgages. For this reason, an in-depth examination of these two secondary market operators is included next.

Federal National Mortgage Association (Fannie Mae)

Fannie Mae reported a loss of $29 billion, or $(13.00) per diluted share, in the third quarter of 2008, compared with the second-quarter loss of $2.3 billion, or $(2.54) per diluted share. The third-quarter results were driven primarily by a $21.4 billion non-cash charge to establish a valuation allowance against deferred tax assets, as well as $9.2 billion in credit-related expenses, arising from the ongoing deterioration in mortgage credit conditions and declining home prices.

Net revenue rose 2.4 percent to $4.1 billion in the third quarter from $4.0 billion in the second quarter. Net interest income was $2.4 billion, up 14.5 percent from $2.1 billion in the second quarter, driven by the reduction in short-term borrowing rates, which reduced the average cost of Fannie Mae's debt.

Guaranty fee income was $1.5 billion, down 8.3 percent from $1.6 billion in the second quarter, driven primarily by fair-value losses on certain guaranty assets.

The valuation allowance against deferred tax assets, which was established by taking a non-cash charge, totaled $21.4 billion for the third quarter of 2008.

Credit-related expenses, which are the total provision for credit losses plus foreclosed property expense, were $9.2 billion in the third quarter, compared with $5.3 billion in the second quarter.

Combined loss reserves stood at $15.6 billion on September 30, up from $8.9 billion at the end of the second quarter. The combined loss reserves on September 30 were 53 basis points of their guaranty book of business compared with 31 basis points on June 30.

Net fair-value losses were $3.9 billion in the third quarter, compared with $517 million of fair-value gains in the second quarter. The primary drivers were $2.9 billion in trading securities losses arising from a significant widening of credit spreads and $3.3 billion in derivatives losses driven by interest rate declines, partially offset by gains on hedged mortgage assets.

Net investment losses were $1.6 billion in the quarter, compared with losses of $883 million in the second quarter. The third-quarter loss was driven by other-than-temporary impairments of $1.8 billion recorded primarily on private-label securities backed by Alt-A and subprime mortgages, and reflected a reduction in expected cash flows for a portion of FNMA's private-label securities portfolio.

Nonperforming loans were $63.6 billion, or 2.2 percent of Fannie Mae's total guaranty book of business on September 30, 2008, compared with $46.1 billion, or 1.6 percent, as of June 30, 2008.

Single-Family foreclosure rate was 0.40 percent for the nine months ended September 30, 2008, and was 0.16 percent for the third quarter of 2008, compared with 0.13 percent for the second quarter. The foreclosure rate reflects the number of single-family properties acquired through foreclosure as a percentage of the total number of loans in FNMA's conventional single-family mortgage credit book of business. Their inventory of single-family foreclosed properties was 67,519 on September 30, 2008, compared with 54,173 as of June 30, 2008, and 33,729 as of December 31, 2007.

266

Net Worth was $9.4 billion on September 30, 2008, compared with $41.4 billion on June 30, 2008. Stockholders' equity on September 30, 2008, was $ 9.3 billion.

Delisting on the NYSE

On November 18, 2008, Fannie Mae reported in a filing with the Securities and Exchange Commission that the company has been notified by the New York Stock Exchange that it has failed to satisfy one of the Exchange's standards for continued listing of its common stock.

The NYSE advised the company that it was below the exchange's price criteria for common stock because the average closing price of Fannie Mae's common stock for the 30 consecutive trading days ending November 12, 2008, was less than $ 1.00 per share. As a result, the company's common stock and each of its listed series of preferred stock are subject to suspension and delisting.

The company will have six months from November 12, 2008, to bring its common stock share price and average share price for 30 consecutive trading days above $1.00. Fannie Mae is currently working with its conservator, the Federal Housing Finance Agency, to explore options relating to this deficiency and has not yet determined its response or any specific action that it will take as a result of the exchange's notice.

Fannie Mae's common stock and each of the company's listed series of preferred stock currently remain listed on the exchange under the symbol or prefix "FNM" and will trade on the main platform. Further, each will be assigned a "BC" indicator by the NYSE to indicate to investors that the company is not currently in compliance with the exchange's continued listing standards.

Temporary Suspension of Foreclosures

In order to support the streamlined modification program announced on November 11, 2008, Fannie Mae issued a notice to its loan servicing organizations and retained foreclosure attorneys directing them to suspend foreclosure sales on occupied single-family properties as well as the completion of evictions from occupied single-family properties scheduled to occur from November 26, 2008, until January 9, 2009. This notice was issued on November 20, 2008.

The temporary suspension of foreclosures is designed to allow affected borrowers facing foreclosure to retain their homes while Fannie Mae works with mortgage servicers to implement the streamlined modification program scheduled to launch on December 15, 2008. This program is expected to affect over 10,000 borrowers. Foreclosure attorneys and loan servicers were instructed to use the additional time to reach out to borrowers who have defaulted on their loans and continue to pursue workout options. The initiative applies to loans owned or securitized by Fannie Mae.

The streamlined modification program is aimed at the highest-risk borrower who has missed three payments or more, owns and occupies the primary residence, and has not filed for bankruptcy. The program creates a fast-track method for getting troubled borrowers into an affordable monthly payment through a mix of reducing the mortgage interest rate, extending the life of the loan, and even deferring payments on part of the principal. Servicers have flexibility in the approach, but the objective is to create a more affordable payment for borrowers at risk of foreclosure.

"The streamlined modification program by Fannie Mae, Freddie Mae, Hope Now, and 27 mortgage servicers is an important step forward in addressing the systemic issues driving the increase in foreclosures," said Fannie Mae President and Chief Executive Officer Herb Allison. "Until the streamlined modification program is fully implemented, we felt it was in the best interest of both borrowers and Fannie Mae to take this extra step to ensure that homeowners with the desire and ability to prevent a foreclosure have an opportunity to stay in their homes. We encourage other servicers of non-GSE mortgages to participate in the streamlined modification program to bolster our collective efforts to stem the foreclosure crisis."

"Act Now to Avoid Foreclosure"

On their website, FNMA has some very helpful information for homeowners who may be in jeopardy of having their home foreclosed. The link to the information is entitled "Act Now to Avoid Foreclosure." The following information is quoted directly from their website:

> If you have fallen behind on your mortgage payments, or if your loan has been referred to an attorney, you may still have time to save your home. You should act quickly to avoid losing your home. The most important step you can take is to get help early from your mortgage lender, servicer, or housing counselor.
>
> If you delay and fall further behind in your payments, you are likely to have fewer options. Finding a solution that avoids foreclosure is better for you and better for your mortgage lender. Foreclosure damages your credit rating and your ability to borrow money or buy a home in the future.

It is important to be open and honest about your financial situation with your servicer or counselor. Here are important steps to take immediately:

- Call your lender or loan servicer to talk about your situation. You can find the contact information on your monthly mortgage statement or coupon book.

- If you can't reach your lender or servicer or you do not receive help, contact the Homeownership Preservation Foundation at 1-888-995-HOPE. Experienced counselors can help you develop the best plan for your personal financial situation. This counseling is free.

- Gather the information you will need. You will be asked to provide:

  1. letters or communications from your lender
  2. foreclosure notices
  3. recent mortgage statements showing your loan number
  4. homeowner's insurance policy
  5. last two pay stubs and most recent tax return for all borrowers named on the mortgage
  6. proof of other income, such as child, support, alimony, Social Security, or pension
  7. bank account statements
  8. list of major monthly bills, including child care, utilities, credit cards, and cell phone

- Understand your options. Depending on your situation, you may have several options to discuss with your servicer or counselor. They could include:

- **Repayment Plan**—You may be able to catch up on missed payments by creating a schedule for repaying the past-due amount.

- **Advance**—If your mortgage is owned by Fannie Mae (your servicer has this information), and your missed payments are due to a temporary financial hardship, you may be eligible for an unsecured personal loan, such as HomeSaver Advance™, that is available from your servicer to help you get current with your payments.

- **Modification**—In some cases, mortgage loan terms can be changed on a temporary or permanent basis to make the payment more affordable.

Avoid foreclosure rescue scams. Don't become a victim. Foreclosure scams seek to take advantage of your situation.

Your financial situation may have changed significantly since you qualified for your home due to unemployment, divorce, job change/relocation, or medical issues. You may want or need to sell your home as a result of this change. There are options for borrowers who are worried about possible foreclosure:

Pre-foreclosure or short sale—Servicers work with borrowers to sell their home and use the proceeds to pay off the loan even if the proceeds are not enough to settle the entire balance.

Deed in lieu—Borrowers sign over title to the property to Fannie Mae without the expense of foreclosure.

Mae's, Mac's New Loan Program

In late November 2008, in an effort to push down mounting foreclosures, Fannie Mae and Freddie Mac announced a new mortgage program that would expedite the process for modifying loans, which could help hundreds of thousands of homeowners avoid foreclosure.

Qualifying borrowers would have their interest rates lowered or loan principal reduced. But they would eventually have to pay back the full loan, either by extending the life of the payments or adding a one-time payment, when the house is sold. Monthly payments would not exceed 38 percent of a household's income.

Borrowers would have to show that they can afford a new loan, but they wouldn't have to undergo the underwriting and credit-score process.

To qualify for the loan program:

- Mortgages must be owned or guaranteed by Fannie Mae and Freddie Mac, who own or guarantee 51 percent of the country's single-family mortgages.
- Borrowers must have missed three or more payments.
- Borrowers must contact their mortgage servicer and provide the household's monthly gross income, any association dues or fees, and proof of recent job loss or economic hardship.

Federal Home Loan Mortgage Corporation (Freddie Mac)

On November 14, 2008, Freddie Mac reported a net loss of $25.3 billion, or $(19.44) per diluted common share, for the quarter ended September 30, 2008. This is compared to a net loss of $1.2 billion, or $(2.07) per diluted common share, for the quarter ended September 30, 2007.

As a result of the net loss, as at September 30, 2008, the company's stockholders' equity (deficit) totaled $(13.8) billion. Pursuant to the company's Senior Preferred Stock

Purchase Agreement with the U.S. Department of the Treasury, the Director of the Federal Housing Finance Agency has submitted a request to Treasury under the Purchase Agreement in the amount of $13.8 billion.

The third-quarter results were driven primarily by a non-cash charge of $14.3 billion related to the establishment of a partial valuation allowance against the company's deferred tax assets, $9.1 billion in security impairments on available-for-sale securities and $6.0 billion in credit-related expenses arising from the dramatic deterioration in market conditions during the third quarter, including declining home prices, increasing unemployment, a significant decline in consumer spending, and a considerable tightening of both consumer and business credit.

Net interest income for the third quarter of 2008 was $1.8 billion, up $1.1 billion from $761 million in the third quarter of 2007. This increase was primarily driven by lower funding costs and purchases of fixed-rate assets at wider spreads relative to those funding costs.

Management and guarantee income on PCs and structured securities for the third quarter of 2008 was $832 million, up $114 million, or 16 percent, from $718 million in the third quarter of 2007. This increase primarily reflects growth in the average balance of PCs and structured securities.

Other non-interest loss for the third quarter of 2008 was $12.1 billion, compared to $601 million in the third quarter of 2007. Included in the third quarter of 2008, other non-interest losses were:

- Security impairments on the company's available-for-sale securities of $9.1 billion;
- Losses of $932 million related to the company's trading securities; and
- Mark-to-market losses of $1.3 billion and $1.4 billion on the company's guarantee asset and derivatives portfolio, respectively, both due to the impact of decreasing long-term interest rates.

These loss items were partially offset by income on guarantee obligation of $783 million.

Administrative expenses totaled $308 million for the third quarter of 2008, compared to $428 million for the third quarter of 2007. The decrease is primarily due to a reduction in short-term performance compensation.

Credit-related expenses, consisting of provision for credit losses and REO operation expenses, were $6.0 billion for the third quarter of 2008, compared to $1.4 billion for the third quarter of 2007. The provision for credit losses significantly increased due to continued credit deterioration in the company's single-family credit guarantee portfolio, primarily due to further increases in delinquency rates and higher severity of losses on a per-property basis.

Other non-interest expenses for the third quarter of 2008 were $1.5 billion, compared to $1.2 billion in the third quarter of 2007. Included in other non-interest expenses for the third quarter of 2008 were:

- Securities administrator loss on investment activity, of $1.1 billion, related to investments by Freddie Mac in short-term, unsecured loans to Lehman Brothers Holdings, Inc., in the company's role as securities administrator for certain trust-related assets, and losses on loans purchased, of $252 million.

Freddie Mac to Broaden Support for Troubled Borrowers

Freddie Mac joined representatives from the U.S. Department of Treasury, HUD, the Federal Housing Finance Agency, Fannie Mae, and the HOPE NOW Alliance to announce a streamlined mortgage modification program that will help borrowers across the country at the highest risk of losing their homes.

The new effort promises uniform eligibility requirements and easier processing, and uses less documentation, than other loan modification processes. It builds on Freddie Mac's foreclosure avoidance efforts, which are estimated to provide a workout to three out of five troubled borrowers with Freddie Mac-owned loans.

Freddie Mac is currently finalizing the operational and implementation details and will be communicating additional information to Freddie Mac Servicers. The streamlined modification program is in addition to the many workout options available to, and being used by, Freddie Mac Servicers.

Freddie Mac Announces Funding for Major Southern California Property

Freddie Mac recently purchased a $73.7 million loan from Wells Fargo Bank that enabled borrower Loma Palisades, a California general partnership, to refinance the 546-unit Loma Palisades Apartments. The 68-building, garden-style complex in San Diego was built in 1959. A portion of the proceeds will help complete the rehabilitation of all the units' interiors.

"The deal was rate-locked and funded in 45 days in an extremely volatile rate environment," said Tom Szydlowski, Wells Fargo Multifamily Capital head of production. "The client was impressed with the pricing, execution, and client-focused approach that the team took in underwriting the credit, which helped deepen an important bank relationship."

The transaction benefited from the Freddie Mac Fixed-Rate Mortgage product utilizing the Freddie Mac Early Rate-Lock option. Since the launch of Freddie Mac's multifamily business in 1993, it has provided more than $200 billion in financing for approximately 55,500 multifamily properties.

2009 Fannie Mae Freddie Mac Loan Limits

The Federal Housing Finance Agency (FHFA) has announced that the conforming loan limit will remain at $417,000 for 2009 for most areas in the United States but specified higher limits in certain cities and counties. The conforming loan limit is the maximum size of loans that Fannie Mae and Freddie Mac can purchase in 2009.

According to provisions of the Housing and Economic Recovery Act of 2008 (HERA), the national loan limit is set based on changes in average home prices over the previous year, but cannot decline from year to year.

Loan limits for two- , three- , and four-unit properties in 2009 will remain at 2008 levels as well: $533,850, $645,300, and $801,950, respectively, for homes in the continental U.S. The national limit was left unchanged at $417,000 based on declines in FHFA's monthly and quarterly house price indexes over the past year. The monthly purchase-only index declined 5.9 percent over the 12 months ending August 2008, and the quarterly all-transactions index dropped 1.7 percent from second-quarter 2007 to second-quarter 2008.

Virtually every other measure of house prices has also fallen, with many showing even larger declines. FHFA has not yet determined whether it will continue to use a currently existing FHFA price index to gauge price movements in future years. For this year, however, all reliable metrics point to lower prices, and a price decline of any size is sufficient to determine that the national limit will not change.

Federal Housing Administration (FHA) Update

FHA is Back in Town

The Federal Housing Administration has insured over 35 million home mortgages and 47,205 multifamily project mortgages since 1934. Currently, FHA has 4.8 million insured single-family mortgages and 13,000 insured multifamily projects in its portfolio.

FHA seems to be back in business after many years of being in the background. Low down payment conventional mortgages dominated the market for many years. Possibly, the disastrous mortgage market in 2008 was the cause of the resurgence of FHA. Regardless, the volume of mortgages insured by FHA is up significantly.

In 2006 FHA insured 501,774 loans with an average loan size of $110,211. In 2007 they insured 532,092 loans with an average loan size of $112,455. In the first seven months of 2008, FHA had insured 907,289 loans, with an average size of $146,689. In 2007 FHA financed $59,836,711,331 in mortgage loans. Through July 2008 they had financed $133,089,451,991. Annualizing the 7-month figure would show a 12-month figure of approximately $228,153,346,270. This represents a 127 percent increase in volume in just one year.

They must be serious about doing more business because they now have two websites: www.hud.gov and www.fha.gov.

New (Temporary) Higher Loan Limits

Nearly a quarter of a million more families could be eligible to purchase or refinance their homes using affordable, FHA-insured mortgages, thanks to the economic growth package signed into law by President Bush in 2008. The Economic Stimulus Act of 2008 will allow FHA to temporarily increase its loan limits and insure larger mortgages at a more affordable price in high-cost areas of the country.

Families in high-cost states have been priced out of FHA-backed loans. This has created a vacuum, filled by exotic subprime loans. Families with home loans up to $729,750 will now qualify for an FHA loan, depending on where they live.

FHA is offering temporary loan limits that will range from $271,050 to $729,750. Overall, the change in loan limits will help provide economic stability to America's communities and give nearly 240,000 additional homeowners and homebuyers a safer, more affordable mortgage alternative. The maximum amount of $729,750 will only be applicable to extremely high-cost metropolitan areas such as New York, Los Angeles, San Francisco, and Washington, D.C. Even moderate-cost areas like those in the South and Southwest, such as Dallas, Houston, Augusta, and Tallahassee, will be helped, with most loan limits there rising to $271,050.

There are 75 areas in the United States, out of a total of approximately 3,200, that will be eligible for the highest loan limit of $729,750. Previously, FHA's loan limits in these very-high-cost areas were capped at $362,790. The Economic Stimulus Act of 2008 permits FHA to insure loans for amounts up to 125 percent of the median house price in the area, when that amount is between the national minimum ($271,050) and maximum ($729,750). The new minimum and maximum loan limits are based on 65 percent and 175 percent, respectively, of the conforming loan limits for government-sponsored enterprises in 2008, which is $417,000.

The FHA used a combination of existing government data sets and available commercial information to determine the median sales price for each area, and released the data approximately two weeks after the president signed the stimulus bill. By increasing loan limits nationwide, FHA will provide much needed liquidity and stability to housing markets across the country. Already, as conventional sources of mortgage credit have been contracting, FHA has been filling the void. FHA has a website that can be accessed to determine loan limits in the different areas.

FHA's Refinancing Product

FHASecure, FHA's refinancing product, focuses on 30-year fixed-rate mortgages. FHA helps homeowners avoid and escape the risks associated with exotic subprime mortgage products, which have resulted in rising default and foreclosure rates. In January 2009, FHA's maximum loan limit will return to $362,790, unless the U.S. Congress approves bipartisan legislation to permanently increase loan limits as part of the FHA Modernization Bill.

FHA indicates that the next step must be to modernize the 74-year-old agency. In 2006, before the downturn, an FHA modernization bill was introduced to Congress. The plan offered flexible down payment requirements and higher loan limits. It would also enable the FHA to fairly price premiums, taking risk into account so the market makes rational decisions. FHA modernization could help a quarter of a million families in its first year. It passed the House and Senate in an overwhelmingly bipartisan fashion. But as of December 1, 2008 a final bill had yet to reach the president.

FHASecure helps responsible families who, having paid their bills on time under the original interest rate, find themselves falling behind under the reset rate. For the first time, these delinquent families would be able to qualify for an FHA loan. "Underwater" borrowers and those in the process of foreclosure may also qualify. From August to December of 2008, FHA had helped 110,000 homeowners who were current or past due on their loans refinance, with an additional 200,000 expected in the near future.

FHA Down Payment Rises Slightly

The down payment requirement for an FHA loan is now 3 percent. A recent change, however, prohibits the seller from funding any of the down payment. The buyer can still receive assistance from relatives or other entities that routinely provide down payment assistance. The seller is still allowed to provide up to 6 percent in financial concessions.

Mortgage Insurance for Disaster Victims—Section 203(h)

Under the Section 203(h) program, FHA insures mortgages for victims of a major disaster who have lost their homes and are in the process of rebuilding or buying another home. People are eligible for this program if their home, whether they owned or rented it, is located in an area designated by the president as a disaster area and their home was damaged to such an extent that reconstruction or replacement is necessary. These individuals must qualify for a mortgage through FHA's underwriting guidelines, which are generally more lenient than in the private sector.

No down payment is required under the Section 203(h) program. Potential homeowners are eligible for 100 percent financing of the mortgage. The borrower will pay some closing costs, but often the seller and the lender pay a portion of these costs. Potential homebuyers who are eligible to participate in this program can purchase a home anywhere they wish, in the United States. There are restrictions on the amount of the mortgage.

The amount of the mortgage that HUD will insure ranges from $172,632 to $312,895, depending on the location of the property. Check HUD's website for up-to-date FHA mortgage limits in each area.

Borrowers pay an up-front insurance premium as well as monthly premiums. Both of these may be added to the regular mortgage payment. There is no need to come up with any additional cash at closing to pay insurance premiums. Lenders are more willing to loan to borrowers with mortgages that are insured with FHA. Individuals who have had a financial setback and have problems qualifying for a mortgage in the private sector may qualify under FHA.

More importantly, the lender is required to work with FHA borrowers who have been unable to make their mortgage payment for reasons such as job loss or illness. Under certain circumstances, FHA will make payment(s) on behalf of the homeowners so that they can keep their home. In exchange, the homeowner signs a note with FHA to cover those payments.

The borrower must apply for an FHA-insured mortgage within one year of the president's declaration of the disaster. Applications are made through an FHA-approved lender. A list of lenders is provided online at HUD's website at.

For more information on Section 203(h), contact the HUD National Servicing Center Hotline 1-888-297-8685. HUD also has disaster assistance information on its homepage.

HOPE for Homeowners

In November 2008, U.S. Housing and Urban Development Secretary Steve Preston announced that the *HOPE for Homeowners* (H4H) Board of Directors has approved changes to the program to help more distressed borrowers refinance into affordable, government-backed mortgages. The changes will reduce the program costs for consumers and lenders alike, while also expanding eligibility by driving down the borrower's monthly mortgage payments.

"Clearly, meaningful changes were needed. These modifications should increase lender participation and help more families who are having difficulty paying their existing mortgages, but can afford a new affordable loan insured by HUD's Federal Housing Administration," said Preston.

By taking full advantage of the new authority provided under the *Emergency Economic Stabilization Act (EESA) of 2008*, H4H will provide additional mortgage assistance to struggling homeowners.

Modifications to HOPE for Homeowners include the following:

- Increasing the loan-to-value ratio (LTV) to 96.5 percent for some H4H loans
- Simplifying the process to remove subordinate liens by permitting up-front payments to lien holders
- Allowing lenders to extend mortgage terms from 30 to 40 years

"These changes will further encourage lenders to take a hard look at this program before heading down the path to foreclosure and will provide families with another resource to refinance into a loan they can afford," said FHA Commissioner Brian D. Montgomery. *"HOPE for Homeowners* will continue to serve as another loss mitigation tool that can be used to help families keep their homes."

HOPE for Homeowners will continue to only offer affordable, government-insured fixed-rate mortgages. Further, this program will maintain FHA's long-standing requirement that new loans be based on a family's long-term ability to repay the mortgage. Only owner-occupants are eligible for FHA-insured mortgages.

Increasing the Loan-to-Value and Adjusting Debt-to-Income Ratios

The program will increase the LTV ratio on H4H loans to 96.5 percent for borrowers whose mortgage payments represent no more than 31 percent of their monthly gross income and household debt no more than 43 percent. This change will expand the number of eligible borrowers. Raising the LTV ratio reduces the gap between the existing loan balances and the new H4H loan and decreases losses to the existing primary lienholders.

Alternatively, the program will continue to offer borrowers with higher debt loads a 90 percent LTV ratio on their H4H loans. This LTV ratio will include borrowers with debt-to-income ratios as high as 38 and 50 percent. In conjunction with the LTV change, H4H will eliminate the trial modification that was previously required.

Immediate Payments to Subordinate Lienholders

H4H will offer subordinate lienholders an immediate payment, in exchange for releasing their liens, to allow more borrowers access to the program. Previously, subordinate lienholders who released their liens were only eligible to receive a small recovery payment when the home owned by the H4H borrower was sold. Given the amount of time that would pass between the creation of the H4H and the ultimate sale of the home, as well as the tremendous market uncertainties, subordinate lienholders were not guaranteed any return at all.

Extending Loan Terms from 30 to 40 years

To assure that borrowers are put into the most affordable monthly payment possible, H4H will permit lenders to extend the mortgage term from 30 to 40 years. For borrowers with very high mortgage and household debt loads, extending out the amortization period may reduce their monthly payments enough to make it possible for them to qualify for this rescue product and save their homes.

Consistent with statutory and regulatory requirements, borrowers must continue to meet the following criteria:

- Their mortgage must have originated on or before January 1, 2008.

- They cannot afford their current loan.

- They must have made a minimum of six full payments on their existing first mortgage and did not intentionally miss mortgage payments.

- The loan amount may not exceed a maximum of $550,440.

- The up-front mortgage insurance premium is 3 percent and the annual mortgage insurance premium is 1.5 percent.

- The holders of existing mortgage liens must waive all prepayment penalties and late-payment fees.

- They do not own a second home.

- They did not knowingly or willfully provide false information to obtain the existing mortgage, and they have not been convicted of fraud in the last 10 years.

- They must follow FHA's long-standing and strict policy of fully documented income and employment.

The Board of Directors was charged with establishing underwriting standards to ensure that borrowers, after any write-down in principal, have a reasonable ability to repay their new FHA-insured mortgage. The program began on October 1, 2008, and will end on September 30, 2011.

Longer Term Loans

The 30-year fixed-rate mortgage is the most common home loan in America today. But 5 percent of all new mortgages in the United States (25 percent in California) are now being written for a term of 40 years. And the 40-year mortgage, first introduced in 2005, has since been surpassed in length by the 50-year mortgage. Known as "hybrid ARMs," the 40- and 50-year loans being offered in the mortgage market begin as fixed-rate mortgages but must be converted to an annual adjustable-rate mortgage (ARM) after a specified term. Most 50-year loans require conversion to an annual ARM either five or ten years after origination.

Lenders typically charge an increasing interest rate premium as a loan's amortization period is extended. No hard and fast rule exists to determine the amount of this premium. A reasonable premium is assumed to be 25 basis points or a quarter percent increase in the interest rate for each increment the loan's amortization period is extended. These premiums theoretically compensate for the lender's money being tied up for a longer time, assuming the borrower keeps the loan through final maturity. In reality, most mortgages are refinanced or paid off when the home is sold, well before full amortization occurs.

In an article in the October 2006 edition of *Tierra Grande*, Harold Hunt compares numerous attributes of 15-year, 30-year, 40-year, and 50-year loans. Table 4-8A, Table 4-8B, Table 4-8C and Table 4-8D shows some of the results of Dr. Hunt's comparisons. Using the popular 30-year loan as the benchmark, monthly payments, outstanding loan balances and the amount of interest and principal paid on 15-year, 40-year, and 50-year loans were compared. The borrower's goal was assumed to be lower monthly payments rather than purchasing a larger home with the same payment amount. In this way, any offsetting effects from increased property taxes and insurance were eliminated. Monthly payments were calculated to include principal and interest only. Fixed-rate mortgages that fully amortize in 15, 40, and 50 years were compared with the 30-year note.

Dr. Hunt's comparisons assume a $100,000 loan at a 6.25 percent interest rate for 30 years, 6 percent for 15 years, 6.5 percent for 40 years, and 6.75 percent for 50 years. Based on the assumptions given, the 15-year mortgage is significantly less affordable than the 30-year, requiring a payment higher by $228.14 per month. The 40-year note's monthly payment is $30.26 less than the 30-year. Extending the amortization period from 40 to 50 years results in a mere $2.83 in further payment reduction. Clearly, the payment difference between a 40-year and a 50-year loan is negligible in this case.

Table 4-8a Total Interest Paid and Percent Difference from 30-Year Loan

Loan Terms	After 3 Years	Diff.	After 5 Years	Diff.	After 7 Years	Diff.	After 10 Years	Diff.
30-year @ 6.25%	$18,419.47		$30,280.27		$41,753.84		$58,123.78	
15-year @ 6%	$16,852.86	−8.5%	$26,640.51	−12.0%	$35,097.44	−15.9%	$44,911.79	−22.7%
40-year @ 6.5%	$19,340.97	5.00%	$32,032.59	5.80%	$44,536.00	36.70%	$62,880.42	8.20%
50-year @ 6.75%	$20,173.91	9.50%	$33,525.97	10.70%	$46,787.10	12.10%	$66,479.14	14.40%

Table 4-8b Total Principal Paid and Percent Difference from 30-Year Loan

Loan Terms	After 3 Years	Diff.	After 5 Years	Diff.	After 7 Years	Diff.	After 10 Years	Diff.
30-year @ 6.25%	$3,746.35		$6,662.76		$9,966.41		$15,762.29	
15-year @ 6%	$13,525.99	261.00%	$23,990.90	260.10%	$35,786.53	259.10%	$56,351.03	257.50%
40-year @ 6.5%	$1,735.48	−53.7%	$3,094.82	−53.6%	$4,642.34	−53.4%	$7,374.40	−53.2%
50-year @ 6.75%	$800.61	−78.6%	$1,431.58	−78.5%	$2,153.47	−78.4%	$3,435.95	−78.2%

Table 4-8c Outstanding Balances

Loan Terms	After 3 Years	Diff.	After 5 Years	Diff.	After 7 Years	Diff.	After 10 Years	Diff.
30-year @ 6.25%	$96,253.65		$93,337.24		$90,033.59		$84,237.71	

15-year @ 6%	$86,474.01	10.2%	$76,009.10	18.6%	$64,213.47	28.7%	$43,648.97	48.2%
40-year @ 6.5%	$98,264.52	–2.1%	$96,905.18	–3.8%	$95,357.66	–5.9%	$92,625.60	–10.0%
50-year @ 6.75%	$99,199.39	–3.1%	$98,568.42	–5.6%	$97,846.53	–8.7%	$96,564.05	–14.6%

Table 4-8d Monthly Payment and Difference from 30-Year Loan

Loan Terms	After 3 Years	Diff.
30-year @ 6.25%	$615.72	
15-year @ 6%	$843.86	$228.14
40-year @ 6.5%	$585.46	($30.26)
50-year @ 6.75%	$582.63	($33.09)

Source: Real Estate Center at Texas A&M University

The difference in interest paid on the four loans is noteworthy but not vastly different. Borrowers choosing the 15-year loan would pay 8.5 to 22.7 percent less total interest than a 30-year borrower depending on the holding period. The 50-year borrower would pay 9.5 to 14.4 percent more. There is a considerable difference in principal reduction. A 15-year borrower pays in 257 to 261 percent more principal than a 30- year borrower, depending on the holding period. A 50-year borrower pays about 78 percent less principal than a 30-year borrower during the first ten years.

The result is a wide variation in outstanding balance. The most extreme results occur when loans are held for ten years. The 15-year loan's balance is paid down to $43,648. By contrast, the 30-year and 50-year outstanding balances decline to only $84,237 and $96,564, respectively.

Government National Mortgage Association (Ginnie Mae)

Ginnie Mae helps make affordable housing a reality for millions of low- and moderate-income households by channeling global capital into the nation's housing markets. Specifically, the Ginnie Mae guaranty allows mortgage lenders to obtain a better price for their mortgage loans in the secondary market. The lenders can then use the proceeds to make new mortgage loans available.

Ginnie Mae guarantees investors the timely payment of principal and interest on MBS (Mortgage Backed Securities) backed by federally insured or guaranteed loans. These loans are mainly loans insured by the Federal Housing Administration (FHA) or guaranteed by the Department of Veterans Affairs (VA). Other guarantors or issuers of loans eligible as collateral for Ginnie Mae MBS include the Department of Agriculture's Rural Housing Service (RHS) and the Department of Housing and Urban Development's Office of Public and Indian Housing (PIH).

Ginnie Mae securities are the only MBS to carry the full faith and credit guaranty of the United States government, which means that even in difficult times an investment in Ginnie Mae MBS is one of the safest an investor can make. They carry the same risk as Treasury bills.

Ginnie Mae MBS are created when eligible mortgage loans (those insured or guaranteed by FHA, the VA, RHS, or PIH) are pooled by approved issuers and securitized. Ginnie Mae MBS investors receive a pro-rata share of the resulting cash flows (again, net of servicing and guaranty fees). In addition, the mortgage interest rates must all be the same and the mortgages must be issued by the same issuer. The minimum pool size is $1 million; payments on Ginnie Mae MBS have a stated 14-day delay (payment is made on the 15th day of each month).

Ginnie Mae announces GinnieNet, Version 7.0

On September 22, 2006, Ginnie Mae announced the introduction of Ginnie*NET*, Version 7.0, a web-based application that will accommodate electronic pooling and investor reporting, via the Internet, for both single family and multifamily issuers. The web-based application was being rolled out in two phases, Ginnie*NET*, Version 7.0 (phase 1), and Ginnie*NET*, Version 7.1 (phase 2). Ginnie*NET*, Version 7.0 was available to all issuers and document custodians effective for pools with an issue date of October 1, 2006, and thereafter.

Continued Payment of Private Mortgage Insurance

A controversial subject that has caused a number of lawsuits over the years is whether a borrower is obligated to pay the premium for private mortgage insurance (PMI) after the loan amount declines to less than 80 percent of the property value. The 80 percent Loan To Value Ratio (LTVR) figure is used because lenders do not require PMI coverage if the borrower puts 20 percent or more down.

Since 1997, state law requires lenders to provide borrowers with an annual notice that they may cancel PMI whenever the loan balance is 80 percent or less of current fair market value of the home. Whether an appraisal of the property is required to determine "current fair market value" is not addressed.

A later federal law [the Homeowners Protection Act (HPA)] passed in July 1998, effective July 29, 1999, covering PMI applies only to loans originated on or after July 29, 1999. It requires lenders to notify consumers of their right to cancel private mortgage insurance when the equity in their homes reaches 20 percent. Lenders may ask for an appraisal to prove property value. The law exempts FHA and VA loans. It does not preempt any state statutes in effect before January 2, 1998.

Furthermore, the bill provides for *automatic cancellation* at three different levels, depending on the size and risk of the mortgage. These levels are as follows:

1. For most conventional loans, automatic cancellation is made when the loan reaches 78 percent of the original value of the property.

2. For high-risk mortgages that do not exceed conforming loan limits, automatic cancellation is triggered at the midterm of the loan.

3. For high-risk mortgages that are above the conforming loan limit, trigger for cancellation is 77 percent LTVR.

Because cancellation of PMI at 80 percent LTVR could require an appraisal, many homeowners wait until the 78 percent of original value triggers automatic cancellation.

HERA Money to Go to North Texas

The Housing and Economic Recovery Act has earmarked more than $30 million of the federal government's money to go to several North Texas cities and counties. The money will go to Arlington, Dallas, Fort Worth, Garland, Grand Prairie, and Mesquite, and to Dallas and Tarrant counties. The money will be used to purchase and refurbish foreclosed homes, and to provide down payment assistance to qualified homebuyers who purchase foreclosed homes.

The money is not intended to bail out homeowners who are facing foreclosure but to protect neighborhoods from declining home values. "This money was designed to acquire, rehabilitate . . . . and make these houses homes again," said Brian Sullivan, spokesman for the U.S. Department of Housing and Urban Development (HUD). "It's about making sure these homes don't become sources of blight in the community where the effect becomes almost viral."

The money is expected to begin being used in January or February of 2009 to buy homes and lend to homeowners. Once the cities and counties determine where they will spend the money, they submit their plans to HUD for approval.

AIG's Rescue Package Swelling

According to a press release by the Associated Press and also the Real Estate Center at Texas A&M University, the AIG rescue package is swelling. The government's emergency rescue loan to insurer American International Group (AIG) has ballooned from $85 billion to more than $150 billion, a record for a private company.

Under the new plan, the Fed will provide $60 billion in loans, the Treasury will provide $40 billion to buy up preferred stock, and the government will spend close to $53 billion to buy up mortgage-backed assets and other AIG contracts on debt.

"It's interesting that the day after the $700 billion bailout package passed, we were hearing that this is only a down payment," said Dr. Mark Dotzour, chief economist with the Real Estate Center at Texas A&M University. "They were saying the final price tag would probably be somewhere between $2 trillion and $3 trillion. And that's how the story continues to unfold."

Dotzour said investors are still on the lookout for positive signs that government initiatives are working. "To date, those signs are scarce," he said. For more information on this topic link to the following URL:

http://recenter.tamu.edu/mnews/newsSearch.asp?MODE=RECON&CID-2697

Borrowers Agree to Loan Process

In a recent article in the *New York Times*, it was disclosed that even though the loan process may be longer and more complicated these days, borrowers generally don't seem to mind. This was the result of a J.D. Power and Associates' 12-month study of 4,300 loan customers.

Out of a possible 1,000 points on J.D. Power's customer satisfaction scale, mortgage originators scored 757, up from the industry's average of 750 in the previous two years.

Tim Ryan, director of the financial services practice at J.D. Powers, said the positive results had less to do with the lenders and more to do with lower expectations. "The public has been so inundated with negative stories about the industry, expectations have been beaten down," he said. "Then, when you actually get your loan, it's a more appealing experience."

Ryan said borrowers are now less likely to face inexperienced or incompetent loan officers than two years ago, when the real estate market was stronger and the mortgage industry was awash in new loan officers in search of easy commissions. According to the study, it now takes about 11 days between application and approval, which is one day longer than last year, because lenders are now more likely to seek additional documents such as paycheck stubs and bank statements.

This was the first year the survey asked about the trustworthiness of loan originators. Of the respondents, 43 percent said they felt their loan officer had customers' best interests in mind, while 54 percent felt strongly that their loan officer dealt honestly with them.

Citigroup Will Help At-Risk Homeowners

A little over a week after JPMorgan Chase & Co. announced plans to help keep at-risk borrowers in their homes, Citigroup is stepping up its efforts to help struggling homeowners. Citigroup Inc. announced that it will not initiate a foreclosure or complete a foreclosure sale on any eligible borrower if it is the borrower's principal residence, the homeowner is working in good faith with Citigroup, and the homeowner has sufficient income to make affordable mortgage payments.

Over the next six months, Citigroup plans to reach out to 500,000 homeowners deemed as potentially needing assistance to keep up with their payments. This represents about one-third of all the mortgages that Citigroup owns. Citigroup plans to devote a team of 600 salespeople to assist the targeted borrowers by adjusting their rates, reducing principal, or increasing the term of the loan.

More than four million American homeowners with a mortgage were at least one payment behind on their loans at the end of June 2008, and 500,000 had started the foreclosure process, according to recent data from the Mortgage Bankers Association.

JP Morgan Modifying Loans

JPMorgan Chase & Co. announced in late November 2008 that it is expanding its program to modify mortgages to avoid foreclosures on up to $70 billion in loans, including those from Washington Mutual and EMC. The lender will modify adjustable-rate mortgage loans, which will eliminate the loan's monthly options and not allow for minimum payments.

The program includes an additional 24 regional counseling centers, 300 additional loan counselors, new financing alternatives, and a new process to independently review each loan before it is moved into foreclosure. Changes are expected to be implemented by the end of the first quarter of 2009. Until those changes are made, JPMorgan will not put any loans into foreclosure.

Job Losses Responsible for Growing Number of Foreclosures?

At least one pundit feels that job losses are the reason for the foreclosure rampage. In late November 2008, CNNMoney.com stated that as the economy spirals downward, it is unemployment, not bad loans, that is driving the majority of troubled borrowers into foreclosure.

In June 2008, 45.5 percent of all delinquencies reported by Freddie Mac were due to unemployment or the loss of income, an increase from 36.3 percent in 2006. Nearly one million Americans have lost their jobs in 2008. The Bureau of Labor Statistics reports that 159,000 private-sector jobs were lost in September 2008.

Foreclosures spiked 71 percent in September 2008 alone, according to RealtyTrac, and the rise in job losses will increase and extend the delinquency trend.

Predatory Lending

Much has been said about the abuse of predatory lending, but the definition of such remains ill defined. In an effort to identify what this practice really is, along with its plan of comprehensive reform of the mortgage industry, the Mortgage Bankers Association has identified 12 practices considered to be predatory. These are:

1. Steering borrowers to high-rate lenders.
2. Engaging in the practice of intentionally structuring high-cost loans with payments the borrower cannot afford.
3. Falsifying loan documents.
4. Making loans to mentally incapacitated homeowners.
5. Forging signatures on loan documents.
6. Changing the loan terms at closing.
7. Requiring credit insurance.
8. Falsely identifying loans as lines of credit or open-end mortgages.
9. Increasing interest charges when loan payments are late.
10. Charging excessive prepayment penalties.

11. Failing to report good payment on borrower's credit reports.

12. Failing to provide accurate loan balance and payoff amounts.

Shoddy Appraisals Help Predatory Lenders

Lenders alone should not be the only target of efforts to tackle the problem of predatory lending. HUD Secretary Martinez has said, "A home loan cannot be flipped without a fraudulent appraisal." Flipping schemes occur when a property is resold shortly after it is acquired at an inflated price. This can be caused by an inaccurate appraisal, or it may be sold before receiving the extensive rehabilitation needed to justify the increase in price.

The term *flipping* also applies to the practice of unscrupulous lenders soliciting multiple refinancing with loan terms that are not favorable to consumers. This practice also leans on shoddy appraisals. There are laws in place that provide guidelines that appraisers must follow. Every state has an appraisal commission that sets requirements for licensing, but state governments inconsistently enforce the laws.

To help avoid becoming a victim of loan fraud, HUD has provided 11 tips on being a smart consumer. These tips are available by going to the HUD Web site—*http://www.hud.gov*—click on "Consumer Information" and then click on "Predatory Lending."

Since the spring of 1999, HUD has been actively involved in combating predatory lending through research, regulation, consumer education and enforcement actions against lenders, appraisers, real estate brokers, and other companies and individuals that have victimized homebuyers. In the event that one believes they have become a victim of predatory lending practices, there is a list of federal agencies on the Web site that can help.

State Predatory Lending Bills

Even though the practice is still not well defined, the concern that some consumers with flawed credit histories are being taken advantage of in subprime loans has brought many state legislatures into possible action. Abusive practices in this expanding market do harm some consumers and harms reputable lenders who suffer from guilt by association.

A few states have passed legislation, and most other states are considering such action. The state bills lower the threshold found in federal law, such as the Truth-in-Lending Act. Some curtail the ability of mortgage lenders to charge points and fees. To avoid a growing patchwork of laws that could create burdensome compliance tasks, the Mortgage Bankers Association is trying to work with the various states and with Congress to promote more uniform and practical legislation in this area.

So far, the Texas Legislature has not passed any law that targets the ill-defined area of predatory lending.

Mortgage Fraud

Increases in mortgage fraud are due, in part, to the fact that it has become much easier to perpetrate. An example is an e-mail sent out from an Indiana firm offering a "new identity" for $19.95. It offered a new name, credit file, Social Security number, picture ID, and any major credit card. The increase of fraud is caused by new and creative forms of financing; automated underwriting encouraging faster qualification, which can compromise due diligence; and availability of low-cost quality computer equipment, printers, and copy machines, which can produce high-quality fraudulent documents.

People with tarnished credit who are anxious to buy a home are sometimes victims of unscrupulous operators. The victim is offered "guaranteed homeownership" and asked for an advance fee. The fee is pocketed and no attempt is made to obtain any kind of mortgage loan. Authorities in Massachusetts found a "mortgage assistance company" had defrauded more than a million dollars from low-income people with poor credit—those who can least afford the loss. Because there is no clear paper trail that usually accompanies mortgage fraud, prosecutors have successfully utilized wire and mail fraud laws to prosecute mortgage-related scams. The possibility of a loan to achieve homeownership is attractive to many, but one should always beware of paying a fee in advance to obtain a loan.

Foreclosure "Rescue" Scam

Convinced that home foreclosures will rise dramatically in the next two years, Dr. Mark Dotzour, the chief economist for the Real Estate Center at Texas A&M University, warns that a new scam threatens homebuyers desperately looking for a way out of financial stress. Homebuyers who purchased homes with subprime loans are especially vulnerable. Predatory lenders are targeting subprime borrowers who have some equity built up in a home but who are having difficulty meeting monthly mortgage payments.

"Predatory lenders now offer what they call 'rescue loans,'" said Dr. Mark Dotzour, "but homebuyers are neither rescued nor do they actually receive loans." Homebuyers with impaired or nonexistent credit histories often turn to subprime loans despite the higher interest that comes with them. According to Dotzour, many are about to discover that their "American dream" has turned into a nightmare.

The scam works as follows. The homebuyer gets behind on mortgage payments. The predatory lender offers a "loan to get caught up" on the delinquent mortgage payments. In exchange for the rescue, the homeowner signs over the title to the predator, who promises that the homebuyer may remain in the home while paying rent. The predator then sells the house to someone else, and the original homeowner gets an eviction notice. About a dozen states have passed laws designed to deter rescue loan fraud, but Texas is not one of them.

"The scam is called a loan, but it is not," says Dotzour. "It really is a buy-out with a leaseback." Dotzour fears the problem is going to get much worse. As of Oct. 31, 2007, some 4 percent of borrowers who obtained subprime loans in 2006 were 60 days or more behind on payments. He said the delinquency rate is running twice that of a year ago. "Foreclosures are up 27 percent in the last 12 months," said the noted economist, "but that's still low in my books." Dotzour expects that figure to double within a few months.

Subprime mortgage volume has increased fivefold in five years. The Mortgage Bankers Association estimates that $1.1 trillion to $1.3 trillion in subprime loans are due to adjust to higher interest rates in 2007. "Obviously there will be a much higher foreclosure rate in the next five years," said Dotzour, "regardless of whether there is an upswing or downswing in the economy."

Deed in Lieu of Foreclosure

Financial troubles could be in store for thousands of Texas homeowners if the dire foreclosure forecasts come true. But homeowners facing foreclosure do have options, says Judon Fambrough, a lawyer with the Real Estate Center at Texas A&M University. "They can pay off the debt before the foreclosure sale begins, refinance the debt with another lender, or sell the property and pay off the debt," he said. "However, these options may not be practical for homeowners who lack funds, good credit, or the time necessary to sell the property before foreclosure."

Fambrough says another, lesser-known option is available. The homeowner can request a deed in lieu of foreclosure (DILF). A DILF conveys the property back to the lender in exchange for cancelling the debt. The lender's consent and cooperation are required. DILFs offer several advantages over traditional nonjudicial foreclosures under deeds of trust, the most significant of which is that the homeowner's credit is unaffected.

In addition, Fambrough says DILFs are quicker, requiring fewer than the minimum 41 days needed to foreclose on a home under a deed of trust. DILFs are also more confidential and less expensive. "The major costs of a DILF are deed preparation and the recording fee," Fambrough said. "But lenders may require the debtor to pay for a title search and an appraisal before agreeing to the DILF." The title search determines whether there are other liens on the property, and an appraisal substantiates the property value. Often, if a property has more than one lien, or if the property value does not greatly exceed the amount of the debt, lenders will not agree to the DILF.

Under certain circumstances, a lender can void the arrangement or foreclose even after agreeing to a DILF. "The arrangement could be voided if there was a lien or encumbrance on the property that the homeowner did not disclose or that the lender had no knowledge of," Fambrough said. Likewise, in some cases, homeowners may find foreclosure a more attractive option than a DILF. If the property value exceeds the debt, and the debtor decides to foreclose, any excess revenue generated by the foreclosure sale will go to the debtor. This is not the case with a DILF. Debtors forfeit their equity.

Before executing a DILF, Fambrough recommends the homeowner talk to a financial advisor about possible income tax consequences that could result from the debt forgiveness. Forgiven debt will most likely be considered as taxable income. For more information, read "DILF or No DILF" in the January, 2007 issue of Tierra Grande, the Center's quarterly real estate journal.

Investing IRA Dollars in Real Estate

Most people are familiar with the concept of their retirement funds being invested in stocks, bonds, mutual funds, and other traditional investment vehicles. However, more people are looking to diversify their portfolio by investing their retirement funds in real estate. This can be done if the investor has a self-directed IRA.

A self-directed IRA is like other IRAs in every respect, except that it allows account holders to direct their own investments. Account holders can buy and sell investment real estate while deferring the tax consequences. Real estate practitioners can earn commissions by helping investor clients buy and sell real estate through self-directed IRAs.

The IRS allows retirement money to be used to buy real estate in any form: houses, raw land, office buildings, shopping centers, and so on. The holder can buy property and develop it or hold the property to sell at a profit at a later date. Once the property is sold, all proceeds go back into the IRA, which continues to grow tax-deferred.

Properties can be bought, sold, or used as rental property in a self-directed IRA. For rentals, all maintenance and improvement costs, taxes, insurance, and property management fees must be paid from the IRA, and all rental income must go back into the IRA. However, that rental income becomes part of the IRA balance and may be used to buy other types of investments, such as mutual funds, stocks, bonds, CDs, and T-bills.

Custodians typically require that any real estate purchased through an IRA be bought outright with no financing. In addition, the property must be used for investment purposes only and cannot be used personally while maintained in the IRA.

Identity Theft

There's a new type of Internet piracy called "phishing." It's pronounced "fishing," and that's exactly what these thieves are doing: "fishing" for personal financial information. What they want are account numbers, passwords, Social Security numbers, and other confidential information that they can use to loot checking accounts or run up bills on credit cards. In the worst case, one could become a victim of identity theft. With the sensitive information obtained from a successful phishing scam, these thieves can take out loans or obtain credit cards and even driver's licenses in the victim's name. They can do damage to financial history and personal reputation that can take years to unravel. But if potential victims understand how phishing works and how to protect themselves, they can help stop this crime.

Here's how phishing works:

In a typical case, you will receive an e-mail that appears to come from a reputable company that you recognize and do business with, such as your financial institution. In some cases, the e-mail may appear to come from a government agency, including one of the federal financial institution regulatory agencies.

The e-mail will probably warn you of a serious problem that requires your immediate attention. It may use phrases, such as "Immediate attention required," or "Please contact us immediately about your account." The e-mail will then encourage you to click on a button to go to the institution's Web site.

In a phishing scam, you could be redirected to a phony Web site that may look exactly like the real thing. Sometimes, in fact, it may be the company's actual Web site. In those cases, a pop-up window will quickly appear for the purpose of harvesting your financial information. In either case, you may be asked to update your account information or to provide information for verification purposes: your Social Security number, your account number, your password, or the information you use to verify your identity when speaking to a real financial institution, such as your mother's maiden name or your place of birth.

If you provide the requested information, you may find yourself the victim of identity theft. The Federal Trade Commission has provided information on their Web site to help consumers avoid identity theft.

http://www.ftc.gov/bcp/edu/microsites/idtheft//index.html

This Web site is a one-stop national resource to learn about the crime of identity theft. It provides detailed information to help you deter, detect, and defend against identity theft. On this site, consumers can learn how to avoid identity theft – and learn what to do if their identity is stolen. Businesses can learn how to help their customers deal with identity theft, as well as how to prevent problems in the first place. Law enforcement can get resources and learn how to help victims of identity theft.

Reverse Mortgages Growing Trend

Reverse mortgages have been around for many years. They began as an expensive idea first tried by independent bankers 30 years ago. They evolved into a "demonstration program" sponsored by HUD in 1993 and are now a permanent, refined economic vehicle. More than 16,000 loans were generated in fiscal 2003.

HUD insures the nation's leading reverse mortgage product, the Home Equity Conversion Mortgage (HECM). HUD recently announced that reverse mortgage lenders would be able to "lock" loans at application, eliminating the possibility of rates rising between application and closing. In addition, mortgage lenders offering HECMs no longer need to recalculate the principal limit on the day of closing. Lenders are not allowed to charge a fee for the 60-day lock.

In some reverse mortgage packages, the cash can be put toward a line of credit and used as the consumer needs the funds. Reverse borrowers make no monthly payments on their mortgage during its term. The loan comes due when the borrower permanently moves out of his or her home.

Reverse mortgage borrowers can outlive the value of their home without being forced to move. The homeowner cannot be displaced and forced to sell the home to pay off the mortgage even if the principal balance exceeds the value of the property. If the value of the house exceeds what is owed at the time of the homeowner's death, the excess goes to the estate.

To qualify, the borrower must be at least 62 years of age and own his or her home. The home does not need to be free and clear, but the greater the equity, the greater the reverse loan amount. Age, location, and loan type also factor into the calculation of the reverse mortgage amount.

The Veterans Housing Opportunity and Benefits Act of 2006

On June 15, 2006, the president signed P. L. 109233, the Veterans Housing Opportunity and Benefits Act of 2006. Several items in the Act impact the Loan Guaranty Program. The law authorizes VA to provide Specially Adapted Housing (SAH) assistance to veterans who are temporarily residing in a home owned by a family member. This assistance would be in the form of a grant to assist the veteran in adapting the family member's home to meet his or her special needs. Those eligible for the grant would be permitted to use up to $14,000 of the maximum grant amount for a 2101(a) grant or up to $2,000 of the maximum grant amount for a 2101(b) grant. This new provision does not authorize VA to make such grants available to assist active duty service members.

The law changes the onetime only usage of grant benefits. Although a veteran may now use his or her benefits up to a total of three times, the aggregate amount of assistance cannot exceed the maximum amounts allowable for either the 2101(a) or 2101(b) grant.

The law reestablishes VA's authority to make SAH grants (but not the temporary grants referred to above) to active duty service personnel awaiting disability discharge. No temporary grant assistance may be provided after June 15, 2011. The benefits administered under chapters 17, 21, and 31 of Title 38 cover assistance provided under the Home Improvement and Structural Alteration (HISA), SAH, and Independent Living (IL) benefit programs.

Texas Veterans Land Board

Housing Assistance

For qualified veterans, the Veterans Housing Assistance Program (VHAP) provides financing up to $325,000 toward the purchase of a home. Loans for $45,000 or less may be originated through the Texas Veterans Land Board's (VLB) direct loan program.

There is no maximum sales price, however, the VLB can only loan up to $325,000 toward the purchase. The VHAP must be originated in conjunction with FHA, VA, or conventional financing. The VLB also offers a "two-note loan" for veterans needing more than $350,000. These loans as well as any loans over $45,000 must be originated by a participating lender. The two notes are underwritten as co-first liens using one Deed of Trust to secure them.

The VHAP is not a refinancing or equity loan program. It can only be used as a first lien on the purchase of a primary residence. The term of the loan can be 15, 20, 25, or 30 years. Two married, eligible veterans may have only one active VHAP loan at one time.

Land Loans

The VLB will finance the LEAST of the following options:

- $80,000, or

- 95% of the final agreed-upon purchase price, or

- 95% of the appraised value of the land.

The veteran must have AT LEAST a 5 percent down payment invested as cash equity in the property. At closing, the TVLB will purchase the land and sell it to the veteran on a "contract for deed."

Home Improvement Loans

The Texas Veterans Land Board (VLB) will lend eligible Texas veterans up to $25,000 for up to 20 years on a fixed-rate note to make substantial repairs to their existing primary residence. No down payment is required. For loans of less than $10,000, the maximum term of the loan will be 10 years. All loans are FHA-insured. The VLB must be in a first or second lien position. The veteran cannot advance any funds to the contractor or purchase materials prior to receipt of loan proceeds from the VLB. All property improvements should be completed within 6 months from the date of disbursal of loan proceeds.

If the veteran is required to vacate the home while the improvements are being made, the veteran must re-occupy it within 60 days after completion of the construction. The Home Improvement Program cannot be used for refinancing.

Public Improvement Districts (PIDs)

When a subdivision, a community, or an area with common interests has a need for capital improvements, such as street improvements, water, sewer, drainage, bulkheads, sand socks, or any other infrastructure, finding the funds may be problematic. Public Improvement Districts may be excellent vehicles for obtaining the necessary funds.

Many communities along the Gulf Coast feel that sand socks may be very beneficial in protecting their property against hurricanes and tidal surges. Sand socks are large "socks" that are filled with sand and augment the benefits of the sand dunes. In areas where the sand socks have been installed, they have suffered less property damage than those areas without sand socks. For example, the GeoTubes in front of Pirates Beach in Galveston provided more protection against Hurricane Claudette (2003) and Rita (2005) than the traditional sand dunes provided other properties. That is the good news, but the bad news is that the sand socks can be very costly. The cost in some areas could be as much as $10,000 per lot. As a one-time assessment this could be prohibitive; however, if it could be paid for over 10 or 20 years, it would be far less burdensome to the property owners.

To attempt to borrow the money for the improvements would be virtually impossible because there is no entity that the lender could look to for repayment. An excellent vehicle for financing such improvements is a PID or Public Improvement District. If over 50% of the property owners in a discrete area petition the city for formation of a PID, the city will schedule a public hearing. Based on the results of the hearing, the city will decide whether to create the PID.

The city then issues bonds to raise money to pay for the improvements. The property owners create the management plan and establish budgets for the district but the city is in total control of the district. Once the public infrastructure is constructed, each property owner in the area will be charged or assessed its pro-rata share of the total cost. When the construction is completely finished, the city will hold a public hearing to present the cost of the project and the assessment amount for each lot. Once the public hearing is held, the city will levy the assessment. Once the assessment is levied, it does not change. The assessment lies between a tax lien and a first mortgage lien in priority.

How Can This Assessment Be Paid?

A PID assessment can be paid in one of three ways:

1. The property owner can pay it in full at closing and will not have any further annual payments; or

2. The property owner can pay the assessment in annual installments over 5, 10, or 20 years (the payout can be over any period of time established by the PID); or

3. The property owner may incorporate the PID amount into their home loan, thereby including the PID amount into their monthly mortgage payment. This assumes the PID is a residential area and that the homeowner has worked this out with their mortgage company. PIDs can also be used to finance the infrastructure of a new development.

How Is This Assessment Different from a MUD (Municipal Utility District) Tax?

A MUD has the authority to construct public infrastructures, sell bonds to finance the infrastructure, and to levy a tax each year in an amount sufficient to pay the bonds and operate the MUD. Each year the tax rate can vary and as the MUD builds out, additional bonds can be sold, extending the life of the MUD. In a PID, each property that benefits from the improvements pays only for its particular pro-rata share of the cost. Once the PID assessment is paid, the property owner does not pay a portion of expansions in the subdivision. PID bonds can be sold, but only the revenue from existing PID assessments can be used to repay the bonds.

Management Districts

The property owners in a large commercial area of a major Texas city desired to make some extensive capital improvements to enhance the attractiveness of the area. The improvements consisted of massive arches across the major streets in the area, attention-getting signage, landscaping, and other items to give the area a unique character. To pay for the improvements by special assessment would have been a big burden on the property owners and collection of the assessments could not be enforced. As with PIDs, any attempt to borrow the money for the improvements was virtually impossible because there was no entity for the lender to hold responsible.

The property owners chose to form a management district as a vehicle for financing the improvements. A management district is somewhat similar to a PID with certain exceptions. The creators of the management district maintain control of the project as opposed to the PID being run by the city. Also, the formation is different in that the management district is established by the state legislature. Probably the big advantage of a management district is the flexibility of operation once the district has been formed. There are 26 such districts in the city of Houston alone.

Real Estate Center

Real estate licensees have an advantage in Texas through the benefits of a Real Estate Center that actively supports the industry with its research and education programs. It has made available to licensees a substantial library of information on the many facets of real estate. The information is in the form of numerous publications covering topics from appraisal to zoning and a reservoir of real estate price data. The Center's staff is willing to explore new fields of information that are helpful to all real estate licensees.

Under the direction of Gary Maler, the Center continues to expand its outreach throughout the state. Its professional staff is frequently called upon to meet with local organizations to explain economic, marketing, and legal questions pertinent to real estate issues. Their most current contribution to the industry is the creation of the new mandatory MCE courses, the 3-hour legal update, and the 3-hour ethics segment.

Periodically the Center holds a 1-day refresher seminar to which all Texas real estate instructors are invited in cooperation with the Texas Real Estate Teachers Association (TRETA).

The Center is funded by real estate licensees. A portion of each license paid to the Texas Real Estate Commission is reserved for the operation of the Center at Texas A&M University in College Station. The 1995 legislature set the Real Estate Center's annual portion of licensee fees at $20 for brokers and $17.50 for salespersons. Although the funding varies with the number of licensees paying fees each year, the average annual budget is now about $2 million. Because of this method of financing, every licensee has a vested interest in the Center.

Real Estate Center Advisory Committee

To maintain close contact with the real estate community, the Center has an Advisory Committee consisting of nine members appointed by the governor. Six are real estate brokers licensed for at least 5 years, representing each of the following specialties: brokerage, finance, improvements, residential properties, commercial properties, and industrial properties. The other three members represent the general public. In addition, the chairperson of the Texas Real Estate Commission or a designee is an ex officio member.

Publications

Texas real estate licensees automatically receive *Tierra Grande*, a quarterly magazine detailing research results and trends. This publication now includes Judon Fambrough's "Law Letter."

Upon request, licensees may receive *Trends*, an 8-page monthly statistical report on the 27 major Texas markets.

More than 12,000 pages of free news, information, and statistical data are available on the Center's Web site at *http://recenter.tamu.edu*. Real Estate Center *Online News* (RECON) is a free weekly update of Texas-relevant real estate news; signing up can be done on their Web site.

Much of the information in this chapter has been obtained from data and publications available on the Texas Real Estate Web site. All of the recent editions of *Tierra Grande* are available in their entirety. There are also many other resources that are available to the real estate professional as well as the general public. The Center does an excellent job of researching current trends in real estate, particularly as they affect Texas. Real estate license fees provide funding for this valuable asset and therefore licensees should take advantage of this resource.

The Center also has several videotapes on a variety of topics. A free catalog is available for the asking. Contact:

Publications
Real Estate Center
Texas A&M University
College Station, Texas 77843-2115
Phone: 979-845-2031
FAX: 979-845-0460
E-mail: info@recenter.tamu.edu
Web site: *http://recenter.tamu.edu*

Current Issues in Commercial Real Estate

Pre-Assessment Evaluation

Please answer the following questions.

1.   Certificates of Convenience and Necessity are issued by the Texas Commission on Environmental Quality and confer the exclusive right to supply specified utility services to an identified geographic area.

        True   **False**

2.   Soil surveys are now available online for a moderate fee.

        True   **False**

3.   Land, buildings, improvements, tangible personal property, and leasehold interests in nonexempt properties are eligible for tax abatement.

        True   **False**

4.   Liability for toxic cleanup is joint and several, but not strict.

        True   **False**

5.   It may be possible for a landowner with a wetlands area on the land to be developed to purchase acreage in a mitigation bank and thus meet Corps of Engineering requirements allowing a permit to be issued to fill in the existing wetlands.

        True   **False**

Certificates of Convenience and Necessity (CCN)

Certificates of Convenience and Necessity (CCNs) are issued by the Texas Commission on Environmental Quality (TCEQ) and confer on its holder the exclusive right to supply specified utility services to an identified geographic area. That right can cover water or wastewater service for all land in the CCN territory.

The CCN also obligates its holder to provide continuous and adequate service for every consumer in the area. If the holder fails to provide service, a decertification process through TCEQ can revoke the CCN. If the utility has outstanding debt with an entity of the federal government, however, decertification cannot occur because federal law prohibits changes in the CCN boundaries.

In the past, many CCNs were issued without the knowledge of affected landowners or without a demand for service. Some utilities obtained the certificates but lacked the resources needed to provide service. Further, the boundaries of CCNs sometimes were unclear from official documents. Because the Texas Water Code did not require notification of affected landowners in the past, many landowners did not discover the CCNs until they prepared to develop their properties. Some found that dealing with a CCN holder to secure service complicated or even blocked the subdivision process.

In the worst-case scenario, an owner who did not know the CCN existed would develop a subdivision and install a private water system to supply the new neighborhood. After building the system, the developer would discover the existence of a CCN for water service in that area. The CCN holder could be a city, water supply district, investor-owned utility, or other special district. In that situation, the developer would be prohibited from operating the private utility and would have no choice but to transfer the water system to the CCN holder.

Negotiations typically involve paying CCN holders fees for infrastructure transferred plus damages to the CCN holder's plans for future service to the remaining CCN area. Some landowners find CCN holder demands so onerous that they abandon their development plans. Nearly half of Texas cities have CCNs. An estimated 100 cities have obtained CCNs beyond their extraterritorial jurisdiction (ETJ), effectively projecting city controls into rural areas.

Because of the frequent conflicts, a crusade for changes in the CCN process emerged. In September 2005, rules designed to implement the bill were adopted by TCEQ in December 2005 and became effective in January 2006. Under the new law, landowners must be notified when a CCN is created or amended. CCN applicants must define proposed service areas and sources of funding, and landowners may become a part of the certification process. The bill also shortens and simplifies the decertification process to 180 days, and it limits cities' ability to extend CCNs beyond their ETJs.

Trends Affecting the Retail Industry

There are two major socioeconomic trends that are affecting the retail industry and having noticeable effects on retail developers and investors. The first trend is the accelerating speed at which change occurs in the industry. Because shoppers' attention spans are shorter, and fads are coming and going faster, shoppers do not have the luxury of leisurely shopping as they used to have. To compete, retailers must continually change their products and presentation, offering shoppers a "new" experience.

The other trend is known as *commoditization*. Customers want assurance that retailers are offering a "value proposition." That is, each retailer and shopping center must feature something that compels people to shop there. If retailers do not have a value proposition, they become nothing more than a commodity. And in the commodity market, sellers must run as fast as they can to earn even a small profit.

High-end retail malls are thriving. A great location and proximity to high-income buyers is still a great combination for retail success. Well-located malls offering entertainment, interesting shops and convenience are succeeding. New restaurants such as Cheesecake Factory and Maggianos are drawing traffic wherever they go. JC Penney is successfully engineering a turnaround. Its link with beauty retailer Sephora signals a move toward a different client base: younger customers with spending power. Since then, JC Penney has been repositioning itself to be "hip" and attractive to young clothing shoppers.

Wal-Mart will remodel many of its stores and upgrade its product lines. It is looking to sell to customers in the middle 80 percent of the income distribution. Wal-Mart strives to achieve 30 percent market share in all its product categories. Wal-Mart has already crushed the toy and food markets. Now it is focusing heavily on electronics. Best Buy is successfully competing with Wal-Mart by getting new products onto its shelves faster.

Apparel companies are struggling to differentiate themselves by offering designer brands that cannot be found at other stores in addition to their own private labels. Wal-Mart's apparel brand "George," however, is not very strong, and the company will not become a dominant apparel player until it improves its brand. The supermarket industry is engaged in a pitched battle, with Wal-Mart currently the dominant player. The company opened 55 supercenters in January of 2006. Home Depot may open convenience stores by 2010.

Other supermarket chains are finding it difficult to compete with Wal-Mart on price. Dollar Stores are adding food and pharmaceuticals. Convenience stores are expanding food inventories. Meanwhile, dining out is growing as fast as dining in. Internet sales are increasing. L.L. Bean sells more products through its Web site than through its catalogue. Big retailers have greatly improved their Internet capabilities. Catalogue distribution is likely to decline. However, Internet sales amount to only 6 percent of U.S. retail sales, so a lot of business is still being done in traditional stores.

Each year, retailers and the shopping center development industry meet in Las Vegas for spring meetings of the International Council of Shopping Centers (ICSC). Attendance at the 2007 ICSC convention approached a record 50,000. Clearly, developers and municipalities are still enthusiastic about retail development, and American consumers, who continue to accumulate monumental debt, are still shopping. In the October 2007 edition of Tierra Grande, chief economist Dr. Mark Doutzer reports on the convention. The following are excerpts from his report.

Mixed-Use Projects

Zoning ordinances over the past 50 years have separated residential and commercial land uses, leaving people to commute long distances from home to work and entertainment venues. Now that gas prices are painfully high and concern about environmental issues is increasing, developers are building mixed-use developments that combine housing with office, retail, and hotels in one area. Proximity allows people to walk to and from destinations.

Mixed-use projects are complex. They can be created in urban, suburban, in-fill and reuse scenarios. Developers often seek zoning changes to allow higher density and taller buildings, but sometimes conflicts arise between area residents and city officials.

When the public gets involved, debate over new development must be done in the glare of the public spotlight, making negotiations more difficult. Mixed-use deals often are done with financial support from the local municipality in the form of tax abatements or infrastructure improvements. Because municipal government spending is funded by retail sales taxes paid by local shoppers, mayors are keen to attract big retailers to their cities. And of course, housing and retail development go together because there is no retail demand without the houses full of shoppers.

Big-city mayors at the convention advised developers that successful development projects must help the city achieve its long-term goals. For example, Atlanta is currently focusing on providing retail developments that include locally owned businesses.

"Workforce housing" is the new euphemism for what used to be called "affordable housing." Mixed-use developments may include workforce housing, in some cases across the street from million-dollar condos. Tax credits for developing affordable housing and preserving historical buildings can reduce costs by 30 to 40 percent. New Markets Tax Credits and Historic Preservation Credits are two examples.

Underserved Urban Retail Markets

Lower-income residents living in the core of American cities often have no retail to support them. In some cases, they have to travel miles to shop for groceries and other necessities. This market, which convention speakers referred to as the "new frontier" for retail development, faces serious challenges. Perceptions of high crime, inventory losses, and lack of disposable income have made debt and equity investors skeptical about entering these markets. However, a few success stories are providing encouraging momentum.

Urban retail often entails the reuse of existing buildings. Urban settings frequently include multistory buildings, which traditionally have been anathema to retailers, who prefer to be on the "pedestrian" ground floor. Mixed-use projects can take a long time to develop, often longer than the terms of the mayors and council members who supported them.

One of the biggest challenges for developers is getting national retailers to commit to locations in the urban core. The mayor of Atlanta suggested developers turn to locally owned retailers to fill the gap.

Former Los Angeles Lakers basketball star "Magic" Johnson has formed a development company and a partnership with Starbucks to open coffee shops in the urban core. He has also partnered with TGI Friday's and AMC Entertainment to provide restaurants and movie theaters in minority urban and suburban markets. These retail developments already exist in Dallas and Houston.

A panel of mayors from across the United States suggested that it takes a strong mayor and city council commitment to make urban retail work. Hence, these developments are almost exclusively public–private partnerships. The developer brings the capital and expertise; the city provides public services, infrastructure and financial subsidies. Several mayors agreed that mayors must not be just chief financial officers for their cities but also chief marketing officers.

Unionization and Its Effect on Building Owners

In an attempt to revive private-sector membership, a number of labor unions are setting their sights on America's service sector employees. The Service Employees International Union (SEIU) was one of seven unions that broke away from the AFL-CIO in 2005 to form the Change to Win (CTW) labor federation. The two organizations have different ideas regarding the most effective way to reverse the decline in union membership and reestablish organized labor as a force in today's workplace. The seven CTW unions primarily represent women, immigrants, and people of color working in the service sector.

More than 225,000 janitors already belong to SEIU, which first began its "Justice for Janitors" campaign in 1985. Since that time, SEIU has negotiated labor contracts for janitors in twenty-seven markets across the United States. SEIU membership is about 1.8 million nationwide.

SEIU is targeting five national firms that provide janitorial services to about 75 percent of Houston's office buildings. They are ABM Janitorial Services, GCA Services Group Inc., OneSource Facility Services Inc., Pritchard Industries Southwest Inc., and Sanitors Services of Texas LP.

In August 2005, the five contractors entered into a "neutrality agreement" with SEIU. Under the agreement, nonsupervisory janitorial employees in Houston were given the option to choose SEIU as their bargaining representative. This was done through a card-check procedure in which janitors could sign membership authorization cards indicating they favored union representation. The janitorial firms, having already negotiated union contracts with SEIU in other cities, agreed to take a neutral position on unionization with their Houston employees.

By the end of November 2005, about 3,000 of a total of 5,300 contract janitors had signed authorization cards. The American Arbitration Association then verified the signatures were legitimate and represented a majority, paving the way for SEIU to represent the janitors in labor contract negotiations.

The Houston chapter of the Institute of Real Estate Management (IREM) reports that janitorial expenses are about 75 cents to $1 per square foot annually for both Class A and B office buildings. Total operating expenses are approximately $10 per square foot for Class-A buildings and $8 to $8.50 per square foot for Class-B buildings. This means janitorial expenses range from 8 to 12 percent of total operating expenses for A and B buildings in the Houston market.

SEIU officials stated it would be a victory to obtain a $1 an hour raise and health benefits for the Houston janitors. The wage increase alone would escalate janitorial costs by about 20 percent annually.

In Houston, the Houston Building Owners and Managers Association estimates that if fully paid health benefits are included, janitorial costs could increase by as much as 50 percent. A 20 to 50 percent increase in janitorial expenses translates into a 2 to 5 percent increase in total operating expenses for Houston office buildings. During the past 10 years, total building operating expenses have increased 2 to 4 percent annually. Recent pressure on other expense categories such as electricity and insurance have prompted speculation that 2006 increases will be in the 10 to 15 percent range. Specific expense pass-through provisions negotiated in each lease will determine whether building owners or tenants shoulder the brunt of the increases.

`SEIU estimates that the turnover rate for Houston janitors is 200 to 300 percent annually. Assuming significant improvements in wages and benefits are secured through union negotiations, turnover rates would be expected to decline.

The efficiency of the workforce should improve, and the contractor's cost to train new employees should be reduced, creating a more stable and productive workforce. A gradual transition from part-time to full-time employees in such a high-turnover industry should limit the need for layoffs.

SEIU reports that the three Harris County public hospitals spent nearly $500 million in 2003 to cover health care services for the uninsured. The CTW federation maintains that 92 percent of union workers nationwide receive job-related health coverage versus only 68 percent of nonunion workers.

SEIU may initially choose to negotiate relatively small increases in wages and benefits to gain a union foothold in Houston's private sector. The average annual raise for union contracts is about 3 percent nationwide, according to Bill Bux, head of the labor and employment law section for Locke Liddell & Sapp. SEIU may also forego collecting union dues early on to build membership.

If SEIU does successfully negotiate a labor contract, the long-term success of unionizing the Houston janitors still is not assured. However, if the movement is successful, look for union interest to extend to other areas of the state and other service personnel affecting commercial real estate, such as security guards and landscaping crews. Janitorial firms servicing other commercial property types will also be potential targets for unionization.

Texas Industrial Market Report

Grubb & Ellis has issued its industrial market report for major Texas cities for the third quarter of 2008. Here is how four Texas markets fared:

Austin—Negative net absorption of 39,556 sf, combined with construction completions of more than 700,000 sf, pushed the citywide vacancy rate to 11 percent, up 90 basis points from the second quarter and its highest point since fourth-quarter 2005. At $7.48 per sf per year, citywide asking rents are down 1.4 percent from the second quarter and 6.5 percent from a year ago. Both the R&D-Flex and warehouse-distribution sectors saw asking rents decrease, whereas general industrial space saw an overall increase.

Dallas–Fort Worth—During third-quarter 2008, net absorption was a positive 1.8 million sf. The previous quarter had 610,820 sf of net absorption. Despite the positive gain, the year-to-date absorption tally is about 3 million sf, which is well below the 10.3 million sf posted during the first nine months of 2007.

Houston—Houston's industrial market posted just over 1 million sf of positive net absorption during third quarter 2008 as the annual growth total rose to just over 3.6 million sf. The majority of the quarterly growth occurred in the warehouse-distribution sector with 812,264 sf. Standard industrial-type properties recorded 172,984 sf of quarterly growth. R&D-Flex properties registered slight absorption gains during the third quarter with 97,722 sf. Overall vacancy remained flat at 6.6 percent. New construction deliveries totaled just over 1 million sf, with the majority of the new products being warehouse-distribution buildings.

San Antonio—The Alamo City posted 127,553 sf of positive absorption during the third quarter. Warehouse-distribution led in absorption with 140,283 sf, and R&D-Flex followed with 25,038 sf. Meanwhile, general industrial space experienced a loss during the quarter with 37,768 sf of negative absorption.

Tax Abatement as an Economic Development Incentive

Businesses that are expanding or relocating operations may not be aware of the advantages of the economic development incentives that local government can provide. These incentives encourage the expansion or relocation and which allow local government to regulate development and control growth.

A tax abatement is the traditional economic development tool available for local government to encourage development. Tax abatement agreements are governed by the Property Redevelopment and Tax Abatement Act, Texas Tax Code, Chapter 312. A tax abatement agreement is a contract under which the participating taxing unit may abate or forgo collection of certain property taxes that would otherwise be due and payable to the taxing unit.

Tax abatement is an exemption administered by the chief appraiser of the central appraisal district. See Tax Code §11.28. The owner or lessee of property to which the tax abatement applies is required to file an annual exemption application with the chief appraiser before May 1 of each year.

Failure to apply for the exemption or the denial of the exemption by the chief appraiser precludes the taxing unit from abating any taxes pursuant to the agreement. When a property owner or lessee breaches a tax abatement agreement and a default is declared or the agreement is terminated, the taxing unit notifies the chief appraiser to remove the exemption and places the applicable property on the tax rolls at full value.

What Types of Property Are Eligible for Tax Abatement?

Land, buildings, improvements, tangible personal property, and leasehold interests in exempt and nonexempt property are eligible for tax abatement. Tangible personal property includes machinery, equipment, furniture, fixtures, vehicles, inventory, and supplies. Cities, counties, and special districts may exempt from taxation all or a portion of the increase in the value of real property, and tangible personal property after the agreement is executed for a period not to exceed 10 years. Tax abatements may not be granted to owners of property that was the subject of a previous 10-year tax abatement.

What Is the Amount of Abatement?

The amount of tax abatement is determined by the Tax Code and by the guidelines adopted by the participating taxing unit. Under the Tax Code, a taxing unit may abate up to 100 percent of the increase in the appraised value of real property, and tangible personal property added to the real property, for a maximum of 10 years. The local guidelines establish the amount or percentage of tax abatement and the number of years that the abatement will be provided.

What Is the Process for Obtaining Tax Abatement Agreements?

There are basically six steps required by the taxing authorities entering into a tax abatement agreement.

1. The taxing unit adopts a resolution stating that it elects to become eligible to participate in tax abatement.
2. Taxing unit adopts, by resolution or by ordinance, tax abatement guidelines that contain the conditions that an applicant must satisfy to be eligible for tax abatement consideration. See Tax Code §312.002(a).
3. The next step is the application process. Prior to pursuing the application process, it is essential to know who are the key players and decision makers. Often times the engagement of a property tax expert, local counsel, or representative can assist in the identification of the key players and decision makers, ease the application process, and improve the subsequent contract negotiations.
4. A formal agreement is negotiated between the parties that contractually obligates the taxing unit to provide abatement conditioned on the property owner or lessee constructing improvements, repairs, redevelopment, or performing certain action during the term of agreement.
5. If it has not already been done, a tax reinvestment zone must be designated.
6. The tax abatement agreement is approved by a majority vote of the governing body of the local government at a regularly scheduled meeting. The calendar year the tax agreement is executed is known as the "base year."

Soil Surveys Now Available Online—Free

For decades, soil surveys conducted by the U.S. Department of Agriculture Natural Resources Conservation Service and its predecessors have provided a wealth of information on soil properties in locations across the country. Farmers, ranchers, engineers, developers, land-use planners, park and recreational area planners, appraisers, homebuyers, and homeowners—all benefit from soil survey data, which are valuable when planning property management strategies.

Farmers use information on soil properties to devise optimal combinations of tillage practices and fertilizer regimens. The data allow them to identify potential crops and expected yields for those crops. Ranchers gain insights into expected grazing yields and suitability for making hay. Engineers and developers use information on depth of soil, shrink-swell properties, wetness, erodibility, flood hazards, and slope to determine the development potential of the property.

Now these soil surveys are available online at the Web Soil Survey (WSS) website (http://websoilsurvey.nrcs.usda.gov/app/). The WSS online database contains soil maps and data for nearly all counties in the nation. The soil map outlines the different soil types found in the geographic area covered by the map. The WSS site contains those maps and volumes of information explaining the terms and concepts underlying the survey.

Accessing the information is free and is done in three steps: first, identifying a property; second, viewing the soil maps and data related to that property; and, finally, creating a customized report. To begin, click the *Start WSS* button. Then define an *area of interest* (AOI) that specifies the geographic boundaries of the target property. This is done using the *Quick Navigation* panel on the left and/or the *Interactive Map* panel on the right. One way to start quickly is to use *Quick Navigation* to view a particular state and county, and then use *Interactive Map* to highlight a tract of land containing the specific property.

After zeroing in on an area, click one of the two AOI tabs at the top of the map to trace an outline of the property boundaries with the cursor. Then right click the mouse to clip the soil map files for that area. Click on the *Soil Map* tab to see a list of soil types found on the property. The soil map can be printed or added to a custom report. Then select the *Soil Data Explorer* tab, which gives access to the *Suitabilities and Limitations for Use* tab and the *Soil Properties and Qualities* tab. The associated pull-down menus offer an abundance of information on soil characteristics affecting possible land uses.

The *Suitabilities and Limitations for Use* tab describes the soil's characteristics in the categories of building site development, disaster recovery planning, land classifications, land management, vegetative productivity, and water and waste management. The *Soil Properties and Qualities* tab details soil chemical properties, soil erosion factors, soil physical properties, soil qualities and features, and water features. If the soil survey database includes data on a particular soil property for the AOI, the system provides a description rating for the soils.

The Soil Data Explorer information can be summarized under the *Soil Reports* tab and then added to the Shopping Cart for a custom report of soils of the area of interest. In addition to production per acre for rangeland, the survey may also provide a breakdown of the kinds of plants seen on a typical site in the area. To produce the final report, go to Check Out. WSS then generates a Custom Soil Resource Report. Users can preview and edit their custom reports in the Table of Contents panel before checkout.

Landowners can combine the information gleaned from the soil survey with financial data to estimate production and income potential for their properties. For example, calculating the soil's carrying capacity is the first step in estimating income potential from a grazing lease (see "Ranching for Rookies" in *Tierra Grande*, January 2008). The data also enable an owner or potential buyer to compare results from current management with expected results. The *Soil Data Explorer* allows a comparison of the relative productivity of all soils in the county. The map assists in identifying the most productive soils in the region.

Although the site requires patience because of the massive amount of data it contains, those willing to devote the time needed to explore its riches of information will find the Web Soil Survey invaluable in evaluating land resources. This information was excerpted from an article in the October 2008 edition of the *Tierra Grande*. For additional information please refer to the article entitled "Downloading Dirt—Reaping Results from Soil Surveys" by Charles Gilliland and Nadiya Nichols.

Section 380.001 Texas Local Government Code

The most underutilized and overlooked economic development incentive to local government in Texas is Section 380.001 of the Texas Local Government Code. This statute provides express statutory authority for municipalities to provide economic development incentives consisting of loans and grants of city funds, use of city personnel, facilities, and services with or without charge for economic development.

The legislature did not expressly provide what such a program should be. In testimony before the Senate Committee on Intergovernmental Relations, the author of Senate Bill 1820, a companion bill to House Bill 3192, stated that the bill would authorize cities to establish loan programs and to use municipal personnel for the purpose of attracting new businesses to the area and assisting businesses to expand.

There is no definitive case law or Attorney General Opinions that describe the limits of a program to promote state or local economic development. The statute literally allows a municipality to make loans and grants of city funds, personnel, facilities, property, and equipment without charge.

Impact Fees

Many Texas communities, especially those in high-growth areas, are assessing impact fees to finance infrastructure construction. Only eligible state-authorized political subdivisions can do this, and those that do must create local impact fee ordinances as described in Chapter 395 of the Texas Local Government Code. In the July 2007 issue of Tierra Grande, the ordinance creation process was examined in detail (see "Impact Fees: Paying for Progress").

Impact Fee Studies

Once the Capital Improvements Plan (CIP) is adopted, the impact fee amount must be calculated, presented and reviewed for final approval and enactment of the ordinance. Typically, this part of the process includes an impact fee study that details the data, assumptions, measures and methodology used to compute the maximum fee amount. By statute, land use and service demand projections must include:

- forecasted new development by individual land uses for at least ten years within a defined service area

- the ratio of service units per land-use category

- projections of service demand by land-use service units

Service Areas

Impact fees are assessed within specifically defined service areas, which are generally limited to the corporate boundaries of the political jurisdiction. If water-wastewater services or flood control and drainage services are provided in areas of the jurisdiction's extraterritorial jurisdiction, those areas may be included in the service area. The service area for water-wastewater capital facilities may include the entire geographic area served by the water-wastewater system.

Land-Use Assumptions

Common areas of concern and review include such details as household size and age, densities, undevelopable land (parks and flood zones, for example) and changes in technology and physical limits on development (wetlands, rivers, and topography). Nonresidential LUA are equally important to ensure that residential growth does not pay a disproportionate share of the costs of required facilities. The amount and timing of nonresidential development may play a significant role in new service demand and costs.

Service Units

A key measure generated from the LUA is the projected total new service units created by new development. This number is the denominator in the equation to compute the maximum impact fee. A service unit is a standard measure of service use or demand per land-use category. The number of service units for each land-use category equals the projected development units for each land use times the demand or usage factor for each land-use type. By formula, this is represented as:

Service unit land use = Development units land use × Use or demand factor land use

For residential uses, a development unit usually corresponds to a projected single-family or multifamily unit. For commercial and industrial properties, a development unit is typically expressed per 1,000 square feet of new development or some other standard measure (number of beds in a hospital, for example). Total development units derive directly from the projected development within the area over the period considered.

Credits

Texas law requires the local jurisdiction to give a credit for future taxes and service revenues from projected new development before computing the maximum amount of an impact fee. The future taxes and revenues may be calculated or, alternatively, the jurisdiction may apply a 50 percent deduction. Most jurisdictions opt for the 50 percent credit, as future taxes and revenues are difficult to project with accuracy and open to debate.

Maximum Allowable Impact Fee

The maximum allowable impact fee equals the eligible capital infrastructure costs identified in the CIP less the credit for future taxes and service revenues divided by the total number of projected new service units. By formula, the maximum impact fee =

$$\text{(eligible CIP costs} - \text{credit for future taxes and service fees)/} \\ \text{projected new service units}$$

Local jurisdictions may elect to impose fees less than the maximum allowable fee.

The Bottom Line

When it comes to reviewing proposed impact fee ordinances, the devil is indeed in the details, as the old adage says. The LUA, the projected types and rate of new development, the CIP, the projected service units, and demand per service unit as well as individual capital improvement costs and the other variables affecting the fee are highly technical, complex, and difficult to quantify accurately.

The law requires that professional engineers and consultants be used to prepare the estimates. But projecting future growth and costs is not an exact science. The estimates should be carefully reviewed before final acceptance, and developers, builders, and the public should get involved in the process as early as possible.

Development Sales Tax

The Development Corporation Act of 1979 authorizes municipalities to form nonprofit corporations to promote the creation of new and expanded industry and manufacturing, industrial or commercial, or retail activities through the imposition of local sales and use tax. There are two types of corporations allowed, Section 4A and 4B Development Corporations.

The Development Corporations are separate corporate entities with a board of directors appointed by the creating municipality. The sales tax for both Section 4A and 4B Development Corporations may be used to encourage development and redevelopment.

Development sales tax is often overlooked by real estate professionals and local governments. If the city or other applicable taxing units do not offer tax abatement, freeport exemption, or other economic development incentives, Section 4A and 4B Development Corporations can provide incentives or pay the cost of infrastructure improvements, relocation expenses, rent subsidies, or funding for land and equipment acquisitions, and thereby encourage real estate development.

Section 4A sales taxes are typically used to facilitate manufacturing and industrial activities by funding the acquisition of land, buildings, and equipment for projects such as industrial manufacturing facilities, distribution and warehouse facilities, business-related airports, port-related facilities, recycling facilities, and closed or realigned military bases.

Section 4B sales taxes are typically used to fund acquisition of land, buildings, or equipment for professional and amateur sports facilities, park facilities and events, entertainment and tourist activities and affordable housing.

Environmental Issues

Environmental concerns are a continuing issue in commercial real estate transactions. Residential properties have not been subject to as much environmental concern, but this may be changing. Fairly new discoveries of brain damage to growing children caused by chemicals left in the environment by government projects and industry have caused great concern and some decline of land value in such areas.

Although real estate agents are not expected to be environmental experts, the same disclosure rules apply here as with other facts about a property. That is, *if environmental information is known to the sales agent and would affect a prudent purchaser's decision to buy, it must be disclosed.* Therefore, licensees should be familiar with the nature of these problems as well as the laws and regulations that are intended to protect the consumer and the environment.

The number of laws, how they overlap, and the many agencies involved with implementation make a clear understanding very difficult. Yet failure to comply properly with these laws and regulations can result in massive liabilities and/or the "taking" of property without compensation. In addition, many violations call for criminal penalties. Adding to the dilemma, these laws are, for the most part, broadly written with purposes ill defined, creating substantial potential for innocent and unknowing violations.

For the past three decades, most studies and research about the environment have focused on the detrimental effect that humans have had on it. Indeed, in the 1970s, federal and state laws were directed at protection of the environment from such acts as dumping waste, which inflicted long-term damage on the land, water, and air people depend on for their livelihood. Little study was given to the damaging effects that certain elements of the environment could have on people.

Recognition of the harm some chemicals can bring to humans has been somewhat overshadowed by the recent advances in medicine and diagnostic instruments. These advances have overcome many health problems and will prolong life. Publicity about new vaccines and medical techniques has dominated the news, indicating that better health will result from increased knowledge.

What has been overlooked in too many cases are the possible damaging effects that chemicals in the ground, air, and water may have on a child's physical development while growing up. Studies of children's development have produced concern, but no hard results yet. A child's growth is influenced by so many factors—poverty, parental neglect, inadequate schooling, poor diet, the wrong peers—that it is very difficult to assign actual damage to any one cause.

Even so, enough examples of chemical damage affecting a child's brain development have surfaced to warrant further study. As areas have been discovered that may be the cause of such brain damage, the economic effect on the land has been substantial.

Recently a federally funded study at the State University in New York–Oswego showed that babies who had significant amounts of Polychlorinated Biphenyls (PCBs) in their umbilical cords performed more poorly than unexposed babies in tests assessing visual recognition of faces, the ability to shut out distractions, and overall intelligence. In the 1980s, studies performed on young monkeys for Health Canada indicated that substances such as PCBs and mercury caused cancer or birth defects—the only problems for which they were tested in the United States. The studies also suggested that even at very low levels, these substances could affect the developing human brain.

The Environment and the Economy

Much of the legislation aimed at protecting the environment is not new. Many basic laws were written in the 1970s. However, since the various laws were enacted, a stream of regulations issued by designated agencies has expanded, in many instances, the scope of legislation, making it broader and even more complex. In order to better protect landowners against unnecessary rules and legislation, the 1995 Texas Legislature passed some limitations on state laws and regulations (covered in a later section).

Because it has a direct impact on land value, environmental risk has become an added factor in all real estate transactions. One of the problems is that environmental damage is not always visible on the surface. It may be deep underground or seeping in from neighboring property. Nevertheless, under current law, an owner's ignorance of the problem does not relieve the landowner of liability. This is true regardless of whether the owner had any involvement in contaminating the property. However, the potential risk can be reduced by a professional investigation *prior* to acquiring a property (explained more fully in a later section).

Environmental Assessments for Home Loans

Home loans must be distinguished from residential loans. The term *residential* can include multi-family properties, which are treated as commercial properties with regard to environmental issues. It is owner-occupied dwellings that have been granted, by an Environmental Protection Agency rule, a broad exemption from liability for cleanup of toxic waste sites. In "Policy Toward Owners of Residential Property at Superfund Sites," issued in July 1991, the EPA stated it would not hold homeowners liable for cleanup costs unless an owner knowingly contaminated the property or failed to cooperate with the EPA in its cleanup efforts (for example, by not permitting the EPA access to the Superfund site).

The EPA's policy statement is not a statutory exemption. Rather, it is intended only as guidance for EPA enforcement employees. In other words, the EPA's policy does not amend the Superfund statute, which means homeowners can still be held liable for cleanup costs should the agency decide to rescind the policy. An appraisal for a home loan is expected to report any obvious contamination in or near the property evaluated. Furthermore, homeowners generally are prevented by their mortgage agreement from storing hazardous materials on the property and are required to report to the mortgagee any charges of environmental violations against the homeowner.

Environmental Assessments for Commercial Loans

Almost all commercial loan applications must now include an environmental site assessment. This includes multi-family dwellings. Precisely what is meant by "an environmental site assessment" is not clearly defined, and requirements vary with different lenders. However, this is changing.

The assessment outlined in the Superfund Act that is identified as a defense for an *innocent landowner* is called a *Phase I Assessment*. The scope of Phase I is limited to those hazardous materials specifically creating cleanup liability under the Superfund Act. It does not include all possible environmental problems, such as wetlands or the presence of endangered species. Thus, another term, *environmental site assessment*, has come to mean a broader approach than the more limited Phase I Assessment.

Because market terminology does not always make a distinction between a "Phase I Assessment" and an "environmental site assessment," an agent should make sure there is a mutual understanding of what is involved.

Requirements are changing. An "assessment" must be analyzed to measure future risk and in itself provides no assurance against future loss. To give better protection, lenders are now requiring environmental insurance rather than an assessment to be submitted with a commercial loan application. This insurance covers environmental liability for the collateral property if the loan defaults and contamination is found. If cleanup is required, assurance of payment by an insurance company eliminates any need for litigation. Of course, lenders like the transfer of risk and borrowers do not have to pay for the insurance if the loan is not approved.

Environmental Requirements of the Secondary Market

Whereas the secondary market is dominated by home loans, some commercial loans are moving into the hands of secondary market investors. For multi-family loans, both Fannie Mae and Freddie Mac require (in what they call a "Phase I Assessment") information on asbestos, polychlorinated biphenyls, radon, underground storage tanks, waste sites, lead-based paint, and any other hazardous contaminants. The questions, in an appendix form with the application, must be answered and filed with the loan submittal package.

For single-family loans, both agencies rely on information derived from a property appraisal. They require that an appraiser comment on any known environmental conditions that may adversely affect a property's value. This includes asbestos and urea-formaldehyde foam insulation.

In addition, the agencies also require information on the proximity of the mortgaged property to industrial sites, to waste or water treatment facilities, as well as to nearby commercial establishments using chemicals or oil products in their operations. Although appraisers are not considered to be experts on environmental hazards, they are expected to provide "early warnings" of properties harboring potential environmental problems. Freddie Mac also requires that an appraiser consider environmental factors in reaching a conclusion as to the property's value.

It is becoming more common for lenders with residential and commercial loans to include environmental covenants in the mortgage instruments. For instance, the documents could prohibit a borrower from using hazardous substances on a pledged property. The Fannie Mae/Freddie Mac revised single-family mortgage document requires the borrower to promise to abide by state and federal environmental laws and to refrain from storing or using hazardous materials on the mortgaged property. In addition, the borrower must promise to notify the lender if an investigation or a lawsuit involving hazardous substances is filed against the property.

The "Go Green" Initiative

"2008 Green Survey: Existing Buildings"

According to the second annual national survey of the commercial real estate sector, more than 80 percent of respondents have allocated funds to green initiatives for the year 2008. It seems as though greening commercial buildings remains a priority despite the economic downturn.

Despite a faltering economy, commercial building owners are continuing to allocate funds and resources to green their portfolios. In addition, 45 percent of the respondents said that their sustainability investment will increase in 2009. Findings of the study by Incisive Media's *Real Estate Forum*, the Building Owners and Managers Association (BOMA) International, and the U.S. Green Building Council (USGBC) were released during a press conference at *Greenbuild 2008*, the annual conference and expo sponsored by the USGBC. A full analysis of the survey can be found in the January/February 2009 issue of *The BOMA Magazine*.

Also at *Greenbuild*, the results of an energy-savings survey conducted by FMLink, BOMA International, USGBC, and the Association for Facility Engineers (AFE) were released. The survey found that more and more facility managers are implementing recommissioning and energy audits to measure and improve their building's energy performance. Key findings also indicated that most energy savings successes were the result of aggressive low-cost operational strategies, rather than major capital projects.

Other findings of the survey included the following:

- Energy conservation is the most widely implemented green program in respondent properties, followed by recycling, water conservation, and ENERGY STAR® product programs.

- Some 60 percent of those polled offer educational programs to assist tenants in implementing green programs, up from 49.4 percent last year.

- Almost 70 percent of survey respondents have implemented some type of benchmarking system to monitor energy usage and efficiency, while 80 percent say that their energy efficiency efforts have helped defray rising energy costs.

- Almost 65 percent of respondents feel that their green investments have generated a positive ROI, up from 60.8 percent in 2007.

"The survey findings further support the critical role of energy efficiency and sustainability in the existing building market," said BOMA International Chair and Chief Elected Officer Richard D. Purtell, portfolio manager, Grubb & Ellis Management Services, Inc. "The energy and cost savings, coupled with healthy return on investments, are showing that green investment in commercial buildings is a smart business decision in any economic climate.

The survey focused on the application of green methodologies and technologies in existing commercial buildings and on the financial and marketing benefits of these efforts. It was distributed to Incisive Media's national database of ownership, investment and operational entities, as well as to BOMA International's members. To obtain a copy of the complete survey and results, visit www.globest.com/green.

Incisive Media publishes *Real Estate Forum*; GlobeSt.com, the industry's leading daily news website; and the regional magazines *Real Estate Florida*, *Real Estate New Jersey*, *Real Estate New York*, and *Real Estate Southern California*. Its two targeted e-newsletters focus on the tenant-in-common and net lease sectors of the commercial real estate industry. REM also produces the RealShare conferences, a series of regional and national events targeted at commercial real estate professionals.

About BOMA International—Founded in 1907, the Building Owners and Managers Association (BOMA) International is the leading association representing the existing building stock through an international federation of more than 100 local associations and affiliated organizations. The 17,000-plus members of BOMA International own or manage more than 9 billion square feet of commercial properties in North America and abroad. BOMA is a leader in sustainability and energy efficiency and has developed a number of groundbreaking initiatives that include: the award-winning education programs, the BOMA Energy Efficiency Program (BEEP) and the Sustainable Operations Series (SOS); the 7-Point Challenge, which challenges building owners and managers to reduce their energy consumption by 30 percent by 2012, based on an average building rating of 50 on the ENERGY STAR® benchmark, and has over 100 endorsing member companies and associations; and involvement in founding the Commercial Real Estate Energy Alliance (CREEA) in partnership with the U.S. Department of Energy. Their web address is www.boma.org.

About USGBC—The U.S. Green Building Council (USGBC) is a nonprofit organization composed of leaders from every sector of the building industry working to promote buildings that are environmentally responsible, profitable, and healthy places to live and work. Its more than 11,000 member organizations and the network of 75 regional chapters are united to advance their mission of transforming the building industry to sustainability.

About Incisive Media—Incisive Media is a leading global provider of specialized business news and information, in print, in person, and online. The company's principal markets include commercial real estate, financial services, legal services, marketing services, and risk management. Incisive Media's market-leading brands include *Accountancy Age*, *Computing*, *Investment Week*, *Legal Week*, *Post*, *Real Estate Forum*, and *The American Lawyer*. For more information, visit www.incisivemedia.com.

BOMA International Honored with Green Leadership Award

Bisnow on Business, a Washington, D.C.–based electronic news publisher, awarded the Building Owners and Managers Association (BOMA) International the 2008 Green Leadership Award in recognition of BOMA's commitment to promoting sustainability and energy efficiency among its members. The first annual award was given to 20 organizations in 5 categories, real estate, legal, tech, medical, and trade association, that have implemented impressive green initiatives and are leading the way on sustainability.

BOMA International is the leader in energy efficiency and sustainable initiatives that have helped BOMA member organizations lower energy consumption, reduce greenhouse gas emissions, and save on energy costs. The BOMA Energy Efficiency Program® (BEEP), an operational excellence program developed in partnership with the EPA's ENERGY STAR®, teaches property managers no- and low-cost strategies for reducing energy usage in commercial buildings. To date, more than 10,000 commercial real estate professionals have been trained through BEEP.

BOMA was also recognized by Bisnow for its successful Market Transformation Energy Plan and 7-Point Challenge, a challenge to the industry to reduce energy consumption in commercial buildings by 30 percent by 2012. Through the Challenge, BOMA has called upon its members to work in coordination with building management, ownership, and tenants to achieve the goals of the Challenge. The challenge includes benchmarking energy performance, providing education to property professionals to ensure equipment is properly maintained, performing energy audits, and leading community efforts to reduce commercial real estate's role in global warming. More than 100 BOMA member companies and local associations have endorsed the challenge.

Green Commercial Real Estate Lease

Other green achievements include the publication of the industry's first green lease, the premier resource on "greening" a commercial real estate lease. Also included is the launch of the Sustainable Operations Series (SOS) program, a new education program that builds on BEEP and includes additional practical ways to green building operations. An additional achievement is a collaboration with the Clinton Climate Initiative to develop a ground-breaking energy performance contract model to help building owners perform major energy retrofits to the existing building marketplace. Also considered a green achievement is the development of a partnership with the Department of Energy in the newly established Commercial Real Estate Energy Alliance (CREEA), which will pursue energy efficiency technologies that will transform energy use in the commercial building market.

BOMA International Simplifies Going Green

In October 2008, BOMA announced the launch of the next generation of green education for commercial real estate professionals, the Sustainable Operations Series (SOS). The program consists of four 90-minute Webinars that teach practical strategies and address industry best practices for implementing green commercial building operations. Created by the authors of the award-winning BOMA Energy Efficiency Program® (BEEP), BOMA's SOS program takes sustainability education to the next level by cutting through the overwhelming amount of information on sustainable practices and clearly demonstrating how green operations can effectively enhance the bottom line, improve tenant satisfaction and benefit the environment.

The four new course offerings are the following:

- **Course One: Making Sense of Sustainable Operations**—Covers the basics of greening commercial building operations, defining key terms, exploring the best approaches, and explaining green certification programs.
- **Course Two: Strategies for Reducing and Reusing Building Resources**—Highlights two key components of any good sustainable operations plan: how to reduce consumption of resources—from electricity and gas to paper and metals—and how to inventively reuse resources that have been consumed.
- **Course Three: Rethinking Recycling; Beyond Paper and Cans**—Going beyond typical paper and aluminum can recycling, learn how to identify building materials (from construction waste to light bulbs to office equipment) that can be recycled cost-effectively.
- **Course Four: How Green Is My Building? Tools for Measuring the Total ROI of Sustainability**—The final course demonstrates how to measure total ROI on sustainability (from impact on net operating income to tenant retention) and shows you how to "sustain sustainability" to continuously improve building performance.

Leadership in Energy and Environmental Design (LEED)

A growing number of local government officials and prospective tenants want to know if a building is LEED certified. Likewise, they want to know the building's Energy Star design rating. Cities across the nation are looking for ways to encourage or mandate the private sector to build and renovate to LEED specifications, also known as "green building" or "sustainable development."

Commercial Goes Green

Since 1999 the number of commercial buildings being built according to the LEED Green Building Rating System has grown at an average annual rate of 40 percent. The LEED system has become the nationally accepted benchmark for design, construction, and operation of high performance green buildings.

The City of Austin passed a resolution in June 2000 requiring LEED certification of all public projects over 5,000 square feet. Dallas officials have issued a resolution requiring all city buildings larger than 10,000 square feet to have at least LEED silver certifications. Houston adopted a similar resolution in 2004. Plano's city council recently adopted a building sustainability policy. From now on, that city will use the LEED rating system, requiring the highest level of LEED certification possible for all city facilities.

U.S. Mayors Climate Protection Agreement (CPA)

The City of Hutto recently became the 20th city in Texas to sign the U.S. Mayors, Climate Protection Agreement (CPA), which calls for cities to meet the goals set by the international Kyoto Protocol to address climate change. Although the U.S. government did not sign the Kyoto Protocol, mayors of 755 U.S. cities have signed the CPA, which urges state governments and the federal government to enact policies and programs to meet or beat the 7 percent greenhouse gas emission reduction target suggested for the United States.

According to Energy Star, a joint program of the EPA and the U.S. Department of Energy, 30 percent of the typical office building's costs go to energy use. In fact, energy is a property's single largest operating expense. That cost gets passed to tenants, who want as much as possible of that operating cost off their bottom line. As a result, the market is rapidly approaching the point at which developments that are not LEED certified will be unable to attract the anchor tenants needed to guarantee success.

In many large cities, if a new building is not LEED certified, it has almost no chance of being classified Class A or AAA. Consequently, that building might not rent at top market rates, nor will its value appreciate at a rate equal to that of energy-efficient buildings of similar design. Relatively new Class-A buildings not LEED certified could become Class B simply because the market does not consider them energy efficient.

These factors bring to light a huge problem in the U.S. commercial building stock. The Commercial Buildings Energy Consumption Survey estimates there were nearly 4.9 million existing commercial buildings and more than 71.6 billion square feet of commercial floor space in the United States in 2003. In 2007, only 1,129 buildings were LEED rated; 8,566 under-construction buildings had applied for LEED certification.

The nation's commercial building stock will face stiff competition as certified energy-efficient buildings come online. Building owners and developers are being pressured from all sides to go green. But while owners and developers understand that green building has become a necessary marketing tool, the perception remains among them that the added costs of green building outweigh the benefits.

Major problems occur when building owners implement technological changes without knowing what energy technology to install or how to operate and maintain it. In short, technology alone does not equate to high performance. As a result, a new breed of real estate professionals is emerging called "building commissioners." These experts perform quality assurance, known as building commissioning, which can detect and remedy most deficiencies found in either new or existing building design. Building commissioners look for ways to streamline buildings for energy efficiency.

Commissioning and Retro-Commissioning

Building commissioning confirms a building's energy systems function according to criteria described in the project's construction documents and meet the owner's operational needs. Retro-commissioning, also called recommissioning, is the process of investigating, analyzing, and optimizing system performance in existing buildings. After analyzing the current systems, building commissioners make recommendations that will improve operation and maintenance to ensure continued high performance. Retro-commissioning helps make the building systems perform interactively to meet the owner's and tenants' current facility requirements.

Building commissioners' contributions include acting as consultants, project managers/value engineers, and facilities managers. Their incomes are based on flat consulting fees, a percentage of the annual cost savings realized, maintenance programs involving key performance indicators, or a combination of these.

Analyzing Efficiency

Traditional consulting firms perform "business sustainability value analysis" but may or may not perform or oversee the suggested cost savings initiatives. Some consulting services may include tracking the success of the client's implemented changes. Real estate firms such as Cushman & Wakefield, CB Richard Ellis, and the Staubach Company are expanding into facilities management through "value engineering," which describes the process of commissioning new or recommissioning existing facilities to operate at maximum efficiency.

One Success Story

Cushman and Wakefield's George Denise, project manager for the Adobe Systems Inc. headquarters located in downtown San Jose, Calif., has documented phenomenal success with value engineering. Adobe's headquarters are in three buildings known as Almaden Tower, East Tower, and West Tower, which are 17, 16, and 18 stories, respectively, and at the time of recommissioning were three, nine, and 11 years old. The three buildings total 989,358 square feet of office space, situated above an additional 938,473-square-foot enclosed parking garage.

After analyzing the three towers, Cushman & Wakefield implemented energy saving techniques that reduced per occupant **electricity use by 35 percent, natural gas use by 41 percent,** domestic **water use by 22 percent, CO_2 emissions by 23 percent**, and **landscape irrigation by 76 percent**. In addition, they are diverting solid waste by up to 87 percent. Adobe spent just over $1 million, received about $389,000 in rebates from government agencies and reduced operating costs by some $1.2 million annually. The project had an average payback of 9.5 months with return on investment netting a whopping 121 percent.

Notably, even though these buildings were relatively new at the time of recommissioning, the payback still proved worth the expense. Commissioning and recommissioning buildings is proving extremely valuable to the client. According to Energy Star, along with realized cost savings, recommissioned buildings typically sell for about 5 percent more than similar nonrecommissioned buildings.

The Cost-Effectiveness of Commercial-Buildings Commissioning

In a study entitled "The Cost-Effectiveness of Commercial-Buildings Commissioning," analysis of 224 buildings totaling 30.4 million square feet across 21 states found that commissioning has far broader relevance than simply optimizing energy-efficient systems. Knowledge of day-to-day systems operations is essential. Cost savings are directly affected by the extent to which energy efficiency research, development, and deployment programs are combined with quality assurance in design, delivery, and operations maintenance.

A fan study conducted by the EPA found that 60 percent of building fan systems are oversized by an average 60 percent. The 224-building study found chillers were oversized by 50 to 200 percent. Across the nation, improper installation, inaccurate sizing and poor maintenance are negatively affecting building efficiency. Building commissioners apply an emerging form of cost-effective quality assurance procedures that provide a way to define measurable performance targets and evaluate as-built and as-operated systems.

As part of an integrated strategy for improving building energy performance, commissioning is an effective and far-reaching means of improving energy efficiency across the U.S. building stock. Commissioning professionals are risk managers helping to ensure funds are spent wisely and that intended energy savings targets are actualized. Commissioning provides a way to define measurable performance targets and evaluate existing operating systems.

With more than 99 percent of the nation's existing building stock facing market demand and local governmental pressure for recommissioning, the demand for building commissioning professionals is likely to explode.

Residential Green Initiative

A study released in the summer of 2008 by *McGraw-Hill Construction* and the U.S. Green Building Council (USGBC) found that over the past three years more than 330,000 "market rate" homes with green features were built, making green building a $36 billion per year industry. Of that number of homes, an estimated 60,000 earned third-party property certifications through LEED or another certification program.

The study also surveyed existing owners of green-certified properties in an effort to gauge their attitudes about their homes. An overwhelming 83 percent of respondents stated that their new green home will lower operating costs. Seventy percent of those surveyed said that they would be "more" or "much more" inclined to buy a green home rather than a conventional home in a down market like today's market. The study also found that 78 percent of lower-income consumers would be more inclined to purchase a green home.

Michelle Moore, senior vice president for policy and public affairs at USGBC, states that "our green buildings numbers are really strong, our membership numbers remain strong. In fact, we're at record levels across the board, from registrations and certifications of projects to the number of people taking the LEED AP test. They're all way up."

At the Greenbuild conference in Boston in 2008, Nancy Floyd, founder of the clean tech venture capital firm Nth Power, echoed Moore's sentiments. "The economic downturn will actually be good for this sector," Floyd said, "because the market meltdown is accelerating innovation. There are opportunities now because builders and decision makers have more time to consider new ideas. There also is more competition among builders; so some will differentiate by adopting green building products and practices."

New Broker Designation—EcoBroker®

If more and more green buildings are being built, and consumers are increasingly satisfied with green buildings, the logical conclusion is that green real estate professionals should have more opportunities to help facilitate these transactions. EcoBroker® training ideally positions the broker as the most qualified real estate professional to handle these kinds of deals. Becoming an EcoBroker® can also help the broker capitalize on the continued vitality of green building.

The education requirements for becoming an EcoBroker® are extensive. EcoBroker® is a premiere green designation program for real estate professionals. EcoBroker Certified® professionals help clients market properties with green features, save money, and live comfortably through energy efficiency and environmentally sensitive choices.

Founded in 2002, EcoBroker® was the first and remains the largest green real estate training and communications program in the world. With members in all 50 United States, Canada, Mexico, the Caribbean, Central America, and New Zealand, EcoBroker® and its members serve real estate consumers, communities, and the environment with a level of care, commitment, and follow-up. With the benefit of oversight from the Association of Energy and Environmental Real Estate Professionals (AEERP), EcoBroker® training and communications provide professionals with the resources to be constructive green ambassadors in an ever-changing business and consumer world.

EcoBroker® offers education and tools to real estate professionals that in turn help consumers take advantage of energy efficiency and environmentally sensitive design in real estate properties. Through EcoBroker®'s unique energy and environmental curriculum, real estate professionals acquire the knowledge and resources to become Certified EcoBroker®s. These real estate professionals assist clients in their pursuit of properties that provide affordability, comfort and a healthier environment by, among other things, reducing carbon footprints.

In order to earn the EcoBroker® Designation, licensed real estate agents must fulfill a straight-forward set of requirements. The most important requirement of EcoBroker® Certification is the completion of the energy, environmental, and marketing training programs. For information on how to become an EcoBroker® please access the following website: http://www.ecobroker.com/eb/requirements.aspx

For more information on these and other "Green" topics, please visit the following websites:

Green Homes: *A Bright Spot in the Housing Market*
http://www.fypower.org/res/news/green-homes.html

VC (Venture Capital) Calls Green Building Technologies "Bright Spot" in Economy
http://energypriorities.com/entries/2008/11/nancy_floyd_greenbuild.php

GreenSource. *Green Housing Is Bright Spot on Otherwise Gloomy Market*
http://greensource.construction.com/news/080725GreenHousing.asp

The Architects Newspaper. *What Recession?*
Green firms see bright future in dark times
http://www.archpaper.com/e-board_rev.asp?News_ID=2950

Green Homes

More and more new-home buyers are including green features in their lists of preferred amenities. Whether they are motivated by increased concern for the environment or are interested in energy-efficient or environmentally friendly features because they may reduce overall homeownership costs, the buyers perceive a value attached to green components.

In an article in the April, 2008, edition of *Tierra Grande* entitled "Green House Values," Dr. Harold Hunt examines the benefits of including green features in residential properties. Dr. Hunt is a research economist with the Real Estate Center at Texas A&M University.

Green Price Tag

Some of the benefits of green buildings include relatively inexpensive things, such as cellulose insulation made from recycled paper, as well as extremely expensive ones, such as solar electrical systems. The costs green upgrades add to a new home's price vary widely. However, a 3 to 15 percent premium is a good rule of thumb. According to the National Association of Home Builders (NAHB) and McGraw-Hill Construction, 10 percent of new homes will be constructed using some green elements by 2010.

Value to Initial Homebuyer

For those who view value in nonmonetary terms, the benefit of adding green features to a new home comes from a reduction in the country's energy consumption, less contribution to deforestation and other means of improving the environment as reward enough. Other homebuyers expect to gain more concrete value from the addition of green components by recouping the dollars they spent on the upgrades over time or when they sell the property.

If the buyers added a more efficient, green heating and cooling system to lower utility costs, they could reasonably expect the system to pay for itself. If the new system costs an extra $2,000 and the utility savings amount to $500 per year, the homeowner would recoup the added cost in four years.

Another environmentally beneficial item might be the installation of Bamboo flooring. Bamboo is a rapidly renewable plant, which unlike timber is not killed during harvesting. Bamboo is also harder than wood, resulting in a more durable and longer-lasting product. However, a subsequent purchaser may not be willing to pay a premium for the bamboo flooring.

Consider the conundrum *value in use* and *value in exchange*. Value in use is tied to the satisfaction of the current homeowner and can be measured in monetary or nonmonetary terms. Value in exchange is based on how much subsequent homebuyers in the market would actually pay for a feature or amenity.

Value to Residential Appraisers

Residential appraisers are interested in estimating a home's *value in exchange* only. In a given market, if enough buyers refuse to pay for a particular amenity, appraisers will conclude that the amenity makes no contribution to the market value of a home. Over time, housing markets recognize certain features as having *exchange value*. The critical point occurs when an amenity shifts from having value in use for a few who are willing to try something new to becoming widely accepted. At that point, the amenity shifts from a cost to the initial homebuyer to a feature with measurable *exchange value*.

However, such a transition may take years. The problem with many green features and building techniques today is their newness. Until they move past the pioneer stage in the marketplace, appraisers will have difficulty attributing any value in exchange to them.

Value to Lenders

Private loan purchasers have little incentive to consider purchasing the mortgages of "nonstandard" green homes under the current system. Even if green features yield some value in exchange, homes considered too outside the mainstream may still have a difficult time obtaining financing.

Green Fallout

If green features cannot be included in the mortgage, homebuyers must pay cash for them over and above the required down payment. While some buyers may be financially able to pay a premium for green features, many are not.

One way to assist homebuyers and accelerate the acceptance of green amenities is through government incentives such as tax credits and grants to help pay for green features. For example, the City of Austin offers grants and the federal government offers tax credits for homebuyers who purchase residential photovoltaic solar electric systems and other specified green components (see "Energy Efficiency Pays" in the *Tierra Grande*, April 2007*)*.

Unfortunately, green features are often hidden behind walls. The bulk of homebuyers still see more value in the visible, aesthetic features of a home, such as granite countertops, than they do in green amenities. But protecting the environment and lowering the cost of homeownership is a winning combination that will be hard for homebuyers to resist in the long run.

Insuring Green Buildings

The insurance industry is starting to encourage commercial policyholders to go green. In an industry first, Fireman's Fund launched Green-Gard^{SM}. This policy provides special coverage for certified commercial structures nationwide that the company believes will encourage safe, energy-efficient construction and repairs and give it a competitive advantage. This special coverage has the following features:

Certified Green Building, which restores a green-certified property to its original condition following a loss, including alternative energy systems. "If there's a fire and the building has been selling energy back into the grid, we will pay for that loss of income," stated Steven G. Bushnell, product director for commercial business at Fireman's Fund.

The policy also pays the cost of buying power from the grid while the alternative energy system is repaired. The price of this green coverage is similar to, and in some cases 5 percent less expensive than, existing property-loss policies. Fireman's Fund studies show that green structures present fewer property risks than traditional ones because the commissioning process, required for LEED certification, addresses the major causes of commercial loss: electrical fires, plumbing leaks and heating, ventilating, and air-conditioning (HVAC) failures.

Building Commissioning Expense recommissions heating and cooling systems after a loss in order to meet the LEED standard.

Green Real and Personal Property Upgrade pays for a conventional building to be rebuilt with green alternatives following a loss. Travelers has recently followed suit with a similar product, called Green Building Coverage Enhancements, for midsize buildings.

"For building owners, such coverages further validate the continuing viability of green and sustainable practices in building design, construction and management," the editors of *Buildings* magazine wrote. "In addition to protecting the bottom line, owners have been given another tool to increase their buildings' asset value and attract high-quality tenants."

How Some Executives View Green Space

As reported in the *Dallas Morning News*, corporate real estate executives place a higher priority on sustainability than ever before. However, a recent study shows they are less likely to pay a premium for green office space than they were a year ago.

CoreNet Global and Jones Lang LaSalle's survey of over 400 real estate executives in September and October 2008 found:

- that 42 percent would pay more to lease green space, down from 77 percent last year;
- that 69 percent think sustainability is a critical business issue, compared with 47 percent in 2007;
- that 40 percent rate energy and sustainability as major factors in their companies' location decisions;
- that 60 percent have implemented energy management, which provides the highest potential cost savings; and
- that less than 20 percent have broadly implemented strategies that help the environment but cost more.

A separate study by CoStar Group found that green buildings generate 3.8 percent higher occupancy rates and are up to 30 percent more efficient but also command higher rent and sale prices per square foot.

Wind Energy

In an article entitled "Against the Wind" in the October, 2008, edition of *Tierra Grande*, Judon Fambrough discusses numerous aspects of wind energy. Some of the topics that are discussed here include environmental concerns, nuisance problems, property tax abatements, construction time for wind farms and transmission lines, regulating wind development, and federal estate tax complications.

Environmental Concerns

Even though wind energy is renewable and apparently environmentally beneficial, it seems as though there are some who oppose the wholesale conversion of wind energy into electricity. Perhaps the most vocal opposition to wind energy comes from environmentalists, who object to the destruction caused when birds and bats collide with the spinning wind turbine blades.

An article with the headline "Texas Coast Wind Farms May Put Birds at Risk" appeared in the January 2, 2008, issue of *Houston Chronicle*. The article focused on two wind power projects under construction on the Kenedy Ranch in Kenedy County. The projects will generate about 388 megawatts—enough electricity to power 90,000 homes. A report issued by EDM International Inc. using methodologies developed by the U.S. Fish and Wildlife Service, concluded that the projects could result in the largest and most significant avian mortality event in the history of wind energy.

The Coastal Habitat Alliance Inc., formed in June 2007 to protect the Texas Gulf Coast, filed federal and state lawsuits in December 2007 seeking to halt construction of the two wind farms. The suit alleges that state officials and developers violated the Federal Coastal Zone Management Act by building the farms without an environmental review or permit. Loss of scenic beauty and possible harm to the bat population resulted in a moratorium on wind development in Gillespie County. Edwards County, with its significant bat population in the Devil's Cave, may follow suit.

Several lawsuits were filed against landowners and wind farms in the Sweetwater-Abilene area alleging they constituted an unreasonable interference with the use and enjoyment of nearby property. Loss of view and noise were two of the primary complaints. At the trial level, the lawsuits proved unsuccessful. Texas case law supports the free use of property in a legal, non-nuisance manner. The Real Estate Center's publication entitled *Obstruction of View, Light or Air* summarizes the pertinent case law.

The Texas courts have repeatedly ruled that the owner of real estate may, in the absence of restrictions or other regulations, erect a building, wall, fence or other structure on the premises, even if it obstructs a neighbor's vision, light, or air and even if it depreciates the value of a neighbor's land. The court dismissed the issue of the wind farm's visual degradation by granting the defendants summary judgment. This was appealed.

The trial basically ended when a landowner near the wind farm testified that noise from jet engines at Dyess Air Force Base about 20 miles away drowned out any noise from nearby wind turbines. In August 2008, the 11th Court of Civil Appeals upheld the trial court's decision to grant the defendants summary judgment regarding wind farm's visual impact. Ruling on case precedents, the court said, "Matters that annoy by being disagreeable, unsightly, and undesirable are not nuisances simply because they may to some extent affect the value of property."

Property Tax Abatements

A looming question for Texas wind-farm developers is whether property tax abatements, typically granted by the local county commissioners, will be available. Four conditions are critical to wind-farm development. First, the federal 1.9-cent income tax credit for each kilowatt hour of electricity generated must be in place. The credit is good for 10 years if one kilowatt of electricity is generated by a tower before December 31, 2008, the date the credit expires.

Second, there must be sufficient wind to generate the electricity. Texas has six classes of wind power potential. A region needs to rank class three or higher for wind development. Most of the favorable regions are located in West Texas. (See http://www.seco.cpa.state.tx.us/zzz_re/re_study1995.pdf)

Third, there must be sufficient transmission lines to move the electricity to population centers. And, finally, wind developers need to receive property tax abatements from local officials. In March 2008, the Texas Attorney General (AG) rendered an opinion calling into question wind farms' eligibility for tax abatements.

In Texas, when fixtures and improvements are not owned by the property owner, but by a lessee, for example, the wind company, they are classified as personal property, not real property. Personal property is not eligible for tax abatements under the Texas Tax Code (TC). A month after the AG rendered the opinion, two opponents of wind farms filed a lawsuit against the Taylor County Commissioners Court. The suit alleges tax abatements for the wind farms in that county are illegal because of the personal property classification.

The AG opinion and ensuing lawsuit create uncertainty with respect to past and future property tax incentives deemed vital for wind development in Texas. The Texas Legislature may address the issue in 2009. Tax abatements, if granted, are good for a maximum of 10 years.

Construction Time for Wind Farms and Transmission Lines

Construction time for wind farms is out of sync with construction time for transmission lines needed to transport the electricity. It takes about a year to build a wind farm, but about five years to construct transmission lines to send power to cities. Presently, the capacity to generate electricity in the favorable wind regions exceeds the capacity to move it, resulting in "stranded" electricity.

To alleviate the problem, the 2005 Texas Legislature implemented Section 39.904(g) of the Texas Utilities Code. It directs the Public Utility Commission (PUC), after consulting with appropriate organizations, including the Electric Reliability Council of Texas (ERCOT) to:

- designate Competitive Renewable Energy Zones (CREZs) and
- develop a plan to construct transmission capacity necessary to deliver electricity, in the most beneficial and cost effective manner, to customers from each CREZ.

The code further specifies that ERCOT, the Texas power-grid operator, study the need for increased transmission and generation capacity throughout the state and file a report with the legislature no later than December 31 of each even-numbered year. The results of the studies are intended to provide guidelines for placement of future transmission lines. The installation of the transmission lines will have a tremendous impact on wind development in the regions where the lines are located.

On July 17, 2008, the PUC announced preliminary approval for construction of a massive grid to transmit wind power from West Texas and the Panhandle. The action opens the door for a far-reaching web of transmission lines that, when completed, will create the capacity to transmit an additional 18,456 megawatts. The estimated $5 billion project will take four to five years to complete and will add five dollars monthly to Texas residential consumers' utility bills.

Regulating Wind Development

Another issue discussed in Judon Fambrough's timely and thought-provoking article is that of regulation. One of the items on the agenda for the 2009 Texas Legislature is the possible regulation of wind development. Hearings are already under way. Presently, wind development is unregulated in this state. One question the legislators must answer before imposing any regulations is whether wind is a natural resource. The Texas Constitution mandates that the Legislature pass laws for the *conservation and development* as well as the *preservation and conservation* of all natural resources in the state.

However, the constitution does not define the term *natural resources*. The Texas Natural Resources Code is of no help. It states that "the conservation and development of all the natural resources of this state are declared to be a public right and duty." And "the protection of water and land of the state against pollution or the escape of oil or gas is in the public interest." The only mention of wind in the Texas Constitution deems it more or less a nuisance. The legislature has created *wind erosion districts* which grant the power to create conservation and reclamation districts.

The constitutional language needs some legal interpretation. Do the two words in the constitutional phrase *conserve and develop* apply separately or together? The wording does not say *conserve and/or develop* but *conserve and develop*. While regulating the development of wind sounds reasonable, the conservation of it may not, especially to residents of West Texas.

Federal Estate Tax Complications

Landowners face the loss of special-use valuation when leasing their land for wind farms. The Internal Revenue Code permits farms and ranches to be valued for the purpose of federal gift and estate taxes on the basis of their present use, not their highest and best use. To qualify, several requirements must be met. For one, the deceased should have materially participated in the farm or ranch operations for the five years prior to death. In addition, the "qualified heirs" must continue to materially participate in operations for an additional 10 years after the deceased's death.

Material participation requires active involvement in management and an assumption of the associated financial risks. Cash leasing of the land is prohibited, but crop sharing is permitted. When an estate elects to use the special-use valuation, the IRS imposes a tax lien on the property for10 years. The lien secures repayment of the deferred taxes in the event the deceased's heirs fail to materially participate. If this occurs, a recapture of the tax savings is triggered with a possible foreclosure on the tax lien.

The federal tax lien makes it difficult, if not impossible, for farms and ranches to obtain third-party financing unless the IRS agrees to subordinate the lien. In a recent San Angelo case, a property was subject to the tax lien imposed by Section 6166. The heirs entered a wind lease. The lease required the landowners to get all preexisting liens released or subordinated. When the landowner asked the IRS for a subordination agreement, the IRS not only refused but viewed the wind lease as a disqualifying *cash lease* that triggered the recapture of the tax savings.

The prohibited "cash leases" are generally viewed as leases connected with farm or ranch operations, and not for wind development. If the IRS continues to take this position, it will have a chilling effect on wind energy development. When a wind lease is negotiated, consultation with knowledgeable legal and tax professionals is recommended.

Maker of Energy Production Equipment Setting up Shop in West Texas

As wind farms gain support as a viable source of renewable energy, Martifer Group has made plans to break ground on a $40 million wind tower manufacturing plant in San Angelo. The Portugal-based company expects to have its plant up and running in a year. The plant is projected to bring 225 jobs to the area in the next three years.

According to company officials, the facility will produce 400 towers a year by 2013. Each turbine will retail for about $4 million. The city offered Martifer $5.6 million in incentives and tax abatements, including money for buying the land for the 340,000-sf plant, which will be off Old Ballinger Highway on the city's northern edge. Tom Green County has offered an additional $2 million in abatements. The state, in addition to $945,000 from the Texas Enterprise Fund, is negotiating millions of dollars in rail improvements with the Texas Pacifico Railroad.

Financing Solar Power

The sun's energy is clean, cheap, and plentiful, but the up-front costs of installing solar panels once presented a daunting barrier to entry for many companies. Fortunately, a financing tool known as **Power Purchase Agreements (PPAs)** is clearing the path. Though the details vary from state to state and from company to company, PPAs are based on the same general framework:

- A third-party solar company funds, installs, and maintains a solar energy system for the participating business.

- The solar company then sells electricity to the business, usually on a 15- to 20-year fixed-rate contract, often at prices lower than those typically offered for electricity by the local utility.

In California, Macy's used a mix of PPAs and traditional solar panel purchases to put solar arrays on the rooftops of 26 stores—while upgrading its lighting, heating and cooling, and energy-management systems to boost efficiency. The result is an estimated 40% reduction on its utility bills and an estimated 88,450 metric tons annual reduction in CO_2 emissions.

Other major companies, including Wal-Mart, Whole Foods, Kohl's, Staples, Target, Kinkos, Google, and Microsoft, have also entered into PPAs with various providers. The benefits, for both business and the environment, are multiple:

- Eliminate the financial barrier to entry normally associated with solar power.

- Reduce demand for conventional energy sources.

- Cut CO_2 emissions.

- Add renewable power to the grid.

At a time of volatile energy prices, PPAs also give companies predictable electricity bills and the opportunity to save money on operating costs. Industry analysts predict PPAs will gain 65 to 75 percent market share for commercial solar installation in 2008 alone. However, continued growth is dependent upon the expansion of state and federal solar incentives. PPAs are currently most prevalent in states with favorable government programs, like California and Hawaii.

Valley Town Earns Accolades

San Benito, a valley town tucked away in the southern tip of Texas, has garnered statewide attention for its renewable energy efforts. The Valley town has received the Texas Renewable Energy Industries Association's renewable energy project of the year award for the solar array that will help power its new water treatment plant. Funding for the $325,000 photovoltaic system came from the Environmental Protection Agency through a grant to the Texas General Land Office and its Renewable Energy Program.

Principal Environmental Problems

The need for adequate environmental information is becoming critical in any transaction involving commercial property. As cited earlier, there are constraints on homeowners using or storing hazardous materials on the premises. This brings up these questions: Exactly what comprises an environmental problem? What is the origin of these problems, and what is being done to mitigate the dangers?

The balance of this chapter is devoted to outlining the problems, explaining the principal federal and state laws and regulations that are being applied, and identifying the major impact these changes are having on property values affecting owners and lenders.

To examine the kinds of environmental problems created by pollution, recent developments are studied under the following nine categories. Each category is defined by law, and the principal agencies responsible for implementation of the law are identified.

1. Lead poisoning

2. Indoor air pollution

3. Toxic waste sites

4. Wetlands protection

5. Endangered species protection

6. Underground storage tanks

7. Electromagnetic forces

8. Mold

9. Carbon monoxide

Lead Poisoning

Lead is a heavy, relatively soft, malleable, bluish-gray metal. It cannot be broken down or destroyed. Because of the ease with which it can be shaped, it has been used for centuries as pipe and other building materials. More recently, it has been alloyed for use as solder to secure pipe joints and as a component of paint. Paint containing high levels of lead was found to be more durable and to look fresher longer.

Although lead was useful in buildings, its ingestion by humans can only do harm. Lead can be more damaging to children up to 7 years of age than to adults because children have higher rates of respiration and metabolism. Lead can be most damaging to the brain. Testing in the first and second grades found that children with the lowest IQs, academic achievement, language skills, and attention spans were the children with the highest levels of lead.

Lead was banned for use in paint in 1977, but lead-based paint can be found in nearly 75 percent of occupied houses built prior to 1978. About 3.8 million units are deemed to be serious hazards to their occupants. Its victims are poisoned by lead dust in the house and lead particles in the soil, not by peeling paint chips.

Nevertheless, in May 1997, the Centers for Disease Control and Prevention reported a drop in the number of children under age 6 who had high levels of lead in their blood. From 1988 to 1991, 1.7 million children were so afflicted, dropping to 1 million in the period 1991 to 1994. The reasons for this decline are attributed to federal initiatives to end the use of lead in gasoline, lead solder in the seams of food cans, and lead-based paint in homes.

1996 Lead-Based Paint Rule

On March 6, 1996, HUD and the EPA issued a joint final rule that requires sellers and renters of houses built before 1978 to disclose to potential buyers or tenants the presence of lead-based paint hazards in housing. Texas has a promulgated contract addendum covering this disclosure for use with TREC-promulgated contract forms, which is reproduced in the Appendix.

Texas Law on Lead-Based Paint

The 1997 Texas Legislature expanded lead abatement by passing its House Bill 729, which gives more authority to the Texas Department of Health to control lead paint abatement in *all pre-1978 child-occupied facilities*, not just *target housing*. This includes child care facilities, daycare centers, preschools, kindergartens, and any other facility visited at least 2 days a week for more than 3 hours, or at least 60 hours annually, by children 6 years of age or younger.

Federal Law for Building Renovators

Effective June 1, 1999, *renovators of dwellings* built before 1978 must give owners or occupants a copy of an EPA document whenever more than 2 square feet of paint will be disturbed. This disclosure is in addition to those listed above. The new law requires renovators to provide owners or occupants with the HUD pamphlet *Protect Your Family from Lead in Your Home* at least 60 days prior to any paint-disturbing activities and to obtain proof of delivery by getting signatures. Alternative means of proof may be used when signatures cannot be obtained.

Formaldehyde Gas

Formaldehyde is a colorless, toxic, water-soluble gas with a strong, pungent, pickle-like smell. It can be emitted by a number of building materials, such as urea-formaldehyde foam insulation (UFFI) and formaldehyde-based adhesives used in pressed wood, particleboard, plywood, shelves, cabinets, and office furniture. It can also be found in some draperies and carpeting. This gas can cause health problems ranging from minor eye, nose, and throat irritation to serious effects such as nasal cancer.

Such problems are not normally found in the average building, but pose greater problems in manufactured or mobile homes, extremely energy-efficient houses, tightly constructed newer office buildings, and even schools. Only manufactured homes are required to carry warning labels if they contain products made with formaldehyde. Buyers of manufactured homes must sign statements acknowledging the presence of formaldehyde-based materials. Other buildings have no such requirements. Thus, in other buildings, a real estate agent must disclose any known presence of UFFI or a harmful concentration of formaldehyde gas-producing materials.

Testing

Testing for formaldehyde gas is accomplished in two ways: by a professional or by a testing device. An accurate device called PF-1 is made by Air Quality Research in Research Triangle Park, North Carolina. The PF-1 is a small glass vial that is left in place for 1 week, then sent back to the company for analysis. Two sell for about $59 with analysis and for about $36 without analysis. The company's phone number is 919-918-7191.

Remedies

The best solution to the formaldehyde problem is removal of the gas-emitting material. This may, however, be an extremely complex and expensive process. Increasing ventilation or lowering the temperature and humidity inside a building can reduce the concentration of gas. Another effective procedure is to seal particleboard and other wood products with paints or veneers.

Radon Gas

In 1989, the administrator of the EPA, William Reilly, pronounced radon "the second leading cause of cancer in this country." The EPA estimates that radon causes as many as 20,000 deaths each year. The hazard was not discovered until 1984, when an engineer working on construction of the Limerick Nuclear Plant in Pennsylvania was found to be bringing radiation *into* the plant from his home!

Radon is an invisible radioactive gas. A person cannot smell it, feel it, or see it. Outside it is virtually harmless because it dissipates. It becomes a problem only inside a building, when it accumulates into dangerous concentrations. Radon comes from decaying uranium. Uranium can be found in many places—the earth's soil, black shale, phosphatic rocks, and even granite. It can be found in areas that have been contaminated with industrial wastes, such as by-products of uranium or phosphate mining.

The danger arises when such materials are located directly underneath an inhabited building and the gas seeps inside. Entry into a building can be through cracks in the slab or openings found around pipes. The gas can also enter through well water. In building areas that lack adequate ventilation (for example, a basement), the gas can become concentrated and dangerous.

Although the materials that cause radon gas are widely dispersed, they are not found everywhere. Clues about its possible presence can be obtained from local, state, and federal environmental and health officials or from information gathered about other buildings in the local neighborhood. Although any building can contain radon gas, well-insulated and energy-efficient homes experience higher levels of contamination. If the presence of radon is suspected, air tests should be made.

Testing

The simplest test involves using an activated charcoal filter canister, which can be purchased at hardware stores or home centers. The canister is placed in the basement or at ground level of the building for 4 to 7 days, then returned to a laboratory for analysis. (Radon is not normally a problem in the upper floors of a building.) If professional testing is preferred, the EPA has a list of proficient radon testing contractors. If the building tested is being offered for sale, full disclosure of the test results must be given to prospective buyers.

Remedies

Several remedies reduce the problem of radon gas pollution. Basement floor cracks and pipe openings can be sealed to prevent further seepage. Ventilation devices alone may be sufficient to reduce the radon concentration to a minimal level.

Asbestos

Asbestos is a group of naturally occurring mineral fibers found in rocks. It has been used in such products as patching compounds, wood-burning stoves, siding, roofing shingles, and vinyl floors. Asbestos has a number of advantages. It can strengthen a material, provide thermal insulation, provide acoustical insulation on exposed surfaces, and fireproof a product or material. However, it has at least one disadvantage: it can kill you. That fact has been known since 1924! In that year, the *British Medical Journal* published a report by W. E. Cooke about a young woman who had worked with asbestos and died with extensively scarred lungs.

Asbestos can cause asbestosis, a noncancerous disease that scars the lung tissues. It can also cause several different kinds of cancer in the lungs, esophagus, stomach, and intestines. Yet it is a difficult type of pollution to assess accurately. Media attention to the problems of asbestos as a health hazard in schools and office buildings has increased concern. The same problems can exist in homes, although this concern has received less attention. Nevertheless, recent studies have indicated that the real danger lies with loose asbestos rather than that occurring in hard form.

Construction materials have contained asbestos for hundreds of years. When bonded with another hard material, asbestos can be relatively harmless. This nonfriable condition, common in asbestos siding, usually poses no threat unless drilled or sanded, thus releasing fibers. It is the efforts to remove hard asbestos materials by disturbing them that can cause health hazards.

Soft or crumbling forms (i.e., friable asbestos) pose greater risks. Damaged asbestos insulation around pipes or ceiling tiles may release airborne microscopic fibers. These fibers may, even after many years, cause respiratory diseases. No conclusive studies to date have shown that a health hazard is caused from the ingestion of food or water containing asbestos or that the fibers can penetrate the skin. Asbestos becomes dangerous only when it breaks down and fibers are released into the air.

In a recent court case, it was ruled that even though the National Emission Standards for Hazardous Air Pollutants for Asbestos (Asbestos NESHAP) call for "visible emissions," it does not require the visible observation of particulate asbestos material, only the visible observation of the emissions, which contain invisible particles. The court ruled against the defendant who rehabilitated brake shoes that may have contained asbestos and fined the defendant $50,000. *United States v. Midwest Suspension & Brake*, 49 F3d 1197 (6th Cir., 1995).

Testing

As buyer/investor, seller, or agent, it is important to know whether homes or buildings in the neighborhood have been found to contain asbestos. If there is an indication of problems, an EPA-certified asbestos inspector can determine from bulk samples whether materials contain asbestos. Once a laboratory analysis determines the material's content, the buyer and seller can consider management plan options. Full disclosure to a potential buyer is mandatory.

Economic Consequences

Discovery of asbestos can be a building owner's nightmare. Aside from the problems associated with federal and state laws regarding the handling of asbestos-containing materials, a real problem lies in the economic risks associated with its presence.

Two risks are dominant: (1) the potential of health-related lawsuits and (2) the potential lack of tenants due to fear of the presence of asbestos. This translates into a lower value for the building and difficulty in obtaining adequate insurance coverage. Even so, when faced with such a dilemma, building owners may consider an asbestos management plan as suggested by the EPA.

Toxic Waste Sites

The problem of toxic waste sites first came to national attention with the discovery of a contaminated area in the abandoned Love Canal near Niagara Falls, New York. The federal response was passage of the *Comprehensive Environmental Response, Compensation, and Liability Act of 1980* (CERCLA). It set up a fund totaling $8.5 billion, known as *Superfund*, to evaluate and clean up inactive and abandoned sites throughout the United States.

A toxic waste site is an area identified by the EPA as containing a concentration of hazardous materials. About 1,290 such sites are known of in the country. Thirty of these sites are in Texas, with nearly half (fourteen) located in the Houston area. Although toxic waste sites are no bigger problems than areas polluted by other contaminants, they have attracted popular attention by being very visible. The catch phrase "the polluter pays" has been widely accepted as the way to handle this problem. Unfortunately, it has not worked quite this way because often the major polluter is out of business.

By placing liability for cleanup of these sites on anyone who has used the land, regardless of fault, the Superfund Act has created enormous litigation expenses and very little remedial action. Of the approximately $26 billion spent on toxic waste, the private sector has paid about $5 billion in litigation and the government, another $4 billion. Indeed, a toxic waste site known as the Brio site, just south of Houston, has created an active business for damaged claimants that nearly replaced efforts to clean up the real problem.

Extent of Liability

CERCLA places strict, joint and several liabilities for cleanup costs on all responsible parties. *Strict* means liable regardless of fault, and *joint and several* means the parties are both singularly and jointly liable for all cleanup costs. This is true whether the party involved had anything to do with creating the problem. No minimum amount of contamination is required to create liability for cleanup.

Although only about 250 of some 1,290 designated Superfund waste sites have been cleaned up, a rough estimate of average cost per site thus far has been $25 million. There is no limit on the liability that can be incurred, except for damage to natural resources, which is limited to $50 million.

Liability to the government may not be allocated; however, responsible parties may seek an allocation of costs among themselves. One result has been that much of the money spent on toxic waste problems has been directed to litigation centered primarily on insurance companies' denial of liability.

Hazardous Materials Covered by CERCLA

CERCLA does not include all substances that can be classified as dangerous to a person's health. Thus, liability for cleanup may be more specifically allocated by other laws for non-CERCLA-covered substances. CERCLA defines a hazardous substance as one specifically listed as poisonous by the EPA, comprising about 750 materials at present, in addition to those so designated by any other law.

There are a number of exclusions from the definition of CERCLA's hazardous substances, including petroleum and derivatives thereof, unless expressly listed as a hazardous substance by other statutes. Also excluded are natural gas, natural gas liquids, and synthetic natural gas usable for fuel. Furthermore, the exclusion includes mining wastes, cement kiln dust, and wastes generated from the combustion of coal or other fossil fuels.

Innocent Landowner Defense

An innocent landowner defense against liability for toxic waste cleanup may be sustained in the case of damages caused by a third party, not an employee and not under any contractual relationship with the defendant, *providing* the defendant did not know and had no reason to know that the facility had been used for the disposal of hazardous substances prior to the time the facility was acquired by the defendant.

Environmental Due Diligence Assessment

The purpose of a due diligence assessment is to analyze, evaluate, and manage a potential environmental risk. The method used is (1) to research the historical uses of the subject property, (2) to identify the presence and extent of environmental contamination, and (3) to determine the most feasible method of managing the environmental risk if hazardous substances are found.

Two key elements to making these assessments are not addressed in the Superfund Act. One is that there are no standards to determine what measure of contamination triggers liability for cleanup. Groups involved in the real estate industry have been seeking better clarification. One result has been a set of standards recently developed privately by the American Society for Testing of Materials (ASTM). The other important element not addressed in the act is that there are no legally identified credentials for persons making environmental assessments. Educational programs leading to professional designations that will better identify qualified people are offered through schools in Texas.

As dictated by CERCLA, the environmental assessment should be conducted in phases. A *Phase I Assessment* involves a limited inquiry into how the land has been used *prior to conveyance of title*, focusing on readily available sources of data and culminating in an inspection of the site.

If the assessment reveals actual or potential environmental problems, a *Phase II Assessment* is required. Phase II targets those areas believed to be contaminated and include the collection and chemical analysis of soil samples, surface and groundwater samples, and other relevant investigations and analyses. A *Phase III Assessment* involves defining the extent of soil and groundwater contamination and implementing the most appropriate cleanup activities.

Recovery of Brownfield Areas

Urban land that has become contaminated over the years often lies idle because of the cost and possible liability involved with its cleanup and restoration to good economic use. *Brownfield* is the EPA's term for contaminated areas with the potential for reuse. The EPA estimates there are 450,000 brownfields nationwide. An example of restoration and a return to tax-paying value to the community is the construction of Minute Maid Park in downtown Houston.

Federal agencies have been working with the private sector to help redevelopment of brownfield sites. These agencies include the EPA, the Federal Housing Finance Board, and HUD. The private sector has been slow to become involved due to the availability of greenfields, concerns with liability, the time and cost of cleanup, and a reluctance to invest in older urban areas. Since 1995, the EPA has loosened some of its regulatory oversight. Although developers could technically be held liable for past contamination, nonlitigation agreements between Washington and some states encourage the cleanup of sites with lesser contamination.

The Federal Home Loan Bank system, a government-sponsored enterprise, is now involved in helping to finance redevelopment of city ground use. The FHLB's *Community Investment Cash Advance Program* encourages partnerships between the FHLB and public and private entities to reduce the financing costs for targeted projects. Last year the FHLB made $790 million available in term financing for brownfield redevelopment.

HUD programs, such as Community Development Block grants, Section 108, and the Brownfield Economic Development Initiative, could help stimulate economic development by leveraging private investment and making brownfield projects feasible.

An example of a successful cleanup in operation is in Dallas, Texas. The work is being promoted as the Victory Project by Ross Perot, Jr., CEO of Hillwood Development and son of the former presidential hopeful. The location is a 72-acre former city dump with an aging power plant and a row of abandoned grain silos. The mile-long site was purchased for $12 million, involving 25 parcels of land with virtually no records of possible contaminants. By 2001, the American Airlines Center had been completed, and the 8 million square feet of apartments, offices, stores, and recreation facilities was awaiting further financing. The Victory Project will be a $1 billion development catering to road-weary Dallasites who want to live, work, and play downtown.

Tax Relief for Brownfield Cleanup

In January 2001, legislation was passed to extend the Taxpayer Relief Act of 1997. Owners of brownfield sites can expense their cleanup costs rather than capitalize them until January

1, 2004. Also, the criteria for an eligible site has been expanded to include contaminated areas certified by a state environmental agency.

Wetlands Protection

In the past, swampy, marshy, or water-saturated soils were considered a source of sickness, a breeding place for disease-bearing mosquitoes. Farmers were encouraged to drain or fill such areas. In addition, large areas of wetlands were eliminated for federal flood control projects, canal building, and mosquito control projects. Then, too late in many cases, scientists learned that wetlands could help control flooding, filter out pollution, clean drinking water, and provide habitat for fish and other wildlife. Environmentalists were quick to expand the new intelligence with rather far-reaching and perhaps unintended results.

Wetlands may be natural or manmade. Decorative lakes or water hazards on golf courses, for example, may become protected wetlands. *Wetlands* is not a scientific term, and because of a lack of clear definition, each agency involved has its own definition. If an area that involves a wetland is disturbed before discovering it is so defined, the result can be enforcement action, including the assessment of administrative, civil, and/or criminal penalties.

Regulations did not prohibit *drainage* of a wetland area, but disallowed the dumping of fill material. That seemed to be a loophole, and in 1993, the administration prohibited drainage, as the excavation work of drainage allowed fill material to be dumped in the wetlands. In late 1996, the change in rules was disallowed, restoring drainage as a legal procedure.

Wetlands Definition

As defined by the Corps, wetlands are "areas inundated or saturated by surface or groundwater at a frequency and duration sufficient to support, and that under normal circumstances do support, a prevalence of vegetation typically adapted for life in saturated soil conditions." The definition is broad and leaves many landowners with less than a clear understanding of its consequences.

If cattails are growing in a landowner's swampland, that area is most likely wetlands. However, many areas may or may not qualify depending on how one interprets such words as *normal circumstances* and *prevalence of vegetation*. Because the Corps and the EPA exercise authority over wetlands, in 1987, the two agencies combined to produce the Federal *Wetlands Determination Manual*, which explains the technical criteria in greater detail. However, the manual does not distinguish between natural and manmade wetlands. Thus, a wet area in a cornfield created by a farmer's irrigation ditch would be classified the same as an ancient cypress swamp in the Florida Everglades.

So the only way to be certain whether an area comes under the wetlands definition is to request the Corps to make an inspection and issue its own determination. Each of the twenty-six Corps district offices throughout the country is authorized to make these determinations, which are final unless a landowner brings suit in federal court to overturn them. There is no right to administrative appeal. Texas has two Corps district offices, one in Galveston and one in Fort Worth.

The federal Department of Agriculture enters into the proper usage of such land when it is designated as agricultural land.

Wetlands Mitigation Banking

If a wetlands area must be filled to complete a development project, it is possible to obtain the necessary Corps permit by restoring or creating another wetlands area—usually on a ratio of 1.5 acres of new wetland for every acre of developed wetland—on or near the project site. To obtain a permit for such work, the developers must agree to flood the area; plant trees, grass, and other vegetation; and guarantee to maintain the new wetland in perpetuity. This method leaves many developers facing a big obstacle.

Fortunately, another method may be available. Entrepreneurs are developing large reserves, or banks, comprising 500 acres or more of functioning wetlands in areas that were previously farmed. Costs to develop this new wetlands bank run about $10,000 per acre. The sponsor offers the acres that may be needed for sale, and the developer can use the land as a credit to fulfill the Corps' requirements. Developers can buy the acreage needed, but they do not take title to the land. The sponsor continues to maintain the new wetlands bank.

This method, known as *mitigation banking*, is gaining recognition, as it offers opportunities for commercial real estate developers to go forward with projects that involve existing wetlands areas and for entrepreneurs to work with developing the wetlands bank for sale at a profit.

Enforcement

The Corps and the EPA share enforcement powers for violations of the wetlands program. Under a Memorandum of Agreement between the two agencies executed in January 1989, the Corps handles enforcement actions involving violations of Corps-issued permits and for unpermitted discharges. The EPA is the lead agency only in unpermitted discharge cases that involve repeat violators and flagrant violations.

Enforcement action can also be instigated by citizen groups who sue the regulatory agencies for improper issuance of a permit or the alleged violator for illegal actions. However, these groups are not entitled to compensation for damages they may have suffered, but they can seek compliance and the imposition of civil penalties. Citizen groups can also recover litigation costs if the court thinks the award is appropriate.

Endangered Species Protection

Landowners have recently become more aware of the fact that the Endangered Species Act of 1973 (16 U.S.C.A. Section 1531 et. seq.) can have a profound impact on the value of their land. One reason for the delay in recognizing its importance is that since the initial act was passed, it has been substantially expanded by bureaucratic regulations. The 1973 act was intended to protect endangered species on federal land and passed Congress by a vote of 92-0 in the Senate and 355-4 in the House. In spite of the overwhelming initial support, the act quickly caused serious consternation when it threatened to shut down construction of the Tellico Dam in Tennessee to protect the snail darter. Since then, regulations have focused on controlling land usage, including private land, which may contain an endangered species' habitat, almost without regard to the actual presence of such species.

Implementation and regulation of the act was assigned to the U.S. Fish and Wildlife Service under the Department of the Interior.

Kinds of Endangered Species

The popular concept of what comprises an endangered species (such as bald eagles, elk, bears, and certain fish and plant life) has been expanded to include 1,177 species on the threatened or endangered lists. The list includes such little-known species as the giant kangaroo rat, the Tooth Cave pseudoscorpion, and the furbish lousewort. Regulations prohibit the modification of habitats for any of these.

When Congress passed the initial Endangered Species Act, it mandated that a protected endangered species be determined by the "best scientific and commercial data available." Nevertheless, no standards were set, and the responsible agencies now make their own determinations without peer review. They specifically require that economic consequences shall *not* be considered. A challenge is being made to require consideration of economic consequences to EPA rules.

Taking Is Prohibited

The act prohibits the "taking" of endangered species as listed by the federal government. In this context, taking means the killing of any listed plant, animal, fish, or insect. Also, U.S. Fish and Wildlife Service regulations prohibit any *harm* or *harassment* of an endangered species, including modifying, damaging, or destroying the habitat even though the species may not be present. A recent court ruling held that an unintentional catching of an endangered species of salmon was an allowable incidental taking, even though fishing for salmon was a purposeful activity on the part of the fisheries involved. Plaintiffs in this case challenged the failure of the U.S. Department of Commerce and other federal agencies to respond to the "taking" of three species of salmon listed as endangered. Plaintiffs contended that the fisheries should be barred from harvesting all salmon because they could not distinguish between listed and unlisted species. Defendants argued that the "taking" of an endangered species is incidental to the permitted activity. The court held that Congress could not have intended to penalize the fisheries by wholly denying them the ability to fish for salmon because they cannot distinguish between listed and unlisted species before they are caught. *Pacific NW Generating Coop. v. Brown*, 25 F3d 1443 (9th Cir., 1994).

Although the regulatory definition of a taking is broad, it is not clearly defined by case law. An underlying question is this: Can such prohibitions of land usage entitle the landowner to undertake an inverse condemnation suit against the government entities involved? The 5th Amendment to the U.S. Constitution clearly states "...nor shall private property be taken for public use without just compensation." Earlier opinion interpreted this clause as meaning compensation is due only when title to property is taken under eminent domain. The difficult-to-define gray area that has since arisen concerns the partial taking of property that leaves the landowner with title but with only limited usage.

Incidental Take Permit

A developer or landowner who wants to build on land that is home to a threatened or endangered species must apply for an *incidental take permit*. The process can be lengthy and complex. The application for an incidental take permit must be accompanied by a habitat conservation plan (HCP). The purpose of the plan is to ensure that any incidental take and its effects are minimized. Developing such a plan can take from 8 to 24 months.

Underground Storage Tanks (USTs)

The Resources Conservation and Recovery Act of 1976 (RCRA) has been amended so as to require the EPA to develop a comprehensive program to prevent, detect, and correct releases from Underground Storage Tanks (USTs). Under the EPA definition, a UST is any tank that has 10 percent or more of its volume below ground and contains either petroleum or hazardous substances. The EPA estimates that 2 million USTs are covered by the regulations and that 95 percent of those are used to store petroleum and its products.

Certain tanks are excluded from the definition, including farm or residential tanks of 1,100 gallons or less storing fuel for noncommercial purposes, heating oil tanks holding oil for consumption on the premises, septic tanks, wastewater collection systems, and storage tanks located in an enclosed underground area (basement). Although excluded by the EPA, these types of tanks may be covered by state or local laws.

UST owners must provide certain safety precautions, including corrosion protection, leak detection by monthly monitoring or inventory control, and tank-tightness testing, in addition to spill and overflow devices. Compliance has been phased in over 5 years and now applies to all USTs.

USTs installed after December 1988 must have all requirements in place upon installation. Qualified contractors must install new tanks according to code, and tank owners must provide the EPA with certification of proper installation. The same is true for tank removal.

There are reporting requirements for containment of leaks and spills; also, various records must be kept to evidence a tank owner's ongoing compliance with the regulations. Since October 1990, owners and operators of USTs must demonstrate responsibility for corrective actions and be able to compensate for injury or property damage from $500,000 to $4 million, depending on the number of tanks owned. If a landowner finds an underground tank on the property, he must find out what it contains and what condition it is in. Some abandoned tanks have been filled with sand, gravel, or other inert material. If the tank contains a liquid, the landowner needs to find out what the liquid is so it can be properly disposed of and whether the tank has leaked or is leaking. A professional may need to perform a tank-tightness test. If a hazardous substance is involved, a report to the EPA may be necessary.

Landlords whose tenants have tanks, mortgagees whose borrowers have tanks, and purchasers of property on which tanks are located must make sure they are in compliance with the regulations. Familiarity with these regulations will enable a real estate agent to provide competent, professional suggestions in transactions involving USTs.

Electromagnetic Forces

Most environmental concerns are real and should be considered when dealing with land and what may be built on it. Yet there is no doubt that some people profit from environmental scares. Whether electromagnetic force is a scare tactic or a real concern has yet to be determined. Nevertheless, because it could be a consideration in buying property or evaluating some, electromagnetic force is a subject the agent needs to know about.

Electromagnetic fields (EMFs) fit nicely into scare tactics. They are silent and invisible, and few nonscientists know what they are or where they come from. Yet they exist anywhere electrons zip through transmission lines, in the innards of appliances, and in electric blankets, making them nearly impossible to avoid.

Over the years, various studies have linked electromagnetic fields to cancer. In 1979, epidemiologists found that children living near high-current power lines in Denver got leukemia at 1.5 times the expected rate. However, these studies are hobbled because it is nearly impossible to monitor actual EMFs continuously inside thousands of houses. So a stand-in for EMF exposure is used. The stand-in is called a wire-code rating and reflects a home's distance from a power line and the size of wires close by. When researchers actually measure EMFs, they find that fields are no higher in homes with leukemia cases than in homes without.

Thus far, there has been no clear relationship between the strength of an EMF and the incidence of leukemia. In November 1996, the National Research Council, after 3 years of examining more than 500 studies, issued its report. Quoting from the report, "The current body of evidence does not show that exposure to these fields presents a human health hazard." There is one possible exception—everyday levels of EMFs do suppress a cell's production of melatonin. This hormone slows the growth of breast cells on their way to becoming cancerous.

Mold

Mold exists everywhere all of the time. Usually, it does not bother anyone. However, at times, mold can be a problem, particularly for people who are unusually sensitive to it. Some people experience respiratory problems when they are exposed to mold, and they can become very ill. Certain molds, in particular the "black mold," seem to make people ill. Even though mold exists everywhere, it thrives in dark, moist areas, such as dirty heating ducts. A roof that has leaked, no matter how slowly, for a long time can create moisture and encourage mold growth. Combine mold with a particularly sensitive person, and a lawsuit may result.

As a result, real estate practitioners and inspectors need to understand the mold issue. The presence of mold or mold-causing conditions, such as previous water damage, should be disclosed by sellers—especially when a homeowner knows about an ongoing mold problem that may not be apparent from a basic inspection. When to disclose is a fact-specific legal issue, but mold disclosure will probably not be uncommon in the near future.

Landlords also need to be vigilant about the mold issue. A chronic leaky roof, leaky water pipes, bathroom moisture, or a poorly maintained ventilation system may be an invitation to a lawsuit. If science establishes a causal relationship between the presence of mold and human illness, legal exposure will rise.

Landlords must take reasonable means to avoid harmful mold growth. Indoor air quality experts are available to provide assistance. If mold repairs are needed, an experienced mold remediation company should be contacted. Certain protocols should be followed, and real estate practitioners will want to ensure that they can prove that the job was done correctly.

Carbon Monoxide

Carbon monoxide (CO) is an odorless, colorless gas produced by the combustion of fuels such as natural gas, oil, and propane in devices such as furnaces, water heaters, and stoves. These items are normally designed to vent the CO to the outside, but harmful interior levels of CO can result from incomplete combustion of fuel, improper installation, or blockages, leaks, or cracks in the venting systems. Homeowners can take action against potential CO poisoning by following the steps given below:

- Have all fuel-burning appliances professionally inspected yearly, preferably before the start of the cold-weather season when heaters and furnaces are first used.

- These appliances include gas stoves and ovens, furnaces and heaters, water heaters, generators, and clothes dryers.

- All such devices should be properly installed and vented to the outside whenever possible.

- If repairs are necessary, be sure they are performed by a qualified technician.

- Always use the proper fuel specified for the device.

- Have flues and chimneys for fuel-burning fireplaces or wood stoves inspected regularly for cracks, leaks, and blockages that may allow a buildup of CO to occur.

- Never use gas stoves or ovens to heat the home, even temporarily.

- Do not start or idle a vehicle in a garage, even with the outer garage door open.

- For additional protection, purchase a CO detector (either battery operated or plug-in) and follow the manufacturer's instructions for proper location and installation.

- Learn what to do should the CO alarm activate.

If anyone in the home experiences symptoms such as fatigue, dizziness, blurred vision, nausea, or confusion, everyone should leave immediately and seek medical attention. If no symptoms are felt, open doors and windows immediately and shut off all fuel-burning devices that may be potential sources of CO.

TCEQ Penalties

In January of 2006, The Texas Commission on Environmental Quality (TCEQ) approved penalties totaling $503,051 against 69 regulated entities for violations of state environmental regulations.

The TCEQ's three commissioners approved agreed orders in the following enforcement categories: thirteen air quality; one municipal solid waste; one Edwards Aquifer; one industrial hazardous waste; five industrial waste discharge; three licensed irrigator; one multi-media; ten municipal waste discharge; fifteen petroleum storage tank; fifteen public water system; and two water quality. The commissioners also approved; one public water system default order; one industrial hazardous waste default order; and one water quality default order.

Included in the total fine figure is a penalty of $123,608 against Cemex, Inc., in Ector County for air violations. The agreed order resulted from eight violations found during investigations in 2004, and include exceeding permit emissions limits; failure to submit and submit timely various reports and compliance certifications; failure to notify TCEQ of emission events; failure to comply with opacity limits; failure to operate consistently with plant plans; failure to properly operate emissions equipment; and failure to comply with monitoring requirements. As a condition of the agreed order, Cemex will contribute $61,804 of the fine for a Supplemental Environmental Project to fund an education and recycling/disposal program by Keep Odessa Beautiful, Inc.

Agenda items from all commission meetings and work session agendas can be viewed on the TCEQ Web site.

Environmental Websites

For additional research on the numerous environmental issues, please consult the following websites:

Radon Sites and Links of Interest:

Gardner, Marilyn, "Easy on the Eyes and the Environment," *The Christian Science Monitor*, March 3, 2004. Accessed on August 2, 2005, from
http://www.csmonitor.com/2004/0303/p11s01-lihc.html

A Citizen's Guide to Radon
http://www.epa.gov/radon/pubs/citguide.html

Buyer's and Seller's Guide to Radon
 http://www.epa.gov/radon/pubs/hmbyguid.html

Table of Action Levels for Radon
http://www.co.jefferson.co.us/health/health_T111_R42.htm#epa

EPA radon page
www.epa.gov/iaq/radon
National Environmental Health Association, radon page,
http://radongas.org/

Colorado Department of Public Health and Environment, radon page,
www.cdphe.state.co.us/hm/rad/radon/index.htm

Other Resources

- Jefferson County Environmental Health Services: 303-271-5700
- Western Regional Radon Training Center: 1-800-513-8332
- Colorado Radon Hot Line: 1-800-846-3986

Lead Sites and Links of Interest:

EPA—Protect Your Family from Lead in Your Home
http://www.epa.gov/lead/pubs/leadpdfe.pdf

Finding a Qualified Lead Professional for Your Home
http://www.epa.gov/lead/pubs/broch32e.pdf

Testing Your Home for Lead
http://www.epa.gov/lead/pubs/leadtest.pdf

Reducing Lead Hazards When Remodeling Your Home
http://www.epa.gov/lead/pubs/rrpamph.pdf

Water Quality Sites and Links of Interest:

Drinking Water and Health—What You Need to Know!
http://www.epa.gov/safewater/dwh/dw-health.pdf

Water System Council
http://www.wellcarehotline.org/

WellOwner.org
http://www.wellowner.org/

EPA—Drinking Water From Household Wells
fhttp://www.epa.gov/safewater/privatewells/

All About Your Water—Domestic Well Analysis
https://www.ecobroker.com/userdef/PDFs/example_well_water_results_letter.pdf

Mold Sites and Links of Interest:

A Brief Guide to Mold, Moisture, and Your Home
http://www.epa.gov/mold/pdfs/moldguide.pdf

Asbestos Sites and Links of Interest:

EPA—Asbestos in Your Home
http://www.epa.gov/asbestos/pubs/ashome.html

EPA—Asbestos Containing Materials
http://www.epa.gov/Region06/6pd/asbestos/asbmatl.htm

Indoor Air Quality Sites and Links of Interest:

EPA—An Introduction to Indoor Air Quality (IAQ)
http://www.epa.gov/iaq/ia-intro.html

EPA—Indoor Air Quality in Large Buildings
http://www.epa.gov/iaq/largebldgs/index.html

EPA—Inside IAQ
http://www.epa.gov/appcdwww/iemb/insideiaq/fw98.pdf

EPA—The Inside Story: A Guide to Indoor Air Quality
http://www.epa.gov/iaq/pubs/insidest.html

Toxic Waste Sites and Links of Interest:

EPA—Environmental Indicators Initiative
http://www.ecobroker.com/userdef/PDFs/EPABetterProtectedLand.pdf

EPA—National Priorities List Sites in the United States
http://www.epa.gov/superfund/sites/npl/npl.htm

EPA—Search Your Community
http://www.epa.gov/epahome/commsearch.htm

EPA Targeted Brownfields Assessments—The Basics
http://www.epa.gov/swerosps/bf/facts/tba_0403.pdf

Brownfields
https://www.ecobroker.com/misc/articleview.aspx?ArticleID=37

National Priorities List in Texas
http://www.epa.gov/superfund/sites/npl/tx.htm

Brio Site
http://cfpub.epa.gov/supercpad/cursites/csitinfo.cfm?id=0602601

Green Buildings and Health Sites and Links of Interest:

Benefits of Owning a Built Green Home
http://www.builtgreen.org/homebuyers/benefits.htm

Environmental Features and Benefits
http://www.builtgreen.org/homebuilders/environment.htm

About ENERGY STAR New Homes
http://www.energystar.gov/index.cfm?c=new_homes.hm_earn_star

Tight Construction Reduced Air Infiltration
http://www.energystar.gov/index.cfm?c=new_homes_features.hm_f_reduced_air_infiltration

Residential Energy Services Network
http://www.natresnet.org/

Documents and Forms

06-30-08

PROMULGATED BY THE TEXAS REAL ESTATE COMMISSION (TREC)

NOTICE OF BUYER'S TERMINATION OF CONTRACT

CONCERNING THE CONTRACT FOR THE SALE OF THE PROPERTY AT

_____

(Street Address and City)

BETWEEN THE UNDERSIGNED BUYER AND_____

_____ (SELLER)

Buyer notifies Seller that the contract is terminated pursuant to the following:

☐(1) the unrestricted right of Buyer to terminate the contract under Paragraph 23 of the contract.

☐(2) Buyer cannot obtain Financing Approval in accordance with the Third Party Financing Condition Addendum to the contract.

☐(3) the Property does not satisfy the lenders' underwriting requirements for the loan under Paragraph 4A(1) of the contract.

☐(4) Buyer elects to terminate under Paragraph A of the Addendum for Property Subject to Mandatory Membership in a Property Owners' Association.

☐(5) Buyer elects to terminate under Paragraph 7B(2) of the contract relating to the Seller's Disclosure Notice.

☐(6) Other (identify the paragraph number of contract or the addendum): _____

_____

_____

_____

NOTE: Release of the earnest money is governed by the terms of the contract.

_____   _____
Buyer   Date   Buyer   Date

TREC No.38-2

Reprinted by permission of Texas Real Estate Commission.

TEXAS ASSOCIATION OF REALTORS®

INTERMEDIARY RELATIONSHIP NOTICE

USE OF THIS FORM BY PERSONS WHO ARE NOT MEMBERS OF THE TEXAS ASSOCIATION OF REALTORS® IS NOT AUTHORIZED.
©Texas Association of REALTORS®, Inc. 2004

To: _____ **(Seller or Landlord)**

and _____ **(Prospect)**

From: _____ **(Broker's Firm)**

Re: _____ **(Property)**

Date: _____

A. Under this notice, "owner" means the seller or landlord of the Property and "prospect" means the above-named prospective buyer or tenant for the Property.

B. Broker's firm represents the owner under a listing agreement and also represents the prospect under a buyer/tenant representation agreement.

C. In the written listing agreement and the written buyer/tenant representation agreement, both the owner and the prospect previously authorized Broker to act as an intermediary if a prospect who Broker represents desires to buy or lease a property that is listed by the Broker. When the prospect makes an offer to purchase or lease the Property, Broker will act in accordance with the authorizations granted in the listing agreement and in the buyer/tenant representation agreement.

D. Broker ❑ will ❑ will not appoint licensed associates to communicate with, carry out instructions of, and provide opinions and advice during negotiations to each party. If Broker makes such appointments, Broker appoints:

_____ to the owner; and

_____ to the prospect.

E. By acknowledging receipt of this notice, the undersigned parties reaffirm their consent for broker to act as an intermediary.

F. Additional Information: *(Disclose material information related to Broker's relationship to the parties, such as personal relationships or prior or contemplated business relationships.)*

The undersigned acknowledge receipt of this notice

_____	_____	_____	_____
Seller or Landlord	Date	Prospect	Date
_____	_____	_____	_____
Seller or Landlord	Date	Prospect	Date

(TAR-1409) 1-7-04   Page 1 of 1

06-30-08

PROMULGATED BY THE TEXAS REAL ESTATE COMMISSION (TREC)
ONE TO FOUR FAMILY RESIDENTIAL CONTRACT (RESALE)
NOTICE: Not For Use For Condominium Transactions

1. PARTIES: The parties to this contract are _____(Seller) and _____(Buyer). Seller agrees to sell and convey to Buyer and Buyer agrees to buy from Seller the Property defined below.

2. PROPERTY:
   A. LAND: Lot _____ Block_____,
   _____Addition, City of
   _____ , County of _____,
   Texas, known as _____(address/zip code), or as described on attached exhibit.
   B. IMPROVEMENTS: The house, garage and all other fixtures and improvements attached to the above-described real property, including without limitation, the following **permanently installed and built-in items,** if any: all equipment and appliances, valances, screens, shutters, awnings, wall-to-wall carpeting, mirrors, ceiling fans, attic fans, mail boxes, television antennas and satellite dish system and equipment, heating and air-conditioning units, security and fire detection equipment, wiring, plumbing and lighting fixtures, chandeliers, water softener system, kitchen equipment, garage door openers, cleaning equipment, shrubbery, landscaping, outdoor cooking equipment, and all other property owned by Seller and attached to the above described real property.
   C. ACCESSORIES: The following described related accessories, if any: window air conditioning units, stove, fireplace screens, curtains and rods, blinds, window shades, draperies and rods, controls for satellite dish system, controls for garage door openers, entry gate controls, door keys, mailbox keys, above ground pool, swimming pool equipment and maintenance accessories, and artificial fireplace logs.
   D. EXCLUSIONS: The following improvements and accessories will be retained by Seller and must be removed prior to delivery of possession:_____
   _____.
   The land, improvements and accessories are collectively referred to as the "Property".

3. SALES PRICE:
   A. Cash portion of Sales Price payable by Buyer at closing................. $_____
   B. Sum of all financing described below (excluding any loan funding fee or mortgage insurance premium).................................. $_____
   C. Sales Price (Sum of A and B).. $_____

4. FINANCING: The portion of Sales Price not payable in cash will be paid as follows: (Check applicable boxes below)
   ❑ A. THIRD PARTY FINANCING: One or more third party mortgage loans in the total amount of $_____ (excluding any loan funding fee or mortgage insurance premium).
      (1) Property Approval: If the Property does not satisfy the lenders' underwriting requirements for the loan(s), this contract will terminate and the earnest money will be refunded to Buyer.
      (2) Financing Approval: (Check one box only)
         ❑(a) This contract is subject to Buyer being approved for the financing described in the attached Third Party Financing Condition Addendum.
         ❑(b) This contract is not subject to Buyer being approved for financing and does not involve FHA or VA financing.
   ❑ B. ASSUMPTION: The assumption of the unpaid principal balance of one or more promissory notes described in the attached TREC Loan Assumption Addendum.
   ❑ C. SELLER FINANCING: A promissory note from Buyer to Seller of $_____, secured by vendor's and deed of trust liens, and containing the terms and conditions described in the attached TREC Seller Financing Addendum. If an owner policy of title insurance is furnished, Buyer shall furnish Seller with a mortgagee policy of title insurance.

5. EARNEST MONEY: Upon execution of this contract by all parties, Buyer shall deposit $_____ as earnest money with _____, as escrow agent, at _____ (address). Buyer shall deposit additional earnest money of $_____ with escrow agent within _____ days after the effective date of this contract. If Buyer fails to deposit the earnest money as required by this contract, Buyer will be in default.

6. TITLE POLICY AND SURVEY:
   A. TITLE POLICY: Seller shall furnish to Buyer at ❑Seller's ❑Buyer's expense an owner policy of title insurance (Title Policy) issued by _____ (Title Company) in the amount of the Sales Price, dated at or after closing, insuring Buyer against loss under the provisions of the Title Policy, subject to the promulgated exclusions

Initialed for identification by Buyer_____ _____ and Seller _____ _____   TREC NO. 20-8

Contract Concerning _____ Page 2 of 8   06-30-08
(Address of Property)

(including existing building and zoning ordinances) and the following exceptions:
(1) Restrictive covenants common to the platted subdivision in which the Property is located.
(2) The standard printed exception for standby fees, taxes and assessments.
(3) Liens created as part of the financing described in Paragraph 4.
(4) Utility easements created by the dedication deed or plat of the subdivision in which the Property is located.
(5) Reservations or exceptions otherwise permitted by this contract or as may be approved by Buyer in writing.
(6) The standard printed exception as to marital rights.
(7) The standard printed exception as to waters, tidelands, beaches, streams, and related matters.
(8) The standard printed exception as to discrepancies, conflicts, shortages in area or boundary lines, encroachments or protrusions, or overlapping improvements. Buyer, at Buyer's expense, may have the exception amended to read, "shortages in area".

B. COMMITMENT: Within 20 days after the Title Company receives a copy of this contract, Seller shall furnish to Buyer a commitment for title insurance (Commitment) and, at Buyer's expense, legible copies of restrictive covenants and documents evidencing exceptions in the Commitment (Exception Documents) other than the standard printed exceptions.   Seller authorizes the Title Company to deliver the Commitment and Exception Documents to Buyer at Buyer's address shown in Paragraph 21. If the Commitment and Exception Documents are not delivered to Buyer within the specified time, the time for delivery will be automatically extended up to 15 days or the Closing Date, whichever is earlier.

C. SURVEY: The survey must be made by a registered professional land surveyor acceptable to the Title Company and Buyer's lender(s). (Check one box only)
☐ (1) Within _____ days after the effective date of this contract, Seller shall furnish to Buyer and Title Company Seller's existing survey of the Property and a Residential Real Property Affidavit promulgated by the Texas Department of Insurance (Affidavit). If the existing survey or Affidavit is not acceptable to Title Company or Buyer's lender(s), Buyer shall obtain a new survey at ☐ Seller's ☐ Buyer's expense no later than 3 days prior to Closing Date. **If Seller fails to furnish the existing survey or Affidavit within the time prescribed, Buyer shall obtain a new survey at Seller's expense no later than 3 days prior to Closing Date.**
☐ (2) Within _____ days after the effective date of this contract, Buyer shall obtain a new survey at Buyer's expense. Buyer is deemed to receive the survey on the date of actual receipt or the date specified in this paragraph, whichever is earlier.
☐ (3) Within _____ days after the effective date of this contract, Seller, at Seller's expense shall furnish a new survey to Buyer.

D. OBJECTIONS: Buyer may object in writing to defects, exceptions, or encumbrances to title: disclosed on the survey other than items 6A(1) through (7) above; disclosed in the Commitment other than items 6A(1) through (8) above; or which prohibit the following use or activity: _____
_____.
Buyer must object the earlier of (i) the Closing Date or (ii) _____ days after Buyer receives the Commitment, Exception Documents, and the survey. Buyer's failure to object within the time allowed will constitute a waiver of Buyer's right to object; except that the requirements in Schedule C of the Commitment are not waived.   Provided Seller is not obligated to incur any expense, Seller shall cure the timely objections of Buyer or any third party lender within 15 days after Seller receives the objections and the Closing Date will be extended as necessary. If objections are not cured within such 15 day period, this contract will terminate and the earnest money will be refunded to Buyer unless Buyer waives the objections.

E. TITLE NOTICES:
(1) ABSTRACT OR TITLE POLICY: Broker advises Buyer to have an abstract of title covering the Property examined by an attorney of Buyer's selection, or Buyer should be furnished with or obtain a Title Policy. If a Title Policy is furnished, the Commitment should be promptly reviewed by an attorney of Buyer's choice due to the time limitations on Buyer's right to object.
(2) PROPERTY OWNERS' ASSOCIATION MANDATORY MEMBERSHIP: The Property ☐ is ☐ is not subject to mandatory membership in a property owners' association. If the Property is subject to mandatory membership in a property owners' association, Seller notifies Buyer under §5.012, Texas Property Code, that, as a purchaser of property in the residential community identified in Paragraph 2A in which the Property is located, you are obligated to be a member of the property owners' association. Restrictive covenants governing the use and occupancy of the Property and a dedicatory instrument governing the establishment, maintenance, and operation of this residential community have been or will be recorded in the Real Property Records of the county in which the Property is located. Copies of the restrictive covenants and dedicatory instrument may be obtained from the county clerk. You are obligated to pay assessments to the property owners' association. The amount of the assessments is subject to change. Your failure to pay the

Initialed for identification by Buyer_____ _____ and Seller _____ _____   TREC NO. 20-8

Contract Concerning _____ Page 3 of 8   06-30-08
(Address of Property)

assessments could result in a lien on and the foreclosure of the Property. **If Buyer is concerned about these matters, the TREC promulgated Addendum for Property Subject to Mandatory Membership in a Property Owners' Association should be used.**

(3) STATUTORY TAX DISTRICTS: If the Property is situated in a utility or other statutorily created district providing water, sewer, drainage, or flood control facilities and services, Chapter 49, Texas Water Code, requires Seller to deliver and Buyer to sign the statutory notice relating to the tax rate, bonded indebtedness, or standby fee of the district prior to final execution of this contract.

(4) TIDE WATERS: If the Property abuts the tidally influenced waters of the state, §33.135, Texas Natural Resources Code, requires a notice regarding coastal area property to be included in the contract. An addendum containing the notice promulgated by TREC or required by the parties must be used.

(5) ANNEXATION: If the Property is located outside the limits of a municipality, Seller notifies Buyer under §5.011, Texas Property Code, that the Property may now or later be included in the extraterritorial jurisdiction of a municipality and may now or later be subject to annexation by the municipality. Each municipality maintains a map that depicts its boundaries and extraterritorial jurisdiction. To determine if the Property is located within a municipality's extraterritorial jurisdiction or is likely to be located within a municipality's extraterritorial jurisdiction, contact all municipalities located in the general proximity of the Property for further information.

(6) PROPERTY LOCATED IN A CERTIFICATED SERVICE AREA OF A UTILITY SERVICE PROVIDER: Notice required by §13.257, Water Code: The real property, described in Paragraph 2, that you are about to purchase may be located in a certificated water or sewer service area, which is authorized by law to provide water or sewer service to the properties in the certificated area. If your property is located in a certificated area there may be special costs or charges that you will be required to pay before you can receive water or sewer service. There may be a period required to construct lines or other facilities necessary to provide water or sewer service to your property. You are advised to determine if the property is in a certificated area and contact the utility service provider to determine the cost that you will be required to pay and the period, if any, that is required to provide water or sewer service to your property. The undersigned Buyer hereby acknowledges receipt of the foregoing notice at or before the execution of a binding contract for the purchase of the real property described in Paragraph 2 or at closing of purchase of the real property.

(7) PUBLIC IMPROVEMENT DISTRICTS: If the Property is in a public improvement district, §5.014, Property Code, requires Seller to notify Buyer as follows: As a purchaser of this parcel of real property you are obligated to pay an assessment to a municipality or county for an improvement project undertaken by a public improvement district under Chapter 372, Local Government Code. The assessment may be due annually or in periodic installments. More information concerning the amount of the assessment and the due dates of that assessment may be obtained from the municipality or county levying the assessment. The amount of the assessments is subject to change. Your failure to pay the assessments could result in a lien on and the foreclosure of your property.

7. **PROPERTY CONDITION:**

    A. ACCESS, INSPECTIONS AND UTILITIES: Seller shall permit Buyer and Buyer's agents access to the Property at reasonable times. Buyer may have the Property inspected by inspectors selected by Buyer and licensed by TREC or otherwise permitted by law to make inspections. Seller at Seller's expense shall turn on existing utilities for inspections.

    B. SELLER'S DISCLOSURE NOTICE PURSUANT TO §5.008, TEXAS PROPERTY CODE (Notice): (Check one box only)
      ❑ (1) Buyer has received the Notice.
      ❑ (2) Buyer has not received the Notice. Within _____ days after the effective date of this contract, Seller shall deliver the Notice to Buyer. If Buyer does not receive the Notice, Buyer may terminate this contract at any time prior to the closing and the earnest money will be refunded to Buyer. If Seller delivers the Notice, Buyer may terminate this contract for any reason within 7 days after Buyer receives the Notice or prior to the closing, whichever first occurs, and the earnest money will be refunded to Buyer.
      ❑ (3) The Seller is not required to furnish the notice under the Texas Property Code.

    C. SELLER'S DISCLOSURE OF LEAD-BASED PAINT AND LEAD-BASED PAINT HAZARDS is required by Federal law for a residential dwelling constructed prior to 1978.

    D. ACCEPTANCE OF PROPERTY CONDITION: (Check one box only)
      ❑ (1) Buyer accepts the Property in its present condition.
      ❑ (2) Buyer accepts the Property in its present condition provided Seller, at Seller's expense, shall complete the following specific repairs and treatments: _____
            .

    E. LENDER REQUIRED REPAIRS AND TREATMENTS: Unless otherwise agreed in writing, neither party is obligated to pay for lender required repairs, which includes treatment

Initialed for identification by Buyer_____ _____ and Seller _____ _____   TREC NO. 20-8

for wood destroying insects. If the parties do not agree to pay for the lender required repairs or treatments, this contract will terminate and the earnest money will be refunded to Buyer.   If the cost of lender required repairs and treatments exceeds 5% of the Sales Price, Buyer may terminate this contract and the earnest money will be refunded to Buyer.

F. COMPLETION OF REPAIRS AND TREATMENTS: Unless otherwise agreed in writing, Seller shall complete all agreed repairs and treatments prior to the Closing Date. All required permits must be obtained, and repairs and treatments must be performed by persons who are licensed or otherwise authorized by law to provide such repairs or treatments. At Buyer's election, any transferable warranties received by Seller with respect to the repairs and treatments will be transferred to Buyer at Buyer's expense. If Seller fails to complete any agreed repairs and treatments prior to the Closing Date, Buyer may do so and receive reimbursement from Seller at closing. The Closing Date will be extended up to 15 days, if necessary, to complete repairs and treatments.

G. ENVIRONMENTAL MATTERS: Buyer is advised that the presence of wetlands, toxic substances, including asbestos and wastes or other environmental hazards, or the presence of a threatened or endangered species or its habitat may affect Buyer's intended use of the Property. If Buyer is concerned about these matters, an addendum promulgated by TREC or required by the parties should be used.

H. RESIDENTIAL SERVICE CONTRACTS: Buyer may purchase a residential service contract from a residential service company licensed by TREC. If Buyer purchases a residential service contract, Seller shall reimburse Buyer at closing for the cost of the residential service contract in an amount not exceeding $_____. Buyer should review any residential service contract for the scope of coverage, exclusions and limitations. **The purchase of a residential service contract is optional. Similar coverage may be purchased from various companies authorized to do business in Texas.**

8. **BROKERS' FEES:** All obligations of the parties for payment of brokers' fees are contained in separate written agreements.

9. **CLOSING:**
   A. The closing of the sale will be on or before _____, 20____, or within 7 days after objections made under Paragraph 6D have been cured or waived, whichever date is later (Closing Date). If either party fails to close the sale by the Closing Date, the non-defaulting party may exercise the remedies contained in Paragraph 15.
   B. At closing:
      (1) Seller shall execute and deliver a general warranty deed conveying title to the Property to Buyer and showing no additional exceptions to those permitted in Paragraph 6 and furnish tax statements or certificates showing no delinquent taxes on the Property.
      (2) Buyer shall pay the Sales Price in good funds acceptable to the escrow agent.
      (3) Seller and Buyer shall execute and deliver any notices, statements, certificates, affidavits, releases, loan documents and other documents required of them by this contract, the Commitment or law necessary for the closing of the sale and the issuance of the Title Policy.
      (4) There will be no liens, assessments, or security interests against the Property which will not be satisfied out of the sales proceeds unless securing the payment of any loans assumed by Buyer and assumed loans will not be in default.

10. **POSSESSION:** Seller shall deliver to Buyer possession of the Property in its present or required condition, ordinary wear and tear excepted: ☐ upon closing and funding ☐ according to a temporary residential lease form promulgated by TREC or other written lease required by the parties. Any possession by Buyer prior to closing or by Seller after closing which is not authorized by a written lease will establish a tenancy at sufferance relationship between the parties. **Consult your insurance agent prior to change of ownership and possession because insurance coverage may be limited or terminated. The absence of a written lease or appropriate insurance coverage may expose the parties to economic loss.**

11. **SPECIAL PROVISIONS:** (Insert only factual statements and business details applicable to the sale. TREC rules prohibit licensees from adding factual statements or business details for which a contract addendum, lease or other form has been promulgated by TREC for mandatory use.)

Initialed for identification by Buyer_____ _____ and Seller _____ _____   TREC NO. 20-8

12. SETTLEMENT AND OTHER EXPENSES:
   A. The following expenses must be paid at or prior to closing:
   (1) Expenses payable by Seller (Seller's Expenses):
   (a) Releases of existing liens, including prepayment penalties and recording fees; release of Seller's loan liability; tax statements or certificates; preparation of deed; one-half of escrow fee; and other expenses payable by Seller under this contract.
   (b) Seller shall also pay an amount not to exceed $ _____ to be applied in the following order: Buyer's Expenses which Buyer is prohibited from paying by FHA, VA, Texas Veterans Land Board or other governmental loan programs, and then to other Buyer's Expenses as allowed by the lender.
   (2) Expenses payable by Buyer (Buyer's Expenses):
   (a) Loan origination, discount, buy-down, and commitment fees (Loan Fees).
   (b) Appraisal fees; loan application fees; credit reports; preparation of loan documents; interest on the notes from date of disbursement to one month prior to dates of first monthly payments; recording fees; copies of easements and restrictions; mortgagee title policy with endorsements required by lender; loan-related inspection fees; photos; amortization schedules; one-half of escrow fee; all prepaid items, including required premiums for flood and hazard insurance, reserve deposits for insurance, ad valorem taxes and special governmental assessments; final compliance inspection; courier fee; repair inspection; underwriting fee; wire transfer fee; expenses incident to any loan; and other expenses payable by Buyer under this contract.
   B. Buyer shall pay Private Mortgage Insurance Premium (PMI), VA Loan Funding Fee, or FHA Mortgage Insurance Premium (MIP) as required by the lender.
   C. If any expense exceeds an amount expressly stated in this contract for such expense to be paid by a party, that party may terminate this contract unless the other party agrees to pay such excess. Buyer may not pay charges and fees expressly prohibited by FHA, VA, Texas Veterans Land Board or other governmental loan program regulations.

13. PRORATIONS: Taxes for the current year, interest, maintenance fees, assessments, dues and rents will be prorated through the Closing Date. The tax proration may be calculated taking into consideration any change in exemptions that will affect the current year's taxes. If taxes for the current year vary from the amount prorated at closing, the parties shall adjust the prorations when tax statements for the current year are available. If taxes are not paid at or prior to closing, Buyer shall pay taxes for the current year.

14. CASUALTY LOSS: If any part of the Property is damaged or destroyed by fire or other casualty after the effective date of this contract, Seller shall restore the Property to its previous condition as soon as reasonably possible, but in any event by the Closing Date. If Seller fails to do so due to factors beyond Seller's control, Buyer may (a) terminate this contract and the earnest money will be refunded to Buyer (b) extend the time for performance up to 15 days and the Closing Date will be extended as necessary or (c) accept the Property in its damaged condition with an assignment of insurance proceeds and receive credit from Seller at closing in the amount of the deductible under the insurance policy. Seller's obligations under this paragraph are independent of any other obligations of Seller under this contract.

15. DEFAULT: If Buyer fails to comply with this contract, Buyer will be in default, and Seller may (a) enforce specific performance, seek such other relief as may be provided by law, or both, or (b) terminate this contract and receive the earnest money as liquidated damages, thereby releasing both parties from this contract. If, due to factors beyond Seller's control, Seller fails within the time allowed to make any non-casualty repairs or deliver the Commitment, or survey, if required of Seller, Buyer may (a) extend the time for performance up to 15 days and the Closing Date will be extended as necessary or (b) terminate this contract as the sole remedy and receive the earnest money. If Seller fails to comply with this contract for any other reason, Seller will be in default and Buyer may (a) enforce specific performance, seek such other relief as may be provided by law, or both, or (b) terminate this contract and receive the earnest money, thereby releasing both parties from this contract.

16. MEDIATION: It is the policy of the State of Texas to encourage resolution of disputes through alternative dispute resolution procedures such as mediation. Any dispute between Seller and Buyer related to this contract which is not resolved through informal discussion ☐will ☐will not be submitted to a mutually acceptable mediation service or provider. The parties to the mediation shall bear the mediation costs equally. This paragraph does not preclude a party from seeking equitable relief from a court of competent jurisdiction.

17. ATTORNEY'S FEES: A Buyer, Seller, Listing Broker, Other Broker, or escrow agent who prevails in any legal proceeding related to this contract is entitled to recover reasonable attorney's fees and all costs of such proceeding.

Initialed for identification by Buyer_____ _____ and Seller _____ _____   TREC NO. 20-8

18. ESCROW:

    A. ESCROW: The escrow agent is not (i) a party to this contract and does not have liability for the performance or nonperformance of any party to this contract, (ii) liable for interest on the earnest money and (iii) liable for the loss of any earnest money caused by the failure of any financial institution in which the earnest money has been deposited unless the financial institution is acting as escrow agent.

    B. EXPENSES: At closing, the earnest money must be applied first to any cash down payment, then to Buyer's Expenses and any excess refunded to Buyer. If no closing occurs, escrow agent may require payment of unpaid expenses incurred on behalf of the parties and a written release of liability of escrow agent from all parties.

    C. DEMAND: Upon termination of this contract, either party or the escrow agent may send a release of earnest money to each party and the parties shall execute counterparts of the release and deliver same to the escrow agent. If either party fails to execute the release, either party may make a written demand to the escrow agent for the earnest money. If only one party makes written demand for the earnest money, escrow agent shall promptly provide a copy of the demand to the other party. If escrow agent does not receive written objection to the demand from the other party within 15 days, escrow agent may disburse the earnest money to the party making demand reduced by the amount of unpaid expenses incurred on behalf of the party receiving the earnest money and escrow agent may pay the same to the creditors. If escrow agent complies with the provisions of this paragraph, each party hereby releases escrow agent from all adverse claims related to the disbursal of the earnest money.

    D. DAMAGES: Any party who wrongfully fails or refuses to sign a release acceptable to the escrow agent within 7 days of receipt of the request will be liable to the other party for liquidated damages in an amount equal to the sum of: (i) three times the amount of the earnest money; (ii) the earnest money; (iii) reasonable attorney's fees; and (iv) all costs of suit.

    E. NOTICES: Escrow agent's notices will be effective when sent in compliance with Paragraph 21. Notice of objection to the demand will be deemed effective upon receipt by escrow agent.

19. REPRESENTATIONS: All covenants, representations and warranties in this contract survive closing. If any representation of Seller in this contract is untrue on the Closing Date, Seller will be in default. Unless expressly prohibited by written agreement, Seller may continue to show the Property and receive, negotiate and accept back up offers.

20. FEDERAL TAX REQUIREMENTS: If Seller is a "foreign person," as defined by applicable law, or if Seller fails to deliver an affidavit to Buyer that Seller is not a "foreign person," then Buyer shall withhold from the sales proceeds an amount sufficient to comply with applicable tax law and deliver the same to the Internal Revenue Service together with appropriate tax forms. Internal Revenue Service regulations require filing written reports if currency in excess of specified amounts is received in the transaction.

21. NOTICES: All notices from one party to the other must be in writing and are effective when mailed to, hand-delivered at, or transmitted by facsimile or electronic transmission as follows:

To Buyer	**To Seller**
at: _____	at: _____
_____	_____
_____	_____
_____	_____
Telephone: ( )_____	Telephone: ( )_____
Facsimile: ( )_____	Facsimile: ( )_____
E-mail: _____	E-mail: _____

Initialed for identification by Buyer_____ _____ and Seller _____ _____   TREC NO. 20-8

Contract Concerning _____ Page 7 of 8 06-30-08
(Address of Property)

22. AGREEMENT OF PARTIES: This contract contains the entire agreement of the parties and cannot be changed except by their written agreement. Addenda which are a part of this contract are (Check all applicable boxes):

☐ Third Party Financing Condition Addendum

☐ Seller Financing Addendum

☐ Addendum for Property Subject to Mandatory Membership in a Property Owners' Association

☐ Buyer's Temporary Residential Lease

☐ Seller's Temporary Residential Lease

☐ Addendum for Sale of Other Property by Buyer

☐ Addendum Containing Required Notices Under §5.016, §420.001 and §420.002, Texas Property Code

☐ Addendum for "Back-Up" Contract

☐ Addendum for Coastal Area Property

☐ Environmental Assessment, Threatened or Endangered Species and Wetlands Addendum

☐ Addendum for Property Located Seaward of the Gulf Intracoastal Waterway

☐ Addendum for Seller's Disclosure of Information on Lead-based Paint and Lead-based Paint Hazards as Required by Federal Law

☐ Other (list): _____
  _____

23. TERMINATION OPTION: For nominal consideration, the receipt of which is hereby acknowledged by Seller, and Buyer's agreement to pay Seller $ _____ (Option Fee) within 2 days after the effective date of this contract, Seller grants Buyer the unrestricted right to terminate this contract by giving notice of termination to Seller within _____ days after the effective date of this contract. If no dollar amount is stated as the Option Fee or if Buyer fails to pay the Option Fee to Seller within the time prescribed, this paragraph will not be a part of this contract and Buyer shall not have the unrestricted right to terminate this contract. If Buyer gives notice of termination within the time prescribed, the Option Fee will not be refunded; however, any earnest money will be refunded to Buyer. The Option Fee ☐ will ☐ will not be credited to the Sales Price at closing. **Time is of the essence for this paragraph and strict compliance with the time for performance is required.**

24. CONSULT AN ATTORNEY: Real estate licensees cannot give legal advice. READ THIS CONTRACT CAREFULLY. If you do not understand the effect of this contract, consult an attorney BEFORE signing.

Buyer's
Attorney is: _____

Telephone: (___) _____

Facsimile: (___) _____

E-mail: _____

Seller's
Attorney is: _____

Telephone: (___) _____

Facsimile: (___) _____

E-mail: _____

EXECUTED the _____ day of _____, 20____ (EFFECTIVE DATE).
(BROKER: FILL IN THE DATE OF FINAL ACCEPTANCE.)

_____
Buyer

_____
Buyer

_____
Seller

_____
Seller

TREC NO. 20-8

Reprinted by permission of Texas Real Estate Commission.

BROKER INFORMATION AND RATIFICATION OF FEE

Listing Broker has agreed to pay Other Broker _____ of the total sales price when Listing Broker's fee is received. Escrow Agent is authorized and directed to pay Other Broker from Listing Broker's fee at closing.

Other Broker _____ License No. _____

represents ☐ Buyer only as Buyer's agent
☐ Seller as Listing Broker's subagent

Associate _____ Telephone _____

Broker's Address _____

City _____ State _____ Zip _____

Facsimile _____

Email Address _____

Listing Broker _____ License No. _____

represents ☐ Seller and Buyer as an intermediary
☐ Seller only as Seller's agent

Listing Associate _____ Telephone _____

Listing Associate's Office Address _____ Facsimile _____

City _____ State _____ Zip _____

Email Address _____

Selling Associate _____ Telephone _____

Selling Associate's Office Address _____ Facsimile _____

City _____ State _____ Zip _____

Email Address _____

OPTION FEE RECEIPT

Receipt of $_____ (Option Fee) in the form of _____ is acknowledged.

_____   _____
Seller or Listing Broker   Date

CONTRACT AND EARNEST MONEY RECEIPT

Receipt of ☐ Contract and ☐ $_____ Earnest Money in the form of _____
is acknowledged.
Escrow Agent: _____   Date: _____

By: _____

_____
Address

_____
City   State   Zip

Email Address _____

Telephone (_____) _____

Facsimile: (_____) _____

TREC NO. 20-8

Reprinted by permission of Texas Real Estate Commission.

PROMULGATED BY THE TEXAS REAL ESTATE COMMISSION (TREC)   06-30-08

ADDENDUM FOR PROPERTY SUBJECT TO MANDATORY MEMBERSHIP IN A PROPERTY OWNERS' ASSOCIATION

(NOT FOR USE WITH CONDOMINIUMS)

ADDENDUM TO CONTRACT CONCERNING THE PROPERTY AT

_____

(Street Address and City)

_____

(Name of Property Owners' Association)

A. SUBDIVISION INFORMATION: "Subdivision Information" means: (i) the restrictions applying to the subdivision, (ii) the bylaws and rules of the Property Owners' Association (Association), and (iii) a resale certificate, all of which comply with Section 207.003 of the Texas Property Code. (Check only one box):

❏ 1. Within _____ days after the effective date of the contract, Seller shall at Seller's expense deliver the Subdivision Information to Buyer. If Buyer does not receive the Subdivision Information, Buyer may terminate the contract at any time prior to closing and the earnest money will be refunded to Buyer. If Seller delivers the Subdivision Information, Buyer may terminate the contract for any reason within 7 days after Buyer receives the Subdivision Information or prior to closing, whichever first occurs, and the earnest money will be refunded to Buyer.

❏ 2. Buyer has received and approved the Subdivision Information before signing the contract.

❏ 3. Buyer does not require delivery of the Subdivision Information.

If Seller becomes aware of any material changes in the Subdivision Information, Seller shall promptly give notice to Buyer. Buyer may terminate the contract prior to closing by giving written notice to Seller if: (i) any of the Subdivision Information provided was not true; or (ii) any material adverse change in the Subdivision Information occurs prior to closing, and the earnest money will be refunded to Buyer.

B. FEES: Buyer shall pay any Association fees resulting from the transfer of the Property not to exceed $_____ and Seller shall pay any excess.

NOTICE TO BUYER REGARDING REPAIRS BY THE ASSOCIATION: The Association may have the sole responsibility to make certain repairs to the Property. If you are concerned about the condition of any part of the Property which the Association is required to repair, you should not sign the contract unless you are satisfied that the Association will make the desired repairs.

_____   _____
Buyer   Seller

_____   _____
Buyer   Seller

TREC NO. 36-5

Reprinted by permission of Texas Real Estate Commission.

PROMULGATED BY THE TEXAS REAL ESTATE COMMISSION (TREC)

02-13-06

AMENDMENT
TO CONTRACT CONCERNING THE PROPERTY AT

_____
(Street Address and City)

Seller and Buyer amend the contract as follows: (check each applicable box)

☐(1) The Sales Price in Paragraph 3 of the contract is:
    A. Cash portion of Sales Price payable by Buyer at closing ....$_____
    B. Sum of financing described in the contract...$_____
    C. Sales Price (Sum of A and B) ....$_____

☐(2) In addition to any repairs and treatments otherwise required by the contract, Seller, at Seller's expense, shall complete the following repairs and treatments:

☐(3) The date in Paragraph 9 of the contract is changed to _____, 20_____.

☐(4) The amount in Paragraph 12A(1)(b) of the contract is changed to $_____.

☐(5) The cost of lender required repairs and treatment, as itemized on the attached list, will be paid as follows: $ _____ by Seller; $ _____ by Buyer.

☐(6) Buyer has paid Seller an additional Option Fee of $ _____ for an extension of the unrestricted right to terminate the contract on or before _____ , 20_____. This additional Option Fee ☐ will ☐ will not be credited to the Sales Price.

☐(7) Buyer waives the unrestricted right to terminate the contract for which the Option Fee was paid.

☐(8) The date for Buyer to give written notice to Seller that Buyer cannot obtain Financing Approval as set forth in the Third Party Financing Condition Addendum is changed to _____, 20_____.

☐(9) **Other Modifications**: (Insert only factual statements and business details applicable to this sale.)

EXECUTED the _____day of _____, 20_____ . (BROKER: FILL IN THE DATE OF FINAL ACCEPTANCE.)

_____   _____
Buyer   Seller

_____   _____
Buyer   Seller

TREC NO. 39-6

12-10-07

PROMULGATED BY THE TEXAS REAL ESTATE COMMISSION (TREC)

THIRD PARTY FINANCING CONDITION ADDENDUM

TO CONTRACT CONCERNING THE PROPERTY AT

_____

(Street Address and City)

Buyer shall apply promptly for all financing described below and make every reasonable effort to obtain approval for the financing (Financing Approval). Buyer shall furnish all information and documents required by lender for Financing Approval. Financing Approval will be deemed to have been obtained when (1) the terms of the loan(s) described below are available and (2) lender determines that Buyer has satisfied all of lender's financial requirements (those items relating to Buyer's assets, income and credit history). If Buyer cannot obtain Financing Approval, Buyer may give written notice to Seller within _____ days after the effective date of this contract and this contract will terminate and the earnest money will be refunded to Buyer. **If Buyer does not give such notice within the time required, this contract will no longer be subject to Financing Approval. Time is of the essence for this paragraph and strict compliance with the time for performance is required.**

NOTE: Financing Approval does not include approval of lender's underwriting requirements for the Property, as specified in Paragraph 4.A.(1) of the contract.

Each note must be secured by vendor's and deed of trust liens.

CHECK APPLICABLE BOXES:

❏ A. CONVENTIONAL FINANCING:

    ❏ (1) A first mortgage loan in the principal amount of $ _____ (excluding any financed PMI premium), due in full in _____ year(s), with interest not to exceed _____% per annum for the first _____year(s) of the loan with Loan Fees (loan origination, discount, buy-down, and commitment fees) not to exceed _____% of the loan.

    ❏ (2) A second mortgage loan in the principal amount of $_____(excluding any financed PMI premium), due in full in _____year(s), with interest not to exceed _____% per annum for the first _____year(s) of the loan with Loan Fees (loan origination, discount, buy-down, and commitment fees) not to exceed _____% of the loan.

❏ B. TEXAS VETERANS LOAN: A loan(s) from the Texas Veterans Land Board of $_____ for a period in the total amount of _____years at the interest rate established by the Texas Veterans Land Board.

❏ C. FHA INSURED FINANCING: A Section _____ FHA insured loan of not less than $_____ (excluding any financed MIP), amortizable monthly for not less than _____years, with interest not to exceed _____% per annum for the first _____year(s) of the loan with Loan Fees (loan origination, discount, buy-down, and commitment fees) not to exceed _____ % of the loan. As required by HUD-FHA, if FHA valuation is unknown, _"It is expressly agreed that, notwithstanding any other provision of this contract, the purchaser (Buyer) shall not be obligated to complete the purchase of the Property described herein or to incur any penalty by forfeiture of earnest money deposits or otherwise unless the purchaser (Buyer) has been given in accordance with HUD/FHA or VA requirements a written statement issued by the Federal Housing Commissioner, Department of Veterans Affairs, or a Direct Endorsement Lender setting forth the appraised value of the Property of not less than $_____. The purchaser (Buyer) shall have the privilege and option of proceeding with consummation of the contract without regard to the amount of the_

Initialed for identification by Buyer____ _____ and Seller_____ _____   TREC NO. 40-3

Third Party Financing Condition Addendum Concerning

(Address of Property)

appraised valuation. The appraised valuation is arrived at to determine the maximum mortgage the Department of Housing and Urban Development will insure. HUD does not warrant the value or the condition of the Property. The purchaser (Buyer) should satisfy himself/herself that the price and the condition of the Property are acceptable."
NOTE: HUD 92564-CN "For Your Protection: Get a Home Inspection" must be attached to this Addendum.

☐ D. VA GUARANTEED FINANCING: A VA guaranteed loan of not less than $_____ (excluding any financed Funding Fee), amortizable monthly for not less than_____years, with interest not to exceed_____% per annum for the first _____year(s) of the loan with Loan Fees (loan origination, discount, buy-down, and commitment fees) not to exceed _____% of the loan.

VA NOTICE TO BUYER: *"It is expressly agreed that, notwithstanding any other provisions of this contract, the Buyer shall not incur any penalty by forfeiture of earnest money or otherwise or be obligated to complete the purchase of the Property described herein, if the contract purchase price or cost exceeds the reasonable value of the Property established by the Department of Veterans Affairs. The Buyer shall, however, have the privilege and option of proceeding with the consummation of this contract without regard to the amount of the reasonable value established by the Department of Veterans Affairs."*

If Buyer elects to complete the purchase at an amount in excess of the reasonable value established by VA, Buyer shall pay such excess amount in cash from a source which Buyer agrees to disclose to the VA and which Buyer represents will not be from borrowed funds except as approved by VA. If VA reasonable value of the Property is less than the Sales Price, Seller may reduce the Sales Price to an amount equal to the VA reasonable value and the sale will be closed at the lower Sales Price with proportionate adjustments to the down payment and the loan amount.

Buyer hereby authorizes any lender to furnish to the Seller or Buyer or their representatives information relating only to the status of Financing Approval of Buyer.

_____   _____
Buyer   Seller

_____   _____
Buyer   Seller

TREC NO. 40-3

PROMULGATED BY THE TEXAS REAL ESTATE COMMISSION (TREC)   12-15-08

ADDENDUM FOR RESERVATION OF OIL, GAS, AND OTHER MINERALS

ADDENDUM TO CONTRACT CONCERNING THE PROPERTY AT

_____

(Street Address and City)

_____

NOTICE: For use only if Seller reserves all or a portion of the Mineral Estate.

A. "Mineral Estate" means all oil, gas, and other minerals in or under the Property, any royalty under any existing or future lease covering any part of the Property, surface rights (including rights of ingress and egress), production and drilling rights, lease payments, and all related benefits.

B. The Mineral Estate owned by Seller, if any, will be conveyed unless reserved as follows (check one box only):

☐ (1) Seller reserves all of the Mineral Estate owned by Seller.

☐ (2) Seller reserves an undivided _____% interest in the Mineral Estate owned by Seller. *NOTE: If Seller does not own all of the Mineral Estate, Seller reserves only this percentage of Seller's interest.*

C. Seller ☐ waives ☐ does not waive Seller's surface rights (including rights of ingress and egress). *NOTE: Any waiver of surface rights by Seller does not affect any surface rights that may be held by others.*

D. If B(2) applies, Seller shall, on or before the Closing Date, provide Buyer contact information known to Seller for any existing lessee.

If either party is concerned about the legal rights or impact of the above provisions, that party is advised to consult an attorney BEFORE signing.

TREC rules prohibit real estate licensees from giving legal advice.

_____   _____
Buyer   Seller

_____   _____
Buyer   Seller

The form of this addendum has been approved by the Texas Real Estate Commission for use only with similarly approved or promulgated forms of contracts. Such approval relates to this contract form only. TREC forms are intended for use only by trained real estate licensees. No representation is made as to the legal validity or adequacy of any provision in any specific transactions. It is not intended for complex transactions. Texas Real Estate Commission, P.O. Box 12188, Austin, TX 78711-2188, 1-800-250-8732 or (512) 459-6544 (http://www.trec.state.tx.us) TREC No. 44-0.

TREC NO. 44-0

PROMULGATED BY THE TEXAS REAL ESTATE COMMISSION (TREC)   12-15-08

SHORT SALE ADDENDUM

ADDENDUM TO CONTRACT CONCERNING THE PROPERTY AT

_____

(Street Address and City)

A. This contract involves a "short sale" of the Property. As used in this Addendum, "short sale" means that:

  (1) Seller's net proceeds at closing will be insufficient to pay the balance of Seller's mortgage loan; and

  (2) Seller requires:

    (a) the consent of the lienholder to sell the Property pursuant to this contract; and

    (b) the lienholder's agreement to:

      (i) accept Seller's net proceeds in full satisfaction of Seller's liability under the mortgage loan; and

      (ii) provide Seller an executed release of lien against the Property in a recordable format.

B. As used in this Addendum, "Seller's net proceeds" means the Sales Price less Seller's Expenses under Paragraph 12 of the contract and Seller's obligation to pay any brokerage fees.

C. The contract to which this Addendum is attached is binding upon execution by the parties and the earnest money and the Option Fee must be paid as provided in the contract. The contract is contingent on the satisfaction of Seller's requirements under Paragraph A(2) of this Addendum (Lienholder's Consent and Agreement). Seller shall apply promptly for and make every reasonable effort to obtain Lienholder's Consent and Agreement, and shall furnish all information and documents required by the lienholder. Except as provided by this Addendum, neither party is required to perform under the contract while it is contingent upon obtaining Lienholder's Consent and Agreement.

D. If Seller does not notify Buyer that Seller has obtained Lienholder's Consent and Agreement on or before _____ this contract terminates and the earnest money will be refunded to Buyer. Seller must notify Buyer immediately if Lienholder's Consent and Agreement is obtained. For purposes of performance, the effective date of the contract changes to the date Seller provides Buyer notice of the Lienholder's Consent and Agreement (Amended Effective Date).

E. This contract will terminate and the earnest money will be refunded to Buyer if the Lienholder refuses or withdraws its Consent and Agreement prior to closing and funding. Seller shall promptly notify Buyer of any lienholder's refusal to provide or withdrawal of a Lienholder's Consent and Agreement.

F. If Buyer has the unrestricted right to terminate this contract, the time for giving notice of termination begins on the effective date of the contract, continues after the Amended Effective Date and ends upon the expiration of Buyer's unrestricted right to terminate the contract under Paragraph 23.

G. For the purposes of this Addendum, time is of the essence. Strict compliance with the times for performance stated in this Addendum is required.

H. Seller authorizes any lienholder to furnish to Buyer or Buyer's representatives information relating to the status of the request for a Lienholder's Consent and Agreement.

I. If there is more than one lienholder or loan secured by the Property, this Addendum applies to each lienholder.

_____   _____
Buyer   Seller

_____   _____
Buyer   Seller

TREC NO. 45-0

Answers to Pre-Assessment Evaluation

Chapter 1
1. False
2. False
3. True
4. True
5. True

Chapter 2
1. True
2. False
3. False
4. True
5. True

Chapter 3
1. True
2. False
3. True
4. False
5. True

Chapter 4
1. True
2. False
3. True
4. False
5. True

Chapter 5
1. True
2. False
3. True
4. True
5. True

Index